ARCHITECTURE OF THE SACRED

Space, Ritual, and Experience from Classical Greece to Byzantium

A distinguished team of scholars explores how architecture and ritual interact to construct sacred experience. Bringing together case studies from ancient Greek, Roman, Jewish, early Christian, and Byzantine sacred architecture, this book reaches beyond the cultural formulation of the sacred to articulate overarching themes in the creation of sacred experience across multiple religious traditions of the eastern Mediterranean. The authors probe our understanding of the nature (and recoverability) of ritual and the role of architecture as an active agent in the magnification, elevation, and ritualization of actions in sacred cause. Addressing key issues including the reciprocity of architecture and place; negotiation of social and spatial boundaries; passage of the body and the eye; interaction of space and iconography; construction of sacred topography; and the vitality of text, history, and memory in the accumulation of sanctity, the authors demonstrate the powerful ways buildings were enabled to perform as spiritually transformative environments.

Bonna D. Wescoat is Associate Professor of Art History at Emory University and director of excavations at the Sanctuary of the Great Gods, Samothrace, Greece. Her research concentrates on ancient Greek sacred architecture and iconography. Recent works include *Temple of Athena at Assos* (2012) and volume 9 of *Samothrace: Excavations Conducted by the Institute of Fine Arts of New York University, The Monuments of the Eastern Hill* (forthcoming).

Robert G. Ousterhout is Professor of the History of Art at the University of Pennsylvania, where he directs the Center for Ancient Studies. A specialist in Byzantine art and architecture, his research focuses on the vanishing architectural heritage of the eastern Mediterranean. He is the author of numerous books, including *Master Builders of Byzantium* (second paperback edition, 2008), *The Byzantine Monuments of the Evros/Meric River Valley* (2007, with Ch. Bakirtzis), and *A Byzantine Settlement in Cappadocia* (second paperback edition, 2011).

ARCHITECTURE OF THE SACRED

Space, Ritual, and Experience from Classical Greece to Byzantium

Edited by

BONNA D. WESCOAT
Emory University

ROBERT G. OUSTERHOUT
University of Pennsylvania

CAMBRIDGE UNIVERSITY PRESS
Cambridge, New York, Melbourne, Madrid, Cape Town,
Singapore, São Paulo, Delhi, Mexico City

Cambridge University Press
32 Avenue of the Americas, New York, NY 10013-2473, USA

www.cambridge.org
Information on this title: www.cambridge.org/9781107008236

First published 2012

Printed in the United States of America

A catalog record for this publication is available from the British Library.

Library of Congress Cataloging in Publication data
Architecture of the sacred : space, ritual, and experience from classical
Greece to Byzantium / edited by Bonna D. Wescoat and Robert G. Ousterhout.
    p.   cm.
  Includes bibliographical references and index.
  ISBN 978-1-107-00823-6 (hardback)
   1. Architecture and religion.   2. Architecture – Mediterranean
Region – Psychological aspects.   3. Sacred space – Mediterranean
Region.   I. Wescoat, Bonna D.   II. Ousterhout, Robert G.
  NA4600.A73   2012
  726′.120918224–dc23   2011021642

ISBN 978-1-107-00823-6 Hardback

CONTENTS

LIST OF ILLUSTRATIONS

CONTRIBUTING AUTHORS

Joan R. Branham is Professor of Art History at Providence College. She has served as Vice President and Chair of Fellowships at the W. F. Albright Institute of Archaeological Research in Jerusalem and as Acting Director of the Women's Studies in Religion Program at Harvard University. She is the author of several critical studies on sacred space in ancient Judaism, early Christianity, and modern culture, and she is interested in the role of gender, blood, and sacrifice in these traditions.

Slobodan Ćurčić is Professor Emeritus of Art and Archaeology at Princeton University. A specialist in Late Antique and Byzantine architecture and art, his most recent work includes *Secular Medieval Architecture in the Balkans, 1300–1500, and Its Preservation* (with E. Hadjitryphonos, Thessaloniki, 1997); *Naupara* (with S. Popovic, Belgrade, 2001); and *Architecture in the Balkans from Diocletian to Süleyman the Magnificent (ca. 300–ca. 1550)* (New Haven and London, 2010). He also cocurated (with E. Hadjitryphonos) the exhibit "Architecture as Icon," with an edited catalog, *Architecture as Icon: Perception and Representation of Architecture in Byzantine Art* (New Haven and London, 2010).

Jaś Elsner is Humfry Payne Senior Research Fellow in Classical Art and Archaeology, Corpus Christi College, Oxford, and visiting Professor of Art History at the University of Chicago. He works on issues of art and religion in antiquity and the early Christian and Jewish worlds and the history of the reception of these themes in later European culture, including such topics as the collecting of objects, the phenomena of pilgrimage, and the description of art and sites. Recent works include *Art and the Roman Viewer: Transformation of Art from the Pagan World to Christianity* (Cambridge, 1995), *Imperial Rome and Christian Triumph* (Oxford, 1998), and *Roman Eyes: Visuality and Subjectivity in Art and Text* (Princeton, 2007).

Mary B. Hollinshead is Associate Professor of Art History at the University of Rhode Island. Her chief interest is Greek architecture, particularly the use of temples in relation to the back room sometimes labeled "adyton." She has also written about Bronze Age painting and Roman sculpture. Her chapter in this volume is a preliminary study for a book she is completing on monumental steps in Greek architecture.

Jodi Magness is Kenan Distinguished Professor for Teaching Excellence in Early Judaism in the Department of Religious Studies at the University of North Carolina at Chapel Hill. Magness's research interests focus on Palestine in the Roman, Byzantine, and early Islamic periods and Diaspora Judaism in the Roman world. Her book, *The Archaeology of Qumran and the Dead Sea Scrolls* (Eerdmans, 2002), won the 2003 Biblical Archaeology Society's Award for Best Popular Book in Archaeology in 2001–2002 and was selected as an "Outstanding Academic Book for 2003" by *Choice* magazine. Magness's book *The Archaeology of the Early Islamic Settlement in Palestine* (Eisenbrauns, 2003) was awarded the 2006 Irene Levi-Sala Book Prize in the category of nonfiction on the archaeology of Israel.

Vasileios Marinis is Assistant Professor of Christian art and architecture at the Institute of Sacred Music and the Divinity School, Yale University. His research focuses on the interaction of architecture and ritual in the Byzantine churches of Constantinople. He is the author of "Tombs and Burials in the Monastery *tou Libos* in Constantinople," *Dumbarton Oaks Papers* 63 (2009), and "Defining Liturgical Space," in P. Stephenson, ed., *The Byzantine World* (New York, 2010).

Margaret M. Miles is Professor of Art History and Classics at the University of California, Irvine, and the Andrew W. Mellon Professor of Classical Studies at the American School of Classical Studies in Athens, Greece, where she is the head of the academic program for North American graduate students in Classics, History, and Archaeology. Her previous publications include a study of the Temple of Nemesis at

Rhamnous; a volume on the City Eleusinion (the Sanctuary of Demeter and Persephone) in the Athenian Agora; and *Art as Plunder*, a study of the impact of Cicero's ideas about the ethics of collecting art on our modern concept of cultural property.

Robert G. Ousterhout is Professor of Byzantine art and architecture at the University of Pennsylvania, where he directs the Center for Ancient Studies. His research focuses on the vanishing architectural heritage of the eastern Mediterranean. He is the author of *Master Builders of Byzantium* (second paperback edition, Philadelphia, 2008), *The Byzantine Monuments of the Evros/Meric River Valley* (with Ch. Bakirtzis, Thessaloniki, 2007), and *A Byzantine Settlement in Cappadocia* (Washington, DC, 2005).

Ellen Perry is Associate Professor of Classics at the College of the Holy Cross. Her interests include Roman art and architecture, ancient rhetoric, and ancient aesthetics. Her publications include the book *The Aesthetics of Emulation in the Visual Arts of Ancient Rome* (Cambridge, 2005).

C. Brian Rose is James B. Pritchard Professor of Mediterranean Archaeology in the Department of Classical Studies at the University of Pennsylvania and Deputy Director of the Penn Museum. Since 1988 he has been Head of Post–Bronze Age excavations at Troy and English language editor of *Studia Troica*, the annual journal of the Troy excavations. He is codirector of the Gordion Excavation Project.

Bonna D. Wescoat is Associate Professor of Art History at Emory University and director of excavations at the Sanctuary of the Great Gods, Samothrace, Greece. Her research concentrates on ancient Greek sacred architecture and iconography. Recent works include *Temple of Athena at Assos* (Oxford, 2012) and *Samothrace: Excavations Conducted by the Institute of Fine Arts of New York University, Volume 9: The Monuments of the Eastern Hill* (American School of Classical Studies at Athens, forthcoming).

Ann Marie Yasin, Associate Professor of Classics and Art History at the University of Southern California, specializes in Roman and late antique art and architecture. Her book *Saints and Church Spaces in the Late Antique Mediterranean: Architecture, Cult, and Community* (Cambridge, 2009) examines the social, political, and commemorative dimensions of early

Christian churches and saints' shrines. Her current work explores various aspects of the materiality and temporality of Roman and early Christian buildings, examining the shifting meanings of ancient structures as they are used, appropriated, altered, and/or forgotten over time.

ACKNOWLEDGMENTS

Although the coeditors have long been interested in the reciprocity of space, experience, ritual, and architecture, the idea for collaborating on this volume emerged from a session we organized for the annual meeting of the College Art Association in 2005 entitled "Ritual and Sacred Space in Pre-Modern Architecture." A second colloquium held at the annual meeting of the Archaeological Institute of America in 2006, "Circular Space and Performance," was also important to the formation of ideas presented here. We are grateful to the participants in these colloquia, Lisa Victoria Ciresi, Meredith Cohen, Mary Hollinshead, Vasileios Marinis, Margaret Miles, and Caroline K. Quenemoen at CAA, and Chrysanthos Kannelopoulos, Charalambas Kritsas, Rush Rehm, Peter Schultz, and Bronwen Wickkiser at the AIA, for generously sharing their ideas. While we have an interest in premodern sacred architecture generally, this volume focuses on the architecture of several historical religious traditions centered in the eastern Mediterranean.

We are grateful to Emory University and the Williams Fund of the History of Art Department at the University of Pennsylvania for their generous subvention for the illustrations. We wish to thank Alexandra Morrison, SIRE research student at Emory, for her help in assembling the manuscript, and Kathleen Carroll, who helped in numerous ways. We very much appreciate our editor Beatrice Rehl's support of this book project, the advice of the anonymous reviewers, and the patient assistance of Amanda Smith in seeing the manuscript through. To the authors of this volume we offer heartfelt thanks for their contributions.

November 2010

PREFACE

In the Western world, it is nearly impossible to think of sacred actions
without conjuring up some image of accompanying architecture, be it
the altar, temple, synagogue, mosque, basilica, or church. In fact, until
the twentieth century, almost the entire history of architecture could
be recounted in terms of sacred structures, for they played the dominant architectural role in fixing social and cultural identity. Despite
the obvious connection between architecture as a creator and signifier
of sacred space and the actions that concretized religious belief, archaeologists and historians of architecture of the historical, premodern
Mediterranean world have lagged behind scholars in other disciplines
in mining the rich interplay of architecture and ritual actions. Partly
in reaction to nineteenth- and early-twentieth-century trends of the
Cambridge School to invest ritual with meaning reflective of contemporary circumstances, archaeologists in the second half of the twentieth century aimed for less invested and more value-neutral description,
explication, and historical precision – that is to say, what and how
took definite priority over why. The attitude toward ritual theory often
resembled the medieval opinion of pagan statuary: while the subject
intrigues, it is regarded as vaguely malevolent, potentially dangerous,
and best avoided. In 1981, Bryony Orme could write, "Ritual and religion are taboo subjects in archaeological circles, denounced by the
brave and avoided by the sensible; only a perverse few continue their
studies in this dangerous field."[1]

Studies of ritual are now front and center, as Jaś Elsner lays out in this volume. But within the ever-burgeoning archaeological literature addressing excavated sacred sites and the standing remains of Mediterranean temples, sanctuaries, churches, and monasteries, only a few attempts have been made to situate the sites and physical remains within a broad theoretical or ritual context. Whereas emphasis has been placed recently on the domestic, civic, or funerary setting of ritual, as well as on the significance of pilgrimage, sacred contexts remain in the "dangerous" category.[2] On the one hand, the assumption that sacred architecture frames ritual appears so obvious as to not warrant comment; while on the other hand, the ritual actions have vanished to the point that their re-creation would seem to be a hopelessly speculative process. Discussions of specific ritual contexts or actions in the context of architecture are usually offered as brief and tentative speculations at the end of extensive "solid" discussions of the archaeological and architectural tangibles. By the same token, many excellent explorations of ritual, both theoretical and practiced, are often discussed in a nonspatial and non-site-specific context. Current ritual studies addressing sacred space focus on its political construction, its social and hierarchical dimensions, the dichotomy of status and power; it serves as the backdrop for change.[3] When the specific architectural setting of ritual is discussed, however, it is usually limited to the organization of levels of purity or sanctity, and the movement of human participants through space. These aspects are, to be sure, important, but exploration of ritual too easily devolves to the negotiation of boundaries, with architecture appearing simply as the passive setting of actions. It is therefore a matter of some urgency that we again attempt to examine the interaction of architecture and ceremony in sacred places for its sacred value.[4] The contributors to this volume, primarily archaeologists and architectural historians deeply rooted in the primacy of physical evidence, desire to make sense of that evidence in terms of the ritual actions that animate and give meaning to it in a sacred context.

The issues we address are basic to the discussion of sanctity and sacred ritual. How did a place or space become sacred? What or who were the active agents involved in the process of sanctification? How does the idea of inviolability become manifest in the built environment? By what process of invention and response do architects and patrons develop architectural forms and craft spaces that meet ritual needs? How does architectural form shape ritual actions? How does it define them?

We contend that in premodern historical societies the architectural setting was an active agent in the ritual process; architecture did not simply house or frame events, it magnified and elevated them and it could also interact with them and engender the construction of ceremonial. In this volume, we hope to reassert the connection of ritual in architecture through close archaeological and architectural analysis of particular places and buildings. Each brings its constellation of questions; collectively, they may serve as building blocks to larger theoretical concerns. In the Sanctuary of the Great Gods at Samothrace or the Church of the Holy Sepulchre in Jerusalem (to cite two examples studied by the editors) the ceremonial settings developed in direct response to the changing nature of the rituals and the sacred presences they housed. Although the benchmark of ritual is its recognizability and repeatability, ritual itself was never static; neither was its setting. The complex relationship of ritual to sacred space, and particularly the ways in which each had the power to transform the other over a long history, deserves closer scrutiny.

In this volume, we propose to examine the active agency of architecture in the ritual processes of premodern historical societies of the Mediterranean, focusing on the archaeological evidence from the Greek, Roman, Early Christian, Jewish, and Byzantine civilizations of the eastern Mediterranean. Architecture is interpreted broadly to include individual structures, complexes of buildings, and other forms of human intervention in the landscape (and in one instance, the landscape of the human body). In examining ritual and sacred space across cultures and religions with fundamentally differing bases and goals, we aim to demonstrate the centrality of architecture and reassert its claim to shape the human experience of the sacred.

Notes

1. Orme 1981, p. 218. An outlier in the study of architecture and ritual is, of course, Thomas Mathews's 1971 account of the interaction of architecture and liturgy in the early churches in Constantinople.
2. For domestic, see Parker Pearson and Richards 1994; civic, Goldhill and Osborne 1999; for studies characterizing scholarship of the 1990s, note Schechner 1993, Ahlbäck 1993; for later work see Elsner, this volume. For pilgrimage, Eade and

Sallnow 1991, Morinis 1992, Elsner and Rutherford 2003. For changes and transformations, Chaniotis 2005, Mylonopoulos 2008.
3. Notably, Smith 1987.
4. See Jones 2000 for an exploration of the sacred in architecture, although as intrinsic to the architecture and not in active relation to ritual practice.

Works Cited

Ahlbäck, T., ed. 1993. *The Problem of Ritual, Based on Papers Read at the Symposium on Religious Rites Held at Åbo, Finland, on the 13th–16th of August 1991*, Åbo.

Bell, C. 1992. *Ritual Theory, Ritual Practice*, New York.

Chaniotis, A. 2005. "Ritual Dynamics in the Eastern Mediterranean: Case Studies in Ancient Greece and Asia Minor," in *Rethinking the Mediterranean*, ed. W. Harris, Oxford, pp. 141–66.

Eade, J., and M. Sallnow, eds. 1991. *Contesting the Sacred: The Anthropology of Pilgrimage*, New York.

Elsner, J., and I. Rutherford, eds. 2003. *Pilgrimage in Graeco-Roman and Early Christian Antiquity: Seeing the Gods*, Oxford.

Goldhill, S., and R. Osborne, eds. 1999. *Performance Culture and Athenian Democracy*, Cambridge.

Jones, L. 2000. *The Hermeneutics of Sacred Architecture: Experience, Interpretation, Comparison*, vols. 1–2, Cambridge, MA.

Mathews, T. F. 1971. *The Early Churches of Constantinople: Architecture and Ritual*, University Park.

Morinis, A., ed. 1992. *Sacred Journeys; The Anthropology of Pilgrimage*, Westport, Conn.

Mylonopoulos, J. 2008. "The Dynamics of Ritual Space in the Hellenistic and Roman East," *Kernos* 21, pp. 49–79.

Orme, B. 1981. *Anthropology for Archaeologists*, Ithaca.

Parker Pearson, M., and C. Richards, eds. 1994. *Architecture and Order: Approaches to Social Space*, New York.

Schechner, R. 1993. *The Future of Ritual: Writings on Culture and Performance*, New York.

Smith, J. Z. 1987. *To Take Place: Toward a Theory of Ritual*, Chicago.

CHAPTER ONE

MATERIAL CULTURE AND RITUAL:
STATE OF THE QUESTION

Jaś Elsner

The last twenty years have seen a remarkable increase in the use of ritual as an analytic and conceptual tool across the range of material-cultural disciplines – archaeology, architectural history, the history of art. This very book is one example of that efflorescence. Certainly there can be no doubt about the rich range of rituals and ritual cultures that not only gave rise to images and objects for use and even veneration in ceremonial, but were themselves in fundamental ways determined by the deployment of artifacts within them and the constraints of material culture around them. In particular, the establishment of spatial boundaries through the markings of landscape and the placement of architecture, and the decorative embellishment of such spaces with art that was in some cases descriptive of sacred histories but was often potentially prescriptive of initiatory and ritualistic experience, is a ubiquitous feature of artistic and archaeological survivals from prehistoric antiquity into the middle ages and beyond. A number of classic anthropological studies and works in the history of religions in the twentieth century have laid the foundations for the study of material culture in its ritual aspects – as liminal space, as sacred centre, as participatory artefact within ritual.[1] Indeed – given the very different disciplinary demands of such fields as Neolithic prehistory, Classical archaeology, Byzantine aesthetics and the architectural history of the middle ages (all of which may at different points need to draw deeply on the study of ritual) – one might argue that what all these material-cultural subject-areas have in common (apart, that is, from a focus on material culture) is a shared interest in the study of ritual, which means in modern academia especially its anthropological and history-of-religions literature.[2]

My aim in this brief introduction is not to justify the current interest in ritual, which is hardly necessary, nor indeed to attack it, nor to attempt any kind of unified approach to ritual on the part of the great diversity of material-culture-centered disciplines that have had recourse to its study, and are well represented in this volume. Rather, I want to examine some of the assumptions we commonly make in looking to ritual as an explanatory system and to worry a little about whether they have all been sufficiently justified or grounded in argument. I will turn at the end from discussion of the general issues of material culture and ritual which must necessarily underlie many of the ramifications of the essays in this volume to the specific problems of architecture, sacred space and experience. The question of architecture is a special case of the theme of ritual and art, since it is about the orchestration of (performative) space – the frames within which people were constructed as ritual subjects – as opposed to the specific artifacts used by people within ritual. In general, whereas artifacts within ritual are so often manipulated by bodies, the special case of architecture, alongside large-scale sacred topographies, relates to its enclosure of bodies within a space at least potentially and on occasion reserved for ritual action. Moreover, insofar as architecture is an invitation into and an announcement of sacred space, it serves a material function analogous to some qualities of ritual itself. Notably, insofar as ritual is about liminality and the articulation of boundaries between sacred and profane, architecture is potentially one of its supreme material formulations.

Issues of Method. The rediscovery of ritual is certainly part of the cognitive movement in archaeology,[3] but it is also part of the rebellion of what was in the 1980s called "the new art history" against stylistic formalism and iconographical studies,[4] and in particular a turn towards more religious and anthropologically-focused interests away from the semiotic formalism and Marxist inflections that initially dominated the new art history. Certainly ritual has come to be seen in recent years as a critical concept in both prehistoric and historical archaeology,[5] as well as a critical term of art history.[6] Indeed, specifically in the arena of classical archaeology, the study of ritual through iconography has come to be established as a prime model for the study of ancient religion through the magisterial volumes of the *Thesaurus cultus et rituum antiquorum*, known as ThesCRA, which have used the concept of ritual as represented in art and in texts as a means to unite both visual and historical approaches to the study of ancient religion.[7] Although hardly the prime purpose of this emphasis on ritual studies, the alignment of material-cultural with historical approaches that has been part of its effect is certainly to be warmly welcomed.[8]

The birth of a new emphasis on ritual in archaeologically inflected studies from the 1980s, associated with such signal contributions as Colin Renfrew's *The Archaeology of Cult* and Simon Price's *Rituals and Power*,[9] took place at the same time as a burgeoning revitalization of interest in ritual on the part of historians of religion and anthropologists. These latter created the *Journal of Ritual Studies* in 1987; and certainly the anthropological exploration of ritual has been hugely creative in the last two decades with a number of seminal works published since the late 1980s. In the same decade, art history saw the birth of the journal *Res* from 1981, subtitled *anthropology and aesthetics* (although over the years it has not been notably ritual-centered in the kinds of anthropology its contributors have drawn on) and ancient history created the journal *Kernos* (from 1988) which has a strong ritual focus as part of its main remit for the study of ancient Greek religion, and *Archiv für Religionsgeschichte* (from 1999) whose focus extends beyond Greece and Rome to Israel, India, and pre-Columbian America.

What is surprising is the relative lack of cross-fertilization between what one might have imagined were kindred fields. Of major recent anthropological studies of ritual, there is almost not a word on material culture – whether on objects as implements within rituals, on buildings, enclosures or landscapes as spatial or geographic frames for rituals, on visual adornments as cues or potential non-written prescriptions for rituals – in the many acute pages of, for example, Bell 1992 and 1997; Boyer 1994, pp. 185–223; Humphrey and Laidlaw 1994; Rappaport 1999; Whitehouse 2000 and 2004; let alone the monumental pair of volumes edited by Kreinath, Snoek, and Stausberg 2006 and 2007. In the more than twenty years in which the *Journal of Ritual Studies* has flourished, only one early issue (vol. 6, no. 1, 1992) has been devoted to "Art and Ritual in Context" and as far as I can tell only two articles in the entire run outside this single issue (mainly consisting of papers by art historians) have touched on material culture at all.[10] There has been some discussion of the aesthetics of ritual,[11] but arguably this is not the same issue as the place of material culture as part of the frame and structure of ritual. While the anthropology of the subject has remained strikingly immune from contagion with the concerns of material culture,[12] it is also true that much art history and archaeology has not progressed far into the theoretics of ritual studies beyond the pre-1980s world of the works of such as Van Gennep, Victor Turner, and Clifford Geertz.[13]

Although anthropology, on the one hand, and the historical study of material culture, on the other, may agree on the importance of ritual, it is worth stressing a fundamental methodological difference between them. In anthropology, rituals are empirically observed data. That data may of course be wrongly interpreted as ritual by a misguided anthropologist, but in principle for a ritual to have been recorded in anthropology, it must have been directly and empirically attested. In art history, archaeology, or architectural history, ritual is not an empirical observation but rather an *inference*, a best guess, derived from material culture with the help of any other evidence (contextual, written, comparative) that can be supplied to help the argument work.

In both sets of disciplines, ritual represents a move to cognitive conclusions.[14] But what is meant by cognition is not quite the same in the two sets of fields. Anthropology has looked toward "intentional states behind ritual actions … located at least partly outside the mind of the actor,"[15] to all kinds of emotions,[16] from "high arousal" to boredom,[17] not to speak of failure.[18] In other words, it has begun to develop a rich and differentiated picture of the varieties of cognitive response to ritual, which may also be cognitive motors of ritual activity.[19] By contrast, in material-cultural disciplines, ritual is itself taken as a virtually cognitive category in its own right, in that it at least adumbrates a dimension of "past ways of thought as inferred from material remains,"[20] a "cognitive space."[21] In particular – and we will discuss this shortly – the category of "ritual" has come swiftly to elide into that of "religion."[22] In other words, it is not always clear exactly what is meant by "ritual" when it is evoked in archaeology or art and architectural history. Is it religion, with the dread name and implications of "religion" avoided? Is it something other than religion? In which case, is it something that overlaps with religion or is entirely different from it? Or has "ritual" become a kind of dust-bin category for all kinds of not terribly precise sacred, mystical, and emotional urges.[23]

However, before pressing the question of definition, it is worth staying with method. The use of material culture as evidence from which to infer ritual is one thing; the assumption that the ritual (whether a specific ritual, a ritual process or a culture that was in certain ways ritually invested) is what gave rise to the evidence of material culture before us, is quite another. In other words, there is a danger of circularity in inferring ritual from archaeologically attested artifacts and then arguing that the ritual, which is the result of our inference from those objects, was in some sense the cause of those objects. Circularity in itself may not always vitiate an argument, but one had better be strongly self-aware about the issue before pressing it. Yet why should we infer ritual unless we are seeking a generative context, which is in some respect causal of the objects or spaces under discussion?[24] In other words, the interest in the move from physical to cognitive,[25] is at least about reinforcing material culture with a deeper structure of meanings and mental intentions, and is often a matter of providing it with causes. But what are presented as causes are (in this case) inferences from what we take to be their artifactual effects.

Now here there are some differences between material cultural studies in historical periods and those from prehistory. In the former, artifacts and buildings can be placed beside other products of those periods (especially texts) and together the two bodies of evidence can be used to throw cultural light on bigger questions. In the latter, we have very little by way of corroborative evidence except for other comparanda – often from other cultural contexts and periods. Historiographically speaking, both these areas have been very reluctant to let objects – images, buildings, artifacts, works of art – stand simply as themselves. Both have wanted to supply a deeper structure of meanings to underpin the material evidence (hence the urge to go cognitive). It is not entirely obvious to me why this should be the case, or why it should be desirable; but if we want to apportion blame, then clearly the Iconology of Erwin Panofsky, defined as the "intrinsic meaning or content," "the symbolic values" of a culture, as re-presented in any one of its artifacts,[26] is a good candidate on account of its huge and still pervasive influence, even if Panofsky is no longer so often explicitly cited or read as he was until relatively recently.[27]

This is not the place to examine the complex origins of Panofsky's theory, but the point is that in the art and archaeology of the prehistoric periods (or shall we say the ones from which no writing survives?), the notion of ritual as a theoretical postulate has come to provide some of the deeper structure of "intrinsic meaning" and "symbolic values" that can hardly be supplied any other way. Of course it inevitably comes with dangers of anachronism, especially the reading back of Christianizing (or anti-Christian) models of religion and ritual into the past. In the historical disciplines – especially classical archaeology and the study of medieval art – we are fortunate in the ritual-centeredness of many of our surviving texts that make any mention of images. Most striking in this regard for antiquity is the travel book by Pausanias written in the second century C.E., which is certainly a ritual-centered and religiously inflected account of the art and monuments of Greece.[28] But if Pausanias was indeed a repetitive pilgrim with his text itself a ritualized version of his travels,[29] then it is hardly surprising if his record is weighted in that direction. It makes him an excellent witness to the *imaginaire* and even the precise realities of Greek ritual in the Roman period (by no means the same thing as Greek ritual in archaic, classical, or Hellenistic times, despite the fact that the text is repeatedly used in that way), but not necessarily a good guide as to how everyone else saw the material culture which he so insistently aligns in a ritual-centered direction.[30] Other sources, like Pliny the Elder, have very little interest in ritual as it relates to works of art. In other words, the reflex to Pausanias in so many studies that emphasize ritual[31] may be misleading in that they skew the evidence in the direction of a very particular but by no means universal or dominant set of "intrinsic meanings" and "symbolic values."

Optimism and Pessimism. The fundamental problem, however, seems to me to rest in two questions. First, the key empirical issue: how can we tell that it is appropriate to infer ritual from any given artifact or space? This was well articulated by Renfrew as "how do I know that this artifact had a ritual significance?"[32] And beyond the initial move of inference lies the problem of whether ritual is the only form of behavior we can infer, even in contexts where it may be a correct inference. In other words, what is the price of deciding for ritual? If we emphasize this, are we precluding other inferences or explanations? The second issue is that of definition: what do we mean by ritual? I shall take them in turn, but arguably they are not so different as distinguishing them into two questions makes it appear. A positive answer to the question "Is this an object of ritual?" is likely also to be aligned to a positive view of the value of ritual as a heuristic category and consequently to an optimistic or extensive view of the ramifications, consequences and meanings of ritual for our historical, social and conceptual understandings of a given culture.

At the opening of *The Archaeology of Cult*, Renfrew refers "with disapproval" to views elegantly advanced over a generation before by C. Hawkes who argued that to infer from archaeological phenomena to the religious institutions and spiritual life of the human groups concerned is the hardest inference of all.[33] Renfrew responds that "there is nothing inherently obscure or problematic" about inferring religious institutions or spiritual life[34] and goes on to argue that "the pessimism expressed by some archaeologists as to the possibility of reconstructing any elements of the content of religious belief from archaeological data alone is misplaced."[35] This conviction represents the bedrock of that optimism about identifying ritual and about what ritual may signify that has come to dominate material-cultural approaches to the topic.

Putting things in terms of optimists and pessimists is a good way to approach the problem. Here is a recent "optimistic" account of the value of ritual in relation to the Aegean Neolithic from M. Nikolaidou:

> There seem to be *inexhaustible* occasions for the ritualization of human actions, that is, *their elevation to a rank of priority over other practices* ... it is their very participation, *body and soul*, in an *act valued higher than the mundane order*, that *enables realization of fundamental symbolic knowledge* ...[36]

Now it is probably always unfair to select and dismantle a single quotation. But this puts the problems of modern scholarly optimism about ritual into firm focus. I have italicized what I take to be the optimistic assumptions. First, there are "inexhaustible occasions" for ritual – that is to say, in human lived experience (at any rate in the past) ritual is assumed to be frequent, perhaps omnipresent; also (implicitly) it is easily recoverable from the archaeological record. Second, by ritualization, we do not mean simply any old repeated or repetitive practice (for example, secular or personal rituals) but, clearly something "valued higher than the mundane order" that offers "realization of fundamental symbolic knowledge." In other words, without the explicit mention of the word "religion" much of what a committed insider to a faith would mean by religion has been imported into "the ritualization of human actions." Now this is very optimistic in its view of all rituals as positive and life-enhancing, as offering a substantive structure of intrinsic meaning and symbolic values (in Panofsky's terminology) underlying the particular data we find attested in the archaeological record, ultimately as not only moving us into cognitive space but giving the cognitive a clear steer.

In the face of this kind of approach, I have to confess my own pessimism by contrast (and here I suspect I agree with Hawkes against Renfrew, let alone Nikolaidou). First, I cannot see on what grounds other than faith one need necessarily make the leap from empirical data to ritual on "inexhaustible occasions," and second I don't see why ritual need in principle mean religion or be a positive category at all.[37] Are there are not endless examples of repetitive and ritualized activity from the nonsacred sphere,[38] from the brushing of one's teeth to the daily taking to and collecting of children from school by parents to all the rules we obey when driving a car to the rituals of the justice system and imprisonment (to move from the personal to the collective level)? To what extent do these deserve the terminology of "ritual"? To what extent can any be excluded? Some of these leave no mark in material culture, others leave as many material remains as a sacred sanctuary might. Such examples militate against any excessively optimistic view of ritual as the avoidance of analytic thought rather than its application.

A good example of taking "ritual" without further definition and without much apparent thought as a core category to mean "religion" are the five volumes of ThesCRA.[39] The literal translation of the title (*Thesaurus cultus et rituum antiquorum*) is "Thesaurus of the cult and rituals of antiquity." The word "ritual" is never defined, but the introduction (repeated at pp. xi–xii of each volume) claims to present "a comprehensive account of all substantial aspects of Greek, Roman and Etruscan *religion*, apart from any assessment of the purely spiritual or philosophical, and only incidentally of the historical" (whatever that means, my italics). What is then offered are a long series of detailed and impressive entries, drawn from visual evidence and iconography alongside epigraphy and other texts, on different kinds of rites (e.g., processions, sacrifice, libation, fumigation, and dedication, to summarize vol. 1), which together, it seems, constitute religion. Notwithstanding the great usefulness of such a compendium, it is frankly a monumental testimony to a series of presumptions and presuppositions grounded in no argument or analytic justification whatsoever. There is no discussion of the assumption that cult and rite can constitute religion, or how they may do so; no definition of either "ritual" or "religion"; no account of the method that translates a range of empirical entries into grand generalizations about cult in different periods and contexts. There is moreover no account of where ritual may cease to be religious, or where the overlaps do not work. This is optimism so extreme that it fails to entertain even a genuflection towards the possible attitudes or responses of the pessimist.

Yet even where we can infer ritual from material culture, there is no need for it always to be religious. A good example of nonreligious ritual (a category for which Renfrew now argues)[40] is the recent discovery of a room from the fourth century C.E. in a late Roman house of thirteen rooms in Trimithis in the Dakhleh Oasis of Egypt.[41] The house has wall paintings (some palimpsests with earlier paintings beneath) that include epic and mythological subjects. One room – only excavated in 2007–2008 – has whitewashed walls with various epigrams inscribed on it, which appear to have been written by a teacher for his students. Now the kind of context might be said to parallel the sorts of cult rooms built into houses in Dura Europos in Syria in the mid-third-century, which had wall-paintings, some palimpsestual, and inscriptions. From these images both a Christian baptistery and a Jewish synagogue have been inferred by the excavators and subsequent scholarship.[42] Yet it is obvious from the Egyptian material that what we have is a schoolroom. All the aspects of prescriptive decoration (here in the form of invocatory texts) and of liminal boundaries to define the space in which the ritual took place are there in the Trimithis house. And the ritual concerned is certainly one of the great ritualized activities of late antiquity, namely the passing on of *paideia*, which is more than merely education but rather the whole gamut of traditional culture, to the young. Indeed, as anyone who spends any time in or sends children to either school or university today is all too aware, education remains one of the great rituals of modern culture. But it is definitively not religious or mind altering in the terms implied by Nikolaidou ("body and soul").

In general, the current era of the application of ritual theory to material culture, and of inferring ritual realities from material culture, is extremely optimistic – much more so that I think is warranted either empirically or analytically. Ritual is now used as a concept to explain the longue-durée of cultural change, communication, and meaning in history.[43] It has become a catch-all category that fills a cognitive space to which empirical observation fails to point quite as often as the data offers grounds for inference. And what is meant by ritual has never been adequately defined, even by those anthropologists who have had the benefit of observing rituals as opposed to the archaeologists who have only inferred them. The assumption that rituals must be capable of communication and redolent of meaning is ubiquitous in the material-cultural literature,[44] despite a significant challenge to this from anthropology and history of religions, in which one strand has argued for the meaninglessness of ritual or at least its noncommunication of meanings.[45] The repetitive nature of ritual has been presented as an argument for the better preservation of this type of human activity than others in the material record,[46] despite the doubts about it being ephemeral which may work to vitiate its place in the record.[47] All this is excessive optimism. And the problem with it is that it leads not only to speculation,[48] but to heavily invested assumptions about culture and causation, evidence and inference, which have no possibility of being tested or justified. That is to say, if we are not careful, the turn to ritual studies will become the avoidance of thought rather than the appropriation of a useful category to think with.

Part of the problem is a pair of too swift leaps in interpretation: from the presence of regularity in the deposition of archaeological evidence to the assumption that this means ritualized behavior, and the move (often unacknowledged) from ritualized behavior (i.e., ritual) to inferring some sort of religious activity. Yet in fact regularity in the material-cultural record need not imply more than stylized or repeated behavior. Insofar as that is communicative (and there is no evidence that it is *always* so) then such stylized communication through artifacts is either with the supernatural world (in which case it does constitute some kind of religion and needs to be read theologically) or with the human world (in which case it ought to be accounted for at least in part politically). Of course, these two need not be wholly separate or mutually exclusive.[49] But in all these cases, it will be necessary to show that regularity occurs within a predictable structure and that if there is communication it will happen between different bits of that structure.

So in making an implicit case for a more cautious and "pessimistic" approach, my aim here is not to evoke despair. Ritual remains both an important category and an evocative one. What is needed in general is a more stringent justification of the empirical question – that is the leap from archaeologically attested visual or material evidence to the inference that it has ritual implications or origins; and at the same time much greater care in defining what ritual means, not indeed in a general or transhistorical or transcultural sense, but for the author of a given paper in relation to the body of material being assessed. I suspect greater awareness of the anthropological literature is necessary in the material cultural disciplines than has so far been usual, in order to come to a satisfactory if pragmatic, instrumental or narrowly based definition.[50] One question that is well worth asking is what are the ideological implications of any given scholarly tradition's turn to "ritual" and in the strange but frequent elision of "ritual" and "religion." Clearly, in prehistory, there is a worrying potential primitivism in "ritual" as a particular concern of the "ancient mind," a primitivism which one fears secularist scholarship may generally wish to apply to religion in any period. Such a position may be defensible by argument, but it ought not to be insinuated through innuendo (and cannot of course be justified or established in that way).

In the course of his brief but extremely interesting *Remarks on Frazer's Golden Bough*, Wittgenstein – here the philosopher in confrontation with anthropology, but also the foreigner commenting on the Briton – touches on two issues that are key to this inquiry. First, he challenges the ease of making inferences from objects:

> Isn't it like when I see a ruin and say: that must have been a house once, for nobody would have built up hewn and irregular stones into a heap constructed like this one. And if someone asked, how do you know that? I could only say: it is what my experience of people teaches me. And even where people do really build ruins, they give them the form of tumbled-down houses.[51]

It is highly dangerous to rely on common sense, "what my experience of people teaches me," to infer a house from ruins (since people really do make ruins, and ones that look like fallen-down houses), or a ritual – in this case, the building process I suppose – from material remains. Moreover, there is an inescapable danger – actually a rather interesting one – of investing one's own present concerns, one's desires and fantasies, into the cognitive space imagined in the past. This emerges in Wittgenstein's more intemperate exclamations against the more dated and parochial of Frazer's Victorian and Edwardian assumptions:

> What narrowness of spiritual life we find in Frazer! And as a result: how impossible for him to understand a different way of life from the English one of his time!
>
> Frazer cannot imagine a priest who is not basically an English parson of our times with all his stupidity and feebleness.[52]

This last is of course the objection of a Viennese in Cambridge writing in about 1930. But with more punch Wittgenstein is surely right – and not only of Frazer but of most explanations and projections of ritual observances in the past, when he writes:

> Frazer is much more savage than most of his savages, for these savages will not be so far from any understanding of spiritual matters as an Englishman of the twentieth century. His explanations of the primitive observances are much cruder than the sense of the observances themselves.[53]

The fundamental problem is that "ritual," and even more so the "religion" for which "ritual" is so often a shorthand, is a space of tremendous force and vibrant potential in the scholar's imagination. It is a "cognitive" space into which one's investments, desires, and fantasies of the past – which may be ideals about the present and may be reactions against the present, which may be about ancestralism and genealogy or may reflect its rejection – cannot but be placed. For all the careful scholarly apparatus of argument and analysis in establishing such rituals (or the possibility, even probability, that they took place) in the end their study is the working of ideology and not of empirical scholarship. That does not make them less interesting; indeed it makes them more so. It does not mean past views of ritual (such as Frazer's) are any less true than modern ones, but rather that they are symptomatic of their time and the varieties of polemics and concerns of that time. Their relevance to the supposed past object of inquiry, which is presented as evidence of them perhaps even caused by them, is less obvious. What is insidious is the pretence that what they really instantiate is anything other than the concerns of modernity.[54]

Beyond Pessimism. The weight of these remarks might imply that we should be negative about the category of ritual altogether.[55] But in fact I remain convinced of the critical value of the concept of ritual for the material-cultural disciplines. The question we must ask is how to employ the category wisely – without succumbing to so much more ideology and without it becoming what I (perhaps provocatively) called "a dustbin" for all kinds of unexamined projections and fantasies associated by the interpreter with the primitive or other idealized myths of the past.

In fact, I think there are many possibilities here. Arguably the category of ritual has become *too* anthropological in that it has been too based on modern observation and experience, theorized and retrojected back into the past. There are obviously differences in inferential potential between prehistoric periods, when there is no collateral evidence beyond the archaeological record, and those periods where other evidence (especially literary and epigraphic) may supplement that of material culture. If we start with the latter – where there is more evidence – we need also to be honest with ourselves about when what we are studying *is* religion, and that aspect of ritual which is part of the constituents of religion, and when it is not. Ritual as a fundamental aspect of religion is not fully synonymous with religion, nor does it constitute all that ritual (or ritualized activity) may be.

In attempting to provide a more propositional sense to our understanding of ritual, one approach would be to return to the substance of ritual-centered texts surviving from those periods from which we do have writing. This is not only literary material, like the travel book of Pausanias or the liturgical writings of the Church Fathers, but also the vast range of documents from votive inscriptions to the epigraphy of sacred laws, from the reports of Church councils to the form of the Mass and the stational liturgies as preserved by ecclesiastical calendars. The material is not simply so much regulation. Nor is it factual information (or disinformation) that may be applied to extend or focus our archaeologically derived knowledge. I mean the use of texts to be *read critically as a series of theological proposals instantiated through liturgical performance and ritual artifacts that offer philosophically distinct and often subtly modulated positions on how the other world can best be related to* by the collective of believers or religious adherents committed to the specific positions adumbrated in a given text. Such texts may relate to a large generality (the Church, for example) or a small subgroup (a sect, perhaps one condemned as "heretical" by others): they may therefore signal difference to and within a bigger spectrum of similar ritual action, much as particular architectural or pictorial choices may signal differences and specific identities.

Now we have to be careful here. As Bonna Wescoat points out to me, texts about one kind of ritual when applied to another have a strong chance of leading to misunderstanding – so that in the case of Samothrace, for instance, the application of too much text may lead to Eleusinianizing the mystery. But what I mean is not the use of text to throw up information or facts, but rather to elicit models of how ritual was *thought*. For example, in the sanctuary to Herakles at Sikyon named the Paedize, Pausanias reports two kinds of rituals (each founded on, or justified by, a different mythological genealogy) that celebrate Herakles at the same site as a god, on the one hand, and a hero, on the other (*Description of Greece* 2.10.1).[56] Here the ritual details, which as usual Pausanias reports with some care, effectively differentiate but also incorporate within a range of liturgical performance some fundamental theological distinctions specific to this site, cult and mythical nexus but in other ways more generally relevant to the culture of divine heroes and hero worship in ancient Greece. In other cases, Pausanias uses ritual to detail a range of kinds of mediation with the gods from imitative role-play where priests and devotees reenact mythical events to very specific exclusions of particular categories of worshippers (by age, gender, chastity-status, initiation, being a priest or not, and so forth) in relation to particular ceremonies or the cultivation of particular images. In certain cases images (whether cult statues or votives) may perform the work of ritual action itself (notably *Description of Greece* 10.18.5).[57] Now the entailments of Pausanias's observations may serve more than one agenda, even in his own account. They may be ethnographic (pointing at activities in different parts of Greece),[58] they may equally be related to historical claims, but it is hard to deny them a substantive religious basis. Likewise, after the end of pagan polytheism, such texts as Pseudo-Dionysius' *Ecclesiastical Hierarchy* (from the sixth century C.E.), Germanos of Constantinople's *On the Divine Liturgy* (from the early-eighth-century Eastern Church) or the Venerable Bede's *On the Temple* and *On the Tabernacle* (from the eighth-century Latin Church), with their varieties of exegesis of scripture, contemplations of church space and artefacts, and meditations on ritual process and meaning, offer rich potential for grasping some aspects of the *imaginaire* of material culture in ritual, at least for some of the more intellectual practitioners and leaders of ecclesiastical liturgy.

The material culture – from cult statues and icons to votives of all kinds, from the architecture of sanctuaries to the manifold means of their decoration (both official, in terms of paintings, mosaics or relief-sculpture, and unofficial in terms of graffiti left by devotees), is *in no way less* theologically propositional than the texts. Given the range of interpretative positions at any particular moment within a given culture about the nature of its gods and its humans' relations with them which we can intimate from the texts, the images and monuments offer both further materially concretised "thought" within these parameters and an extension of the range of written propositions into the world of ritual artefacts themselves. The world of ritual – a sophisticated propositional world of living theology in its own right – to which this combination of material gives us (limited) access, is itself no more than the temporally, physically and performatively instituted thinking of a culture about its relations and mediations with the divine.[59]

Now there is no doubt that a material-cultural approach of this sort to ritual within religion is cognitive. But it is cognitive in that it is theological – using objects and spaces no less than texts or myths as formulations of, and access to, propositions about the other world and relations with the other world. It cannot give us the "whole answer" (whatever that would be) but it can delineate some parameters of the cognitive space that ritual and art within ritual filled, circumscribed and tested in any given context. In the case of pre- or nonliterate cultures, we are necessarily on weaker territory. What is needed – and with great care so that it is clear one is not reading ancestral projections or rejections back into a time whose evidential base cannot refute them – is to use the models derivable from historical periods as a series of speculative hypotheses. Ideally one would construct competing models of ritual and the ritual usage of material culture, which will at least offer broad parameters for the functions of artefacts and the kinds of rites they may point to. Ideally contrasting and mutually exclusive models would provide a basis for competitive plausibility in an always hypothetical set of reconstructions. In this case, one has to be particularly cautious about the possibility that the rituals concerned may not in fact have been religious.

One issue in all this that needs emphasis is that observable differences in the material record may not reflect temporal change (an assumption all too readily leaped upon by the historically minded archaeologist), but rather different forms of theological experiments or philosophical positions. Difference may reflect not cognitive change in a homogenous culture but cognitive multiplicity in the matter of religious thinking within cultures as rich as the ancient polytheism attested by Pausanias or the multiple Christianities (full of "heresies," "heterodoxies," and competing orthodoxies) that define the early Church. The point is well made in the material record of late antiquity, where different cults chose to appropriate the image of ritual action (especially sacrifice) to the cult image, but in ways that are structurally differentiated from each other. Various pagan deities appear pouring libations; Mithras in the stereotypical cult image repeated in hundreds of surviving mithraea conducts the act of sacred slaughter in killing the bull; Jesus – in a brilliant reversal of the model of deity as recipient of sacrifice or instigator of sacrifice – becomes the sacrificial victim, whether represented as a man on a cross or as a lamb.

There are, it seems to me, plenty of grounds for thinking there is promise of interesting work at the interface of material culture and ritual. That promise has, despite a vast amount of scholarship, not really been fulfilled yet. Above all, this is because, for all the necessary talk of the cognitive, those who deal in material culture have shied away from embracing theology. There is in this context obviously a two-way relationship between how particular propositions in thought or belief may guide what people do and what artifacts and rituals they construct in their religion, on the one hand, and how such artifacts and rituals then help to determine the religious views people come to hold, on the other.

◲◱◲

If we turn now to the special case of architecture, it is clear that many of the general issues of material culture and ritual discussed above are relevant. There is no doubt that we have different methodological problems given the difference between historical periods for which we have relevant collateral literary evidence and those for which we do not. Likewise, with buildings or sanctuaries that still stand, where we can at least have some sense of lighting and above-ground architectural orchestration, we are in a different situation from those which need reconstruction from a ground plan. The case of one-off survivals is particularly charged – so, for instance, the Dura Europos synagogue discussed in this book by Jodi Magness offers our one example to date of a complex of historiated wall paintings in a late ancient synagogue, by contrast with copious floor mosaics. Less than half of its murals survive, along with its decorated ceiling tiles (but we have no clue as to the order by which these would have been arranged). It is true that many of the Dura synagogue images focus on priests, rituals (including sacrifice), implements of Jewish liturgy such as the Menorah, temples and so forth. But that is in itself not evidence for what went on in the building, nor for what kinds of relations the synagogue's liturgy may have had with its decoration.

Indeed the example of Pausanias at the Altis – the sacred grove of Zeus at Olympia – one of Greece's most holy sites from archaic antiquity to the end of paganism, remains fundamental and salutary. We know the Altis rather well because of the detail of Pausanias's account and over a century of matching the site's archaeology against this text and the many surviving inscriptions.[60] But at *Description of Greece* 5.14.4 and 5.14.10 Pausanias specifically announces that his account of the altars at Olympia will follow a liturgical order of sacrificial movement according to local ritual practice, despite the way this categorically cuts across any spatial logic of juncture, proximity, or structure. Moreover, this ritual ordering is differently applied from his ordering of other items in the Olympia sanctuary such as statues of Zeus, votive offerings, or victor statues celebrating athletes.[61] This passage is of great significance. For it proves, at least in one case (but that of *the* prime panhellenic sanctuary of Greece) and in an observer unusually sensitive and experienced in both the range of architectural dispositions of sacred sites and the variety of their rituals, that there need be *no relation at all* between the architectural logic of a building or religious enclosure and the ritual logic of what went on inside or around it. Indeed, the two may be in deliberate contradistinction. That is, in focusing on ritual in relation to architecture, we cannot automatically trust *any* of our normal assumptions about the organisation of space through contiguity, sight-lines, apparent processional orchestration, structural order, and so forth. The logic of ritual is perfectly capable of turning this upside down – and certainly did so in ancient Greece's holiest site, at least as experienced by Pausanias in the latter part of the second century C.E.

Let me leap into the Christian era and to absolute modernity but in a building of exceptional sanctity and great antiquity – which happens to be discussed by Bob Ousterhout in his contribution to this volume. In the week before I am writing these words (on 9 November 2008 to be precise), an apparently regular Armenian procession within the church of the Holy Sepulchre in Jerusalem was barred on its route by Greek Orthodox clergy, not very far from the Aedicula (the Tomb of Christ) to judge by the footage shot from cellphones, which was available on the internet. The two sides came to quite a punch-up.[62] Such explosions of feeling are hardly unknown in especially charged sites, particularly when these are contested (as is Jerusalem itself between religions and the Holy Sepulchre between Christian factions). But what is the ritual? Is it the regular (normative?) procession initiated by the Armenians? Or its stopping by the Greeks, which is something that happens relatively regularly although not always with violence and in response to parallel attempts to bar Greek processions by the Armenians? Or is it the outbreak of violence between men of the cloth (in which the media reveled but which too has a long history on that site and many others). Here nothing about the architectural peculiarities or structure of the Holy Sepulchre can tell us much in relation to this ritual and its spontaneities (which may be regarded as its subversion or its extension). And yet the church's territorial subdivision by the various Christian sects which use it has much to do with the rituals practiced there (according to varied ritual calendars) and indeed the urgency of the conflicts instantiated by the fist-fight of 9 November 2008 depends on the sacredness of the space and the depth of the investments in it. The site as we know it architecturally and historically is the necessary setting for such activity, endlessly and not very predictably brought to life in the actions of living people. What this example has in common with Pausanias's observations of ritual at Olympia is that the material-cultural frame of a ritual center – architectural, topographic, decorative – may offer no clues at all as to what people choose to do liturgically within it.

The essays gathered here, by negotiating some of these difficulties in the specific context of architecture, offer two contributions to the bigger picture of material culture and ritual. First, they place architectural history and sacred space firmly on the map as an area in which ritual is both hugely fruitful as a category to think with and in which it has received surprisingly less discussion than in other areas of material culture. Second, they define a related temporal trajectory of continuity and change in the Mediterranean, which challenges with deft assurance the traditional assumptions of a single clean break between pagan polytheism and Christianity as well as between the Christian east and west, at any rate in the early period.

⬚⬚⬚

I am grateful, for their very helpful critiques and comments, to Simon Coleman, Milette Gaifman, Rob Nelson, Robin Osborne, and the two editors of this volume, Bob Ousterhout and Bonna Wescoat. None are to be held responsible for the idiosyncrasy of the views expressed here!

Notes

1. E.g., Van Gennep 1909; Eliade 1959; Eliade 1963; Turner 1969; Geertz 1973; Smith 1987.
2. For an incisive attack on the concept of ritual as "reductionist, too-often vague and essentially alien" when applied to the Christian Middle Ages (ostensibly that most ritualised of cultures), see Buc 2001 passim, but esp. pp. 4–11, 247 (whence the quote), 248–61.
3. E.g., Renfrew and Zubrow 1994.
4. E.g., Rees and Borzello 1986.
5. E.g., Bertemes and Biehl 2001; Kyriakidis 2007a.
6. E.g., Blier 2003.
7. Lambrinoudakis and Balty 2004–6.

8. The specific use of ritual and ritual change as an explanatory model within more strictly historical work is beyond my remit here. But see, e.g., Muir 1997 and Buc 2001, the latter with a very useful discussion of the history of medieval historians' uses of "ritual" at pp. 203–47.
9. Renfrew 1985; Price 1984.
10. These are Boyd and Williams 1989 and Crawford O'Brien 2008. In general, among classic anthropological approaches, Victor Turner's is perhaps most attuned to the ways material culture must nuance the rituals of which it is part – see for instance the discussion of images in Turner and Turner, 1978, pp. 140–71, or the analysis of symbols, pp. 243–51. Among historians of religion Ronald Grimes – one of the founders of the *Journal of Ritual Studies* – has been sympathetic to the place of material culture: See Grimes 1993, pp. 61–126 and Grimes 2006, pp. 3–13 (on the media) and pp. 87–113 (on space).
11. E.g., Williams and Boyd, 2006.
12. The most influential anthropological discussion of material culture in the last twenty years, Gell 1998, is interestingly shy of any discussion of ritual except in the specific issue of the rites for consecrating sacred images (Gell 1998, pp. 143–53). The subtlest anthropological account of material culture in the context of ritual known to me is the work of Susanne Küchler – esp. Küchler 2002, which builds on a number of earlier essays on Malanggan – the making and ritual destruction/sacrifice of funerary effigies in New Ireland, Papua New Guinea.
13. Of the recent works on ritual by classicists known to me, only Stavrianopoulou 2006b cites a wide range of post-1980s anthropology.
14. See, for instance, in recent anthropology the work of McCauley and Lawson, 2002; Whitehouse 2004; Lawson 2006.
15. Whitehouse 2004, pp. 3–4.
16. E.g., Lüddeckens 2006.
17. High arousal: Whitehouse 2004, pp. 71, 72; boredom: Nuckolls 2007.
18. Failure: Hüsken 2007.
19. A rare example of the attempt to find emotions in the ritual inferences that may be drawn from ancient epigraphy is Chaniotis 2006 – although note his overt resort to fiction at pp. 214–16. One might argue that phenomenology in art historical approaches is also a way of exploring the contents of the cognitive: see, e.g., Nelson 2007, esp. 496–500. But again this requires significant imaginative and speculative input on the part of the interpreter.
20. Renfrew 1994a, p. 3.
21. Kyriakidis 2007b, p. 299.
22. Renfrew, 1985, pp. 11–18 and Renfrew 1994b, critiqued to his great credit by Renfrew 2007, pp. 110, 114, 121–2; Marcus and Flannery 1994, p. 60; Lambrinoudakis and Balty 2004–6, passim; Owoc 2008, p. 1923. For an interesting critique of cognitive archaeology's penchant to "study cognition of that which the archaeologist can also cognize, rather than move immediately to the necessarily speculative realm of cognition of the supernatural"; see Osborne 2004, p. 5.
23. For an anthropologist's worries about the concept of ritual having become so broad and wet as to be useless, see Goody 1977.
24. E.g., Mylonopoulos 2008, p. 53 – "a remodelling of space *due to* ritual changes."
25. Kyriakidis 2007b, pp. 298–301.

26. Panofsky 1955, pp. 30–31 and 40.
27. Of particular significance here is Panofsky's development of Karl Mannheim's sociological take on *Weltanschauung* ("worldview") which Mannheim developed especially from reading the art history of Alois Riegl, and Pierre Bourdieu's uses of Panofsky to create a nonreductive sociology. For discussion of Mannheim and Panofsky, see Hart 1993, esp. 534–7 and 541–66; Tanner 2003, pp. 10–12; Tanner forthcoming. For Bourdieu on Panofsky, see Bourdieu 2004. For discussion of Bourdieu and Panofsky, see Tanner 2003, pp. 20–21, 74.
28. E.g., Hutton 2005a; Pretzler 2007.
29. Elsner 1995, pp. 125–58, esp. 144; Rutherford 2001; Hutton 2005b.
30. See, e.g., Pirenne-Delforge 2006, a subtle discussion.
31. E.g., Mylonopoulos 2008.
32. Renfrew, 1985, p. 3.
33. Hawkes 1954, pp. 161–2; Renfrew 1985, p. 1.
34. Renfrew 1985, p. 1.
35. Renfrew 1985, p. 14.
36. Nikolaidou, 2007, p. 183.
37. See Buc, 2001, p. 161: "In an age in which, in academic circles at least, religious belief is not quite understood any longer, the concept of 'ritual' has inherited the mantle of another concept, 'religion', and plays the same structural role in many explanatory models." It is worth noting that there have since the 1980s been a series of substantive contributions to the ritualization of power – which may often draw on religious precedents but need not. See, e.g., Cannadine and Price 1987; Theuws and Nelson 2000; Bertelli 2001; Howe 2007.
38. Moore and Myerhoff, 1977.
39. Lambrinoudakis and Balty, 2004–2006.
40. Renfrew 2007.
41. Cribiore, Davoli, and Ratzan 2008.
42. Kraeling 1956 and 1967.
43. E.g., Chaniotis 2005.
44. This is the governing premise of Stavrianopoulou 2006a.
45. Meaninglessness: esp. Staal 1978 and 1989; Boyer 2001, pp. 264–7; Laidlaw and Humphrey 2006, pp. 271–83.
46. Kyriakidis 2007c, p. 9; cf. Markus 2007, p. 68 on repetition "working in the archaeologist's favour."
47. Stone 1992, pp. 111–12; Ranger 2007.
48. Marcus 2007, p. 43.
49. See, e.g., Osborne 1994 on the ritualization of politics, culture and religion in Democratic Athens.
50. Likewise, it is high time that the anthropology of ritual began to think a little about the objects and spaces that define its area of activity, as have other fields within anthropology such as visual anthropology, the anthropology of technologies and the anthropology of agency.
51. Wittgenstein 1979, 17e.
52. Wittgenstein 1979, 5e.
53. Wittgenstein 1979, 8e.
54. This is not the place to probe one deep and very significant strand in the construction of secular modernity's fantasies about religion (of which its reductive implicit definition as "ritual" is one). But the long history of polemic between

Protestant and Catholic scholarship on issues of what religion should be clearly
includes questions of ritual (including the positions of anthropologists), the
use of decoration and artifacts (including the positions of art historians and
archaeologists), primitivism (both as a positive "simple" category and as a negative precivilized category) and so forth. A good account is Smith 1990, focused
on religions in late antiquity (but not at all on issues of material culture in the
period, on which see further Elsner 2003). On the problem in the history of art
history, see Squire 2009, chs. 1 and 2. On E. B. Tylor and early anthropology, see
Regard 2007.

55. The conclusion of Buc 2001.
56. See Elsner 1996, pp. 523–4.
57. See Elsner 1996, pp. 526–7.
58. See Alcock 1996.
59. See, e.g., Gaifman 2008.
60. Trendelenburg 1914; König 2005, pp. 158–204; Newby 2005, pp. 202–28.
61. See Elsner 2001, pp. 11–18 and, apparently quite independently, Hölscher 2002,
    with Mylonopoulos 2006, pp. 106–8.
62. See, for instance, *http://www.washingtonpost.com/wp-dyn/content/article/2008/11/
    09/AR2008110900726_pf.html* or *http://www.timesonline.co.uk/tol/comment/faith/
    article5121217.ece*

Works Cited

Alcock, S. 1996. "Landscapes of Memory and the Authority of Pausanias," in
    Pausanias historien, ed. J. Bingen, Geneva pp. 241–67.

Bell, C. 1992. *Ritual Theory, Ritual Practice*, Oxford.

Bell, C. 1997. *Ritual: Perspectives and Dimensions*, Oxford.

Bertelli, S. 2001. *The King's Body: Sacred Rituals in Medieval and Early Modern Europe*,
    University Park, PA.

Bertemes, F., and P. Biehl, eds. 2001. *The Archaeology of Cult and Religion*,
    Budapest.

Blier, S. 2003. "Ritual" in R. Nelson and R. Shiff, *Critical Terms for Art History*,
    Chicago, pp. 296–305.

Bourdieu, P. 2004. "Postface" to E. Panofsky, *Architecture gothique et pensée scholas-
    tique*, Paris, Editions de minuit, pp. 135–67.

Boyd, J., and R. Williams. 1989. "Ritual Spaces: An Application of Aesthetic
    Theory to Zoroastrian Ritual," *Journal of Ritual Studies* 6.1, pp. 1–44.

Boyer, P. 1994. *The Naturalness of Religious Ideas: A Cognitive Theory of Religion*,
    Berkeley.

Boyer, P. 2001. *Religion Explained*, London.

Buc, P. 2001. *The Dangers of Ritual: Between Early Medieval Texts and Social Scientific
    Theory*, Princeton.

Cannadine, D., and S. Price. 1987. *Rituals of Royalty: Power and Ceremonial in
    Traditional Societies*, Cambridge.

Chaniotis, A. 2005. "Ritual Dynamics in the Eastern Mediterranean: Case
    Studies in Ancient Greece and Asia Minor," in *Rethinking the Mediterranean*, ed.
    W. Harris, Oxford, pp. 141–66.

Chaniotis, A. 2006. "Rituals between Norms and Emotions: Rituals as Shared Experience and Memory," in Stavrianopoulou 2006a, pp. 211–38.

Crawford O'Brien, S. 2008. "Talking Place: Ritual and Reciprocity at Holy Wells and Mass Stones in the Republic of Ireland," *Journal of Ritual Studies* 22.1, pp. 1–20.

Cribiore, R., P. Davoli, and S. Ratzan. 2008. "A Teacher's Dipinto from Trimithis (Dakhleh Oasis)", *Journal of Roman Archaeology* 21, pp. 170–91.

Eliade, M. 1959. *The Sacred and the Profane: The Nature of Religion*, New York.

Eliade, M. 1963. "Sacred Places: Temple, Palace, 'Center of the World,'" in *Patterns in Comparative Religion*, New York.

Elsner, J. 1995. *Art and the Roman Viewer: The Transformation of Art from the Pagan World to Christianity*, Cambridge.

Elsner, J. 1996. "Image and Ritual: Reflections of the Religious Appreciation of Classical Art," *The Classical Quarterly* 46.2, pp. 515–31.

Elsner, J. 2001. "Structuring Greece: Pausanias' *Periegesis* as a Literary Construct," in *Pausanias: Travel and Memory in Roman Greece*, ed. S. Alcock, J. Cherry and J. Elsner, Oxford, pp. 3–20.

Elsner, J. 2003. "Archaeologies and Agendas: Reflections on Late Ancient Jewish Art and Early Christian Art," *Journal of Roman Studies* 83, pp. 114–28.

Gaifman, M. 2008. "Visualized Rituals and Dedicatory Inscriptions on Votive Offerings to the Nymphs," *Opuscula: Annual of the Swedish Institute at Athens and Rome* 1, pp. 85–103.

Geertz, C. 1973. *The Interpretation of Cultures*, New York.

Gell, A. 1998. *Art and Agency: An Anthropological Approach*, Oxford.

Goody, J. 1977. "Against Ritual: Loosely Structured Thoughts on a Loosely Defined Topic," in Moore and Myerhoff 1977, pp. 25–35.

Grimes, R. 1993. *Reading, Writing and Ritualizing: Ritual in Fictive, Liturgical and Public Places*, Washington, DC.

Grimes, R. 2006. *Rite out of Place: Ritual, Media and the Arts*, Oxford.

Hart, J. 1993. "Erwin Panofsky and Karl Mannheim: A Dialogue on Interpretation," *Critical Inquiry* 19, pp. 534–66.

Hawkes, C. 1954. "Archaeological Theory and Method: Some Suggestions from the Old World," *American Anthropologist* 56, pp. 155–68.

Hölscher, T. 2002. "Rituelle Raüme und politischer Denkmäler im Heiligtum von Olympia," in *Olympia 1875–2000*, ed. H. Kyrieleis, pp. 331–43.

Hüsken, U., ed. 2007. *When Rituals Go Wrong: Mistakes, Failure and the Dynamics of Ritual*, Leiden.

Humphrey, C., and J. Laidlaw. 1994. *The Archetypal Actions of Ritual: A Theory of Ritual Illustrated by the Jain Rite of Worship*, Oxford.

Hutton, W. 2005a. *Describing Greece: Landscape and Literature in the Periegesis of Pausanias*, Cambridge.

Hutton, W. 2005b. "The Construction of Religious Space in Pausanias," in *Pilgrimage in Greco-Roman and Christian Antiquity*, ed. J. Elsner and I. Rutherford, Oxford, pp. 291–317.

König, J. 2005. *Athletics and Literature in the Roman Empire*, Cambridge.

Kraeling, C. H. 1956. *The Excavation at Dura-Europos: Final Report VIII.1: The Synagogue*, New Haven.

Kraeling, C. H. 1967. *The Christian Building: Excavations at Dura-Europos, Final Report VIII.2*, New Haven.

Kreinath, J., J. Snoek, and J. Stausberg, eds. 2006. *Theorizing Rituals: Issues, Topics, Approaches, Concepts*, Leiden.

Kreinath, J., J. Snoek, and J. Stausberg, eds. 2007. *Theorizing Rituals: Annotated Bibliography of Ritual Theory*, Leiden.

Küchler, S. 2002. *Malanggan: Art, Memory and Sacrifice*, Oxford.

Kyriakidis E., ed. 2007a. *The Archaeology of Ritual*, Los Angeles.

Kyriakidis, E. 2007b. "Archaeologies of Ritual," in Kyriakidis (ed.) 2007a, pp. 289–308.

Kyriakidis, E. 2007c. "Finding Ritual: Calibrating the Evidence," in Kyriakidis (ed.), 2007a, pp. 9–22.

Laidlaw, J., and C. Humphrey. 2006. "Action," in Kreinath, Snoek, and Stausberg, 2006, pp. 265–83.

Lambrinoudakis, V., and J. Balty, eds. 2004–6. *Thesaurus cultus et rituum antiquorum*, 2004, Los Angeles, 5 vols. + index.

Lawson, E. T. 2006. "Cognition," in Kreinath, Snoek, and Stausberg 2006, pp. 307–19.

McCauley, R., and E. T. Lawson. 2002. *Bringing Ritual to Mind: Psychological Foundations of Cultural Forms*, Cambridge.

Marcus, J. 2007. "Rethinking Ritual," in Kyriakidis (ed.) 2007a, pp. 43–76.

Marcus, J., and K. V. Flannery. 1994. "Ancient Zapotec Ritual and Religion: An Application of the Direct Historical Method," in Renfrew and Zubrow 1994, pp. 55–74.

Moore, S., and B. Myerhoff, eds. 1977. *Secular Ritual*, Assen.

Muir, E. 1977. *Ritual in Early Modern Europe*, Cambridge.

Mylonopoulos, J. 2006. "Greek Sanctuaries as Places of Communication through Rituals: An Archaeological Perspective," in Stavrianopoulou 2006, pp. 69–110.

Mylonopoulos, J. 2008. "The Dynamics of Ritual Space in the Hellenistic and Roman East," *Kernos* 21, pp. 49–79.

Nelson, R. 2007. "Empathetic Vision: Looking at and with a Performative Byzantine Miniature," *Art History* 30, pp. 489–502.

Newby, Z. 2005. *Greek Athletics in the Roman World: Victory and Virtue*, Oxford.

Nikolaidou, M. 2007. "Ritualized Technologies in the Aegean Neolithic? The Crafts of Adornment," in Kyriakidis 2007a, pp. 183–208.

Nuckolls, L. 2007. "Boring Rituals," *Journal of Ritual Studies* 21.1, pp. 33–48.

Osborne, R. 1994. "Introduction. Ritual, Finance and Politics: An Account of Athenian Democracy," in *Ritual, Finance and Poltics: Athenian Democratic Accounts Presented to David Lewis*, R. Osborne and S. Hornblower, ed., Oxford, pp. 1–25.

Osborne, R. 2004. "Hoards, Votives, Offerings: The Archaeology of the Dedicated Object," *World Archaeology* 36.1: *The Object of Dedication*, pp. 1–10.

Owoc, M. 2008. "Ritual, Religion and Ideology" in *Encyclopedia of Archaeology*, D. Pearsall, ed., Oxford, pp. 1922–32.

Panofsky, E. 1955. "Iconography and Iconology: An Introduction to the Study of Renaissance Art," in *Meaning in the Visual Arts*, Chicago, pp. 26–54.

Pirenne-Delforge, V. 2006. "Ritual Dynamics in Pausanias: The Laphria," in Stavrianopoulou 2006a, pp. 111–29.

Pretzler, M. 2007. *Pausanias: Travel Writing in Ancient Greece*, London.

Price, S. 1984. *Rituals and Power: The Roman Imperial Cult in Asia Minor*, Cambridge.

Ranger, T. 2007a. "Living Ritual and Indigenous Archaeology: The Case of Zimbabwe," in Kyriakidis 2007, pp. 123–53.

Rappaport, R. 1999. *Ritual and Religion in the Making of Humanity*, Cambridge.

Rees, A. L., and F. Borzello, eds. 1986. *The New Art History*, London.

Regard, F. 2007. "The Catholic Mule: E. B. Tylor's Chimeric Perception of Otherness," *Journal of Victorian Culture* 12.2, pp. 225–37.

Renfrew, C. 1985. *The Archaeology of Cult: The Sanctuary at Phylokapi*, London.

Renfrew, C. 1994a. "Towards a Cognitive Archaeology," in Renfrew and Zubrow 1994, pp. 3–12.

Renfrew, C. 1994b. "The Archaeology of Religion," in Renfrew and Zubrow 1994, pp. 47–54.

Renfrew, C. 2007. "Archaeology of Ritual, of Cult and of Religion," in Kyriakidis 2007, pp. 109–22.

Renfrew, C., and E. Zubrow, eds. 1994. *The Ancient Mind: Elements of Cognitive Archaeology*, Cambridge.

Rutherford, I. 2001. "Tourism and the Sacred: Pausanias and the Traditions of Greek Pilgrimage" in *Pausanias: Travel and Memory in Roman Greece*, ed. S. Alcock, J. Cherry, and J. Elsner, Oxford, pp. 40–52.

Smith, J. Z. 1987. *To Take Place: Toward Theory in Ritual*, Chicago.

Smith, J. Z. 1990. *Drudgery Divine: On the Comparison of Early Christianities and the Religions of Late Antiquity*, Chicago.

Squire, M. 2009. *Image and Text in Greco-Roman Antiquity*, Cambridge.

Staal, F. 1978. "The Meaninglessness of Ritual," *Numen* 26, pp. 2–22.

Staal, F. 1989. *Rules without Meaning: Rituals, Mantras and the Human Sciences*, New York.

Stavrianopoulou, E., ed. 2006a. *Ritual and Communication in the Graeco-Roman World*, *Kernos*, suppl. 16, Liége.

Stavrianopoulou, E. 2006b. "Introduction" to Stavrianopoulou 2006a, pp. 7–22.

Stone, A. 1992. "From Ritual in the Landscape to Capture in the Urban Centre: The Recreation of Ritual Environments in Meso-America," *Journal of Ritual Studies* 6, pp. 109–32.

Tanner, J. 2003. *The Sociology of Art*, London.

Tanner, J. 2009. "Karl Mannheim and Alois Riegl: from the History of Art to the Sociology of Culture," *Art History* 32, pp. 755–84.

Theuws, F., and J. Nelson, eds. 2000. *Rituals of Power from Late Antiquity to the Early Middle Ages*, Leiden.

Trendelenburg, A. 1914. *Pausanias in Olympia*, Berlin.

Turner, V. W. 1969. *The Ritual Process: Structure and Antistructure*, Ithaca, New York.

Turner, V., and E. Turner. 1978. *Image and Pilgrimage in Christian Culture*, New York.

Van Gennep, A. 1909. *Les rites de passage*, Paris; translated as A. Van Gennep 1960, *The Rites of Passage*, Chicago.

Whitehouse, H. 2000. *Arguments and Icons: Divergent Modes of Religiosity*, Oxford.

Whitehouse, H. 2004. *Modes of Religiosity: A Cognitive Theory of Religious Transmission*, Walnut Creek.

Williams, R., and J. Boyd 2006. "Aesthetics" in Kreinath, Snoek, and Stausberg, pp. 285–305.

Wittgenstein, L. 1979. *Remarks on Frazer's Golden Bough*, Brynmill.

CHAPTER TWO

MONUMENTAL STEPS AND THE SHAPING OF CEREMONY

Mary B. Hollinshead

Monumental steps, those that are broader than necessity requires, were used from at least the sixth century B.C.E. in Greek sanctuaries, as pathways for processions and as grandstands for observing events.[1] Although they did not constitute the architectural statement of a temple or the ritual focus of an altar, broad steps facilitated and promoted participatory behavior around the central act of sacrifice. Shared experience confers authority on ritual. Sacrifice was important both for its symbolic content and because numbers of people observed and participated in the ritual. Broad steps both increased anticipation of the event in procession and intensified spectators' experience as they massed in a crowd.

Studies of Greek architecture often dissect sanctuaries in terms of form, either as typologies of specific buildings or as arrangements of parts – solids and voids, temples and terraces – as if devoid of people. Studies of ritual and religious behavior, relying on votive objects, inscriptions and literary testimonia, rarely say much about place. In considering spatial aspects of group behavior around animal sacrifice, I will explore how architectural structures built to accommodate crowds of worshippers express and give shape to human activities while enhancing ritual enactment.[2]

At sites in Greece, Asia Minor, and Italy in the sixth through first centuries B.C.E., broad steps that provide routes of access and viewing facilities also integrate sanctuary design by linking architectural components within the temenos into a more coherent unity than in earlier eras. We witness evolutionary changes from built steps that give expression to parading and spectating to architectural complexes that incorporate these activities within a system of organized forms. While accommodating long-established customary behaviors, these structures give shape to their enactment. The study of Greek sanctuaries has emphasized significant developments in architectural configuration; however, studying architecture with plans, reconstruction drawings, and aerial photography rarely reveals how structures were perceived and used at ground level. Studying steps directs attention to interactions between behavior and the built environment. Because the dimensions of steps express a direct relation to body posture (sitting, standing, walking,) we can imagine which activities occurred where within the respective sanctuaries, so as to understand ritual behavior in these sacred spaces.

Dimensions, Behavior, Perception

Steps permit placement of the body on a slope. Humans' perception of gravity imbues steps with an expectation of direction and of potential for movement either up or down. The foot's repeated contact with a sequence of horizontal surfaces at regular, predictable intervals translates to a sense of organization and system. Close intervals and compression of steps express intensity of effort, or conversely, broader spacing brings a slower rhythm.

The absolute dimensions of steps and their relative proportions suggest the nature of activity on them. John Templer's studies of falls and accidents resulted in a recommendation of risers 4.6–7.2 inches (0.117–0.183 m.) high and treads from 11–14 inches (0.279–0.356 m.) wide.[3] There was much less standardization in antiquity and most likely more willingness for humans to adapt than we find now. Nevertheless, steps with risers as tall as 18–20 inches (0.429–0.509 m.) are usually for sitting, an interpretation that can be confirmed by the presence of intermediate smaller steps for easier passage built at intervals along the banks of larger steps, such as seen dividing the *kerkides* of most Greek theaters.

While fixed measurements in general reflect the capabilities of the human body, the ratio of vertical to horizontal can suggest the primary use of steps or stairs as routes of access or as facilities for viewing (some also served as retaining walls). These are arbitrary divisions and not mutually exclusive. To a large extent, context affects which direction (if either) dominates the sense of steps' directionality. There is a kind of iconography embedded in this directionality. A building set atop a flight of steps provides an apex that generates an expectation of upward ascent, involving individual effort, whereas a broad open space lying below steps with no apex promotes a downward focus in a setting conducive to viewing whatever takes place down the slope. This more static configuration also carries a sense of shared experience and communality.

The scale of broad steps, their accessibility to many participants at once, their capacity for large numbers of people gathering together, all convey the power to facilitate, or perhaps generate, social activity. Even when devoid of people, a rank of broad steps expresses its latent capability to accommodate larger crowds than those of everyday scale. Theatral steps that are oriented downward project a potential for participation – active or passive – by groups, defining an event of community (however transitory) by architectural form. Unlike control demonstrated by enclosed structures, in many cases monumental steps constitute intentional and symbolic displays of large-scale participation. The built forms do not indicate conditions for joining any gathering, only the existence of group activities. Who or what entities exercise authority through broad steps in their various forms differs according to contingencies of context.

The sites selected for scrutiny here all have broad steps whose placement, scale, and design reveal the intent to define and enhance the topography of sacred places while simultaneously gathering participants, concentrating and directing them so as to create the audience for sacrificial ritual. My discussion of monumental steps is organized according to their function, as processional ways or as facilities for viewing. Within each of these categories, I consider the sites in a roughly chronological sequence while also incorporating diachronic changes at the respective sanctuaries. The processional steps at Corinth, Labraunda, Lindos, and Kos constituted dominant features of their respective sites through phases of construction and change. Even when a pathway was moved and attendant experience altered, the persistence of built (and rebuilt) steps suggests that the act of processing remained central. Theatral steps at Perachora, Corinth, Argos, Pergamon, and Knidos represent a chronological range of facilities built adjacent to ritual locations, identifiable by votive deposits and constructed features such as altars or pits.

For maximum effect, ritual requires the inclusive collecting of a critical mass of participants, and sufficient control of the group to channel their movement, then focus their attention on the sacred enactment. Meeting these needs, processional and theatral steps magnified communal participation in ritual practices and conveyed that engagement in architectural form.

Steps as Routes of Access: Processions

The introduction of some monumental steps reflected the importance of the *pompe*, or procession escorting the sacrificial animal to the altar, where it was ritually slain, its flesh cooked and distributed to the attending worshippers. A sixth-century B.C.E. black-figure band cup (Fig. 2.1) gives a fine sense of a *pompe* as it portrays Athena with two mortals, an altar, a *kanephoros*, three sacrificial victims-to-be, musicians, worshippers, hoplites, and a horseman.[4] Even if parading en masse to a ritual destination does not entail the degree of symbolic meaning attached to sacrifice, a procession can be considered an auxiliary enactment, since it would take place at a prescribed time and place in a habitual manner, and it would include those about to join in conducting and celebrating the sacrifice.[5] Crowds of worshippers brought the dynamic energy of a group in motion to the altar. The *pompe* was an occasion for display, with musical accompaniment, and vessels for ceremony, and special clothing and finery of many sorts. A second-century B.C.E. civic decree from Magnesia on the Maeander specifies the organization of the procession in honor of Artemis Leukophryne:

> ... the stephanephoros in office together with the male priest and the female priest of Artemis Leukophryne shall ever after lead the procession in the month of Artemision on the twelfth day, and sacrifice the designated bull; that in the procession shall also be the council of elders, the priests, the magistrates, ... the ephebes, the youths, the boys, the victors in the Leukophryne games, and the victors in the other crown-bearing games. The stephanephoros in leading the procession shall carry images of all twelve gods attired as beautifully as possible ... and shall also provide music, a shawm-player, a pan-pipe player and a lyre-player.[6]

The Panathenaic procession is the best known example of a grand *pompe*. The extraordinarily flamboyant procession of Ptolemy

2.1. Black-figure band cup with procession. Private collection.

Philadelphos in Alexandria in 270 B.C.E., described in detail in the *Deipnosophistai*, was an expanded and politicized version of a *pompe*.[7] Such festive participatory parades were common practices (albeit on a lesser scale) at Greek sanctuaries, consistent in concept, but variable according to particular cult and custom. Specifications for participation varied as to such categories as gender, age, and social status. Universally, the *pompe* gathered diverse members of one or more communities out of their daily routine into festive motion together toward a destination. The performative nature of the *pompe* as participants walked alongside the prospective victim(s) brought a tide of energy and anticipation to the impending sacrifice. Broad steps that define a path to the altar constitute the formal articulation of this behavior, and give it permanent expression. Tilley observed that architecture involves deliberate creation and definition of space, not only somatic and perceptual space, but also existential space, that "in a constant process of production and reproduction through the movements and activities of members of a group."[8]

   An individual's experience of a site would be shaped by the pathway (space) and the sequence of perceptions (time) created by a prescribed route of access. Michel DeCerteau described walking as the continuous creation of place in the course of establishing relationships with surrounding spaces and structures.[9] Key constructed elements, such as broad steps, form a preferred path that codifies a visitor's experience of an entire site, as well as of its component parts. We can examine interactions between architecture and auxiliary ritual as represented by processional steps by considering routes of approach at the sanctuaries of Demeter and Kore at Corinth, of Zeus at Labraunda, of Athena at Lindos on Rhodes, and of Asklepios on Kos.

Processional Steps

The sanctuary of Demeter and Kore at Corinth circa 1 kilometer south of the temple of Apollo on the north slope of the massif of Acrocorinth is spread on either side of a long broad stairway (Figs. 2.2–2.5). Extensive deposits of miniature vases in characteristic shapes attest to ritual activity throughout the site; thousands of kalathiskoi, krateriskoi and miniature hydriai, as well as figurines and model offering trays were offered here to honor Demeter and Kore.[10] While cult activity at the site dates from the seventh century B.C.E. and perhaps earlier, it was in the fifth century B.C.E. that this sanctuary underwent substantial architectural enhancement, with structures for ritual dining and a monumental stairway from the road at the lower, northern limit of the sanctuary ascending the hillside to the Middle and Upper Terraces (Figs. 2.2–2.3). Throughout the history of the sanctuary, the Middle Terrace was evidently a focus of ritual, with an enigmatic trapezoidal oikos and stone-lined pits for votives in the fifth century, and continuing evidence of votives and cult activity in the fourth and third centuries B.C.E.[11] In later phases of the sanctuary the stairway was rebuilt, with a ramp alongside it, perhaps for sacrificial animals.[12] Twenty-nine meters long and approximately 3 meters wide, the fifth-century stairway rose in flights of three to four steps punctuated by at least ten landings with entrances to buildings housing dining chambers that flanked the stepped passage on either side.[13] In addition to their width, the generous dimensions of the steps, with low risers (0.14 m.) and broad treads (0.30 m.) easily traversed encourage a slow and easy progression, suggesting that the stairway served for processions. While the stairs link the terraces and the dining facilities in a "unified, more monumental design,"[14] the landings were placed according to the situation of the flanking buildings, and not according to an abstract plan or internal rhythm. The organizing principle is human behavior more than architectural aesthetics. From the fifth

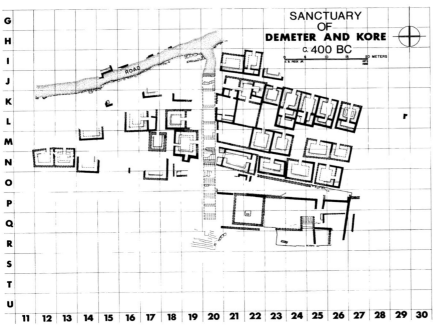

2.2. Corinth, Sanctuary of Demeter and Kore, plan c. 400 B.C.E. After N. Bookidis and R. S. Stroud, *Corinth* XVIII Part III: *The Sanctuary of Demeter and Kore. Topography and Architecture*, Princeton 1997, Plan 4. Courtesy of the Trustees of the American School of Classical Studies at Athens.

century B.C.E., rock-cut steps on the Upper Terrace provided places for viewing events below on the Middle Terrace, as discussed later.

The monumental pathway, and indeed nearly the entire mid-fourth century B.C.E. sanctuary of Zeus at Labraunda in Karia was almost a new creation.[15] An earlier shrine and grove of plane trees attested by Herodotos (5.119) appears to be confirmed by a few fragmentary remains at the site,[16] but it was the Hekatomnid satrap Mausolos, followed by his brother Idrieus who reconfigured the site, adding multiple new structures so as to fashion a sanctuary on a nearly panhellenic scale.[17] Epigraphical evidence suggests that Mausolos expanded the traditional one-day festival of Zeus to last five days, and that he specified the sequence of sacrifices and events.[18] The temple, on the uppermost terrace presumably had an altar in front. The path to it began below, in the southeast corner of the temenos and ascended a succession of three terraces (Figs. 2.6–2.7). In its initial phase (before construction of two propylaia at its base), the path probably continued up at least four steps 10 meters wide, turned

2.3. Corinth, Sanctuary of Demeter and Kore from north. After N. Bookidis and R. S. Stroud, *Corinth* XVIII Part III: *The Sanctuary of Demeter and Kore. Topography and Architecture,* Princeton 1997, Plate 5. Courtesy of the Trustees of the American School of Classical Studies at Athens.

left up a grand 12 meters wide flight of twenty-three steps, turned right up narrower steps (perhaps broader in antiquity) to a terrace with newly built facilities for banqueting at either end, then up another staircase originally 8 meters or more wide to the temple terrace. (There may have been an intermediate terrace, no longer extant.) Each terrace had an *andron,* or banquet hall at the west end, and additional buildings of indeterminate function.[19] While most of the buildings were constructed of local gneiss, the temple, *androns*, and other structures presented marble façades articulated with the Greek architectural vocabulary, however idiosyncratic.[20] The stairs are unequivocally a route of access. Their range of dimensions make for comfortable ascent and descent from terrace to terrace, and an extraordinary roadway outside the sanctuary emphasizes this role. A paved Sacred Way 8 meters wide can be traced (mostly uphill) 15 kilometers from Mylasa, the nearest city.[21] Strabo (14.2.23) described this paved road nearly 60 stades long as the route of sacred processions.

Built structures – the paved roadway and the monumental steps – establish (perhaps) and certainly reinforce ritual behavior that supported

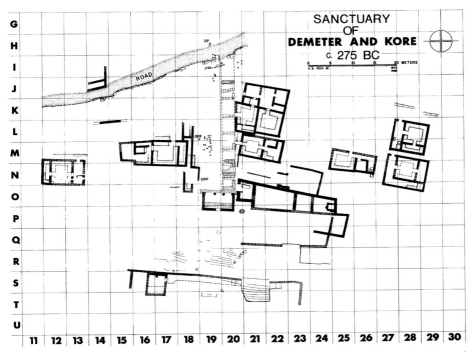

2.4. Corinth, Sanctuary of Demeter and Kore, plan c. 275 B.C.E. After N. Bookidis and R. S. Stroud, *Corinth* XVIII Part III: *The Sanctuary of Demeter and Kore. Topography and Architecture*, Princeton 1997, Plan 5. Courtesy of the Trustees of the American School of Classical Studies at Athens.

Mausolos' expansion of this sanctuary as a festival site. The fine *androns* emphasized the privilege of the banqueting elite, and a stadium (as yet unexplored) attests to athletic contests.[22] The Sacred Way demonstrates that his interest was more in the procession and less in the steps per se. He was promoting the solidarity and spectacle of the *pompe*. However, the pathway had consequences. The route of the procession climbed steadily past his newly built Andron B, adding legitimacy to the respective structures of the new sanctuary by juxtaposition with the grand processional way. The net result of these Hekatomnid projects was an ostentatious sanctuary approached by a ceremonial roadway leading visitors up to the temple of Zeus. Grand processions created ongoing opportunities for display, and yet when the steps were not filled with worshippers, their monumental breadth constituted a visual reminder of the organization and capacity of the lavish celebrations by large numbers of participants.

2.5. Corinth, Sanctuary of Demeter and Kore from northwest. After N. Bookidis and R. S. Stroud, *Corinth* XVIII Part III: *The Sanctuary of Demeter and Kore. Topography and Architecture*, Princeton 1997, Plate 2. Courtesy of the Trustees of the American School of Classical Studies at Athens.

The monumental steps at the sanctuary of Athena Lindia on Rhodes, now thoroughly restored in their third-century form, were not the first at this site.[23] As early as the sixth century B.C.E. there was a 7 meters wide stepped pathway up to the temple on the heights.[24] After a fire destroyed the temple and its dedications in the fourth century B.C.E., major rebuilding of the sanctuary in the third century B.C.E. thoroughly rearranged the site.[25] The sixth-century pathway was obliterated

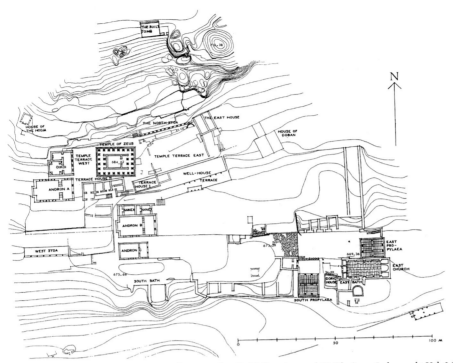

2.6. Labraunda, plan of Sanctuary of Zeus. After P. Hellström and T. Theime, *Labraunda Vol. I.3, The Temple of Zeus,* Stockholm 1982, pl. 26. Courtesy Swedish Labraunda Excavations.

2.7. Labraunda, Sanctuary of Zeus. Broad steps from the southeast. Photo Mary Hollinshead.

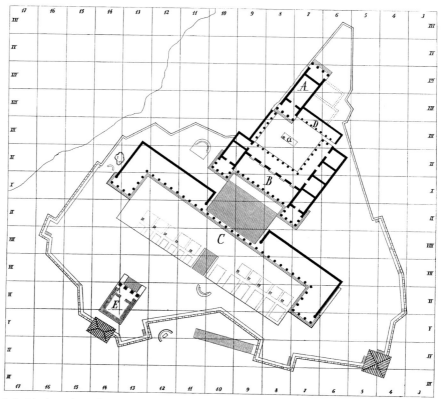

2.8. Lindos, plan of the Sanctuary of Athena. After E. Dygve (based on Chr. Blinkenberg and K. F. Kinch), *Lindos. Fouilles et Recherches 1902–1914 et 1952*, vol. III.2, *Le sanctuaire d'Athana Lindia et l'architecture Lindienne*, Berlin and Copenhagen 1960, p. 532, fig. XIV.6. Courtesy National Museum, Copenhagen, Department of Classical and Near Eastern Antiquities.

by a complex structure usually called the Propylaia (more recently the Upper Stoa) that combined dining chambers, doorways, a colonnaded façade with symmetrical projecting wings (*paraskenia*), and a flight of 37 steps 21.03 meters wide (Figs. 2.8–2.9).[26] This Upper Stoa transformed the process of approach; not only did the angle of view of the temple change, but in fact the temple disappeared behind the colonnade. Instead of Labraunda's segmented linear sequence, breadth and symmetry are emphasized. The excavators envisioned Athenian influence in the projecting wings, drawing comparisons with Mnesikles' Propylaia to the Acropolis.[27] While the Upper Stoa certainly adapted established forms, perhaps even from Athenian concepts, its significance lies in what was new, especially the scale of the staircase and the integrated complexity of the building. Whether or not one chooses to see influence of

2.9. Lindos, model of acropolis from north. After E. Dyggve (based on Chr. Blinkenberg and K. F. Kinch), *Lindos. Fouilles et Recherches 1902–1914 et 1952*, vol. III.2, *Le sanctuaire d'Athana Lindia et l'architecture Lindienne*, Berlin and Copenhagen 1960, p. 531, fig. XIV.3. Photo courtesy National Museum, Copenhagen, Department of Classical and Near Eastern Antiquities.

the Mnesiklean propylaia in the projecting wings, I would propose that broad steps themselves promote symmetry, as most users will choose a path up the middle of a monumental stairway; the projecting wings certainly reinforce the principle here. Lindos' Upper Stoa brings architectural order and coherence to a very difficult site, steep, with limited usable space. Processions would have ascended from the northern edge of the acropolis outcropping, where remnants of a contemporary flight of fifty-five steps are still visible beside the modern path.[28] There is not much scope for a lengthy procession within the temenos. The *pompe* brought important vitality to the act of sacrifice, through the kinetic energy of people and animals in motion, through their anticipation, and through the collective energy of a crowd. Given the steep and uneven terrain, the exceptionally broad staircase captured and concentrated the drive of a procession that probably needed gathering for the final ascent. At the same time, the visual effect of the steps' long horizontal surfaces and the physical rhythm generated in ascending them introduced order and discipline to the process. The architectural changes at Lindos reoriented preexisting processional behavior even as they prepared visitors visually and physically to direct their attention to the upcoming ritual.

The particularities of Lindian worship are not fully understood, and yet the architecture suggests that the temple court was a terminus for the *pompe*, and presumably a locus of ritual activity. The nature and location of sacrifice at this sanctuary has caused controversy. No archaeological remains can be identified with confidence as an altar, but traces of an orthogonal feature in the inner court in front (northwest) of the temple may be remnants of an altar. This court could have held an altar, but it would have been very small (18.20 x 12.80 m.) for the slaughter and butchering of multiple cows.[29]

The spectacular 87 meters long Lower Stoa set symmetrically across the lower part of the Upper Stoa's stairway at Lindos may date as early as the late third century, after the earthquake of 227/6 B.C.E. Its long colonnade expands the built path of approach across the full breadth of the site, while its projecting ends reiterate the design of the Upper Stoa. The stylobate of the Lower Stoa's central colonnade was set over the two lowest steps of the monumental stairway so that immediately inside the colonnade it intersects the ascending steps of the monumental stairway.[30] Although recently Lippolis and other scholars have emphasized the unity of concept with the Upper Stoa, proposing that the entire architectural assemblage of Upper and Lower Stoa were envisioned as an integrated composition from the beginning, I believe that both construction and design argue for a more evolutionary interpretation.[31] The formal compression represented by the Lower Stoa's encroachment on the stairway is significant, especially since the broad steps obviously constituted a major feature of the site, visually and experientially. The Upper Stoa was an innovative structure for the third century but its new developments (stairs, integrated parts) are consistent with trends in contemporary Greek and Karian building, such as a diminished emphasis on the temple alone, and an increased use of terraces and stairs. Planning the entire assemblage of Upper and Lower Stoas linked by stairs seems improbable for the early Hellenistic period. Without conclusive evidence, it is preferable to interpret the structures at Lindos as planned in sequence, as they were constructed.

Lindos provided architectural articulation of the route to the temple from archaic times. Like the broad steps of Labraunda, those at Lindos gave a metonymic presence in built stone to the concept of the *pompe*. The grand stairs of the Upper Stoa at Lindos were designed for display – but the primary display was social more than architectural, of pageantry ordered and concentrated atop the acropolis en route to the sacrifice.

The sanctuary of Asklepios at Kos may be the best known set of broad steps in the Greek world. The well-watered hillside site was initially known for its sacred grove of cypress trees, noted in inscriptions and written sources as a destination for processions.[32] The earliest physical remains at the site date to the fourth century B.C.E., but the first comprehensive building program dates to the third century (Figs. 2.10–2.11). Cult activity was focused on the middle of three terraces, with an altar faced by two small temples, as well as a dining chamber, a spring house and other small structures.[33] On the Upper Terrace a portico of wooden posts framed the sacred grove of cypress trees.[34]

Contemporary with these arrangements, another π-shaped stoa faced uphill below the Middle Terrace.[35] The marble Doric colonnades had a series of rooms behind, most likely associated with the healing process, and perhaps also available to festival-goers. Just west of center in the long northern segment of the colonnade, a propylon embedded in the stoa afforded a near-symmetrical entrance to the large open rectangular Lower Terrace. Leading up to the propylon are foundations and side walls of a broad stairway over 13 meters wide, but none of the steps are preserved.[36] Opposite the propylon and slightly west, another set of broad steps ascended to the Middle Terrace, as indicated by side walls perpendicular to the terrace wall. Again, only side walls and foundations remain of these steps, estimated to have been 10.4 meters wide, rising circa 6 meters high.[37] Ascending worshippers would arrive at the heart of the sanctuary facing the altar-temple axis. By the mid-third century, they would climb broad steps, pass through the lower stoa to the open expanse of the Lower Terrace. From there they would see another broad stairway traversing a terrace wall to the altar and temple of Asklepios, with auxiliary buildings clustered nearby, accentuating the sense of a cult nexus. Close behind these structures was another terrace wall.

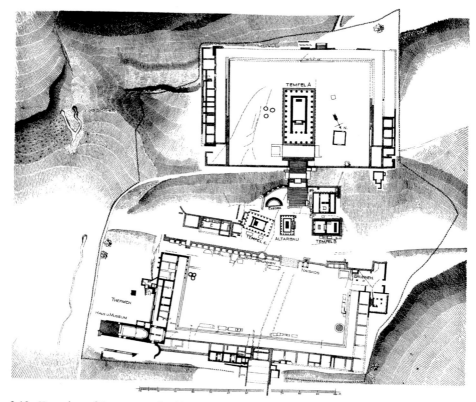

2.10. Kos, plan of Sanctuary of Asklepios. After P. Schazmann and R. Herzog, *Kos. Ergebnisse der deutschen Ausgrabungen und Forschungen vol. I. Asklepieion*, Berlin 1932, pl. 38. Courtesy of the German Archaeological Institute.

Farther up the hillside, the sacred cypress grove would have furnished a visual backdrop for activities on the lower terraces; only the ends of the portico framing it may have been visible. This third-century architectural configuration suggests that people and processions moved purposefully to the altar and the Middle Terrace, which may have become the end point for processions to the grove, or there may have been additional passageways (no longer extant) around either end of the Middle Terrace up to the trees of the Upper Terrace.

A wealth of epigraphic evidence provides unusually specific information as to how the Asklepieion functioned. In 242 B.C.E. a panhellenic pentateric festival, the Great Asklepieia, was established. *Theoroi* solicited grants of *asylia* and contributions from cities and rulers. Processions, sacrifices (in detail) and competitions are attested in inscriptions.[38]

2.11. Kos. Reconstruction of Sanctuary of Asklepios. After P. Schazmann and R. Herzog, *Kos. Ergebnisse der deutschen Ausgrabungen und Forschungen vol. I. Asklepieion*, Berlin 1932, pl. 40. Courtesy of the German Archaeological Institute.

This newly grand sanctuary would have served daily needs, especially for healing; inscriptions tell of an annual festival (*panegyris*) with procession; and every five years, the gala Great Asklepieia attracted visitors from far and wide to join festivities at the sanctuary. The success of Kos' panhellenic venture is documented by the varied sources of *asylia* decrees found in Kos and the varied origins of contestants whose names are preserved in victory lists from the Great Asklepieia. International contacts are attested from Sicily to Samothrace, mainland Greece, Crete, and Asia Minor to Mesopotamia.[39]

By the middle of the second century around 170–150 B.C.E., another major building phase transformed the Asklepieion. New construction on the Upper Terrace replaced the earlier wooden portico with a permanent marble stoa with Doric columns and entablature on the same π-shaped footprint.[40] A massive new terrace wall between the earlier Middle Terrace wall and the sacred grove gave sharp definition to the Upper Terrace. Most striking was the addition of a large new Temple (A) set symmetrically toward the front of the Upper Terrace, with a truly monumental stairway, both broad and long, leading from the altar of the Middle Terrace through the terrace wall to just before the new temple.[41] The marble-faced steps, of which the six lowest were in situ, ascend circa 11 meters in at least two flights (Becker would add additional landings.) The lower, 11.25 meters wide, of perhaps thirty-eight steps, passes over the old terrace wall to a horizontal landing in the intermediate space between old and new terrace walls. Bases for dedications flank the paved intermediate platform and there are slots, perhaps for posts holding banners on either side wall of the upper flight. The upper second flight, 9.25 meters wide of perhaps twenty-seven steps, penetrated the new terrace wall, then expanded to six steps circa 18 meters wide, creating a visual base for the temple.[42] The steps themselves were well suited for walking, with a height of 0.17 meters and a depth of 0.335 meters.[43] Their starting point, in close proximity to the altar and Temple B, suggests that the lower flight could have served double duty as a viewing stand for sacrifices and rituals at the altar, as well as access to the new temple above. Temple A was large, ostentatious and dominant. Its 6 x 11 peripteral Doric form has been compared to the temple of Asklepios at Epidauros only larger. Its scale has been compared to a fragmentary temple once in the gymnasion at Pergamon.[44] Within decades of this large-scale refurbishing, the altar was also rebuilt, around 130 B.C.E.[45] In addition, continuous marble paving was added in the center of the Middle Terrace and between the top step of the grand staircase and Temple A, conveying an experiential message of cultic connection.[46]

Written testimonia note a procession to the cypress grove as part of the worship of Asklepios at Kos. As a *pompe* approached (perhaps coming from the town, 4 km. distant) the new temple provided a visual terminus. The succession of broad staircases direct and channel the procession, concentrating its attention and activity. The steps continue momentum from the altar to the Upper Terrace and the cypress grove, the destination for the procession. The new temple may have changed the visual field more than it did the ritual.

It is not clear whether either the third-century or the second-century improvements to the sanctuary were the consequence of Koan initiative and enterprise, or whether the Asklepieion's dramatic growth reflects donations by major benefactors. Proposals that Ptolemy II Philadelphos, (who was born on Kos in 309/8 B.C.E.) underwrote the third-century expansion of the site, or that Eumenes II of Pergamon gave Kos the temple of the second century B.C.E. remain speculation.[47] Absent explicit confirmation of patronage by specific rulers, it is worth noting that inscriptions record that combined resources, from state donations, cult contributions, and externally solicited funds were all used to carry out rituals and activities at the Asklepieion.[48] There may not have been a single patron, even for improvements on such a grand scale.

These second-century additions projected the principles of axiality and symmetry onto the existing configuration of the Asklepieion. In the third century, the implied passage from propylon to broad steps to altar complex represented a necessary route of approach arranged with an awareness of symmetry, as shown by the π-shaped stoa of the Lower Terrace. But it is only the relentless alignment of second-century structures that suggests an intended formal axis from propylon to Temple A. The new second-century structures would have affected the behavior of worshippers. Were the grand stairway and the Upper Terrace intended to articulate (and facilitate) processions that had always made their way to the sacred grove? Or were they entirely directed toward the temple? Who had authority to reconfigure such a major sanctuary and its essential practices so thoroughly?

Such major renovations can be seen as a question of agency. Would an external if friendly monarch be entitled to change worshippers' behavior by endowing the new temple and its setting? Did sanctuary supervisors solicit a patron or a group of benefactors to underwrite grand new facilities? One can imagine that the Middle Terrace became impossibly cramped as the Asklepieion's renown generated lavish processions and celebrations. Did primary agency lie with worshippers in procession? Even if the route of access changed, gala processions to sacrifice are amply attested as a key feature throughout the life of this sanctuary. It may be that participation in a kinetic performative ritual such as the procession, counted for more than its particular route as it led to the culminating event of sacrifice at a fixed point (the altar) within the sanctuary. As they accommodated crowds of worshippers, the emphatic apex of temple and stairway themselves represented in built form the scale and practice of worship at the Asklepieion.

As at Labraunda and Lindos, changes in the pathway were part of a larger modification of the sanctuary. The display and movement – and destination – were ultimately more important than a fixed or traditional route within the confines of the temenos. The meaning persisted in the act of processing even if the route changed.[49] However, once the procession was given architectural articulation with monumental steps, the built path codified this behavior, bringing the *pompe* that much closer to ritual status. The order, rhythm, and organization intrinsic to the form of steps are essential traits of ritual, making the architecture and its activity mutually reinforcing.

Theatral Steps

Stairs were for descending as well as ascending. It is quite possible that the monumental steps at Kos could also have served a theatral purpose for viewing sacrifice at the altar, whose ongoing importance is shown by its enlargement in the second century, when the grand staircase and temple were built. Comparable configurations of altar, steps, and temple are known to have existed as early as the sixth century B.C.E. (e.g., at Selinous).[50] Active, intensive observation was integral to participation in the act of sacrifice. A fourth-century B.C.E. inscription from Oropos in Attica refers to "the theater by the altar" (now represented by an arc of three decrepit steps, see Fig. 3.13), suggesting that some sanctuaries had facilities constructed for worshippers to observe sacrifice and associated ceremonies.[51] Functionally there had to be space around the altar. Architecturally, this most important spot in the sanctuary derived emphasis by its isolation in space as well as its alignment with a monumental temple. At the sanctuary of Hera at Perachora, of Demeter and Kore at Corinth, of Apollo at Argos, of Demeter at Pergamon, and of Apollo at at Knidos long ranks of steps beside an altar framed the ritual while providing better viewing for worshippers.

The archaic sanctuary in the harbor precinct at Perachora underwent a major building project in the late sixth century, resulting in construction of a new temple, a new altar, and an adjacent rank of at least seven steps (Figs. 2.12–2.13).[52] Reaching a breadth of circa 12 meters, the steps have an average height of 0.23–0.24 meters, providing a facility for observers to view rituals at and around the altar, as well as access to a route to the Middle Terrace above and east of this sanctuary. These steps also served to stabilize the steep hillside, where erosion continues to threaten. Because of their low height, they are not well suited for seated onlookers; spectators must have stood.[53] The rank of steps begins hard up against the base of the altar (Ionic columns added to the altar in

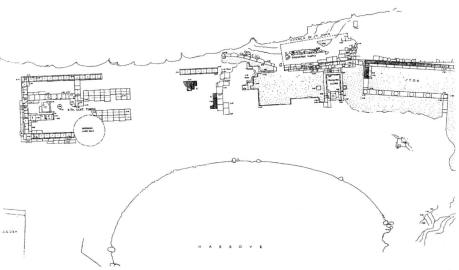

2.12. Perachora, plan of Sanctuary of Hera. After R. A. Tomlinson, "Perachora" in *Le sanctuaire grec. Entretiens (Fondation Hardt)*, ed. A. Schlachter, Geneva 1992, fig. 1. Courtesy R. A. Tomlinson.

2.13. Perachora, steps and adjacent altar (on right) from the southwest. Photo Mary Hollinshead.

the fourth century encroach on the lower steps, which were cut away to make room for them.) Space was tight. However, the grandstand of stone steps was well situated to view any festivities that may have occurred in the modest area between temple and altar, on the shore, or on the water if such activities ever took place within the well-defined enclosure of the harbor.[54]

Revisiting the sanctuary of Demeter and Kore on the north slope of Acrocorinth, we encounter theatral facilities for observing whatever cult activities took place on the Middle Terrace, reached by the processional stairway discussed earlier. From the fifth century on, and possibly as early as the sixth century, the Upper Terrace included stepped rock-cut areas for viewing ceremonies taking place on the Middle Terrace (Figs. 2.4–2.5). A "theatral area" of five steps provided standing room for spectators to view occurrences on the terrace below. Carved out of the rough breccia bedrock (now badly weathered and worn), three areas of steps can be discerned: the southernmost set was aligned with the processional stairway below but extended beyond the sides of the steps.[55] With risers averaging 0.20–0.29 meters in height and treads averaging 0.40 meters wide, these steps could accommodate either standees or seated observers. (The bedrock may have been faced with limestone in antiquity, but that need not have changed the proportions estimated for the steps.) The excavators estimated a capacity of circa fifty people for this intentionally small facility.[56] The steps' dimensions are also well suited for walking, and would have afforded convenient passage up and down this steep slope. In the late fourth or early third century the small viewing area was succeeded – or supplemented – by a more overtly theatral installation nearby to the southeast.[57] This Upper Terrace was designed to provide views of events below. Processions making their way uphill would present pleasing prospects to spectators in this viewing area, but the primary focus must have been on rituals that took place on the Middle Terrace. Unfortunately, we lack sufficient information to know what activity merited such attention. The excavators noted the restrictive aspects of narrow entrances to the Middle Terrace, and observed the small size of the theatral area and its successor, suggesting that this cult may have had aspects of a mystery cult.[58]

Scholars disagree whether the ten (or more) rock-cut steps stretching 27 meters. in breadth behind the altar of Pythian Apollo on the Aspis

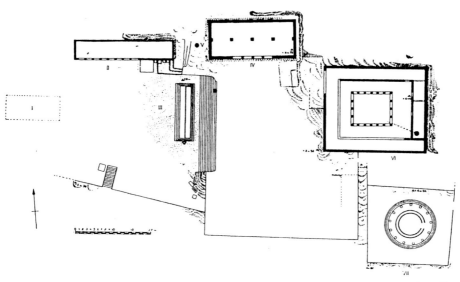

2.14. Argos, plan of Sanctuary of Apollo Pythios. After G. Roux, "Le sanctuaire argien d'Apollon Pythéen," Revue des Études Grecques 70, 1957, fig. 1.

at Argos were solely an aesthetic transition between Lower and Upper Terraces or whether they were intended for spectators (Figs. 2.14–2.15).[59] The area surrounding the altar is reduced to stark bedrock. There are remains of some structures on the Middle Terrace, but no trace of the temple of Apollo alluded to in a third-century inscription from the site.[60] Temples to Apollo and to Athena are reported by Pausanias (2.24.1.), who also mentions an oracular ritual in which a chaste woman prophesied after tasting blood from a sacrificial lamb. The inscription concerns refurbishing the sanctuary of Apollo, and mentions improvements such as moving the altar to the east, and the ὀφρύα (brow), which may indicate the steps, or some formation that preceded their cutting.[61] We surmise that the temple lay west of the altar, opposite the steps. Roux argued that the steps were exclusively ornamental, forming an aesthetic transition between terraces as an artificial stepped retaining wall, while others interpret them as facilities for observing rituals at the altar.[62] If the steps did hold spectators, there would have been room for 540 standees or more. The steps' low risers, 0.21–0.23 meters tall, and treads 0.43–0.45 meters wide would make for cramped seating, so that any use must have involved walking or standing.[63] Whether they also provided monumental access to and from the Upper Terrace is an open question.

2.15. Argos, Sanctuary of Apollo Pythios. Steps adjacent to altar (on left). Photo Mary Hollinshead.

Their close proximity, only 1.48 meters from the altar, would constrict a procession drastically. The placement of the broad steps at this oracular sanctuary implies that they would be the terminus of the procession, gathering worshippers hard by the altar and defining a boundary for the Upper Terrace that may have been restricted to select visitors, or at least to visitors who did not arrive en masse. One role of a viewing facility is to create dense proximity that concentrates the energy and attention of the crowd. The downward facing steps thus consolidate the effect of the *pompe* and intensify the experience of the sacrifice.

At the third-century B.C.E. sanctuary of Demeter at Pergamon, nine rows of seats (with steps at either end for access) 44 m. long, constituted a theatral gallery for eight hundred observers or more overlooking an open terrace with one major and several lesser altars to the east of the temple (Figs. 2.16–2.17). Closed off from the external world, the sanctuary apparently served as a Thesmophorion, with rites restricted to women, linking agrarian and female fertility, as indicated by architectural configuration, votives, and inscriptions. Traces of an early temenos wall and propylaia, as well as a large altar and four smaller altars suggest that a sacred precinct may have existed on the site in the fourth century and possibly earlier.[64] Epigraphical evidence attests to massive

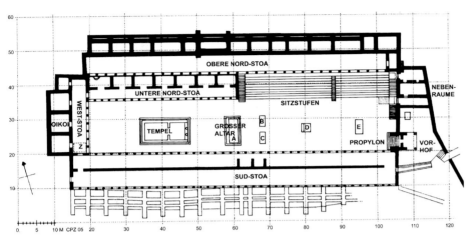

2.16. Pergamon, Sanctuary of Demeter, plan under Apollonis. After C. P. Piok Zanon, "Dank an Demeter: Neue Gedanken zu Architektur und Bedeutung des Demeter-Kultes in Pergamon im späten 3. Jh. v. Chr.," *IstMitt* 57, 2007, fig. 1 p. 326. Courtesy Cornelie Piok Zanon.

2.17. Pergamon, Sanctuary of Demeter from east. Courtesy Cornelie Piok Zanon.

refurbishing in the second quarter of the third century. The entire terrace was enlarged and its surface lowered by removing circa 1 meter of earth. A tetrastyle Ionic temple to Demeter was erected; an inscription on its pronaos stated that Philetairos (281–263 B.C.E.) and his brother Eumenes I (263–241 B.C.E.) dedicated it to Demeter on behalf of their mother Boas.[65] A large new altar east of the temple and aligned with its façade was inscribed with the same message. The four existing small altars extend across the eastern sector of the sanctuary.

The northern side of the temenos, set against a steep slope, was augmented by a long (43.9 m.) rank of nine steps in the eastern half and a stoa in the western half. The dimensions of the steps themselves (0.373 m. high, 0.712 m. wide) are well suited for seated spectators, an interpretation reinforced by the presence of at least two vertical rows of smaller steps, facilitating access like the aisles of Greek theaters.[66] These steps could have accommodated 800–850 spectators. While these seats certainly helped stabilize the precipitous slope, there is no doubt that they served primarily for viewing whatever took place in the open space between temple and propylon, at and near various altars.

Ritual practices in this sanctuary may have differed significantly from elsewhere. The fact that the altar lies west of the grandstand and not directly below it implies variation in the ritual proceedings. On the other hand, there is a conventional temple and altar set, so that we need not discard the grandstand as an example of Hellenistic architectural practices. C. G. Thomas has emphasized that Demeter was worshipped here in the Thesmophoria, restricted to women, and not in the rites of the Eleusinian mysteries.[67] Without knowing the enactment thus viewed, we can nevertheless recall the similar spatial configuration, with spectators looking down on a terrace in front of the "oikos" at the sanctuary of Demeter and Kore in Corinth, suggesting comparable ritual activities. The structures of this closed sanctuary present a clear and distinct message about what to do (sit here) and where ritual activity occurred, even if we are ignorant of the rites viewed from these seats. The scale and placement of the theatral steps at Pergamon's sanctuary of Demeter provide emphatic architectural codification of viewing as participation, a fundamental premise of Greek religious ritual.

At the west end of the city of Knidos, a rank of theatral steps looked down on the sanctuary of Apollo Karneios from above (Figs. 2.18–2.19).[68] A pair of buildings, at least one apparently a nonperipteral temple, faced a large stepped altar ornamented with reliefs of nymphs. An inscribed dedication to Apollo Karneios and also two sculptors' names provides attribution and a second-century B.C.E. date.[69] The extant temple is Roman, but unexplored remains beneath it suggest that there may

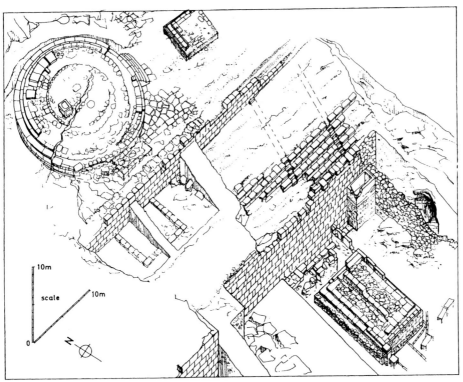

2.18. Knidos, plan of Sanctuary of Apollo. After I. C. Love, "A Preliminary Report of the excavations at Knidos, 1972," *AJA* 77, 1973, fig. 34. Drawing Sheila Gibson. Courtesy I. C. Love.

have been an earlier structure on the site.[70] Close parallels of architectural materials and execution indicate that construction of the round temple of Athena and its small altar on the terrace directly above must be contemporary with the altar of Apollo, and so date to the mid-second century B.C.E.[71]

From the north side of the altar of Apollo an imposing retaining wall of ashlar masonry circa 7 meters high or more defines one side of that lower precinct. Above it, a series of steps for seated observers ascends the steep slope north to a narrow terrace with an altar in front of a naiskos on the west, then another retaining wall that forms the border of the precinct of Athena above, with its round temple, small rectangular altar, and a series of small treasury-like buildings continuing to the east.[72] Although heavily rebuilt in the second century C.E., the steps are thought to have been present in the original arrangement of the sanctuary. Traces of seven rows of steps remain. Each step is 0.35–0. 37 meters high and circa 0.51 meters

2.19. Knidos, Sanctuary of Apollo from southeast. Photo Mary Hollinshead.

deep. While the longest extant row is circa 20 meters long, neither the east nor the west end of the steps has been identified, so that they probably extended farther, especially to the west; this stepped facility could have accommodated three hundred spectators or more. Observers were seated, as suggested by the dimensions of the steps, and confirmed by two intermediate aisles with smaller steps for ease of walking, like those at Pergamon's Demeter sanctuary or between the *kerkides* of a theater.

The close and integrated relationship with the temenos of Apollo below and Athena above imply that a stepped arrangement was part of the second-century-B.C.E. establishment.[73] While recognizing that the steps were a critical connector contributing supplementary support to the terraces above, we can also ask what did observers watch in the precinct of Apollo? In addition to sacrifices and associated events around the altar, contests and festivities in honor of Triopian Apollo mentioned by Herodotos (1.144) may have taken place in the sanctuary of Apollo below.[74] The stepped seating also affords spectacular views of the site of Knidos for a concentration of three hundred or more worshippers, which would have included processions making their way to the sanctuary for sacrifice, contests, and festivities. Their dramatic downward view announces the importance of events at the altar. As architectural forms, these theatral steps beside altars provide visual emphasis by their directionality, sloping down to the center of ritual, and by their framing function, defining edges that articulate ritual space. As important as the form itself is their expression of capacity. When not occupied by worshippers, these ranks of steps advertise the scale of participation at the venue and so add authority to the sanctuary and its ceremonies.

Formal analyses of Hellenistic architecture mention linked pathways, symmetry, and architectural framing among new emphases in sanctuary design. Yet such comprehensive planning may have been a secondary effect. Many examples of broad steps were intended to capture (i.e., direct and enhance) existing human behavior, the processions, and the witnessing of rituals that were expected activities in sanctuaries. A key development in the Hellenistic period is the increase in patronage – not only commissioning specific structures, but more often funding festival activities, such as *pompai*, banquets, and sacrifices. Such financial sponsorship of specific projects by wealthy individuals became widespread in Hellenistic cities and sanctuaries.[75] Expanded display in ritual behavior made possible by the new euergetism led to expanded display in architecture. These patrons, along with cultural expectations around the *pompe* and sacrifice, exercise agency – can the same be said for architecture? Once these monumental stairways and grandstands were built, their expressive form, strategic placement, and perduring stone construction conferred agency upon them. Their form represented utilitarian function on a grand scale while adding traits that complemented and enhanced the enactment of ritual, giving formal expression to the location and scope of celebration. In directing worshippers' movement and attention, monumental steps brought order, rhythm, and energy to the act of sacrifice. The scope of the sacrifice was expanded by increased regularization of the *pompe*.

Monumental steps thus prescribed how both events and structures were experienced. Steps for viewing articulated the locus of enactment and intensified the focus of a crowd by facing them down towards the performed rites. For those processing and viewing, the placement of monumental steps gave meaning to sanctuary architecture by positioning worshippers so as to add emphasis to specific structures and locations. Permanent monumental steps encouraged perpetuation of the activities they were built to serve. Even empty, their form implies group use, and their grand scale and evident capacity carry a message of authority – not the authority of an individual patron or donor, but the communal authority of well-attended ceremonies.

Notes

1. This article is part of a more extensive study of monumental steps supported by the National Endowment for the Humanities, the Graham Foundation, and the Center for the Humanities at the University of Rhode Island. I would also like to thank Georgina Borromeo of the Rhode Island School of Design for timely assistance. For an early study of monumental steps, see Hollinshead 1992. Recent treatments include Becker 2003 and Nielsen 2000, 2002.
2. Maran 2006 (p. 11), citing Parker Pearson and Richards 1994 (pp. 2–3), comments, "architecture is … a medium in which social relations not only take place, but through which they are created, reproduced, and altered." Mylonopoulos 2008 refers to "the dynamics of ritual space."
3. Templer 1992, pp. 25–39.
4. Marangou et al 1995, pp. 86–93 with additional references. Van Straten 1995, pp. 14–15 No. V55. Price 1999, pp. 30–31. Cf. Van Straten 1995, pp. 14–31 for other images of processions.
5. *RE* XXI, 1952, col. 1878, s.v. pompa (F. Bömer). Burkert 1985, pp. 99–101. Connor 1987. Wikander 1992. Chaniotis 1995. Graf 1996. Dillon 1997. Kavoulaki 1999. Chankowski 2005.
6. Sokolowski 1955, no. 32. Price 1999, pp. 174–175 no. 3. Kern 1900, no. 98.
7. Ath. *Deipnosophistai* 197C-203B. Panathenaia: Neils 1992, 1996. Cf. Sourvinou-Inwood 1994 on the City Dionysia in Athens. Procession of Ptolemy Philadelphos: Rice 1983. Wikander 1992. Thompson 2000.
8. Tilley 1994, pp. 16–17.
9. DeCerteau 1984. Tilley 1994, pp. 27–31.
10. *Corinth* XVIII.3, pp. 16–17, 53, 153, 425, 428–9.
11. *Corinth* XVIII.3, p. 432–3.
12. *Corinth* XVIII.3, pp. 224–5, 431.
13. *Corinth* XVIII.3, pp. 94–98, 429. Bookidis and Stroud estimate that there could have been as many as seventeen landings, but there is evidence for only ten.
14. *Corinth* XVIII.3, p. 429.
15. Nearly all of the new construction at Labraunda occurred under Mausolus and his brother Idrieus, and so can be dated to the years 377/6 – 344/3 B.C.E. Upon his death in 353/2, Mausolos was succeeded by his wife Artemisia who had shared his rule for a time. She ruled alone until her own death in 351/0, when Idrieus became satrap. Hornblower 1982, pp. 38–40. For comprehensive and current information about the site, see www.labraunda.org (accessed August 2011).
16. Thieme 1993. Hellstrom 1991, p. 297. *Labraunda* I.2.
17. Hellström 1991 finds strong spatial correlation with Delphi, perhaps intentional. Cf. Hellström 1988b, 1996a. Hornblower 1982, p. 312.
18. *Labraunda* III.2, pp. 81–89, No.53–54a. Two Roman inscriptions of imperial date appear to be copies of fourth-century B.C.E. prototypes.
19. *Labraunda* I.2. Hellström 1991, 1996a. Andron C is Roman in date, but the other two are Hecatomnid.
20. As in the mixed Ionic columns and Doric entablature of the *androns*. Hellström 1988b. Cf. the Doric order with Ionic geison on the oikoi.

21. *Labraunda* I.2, pp. 9–10, fig.2. Improvements to the modern road have obscured some of the details of the ancient route described by Westholm. Bean 1980, p. 47, pl. 11. Hellström (1996, p. 134) speculates that Mausolos must have completed the paved Sacred Way, as it would have been essential for transporting large blocks of marble to the sanctuary.

22. *Labraunda* I.2, pp. 19–20. *Labraunda* III.2, p. 196 notes reference to *agones* in a post-Hekatomnid inscription, no. 11 lines 7 and 10.

23. This site was heavily restored in concrete in the late 1930's, limiting possibilities for reexamining remains. For the Italian policy of restoration 1938–1940 with reinforced concrete, considered a prestigious modern material, see Papadimitriou 1988. Similarly enthusiastic restorations were carried out at this time at the Asklepieion on Kos. Kondis 1963, p. 392. *Lindos* III.2, pp. 25–25.

24. *Lindos* III.2, pp. 59–62, 75, 79, 191. Kondis 1963, pp. 394–5. Papadimitriou 1988, p. 169.

25. Epigraphic evidence from the Lindian chronicle and a list of priests' names indicate that the old temple was destroyed by fire, along with most of the dedications in 392/391 B.C.E. Other epigraphical testimonia about adorning a (the?) statue of Athena are less securely dated; indeed, the presumed date of the temple has been used to place them chronologically. Higbie 2003, pp. 11–12, 146–7, 256–8. Lippolis 1988–1989, pp. 127–132.

26. The Upper Stoa is thought to date shortly after 300 B.C.E., following the reconstruction of the temple. *Lindos* III.2, pp. 276–80. Lippolis 1988–1989, p.134. Higbie 2003, p.13. Kondis 1963. Coulton 1976, pp. 251–2.

27. In *Lindos* III.2, p. 181, Dyggve also cites the Stoa of Zeus in the Athenian Agora and the stoa at Brauron as Attic prototypes for the Lindian stoa. Denied by Kondis 1963, p. 397. Cf. Lippolis 1988–1989, p. 136. Becker 2003, p. 78 n. 398.

28. The dimensions and execution of these steps are similar to those of the Upper Stoa, and pottery fragments beneath them were called "Hellenistic." The steps are 3m. wide, and appear to have turned left at the top, but modern steps have obliterated their uppermost sections and continuation. *Lindos* III.2, pp. 57–58, 73, 76–77. Becker 2003, pp. 85–86 with dimensions.

29. *Lindos* III.2, p. 179, 297. Kondis 1963, pp. 398–9. Dyggve restored a substantial altar in the court before the temple, while Kondis noted a location for a potential large altar in front of the northeast wing of the Lower Stoa. The Lindian Chronicle notes hecatombs sacrificed in honor of such luminaries as Alexander (330 B.C.E.), Ptolemy I (304 B.C.E.) and Pyrrhus (280 B.C.E.). Archaic deposits of animal bones and ash have been found, so that animals were undoubtedly sacrificed somewhere at Lindos. *Lindos* I, p. 183. *Lindos* III.2, pp. 177–178. Lippolis 1988–1989, pp. 137–8. Kostomitsopoulos 1988.

30. Lippolis 1988–1989. *Lindos* III.2, pp. 159, 220.

31. Lippolis 1988–1989, pp.134,150. Becker 2003, pp. 79, 82–83. Pakkanen 1988, pp. 150–154 adopts Lauter's 1986 position pp. 106–8.

32. An epigram of the late fifth century or early fourth century excavated on the Upper Terrace refers to Paeon, a healing god, "ἐν ἄλσει" (in the grove.) Sherwin-White 1978, pp. 55, 338–40. Herzog 1952, p. 33. Laumonier 1958, pp. 691–4. Third century inscriptions indicate that the sanctuary's cypress grove was sacred to Apollo Kyparissios (a site-specific sole occurance of the name) as well as Asklepios. It may be that Zeus as Alseios and Athena as Alseia were also worshipped in association with the cypress grove at the Asklepion, and the grove served as a sacred focus for other Koan cults in the 4th century. Sherwin-White

1978, pp. 294–5, 341. Laumonier 1958, pp. 692–3. Epigraphic and literary references to processions to the cypress grove attest that it was a destination of continuing significance. Herzog 1952, no. 9 (Sokolowski 1969, no. 165) Sherwin-White 1978, pp. 338–9, 356. Herzog 1952. A Pseudo-Hippocratic letter to the residents of Abdera refers to a lavish procession (πομπὴ πολύτελής) to the cypress grove as part of the annual festival of Asklepios. Sherwin-White 1978, maintains that the specificity of other rituals described in the passage means it is more likely to contain accurate information. For the text, see p. 339 n. 423.

33. Sherwin-White 1978, p. 342–3. *Kos I* pp. 34–39, 42, 47–51. Laumonier 1958, p. 693. Along Temple B's south side Building D, often identified as an *abaton* for incubating the sick, more likely served as dining chambers for officiants or elite worshippers; a spring house behind Building D would support either interpretation. *Kos I* pp. 49–51. Sherwin-White 1978, p. 343. Hellstrom 1988a. For comparable structures, see Bergquist 1998, pp. 57–72.

34. *Kos I*, pp. 14–16, Sherwin-White 1978, p. 342.

35. *Kos I*, pp. 61–67. Sherwin-White 1978, p. 342. The lower stoa is dated by architectural details, whose closest comparisons for appear among third-century buildings. *Kos I* pp. 64–67, 74 cites the harbor stoa in Miletos and the older palaestra in Pergamon as parallels. Shoe 1950. Coulton 1976, p. 246 adds a question mark to the date. von Hesberg 1994, p. 179 n. 1486.

36. Becker 2003, p. 56, 58 n. 286. The steepness of the 26 percent slope once thought to be a ramp, led excavators to restore steps as more feasible for ascent and descent: Becker has proposed twenty-nine to thirty steps with landings.

37. Becker 2003, pp. 59–61. Steps B. Becker proposed thirty-six steps, extending farther south into the middle terrace than in published restorations based on Schazmann's publication.

38. See Bosnakis, Hallof, and Rigsby 2010. See also Perrin-Saminadayar 2011 for a summary of the publication history of the inscriptions from Kos. Sherwin-White 1978, pp. 111–14, 357–9. Buraselis 2004. Rigsby 1996, 2004. Sokolowski 1969. Herzog 1928. Musical, athletic and equestrian contests are mentioned, but they may not have taken place within the Asklepieion precinct.

39. Rigsby 1996, pp. 106–53. Sherwin-White 1978, pp. 111–14, 357–8. Herzog and Klaffenbach 1952.

40. *Kos I*, pp. 14–21.

41. *Kos I*, pp. 3–5, 22–24. Sherwin-White 1978, pp. 344. Becker 2003, pp. 65–70.

42. *Kos I*, p. 22–24. Becker (2003, p. 61–66) questions whether there is sufficient evidence for this broadening before the temple. The issue probably cannot be resolved in the light of remains now accessible.

43. *Kos I*, p. 22. Becker 2003, p. 63, 65.

44. Epidauros: von Hesberg 1994, p. 54. Würster 1973 pp. 200–1. Gruben 1966 p. 386. Pergamon: Schwandner 1990. Hellström 1988a speculated that Temple A might be a banquet chamber in the guise of a temple, like the *androns* of Labraunda. For the geometry and planning of Temple A, see Senseney 2007.

45. *Kos I*, pp. 73, 75.

46. *Kos I*, pp. 22–24. Becker 2003, p. 66.

47. Hoepfner 1984. Höghammar 1993, pp. 20–21. Schwandner 1990 identified parallels of form between Temple A and a scarcely preserved temple in the gymnasium at Pergamon. While supporting material is scant for this hypothesis, there is ample epigraphical evidence of close relations over generations between

      Attalid rulers and Kos. Sherwin-White 1978, pp. 163, 358, 369. Herzog 1928 no. 9. Cf. Höghammar 1993, p. 24.

48. Sherwin-White 1978, pp. 344, 358.

49. Mylonopoulos 2008. More broadly, Chaniotis 2005.

50. Selinous Temple M. Pompeo 1999.

51. *IG VII* 4255, 29. Petrakos 1968, pp. 98–99, 180 dates the inscription 338–322 B.C.E. R. Frederiksen 2002, pp. 128–9 and pl. 35. Travlos pp. 301–3 fig. 380. Anti and Polacco 1969. Three steps (0.25 m. high, 0.30–31 m. wide) circa 20 m. long remain, in a broadly curving arc close to the north side of the altar. The center of their arc aligns with the placement of the earliest of three successive altars, suggesting a late-fifth-century date for their initial construction. The inscription records the reuse of the component blocks of the presumably dismantled θέατρον, in a water channel, part of a general refurbishing of the sanctuary. We cannot be sure exactly what the original structure looked like especially since the theater did not assume a canonical form until the 4th century. The term *theatron* encompassed a variety of venues from which people could observe. *LSJ* s.v. θέατρον. Frederiksen 2002, pp. 74–76, special note p. 121.

52. Tomlinson 1992. Date: Plommer and Salviat 1966, pp. 207–15 by juxtaposition and material. Menadier 1995, pp. 75–78, 120. Payne 1940.

53. Width 0.41–0.50 m. is just adequate for sitting, but is cramped in combination with the low height of the risers. Contrast the bench within the nearby hall to the southwest 0.35m high and 0.50 m. wide. Kuhn 1985, pp. 292–293. Menadier 1995. Measurements: Payne 1940.

54. For the harbor, Blackmon 1966.

55. Steps 7–11 in sector Q-R 19–20 are 4.8–5.0 m. wide. *Corinth* XVIII.3, pp. 256–8.

56. *Corinth* XVIII.3, p. 256–7.

57. *Corinth* XVIII.3, pp. 260–6.

58. *Corinth* XVIII.3, pp. 247, 433.

59. There is room at the top for another step or two. Vollgraff 1956, p. 43. Pausanias 2.24.1 calls the site that of Apollo Deiradiotes, after the name of its location on the *deiras*, or ridge.

60. Besides the altar and steps, the lower terrace has foundations of an archaic stoa along the north side, with informal, irregular rock-cut steps giving access to a slope to the upper terrace. Another stoa, with a central row of columns, occupied the north side of the upper terrace, and there are scant remains of a quadrangular building with an interior peristyle, and also of a peripteral tholos on its own square terrace. The two-aisled stoa has been assigned a 4th century date, and the other two buildings have been called Hellenistic. Vollgraff 1956.

61. Vollgraff 1956, p. 112.

62. Roux 1957, p. 480. Roux 1961, pp. 77–78.

63. Vestiges of plaster and the absence of wear reveal that these steps had another surface, whether plaster or a veneer of applied stone slabs.

64. *AvP XVIII* esp. pp. 56–7. Radt 1988, pp. 206–7. Becker 2003, p. 251. Thomas 1998, p. 284, 286–7. Piok Zanon 2007.

65. Umholtz 1999. Thomas 1998, p. 285. Hepding 1910, p. 437. Piok Zanon 2007.

66. *AvP XVIII*. Becker (2003, pp. 249–50) reconstructs two additional aisles in support of symmetrical planning. Unfortunately, the extant remains are too scanty to support or disprove his (plausible) hypothesis.

67. Thomas 1998. Later second-century C.E. Roman enhancements to nymphaeum, temple and altar may have accompanied a shift in ritual focus as well, to a more Eleusinian worship of Demeter and Kore.
68. Bankel 2004. Becker 2003, p. 255. Love 1972, p. 404–5. Love 1973, p. 423.
69. Bankel 1997, pp. 53, 69. Love 1973, p. 423. Stampolides 1984. Bruns-Özgan 1997.
70. Bankel 1997, pp. 59, 67, 69; 2004.
71. Bankel 1997, pp. 53, 69; 2004.
72. Bankel 2004, pp. 101 fig. 2, 104.
73. Bankel 1997, p. 68; 2004, pp. 103–6.
74. The location of the Triopion is far from certain. Bankel 1997, p.69; 2004, favors the location in this sanctuary of Apollo Karneios. However, see Berges and Tuna (Berges 1994. Berges and Tuna 2000, 2001) argue that the Triopion should be located at the site of Emecik farther east on the peninsula.
75. Gauthier 1985. Dignas 2002. Van Bremen 1996. Schmitt-Pantel 1981. For civic and political agendas associated with these practices, see Chaniotis 1995, Chankowski 2005, and Sumi 2004.

Works Cited

Anti, C. and L. Polacco, "Oropos. *To Theatron kata ton Bomon,*" in *Nuove Ricerche sui Theatri Greci Arcaici,* Padua, pp. 163–71.

AvP XIII = C. H. Bohtz, *Das Demeter-Heiligtum,* Berlin 1981.

Bankel, H. 1997. "Knidos. Der hellenistische Rundtempel und sein Altar. Vorbericht," *AA* 1997, pp. 52–71.

Bankel, H. 2004. "Knidos. Das Triopion. Zur Topographie des Stammesheiligtums der Dorischen Hexapolis," in *Macht der Architektur – Architekture der Macht,* ed. E. L. Schwandner and K. Rheidt, Mainz, pp. 100–13.

Becker, T. L. 2003. *Griechische Stufenanlagen,* Münster.

Bean, G. E. 1980. *Turkey Beyond the Maeander* 2nd ed., London and New York.

Berges, D. 1994. "Alt-Knidos und Neu-Knidos," *IstMitt* 44, pp. 5–16.

Berges, D. and Tuna, N. 2000. "Das Apollonheiligtum von Emecik: Bericht uber die Ausgrabungen 1998 und 1999," *IstMitt* 50, pp. 171–214.

Berges, D. and Tuna, N. 2001. "Kult-, Wettkampf- und politische Versammlungsstatte: Das Triopion-Bundesheiligtum der dorischen Pentapolis," *AW* 32, pp. 155–66.

Bergquist, B. 1998. "Feasting of Worshippers or Temple and Sacrifice? The Case of Herakleion in Thasos," in *Ancient Greek Cult Practice from the Archaeological Evidence* ed. R. Hägg, Stockholm, pp. 57–72.

Blackmon D. J. 1966. "The Harbor at Perachora," *BSA* 61, pp. 192–4.

Bömer, F. 1952. *RE* s. v. *Pompa,* cols. 1878–1994.

Bosnakis, D., K. Hallof, and K. Rigsby, ed. 2010. *Inscriptiones Coi insulae: decreta, epistulae, edicta, tituli sacri. IG* XII 4.1, Berlin and New York.

Bruns-Özgan, C. 1997. "Neufunde hellenisticher Skulpturen aus Knidos," in *Sculptors and sculpture of Caria and the Dodecanese* ed. I. Jenkins and G. B. Waywell, London, pp. 99–104.

Buraselis, K. 2004. "Some Remarks on the Koan *Asylia* (242 B.C.) against its International Background," in Hoghammar 2004, pp. 15–20.

Burkert, W. 1985. *Greek Religion* (trans. J. Raffan), Cambridge, MA.

Chaniotis, A. 1995. "Sich selbst feiern? Städtische Feste des Hellenismus im Spannungsfeld von Religion und Politik," in *Stadtbild und Bürgerbild im Hellenismus*, ed. M. Wörrle and P. Zanker, Munich, pp. 147–68

Chaniotis, A. 2005. "Ritual Dynamics in the Eastern Mediterranean: Case Studies in Ancient Greece and Asia Minor," in *Rethinking the Mediterranean*, ed. W. V. Harris, Oxford, pp. 141–66.

Chankowski, A.S. 2005. "Processions et ceremonies d'accueil: une image de la cite de la basse époque hellénistique," in *Citoyenneté et participation à la basse époque hellénistique*, ed. P. Fröhlich and C. Müller, Geneva, pp. 185–206.

Connor, W. R. 1987. "Tribes, Festivals and Processions: civic ceremonial and political manipulation in Archaic Greece," *JHS* 107, pp. 40–50.

Corinth XVIII.3 = N. Bookidis and R. Stroud, *The Sanctuary of Demeter and Kore. Topography and Architecture*, Princeton, 1997.

Coulton, J. J. 1976. *The Architectural Development of the Greek Stoa*, Oxford.

DeCerteau, M. 1984. "Walking in the City" in *The Practice of Everyday Life* (trans. S. F. Rendall), Berkeley, Los Angeles, London, pp. 91–110.

Dignas, B. 2002. *Economy of the Sacred in Hellenistic and Roman Asia Minor*, Oxford.

Dillon, M. 1997. *Pilgrims and Pilgrimage in Ancient Greece*, London and New York.

Frederiksen, R. 2002. "The Greek Theatre. A Typical Building in the Urban Center of the *Polis?*" in *Even More Studies in the Ancient Greek Polis*, ed. T. H. Nielsen, Stuttgart, pp. 65–124.

Gauthier, P. 1985. *Les Cités Grecques et leurs Bienfaiteurs*, (*BCH* suppl. 12), Paris.

Goldhill, S. and R. Osborne eds. 1999. *Performance Culture and Athenian Democracy*, Cambridge.

Graf, F. 1996. "*Pompai* in Greece. Some Considerations about Space and ritual in the Greek *Polis*," in *The Role of Religion in the Early Greek Polis* (Acta Instituti Atheniensis Regni Sueciae 8.14) ed. R. Hägg, Stockholm, pp. 56–65.

Gruben, G. 1966. *Die Tempel der Griechen*, Munich.

Hellström, P. 1988a. "Hellenistic Architecture in Light of Late Classical Labraunda," in *Akten des XIII internationalen Kongresses für Klassisches Archäologie*, Berlin, pp. 243–52.

Hellström, P. 1988b. "Labraunda. Mixed Orders in Hecatomnid Architecture," in Πρακτικά του XII Διεθνούς Συνεδρίου Κλασικής Αρχαιολογίας, Αθήνα 4 – 10 Σεπτεμβρίου, 1983, vol. 4, pp. 70–74.

Hellström, P. 1991. "The Architectural Layout of Hecatomnid Labraunda," *RA* 1991, pp. 297–308.

Hellström, P. 1996a. "The Androns at Labraynda. Dining Halls for Protohellenistic Kings," in *Basileia. Die Paläste der hellenistischen Könige*, ed. W. Hoepfner and G. Brands, Mainz pp. 164–9.

Hellström, P. 1996b. "Hecatomnid Display of Power at the Labraynda Sanctuary," in *Religion and Power in the Ancient Greek World* (*Boreas* 24) ed. P. Hellström and B. Alroth, Uppsala, pp. 133–8.

Hepding, H. 1910. "Die Arbeiten zu Pergamon 1908–1909. Die Inschriften," *AM* 35, pp. 439–42.

Herzog, R. 1928. *Heilige Gesetze von Kos* (AbhBerlin 1928), Berlin.

Herzog, R. and G. Klaffenbach. 1952. *Asylienurkunden aus Kos* (SBBerlin 1952.1) Berlin.

Higbie, C. 2003. *The Lindian Chronicle and the Greek Creation of their Past*, Oxford.

Hoepfner, W. 1984. "ΦΙΛΑΔΕΛΦΕΙΑ. Ein Beitrag zur frühen hellenistischen Architektur," *AM* 99, pp. 358–64.

Höghammar, K. 1993. *Sculpture and Society: A Study of the Connection between Free-Standing Sculpture and Society on Kos in the Hellenistic and Augustan Periods*, Uppsala.

Höghammar, K. 2004. *The Hellenistic Polis of Kos: State, Economy and Culture (Boreas 28. Uppsala Studies in Ancient Mediterranean and Near Eastern Civilizations)*, Uppsala.

Hollinshead, M. B. 1992. "Steps to Grandeur: Monumental Steps and Hellenistic Architectural Complexes," in *The Age of Pyrrhus (Archaeologia Transatlantica vol.11)*, ed. T. Hackens, N. Holloway, R. R. Holloway and G. Moucharte, Louvain-la-Neuve and Providence, pp. 83–96.

Hornblower, S. 1982. *Mausolus*, Oxford.

Kavoulaki, A. 1999. "Processional performance and the democratic polis," in Goldhill and Osborne, pp. 293–320.

Kern, O. 1900. *Die Inschriften von Magnesia am Maeander*, Berlin.

Kondis, I. 1963. Review of E. Dyggve and V. Poulsen, *Lindos* III.2, in *Gnomon* 35, pp. 394–95.

Kos I = P. Schazmann and R. Herzog, *Kos: Ergebnisse der deutschen Ausgrabungen und Forschungen* I. *Asklepieion, Baubeschreibung und Baugeschichte*, Berlin, 1932.

Kostomitsopoulos, P. 1988. "Lindian Sacrifice: An Evaluation of the Evidence Based on New Inscriptions," in *Archaeology in the Dodecanese*, ed. S. Dietz and I. Papachristodoulou, Copenhagen, pp. 125–8.

Kuhn, G. 1985. "Untersuchungen zur Funktion der Saulenhalle in archaischer und klassischer Zeit," *JdI* 100, pp. 169–317.

Labraunda I.2 = A. Westholm, *The Architecture of the Hieron*, Stockholm, 1963.

Labraunda III.2 = J. Crampa, *The Greek Inscriptions* Part II: 13–133, Stockholm, 1972.

Laumonier, A. 1958. *Les cultes indigènes en Carie*, Paris.

Lauter, H. 1986. *Die Architektur des Hellenismus*, Darmstadt.

Lindos I = C. Blinkenberg, *Fouilles de l'Acropole 1902–1914 I. Les Petits Objets*, Berlin, 1931.

Lindos III.2 = E. Dyggve and V. Poulsen, *Fouilles de l'Acropole, 1902–1914 et 1952 III.2 Le sanctuaire d'Athana Lindia et l'architecture lindienne*, Copenhagen, 1960.

Lippolis, E. 1988-1989. "Il santuario di Athana a Lindo," *ASAtene* 48-49, pp. 97–157.

Love, I. C. 1972. "A Preliminary Report of the excavations at Knidos, 1971," *AJA* 76, pp. 393–405.

Love, I. C. 1973. "A Preliminary Report of the excavations at Knidos, 1972," *AJA* 77, pp. 413–24.

Maran, J. 2006. "Architecture, Power and Social Practice – an Introduction," in *Constructing Power: Architecture, Ideology and Social Practice*, ed. J. Maran, C. Juwig, H. Schwengel, and U. Thaler, Hamburg, pp. 9–14.

Marangou, E.-L. I. et al. 1995. *Ancient Greek Art from the Collection of Stavros S. Niarchos*, Athens.

Menadier, B. 1995. "The Sixth Century B.C. Temple and the Sanctuary and Cult of Hera Akraia, Perachora" (diss. Univ. of Cincinnati).

Mylonopoulos, J. 2008. "The Dynamics of Ritual Space in the Hellenistic and Roman East," *Kernos* 28, pp. 49–79.

Neils, J. 1992. "The Panathenaia: An Introduction," in *Goddess and Polis. The Panathenaic Festival in Ancient Athens* ed. J. Neils, Hanover, NH, and Princeton, pp. 13–27.

Neils, J. 1996. "Pride, Pomp and Circumstance: The Iconography of Procession," in *Worshipping Athena: Panathenaia and Parthenon*, ed. J. Neils, Madison, WI., pp. 177–97.

Nielsen, I. 2000. "Cultic theaters and ritual drama in Ancient Greece," *Proceedings of the Danish Institute at Athens* 3, pp. 107–133.

Nielsen, I. 2002. *Cultic Theaters and Ritual Drama*, Aarhus.

Nilsson, M. P. 1916. "Die Prozessionstypen im griechischen Kult," *JdI* 31, pp. 309–39.

Pakkanen, J. 1998. "The Column Shafts of the Propylaia and Stoa in the sanctuary of Athena at Lindos," *Proceedings of the Danish Institute at Athens* 2, pp. 147–159.

Papadimitriou, V. 1988. "The Anastylosis of the Ancient Monuments on the Acropolis of Lindos," in *Archaeology in the Dodecanese* ed. S. Dietz and I. Papachristodoulou, Copenhagen, pp. 169–71.

Parker Pearson, M. and C. Richards. 1994. "Ordering the World: Perceptions of Architecture, Space and Time," in *Architecture and Order: Approaches to Social Space*, ed. M. Parker Pearson and C. Richards, London, pp. 1–37.

Payne, H. 1940. *Perachora: The Sanctuaries of Hera Akraia and Limenia* I, Oxford.

Perrin-Saminadayar, E. 2011. Review of Bosnakis, Hallof, and Rigsby 2010. *BMCR* 2011.04.37.

Petrakos, B. 1968. Ο Ωρωπός και το ιερόν του Αμφιαράου, Athens.

Piok Zanon, C.P. 2007. "Dank an Demeter: Neue Gedanken zu Architektur und Bedeutung des Demeter-Kultes in Pergamon im späten 3.Jh.v.Chr.," *IstMitt* 57, pp. 323–64.

Plommer, H., and F. Salviat. 1966. "The Altar of Hera Akraia at Perachora," *BSA* 61, pp. 207–15.

Pompeo, L. 1999. *Il complesso architettonico del Tempio M di Selinunte: analisi tecnica e storia del monumento*, Florence.

Price, S. 1999. *Religions of the Ancient Greeks*, Cambridge.

Radt, W. 1988. *Pergamon. Geschichte und Bauten, Funde und Erforschung einer antiken Metropole*, Cologne.

Rice, E. E. 1983. *The Grand Procession of Ptolemy Philadelphus*, Oxford.

Rigsby, K. J. 1996. *Asylia. Territorial Inviolability in the Hellenistic World*, Berkeley.

Rigsby, K. J. 2004. "*Theoroi* for the Koan Asklepieia," in Höghammer, 2004, pp. 9–14.

Roux, G. 1957. "Le sanctuaire argien d'Apollon Pythéen," *REG* 70, pp. 474–87.

Roux, G. 1961. *L'Architecture de l'Argolide aux IVe et IIIe siècles avant J.-C.*, Paris.

Schmitt-Pantel, P. 1981. "Le festin dans la fête de la cité grecque hellénistique," in *La Fête, Pratique et Discours d'Alexandrie Hellénistique à la Mission de Besançon*, Paris, pp. 86–99.

Schwandner, E.-L. 1990. "Beobachtungen zur hellenistischen Tempelarchitektur von Pergamon," in *Hermogenes und die hochellenistische Architektur*, ed. W. Hoepfner and E.-L. Schwandner, Mainz am Rhein, pp. 80–102.

Senseney, J. R. 2007. "Idea and Visuality in Hellenistic Architecture: A Geometric Analysis of Temple A of the Asklepieion at Kos," *Hesperia* 76, pp. 555–95.

Sherwin-White, S. M. 1978. *Ancient Cos: An historical study from the Dorian settlement to the Imperial period. Hypomnemata* 51, Göttingen.

Shoe, L. T. 1950. "Greek Mouldings of Kos and Rhodes," *Hesperia* 19, pp. 340–369.

Sokolowski, F. 1955. *Lois sacrées de l'Asie Mineure*, Paris.

Sokolowski, F. 1969. *Lois sacrées des cités Grecques*, Paris.

Sourvinou-Inwood, C. 1994. "Something to do with Athens: Tragedy and Ritual," in *Ritual, Finance, Politics. Athenian Democratic Accounts Presented to David Lewis*, ed. R. Osborne and S. Hornblower, Oxford, pp. 269–90.

Stampolides, N. Chr. 1984. "Der 'Nymphenaltar' in Knidos und der Bildhauer Theon aus Antiochia," *AA* 1984, pp. 113–27.

Sumi, G. 2004. "Civic Self-representation in the Hellenistic world," in *Games and Festivals in Classical Antiquity. BAR International Series 1220*, ed. S. Bell and G. Davies, London, pp. 79–92.

Templer, J. 1992. *The Staircase: Studies of Hazards, Falls, and Safer Design*, Cambridge, MA.

Thieme, T. 1993. "The Architectural Remains of Archaic Labraunda," in *Les grands ateliers d'architecture dans le monde égeen du VIe siècle av. J.-C.* ed. J. des Courtils and J.-C. Moretti, Paris, pp. 47–55.

Thomas, C. M. 1998. "The Sanctuary of Demeter at Pergamon: Cultic Space for Women and its Eclipse," in *Pergamon: Citadel of the Gods*, ed. H. Koester, Harrisburg, pp. 277–98.

Thompson, D. J. 2000. "Philadelphus' Procession: Dynastic Power in a Mediterranean Context," in *Politics, Administration and Society in the Hellenistic and Roman World*, ed. L. Mooren, Louvain, pp. 365–88.

Tilley, C. 1994. *A Phenomenology of Landscape: Places, Paths and Monuments*, Oxford and Providence.

Tomlinson, R. 1992. "Perachora," in *Entretiens.* (Fondation Hardt) *Le sanctuaire grec,* pp. 321–51.

Travlos, J. 1988. *Bildlexikon zur Topographie des Antikem Attika*, Tübingen.

Umholtz, G. 1999. "Queenly Emulation in Early Hellenistic Architecture?" *AJA* 103, p. 302 (abstract).

Van Bremen, R. 1996. *The Limits of Participation: Women and Civic Life in the Greek East in the Hellenistic and Roman Periods*, Amsterdam.

Van Straten, F. 1995. *Hiera Kala: Images of Animal Sacrifice in Archaic and Classical Greece (Religions in the Graeco-Roman World 127)*, Leiden.

Vollgraff, W. 1956, *Le Sanctuaire d'Apollon Pythéen à Argos*, Paris.

von Hesberg, H. 1994. *Formen privater Repräsentation in der Baukunst des 2. und 1. Jahrhunderts v. Chr.*, Cologne, Weimar, Vienna.

Wikander, C. 1992. "Pomp and Circumstance. The Procession of Ptolemaios II," *OpAth* 19, pp. 143–50.

Würster, W. 1973. "Dorische Peripteraltempel mit gedrungenem Grundriss," *AA* 88, pp. 200–11.

CHAPTER THREE

COMING AND GOING IN THE SANCTUARY OF THE GREAT GODS, SAMOTHRACE

Bonna D. Wescoat

In Shakespeare's *As You Like It,* Jaques, libertine turned fool in search of a meaningful identity, wanders through the Forest of Arden, singing apparent nonsense, which he claims "'Tis a Greek invocation, to call fools into a circle" (2.5.58–60). While not the most authentic of Shakespeare's fools, Jaques later makes the famous observation:

> All the world's a stage,
> And all the men and women merely players.
> They have their exits and their entrances (2.7.139–41)

The philosophizing Jaques has hit upon the actions that interest us here: gathering in a circle and coming and going from that circle. Samothrace is the stage; the scene, the Theatral Complex on the Eastern Hill at the entrance to the Sanctuary of the Great Gods; the players, pilgrims who have come to participate in the *mysteria* (Figs. 3.1–3.2, no. 25).[1] In this chapter, I aim to examine the reciprocity of circular form and ritual experience in a construction known as the Theatral Circle. In the essays presented in this volume by Mary Hollinshead and Margaret Miles, traversing, processing, gathering, and witnessing provide key subjects of inquiry. The added component in my investigation involves the particular shape of the gathering space. The basic thesis is hardly novel: architectural form is not the mere handmaiden of function but has semantic value and the capacity to transform the experience of those who engage it spatially, metaphysically, psychologically, emotionally, and associatively.[2]

3.1. Samothrace, Sanctuary of the Great Gods, view of the Theatral Complex from the Propylon of Ptolemy II to the east. Photo Bonna D. Wescoat.

Of course, scholars working with choral performance and the theater long have studied circular space and performance,[3] but most are undoubtedly eager to put an end to discussions of formal origins and associations (whether the *khoros*, "dancing floor" or *halos*, "threshing floor"), not least because they rely on the now disproved hypothesis of an original circular orchestra.[4] The Theatral Circle in the Sanctuary of the Great Gods, however, was unquestionably circular from its inception, and the place where it takes us differs fundamentally from that of a theater's orchestra. The mystery cult of the Great Gods focused on safe-keeping and transformation. The rites – held in silent trust by the community of the initiated – promised not only protection at sea but also the opportunity for initiates to "become both more pious and more just and better in every respect than they were before" (Diod.Sic. 5.48.4–50.1).[5] I argue that the conditions for this transformation were established up front, so to speak, and by means of architecture, right at the Sanctuary's threshold. Moreover, while the Theatral Complex on the Eastern Hill clearly served as a major station upon entering the Sanctuary, I suggest that this architecturally configured space also played a key role in completing the initiates' experience by effecting their final transformation upon leaving the Sanctuary.

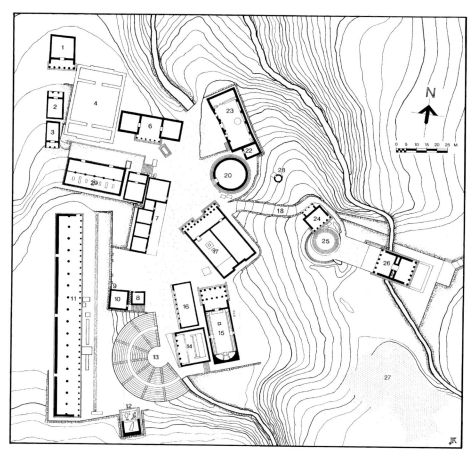

3.2. Samothrace, reconstructed plan of the Sanctuary of the Great Gods. Drawing John Kurtich, Samothrace Excavations.

Prospective initiates into the mysteries of the Great Gods on Samothrace approached the Sanctuary from the east, crossing a deep torrent that formed the boundary of the temenos to enter a paved circular space, roughly nine meters in diameter, surrounded by a grandstand comprised of five steps (Figs. 3.1–3.2 no. 25, and Fig. 3.4).[6] The structure, which we call the Theatral Circle, is the oldest surviving permanent construction in the Sanctuary, and it remained the core of the complex that formed this ritual threshold to the sacred precinct for over half a millennium.[7] The continuous architectural and sculptural elaboration of the area from the late fifth century B.C.E. until the catastrophic destruction of the region by earthquake in the late first or early second century C.E., testifies to the significance of the Theatral

Complex as a primary locus of sacred activity and public display. At the height of its development in the late Hellenistic period, the Theatral Circle was surrounded by a hexastyle Doric building, as well as concentrically deployed platforms and an outer grandstand. These last structures supported more than forty life-size bronze statues that framed the Theatral Circle and, by extension, embraced the participants in the ceremonies enacted here. These essential elements – the orchestra-like space, the grandstands, the ordered architecture, and the bronze sculpture – are all familiar components of Greek civic and sacred spaces, but their concentric configuration on Samothrace stands apart from our general experience of ancient Greek sacred architecture and spatial organization.

We have achieved a good understanding of the design and date, and even know the patron of many of the remarkable monuments in the Sanctuary of the Great Gods, but we have trouble determining their function, a conundrum that includes the Theatral Complex. Although its architectural forms and transitional position in the pilgrim's progress suggest multiple uses, the structures themselves defy functional categories. No extant ancient texts or epigraphic evidence identify the actions associated with the Theatral Complex, a situation that extends to much of the central Sanctuary as well.[8] The excavator, James R. McCredie, followed by Walter Burkert, suggests that an initial sacrifice was offered in the Theatral Circle.[9] Susan Cole thinks that the prospective initiates here received sacred instructions for what was to follow.[10] Kevin Clinton has recently argued that the purificatory rite of *thronosis*, which he suggests may have been performed in this space, constituted preliminary initiation, or *myesis*.[11]

Although we cannot fix the precise ritual or rituals performed in the Theatral Circle, we have the powerful essentials of place, form, and participant; we can examine the impact of the circular space on the participants and derive some understanding from that relationship. The position of the Theatral Circle at the entrance to the Sanctuary, on a sloping ridge separated from the ancient city by a steep torrent bed, was chosen long before the gate that framed the processional passage from the ancient city was built and before the Propylon of Ptolemy II was conceived. The orchestra-like space and framing steps are necessary elements of a theatron, literally a place of watching; in particular, watching performed actions. Here, the concentrically placed circles shape both the space of performance and the place of witness.

The combination sets the Samothracian structure apart from the many other theatra in ancient Greek sanctuaries, whose design reinforces the apposition of audience and performed actions.[12] The impetus for the unusual architectural development of the area might have emerged from the topography itself, but a depression in the landscape is not a sufficient condition for the series of circular elaborations we find. Nor is the shape of actions performed there necessarily the progenitor of form. The early shape of the Greek theater orchestra was not circular, even if the dance performed there was.[13] The circular shape itself does, however, have a semantic value, one that we can trace from its early conception to its heightened exploitation here. How might the interplay of physical form and associative power of circularity have affected the prospective initiates? Can such an exploration help shape our understanding of what this place in the Sanctuary accomplished?

Building History

We cannot doubt the importance of the Theatral Complex within the rites of the *mysteria*, given that the Theatral Circle is among the earliest permanent structures thus far identified in the Sanctuary. Originally, it consisted of a circular zone roughly nine meters in diameter, paved with polygonal fieldstones and framed by at least four concentric steps that were interrupted by a two-meter wide passage set roughly opposite the point where the procession of prospective initiates entered (Fig. 3.3 top). Although the eastern side of the Theatral Circle has been destroyed, pry marks on the foundation indicate that the steps originally continued along this side. Prior to the construction of the Propylon of Ptolemy II and its monumental causeway in the 280s, we imagine that the procession crossed over the sacred boundary formed by the ravine by means of a small bridge and path that met the wide, top step of the Theatral Circle. From here, the participants moved around the perimeter to take their places in the grandstands; eventually, they passed down into the orchestra and out through the passage toward the center of the Sanctuary. The steps are clearly designed for standing, not sitting. They could accommodate approximately 240 participants, if each were accorded half a meter

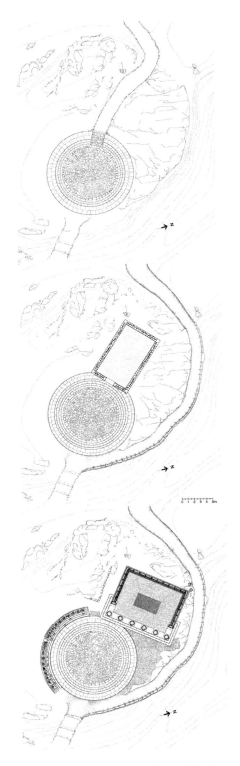

3.3. Samothrace, Sanctuary of the Great Gods, Theatral Circle, restored plan of the first, second, and third phases of construction. Drawings Andrea Day, Samothrace Excavations.

of standing room.[14] In this configuration, the Theatral Circle essentially operated as an enlarged part of the Sacred Way. While the procession surely stopped to perform some action here, the passageway rendered the space fluid; the initiand's trajectory slowed only temporarily. The main goal, passage to the heart of the Sanctuary, remained visually and spatially paramount.[15]

Soon after its construction, however, and certainly no later than the second quarter of the fourth century, the Theatral Circle was radically altered and the full potential of its configuration realized (Fig. 3.3 center). The passage of the Sacred Way through the circle was blocked, the fourth step rebuilt, and a fifth step added. The additional step and filled passageway now allowed for roughly 335 participants. The Sacred Way was redirected northeastward around the bedrock outcrop before turning southwest to rejoin the original path. By making the Theatral Circle tangent to, rather than part of, the Sacred Way, those responsible for the alteration emphasized gathering within the space rather than passage through it. The area became a destination that fully arrested the movement of the procession, rather than an enlarged part of the passage where the procession temporarily paused. The new configuration now consisted of two unbroken circles, blurring the distinction between the orchestra (ostensibly for performing) and the steps (for watching). All subsequent phases of development reassert and elaborate this fundamental change.

The passageway may have been blocked to allow for the construction of a building set axially against the Theatral Circle, but the alterations to the Circle were complete before construction on the new building began.[16] This new building, called the Fieldstone Building, was situated virtually on top of what had once been the Sacred Way, even though there was ample room to place it further to the east. The portions of the north and south walls that survive indicate that the eastern end was set against the outer perimeter of the Theatral Circle. The eastern wall probably rested on the fifth step of the Theatral Circle. A door onto the Circle is the only viable entrance, although none remains. Bedrock outcrops delimit the position of the western wall, but we do not know whether it had a doorway or not.

Although its position over the original Sacred Way is suggestive, the Fieldstone Building could not have served as an inner propylon or framed passageway; its stucco floor would not have withstood the traffic. Although the purpose of the structure remains uncertain, it clearly provided more than an apotheke, for it bears the earliest example in the Sanctuary of interior plaster decoration in imitation of masonry. The exterior was also covered with plaster of a denser consistency, some fragments of which bear graffiti. The building may have been the place where special implements of the cult required in this area could be kept and, perhaps, viewed. It also may have held small offerings such as the fine terracotta figurines and black glaze vessels found on and near its floor.[17] The elegant appointment of the interior also raises the possibility that the Fieldstone Building served as a sheltered gathering place, either for the officials of the cult before meeting prospective initiates or for the initiates themselves. The building stood long enough to require interior renovation, but it was destroyed, perhaps by fire, before the task was completed.

In its place rose a grand marble Doric hexastyle prostyle structure set tangent to the Theatral Circle but turned outward to confront the processional way (Figs. 3.3 bottom, 3.4, 3.6).[18] Owing to the spectacular circumstances of its destruction and the subsequent decision to bury rather than rebuild the Complex, much of this building survives, even though only one fragment of the southeastern corner of the first step remains in situ. The nearly pristine southeast corner and penultimate epistyle blocks bear the beginning of an important dedicatory inscription, ΒΑΣΙΛΕ | ΙΣΦΙΛΙΠΠΟΣ. Five additional letters, three of which cross over a joint face, allow for a full reconstruction:

ΒΑΣΙΛΕ | ΙΣΦΙΛΙΠΠΟΣ | Ạ[ΛΕΞΑΝ]Δ[Ρ] | Ọ[Σ ΘΕΟΙΣΜΕΓ] | Α[ΛΟΙΣ]
KINGS PHILIP [AND] ALEXANDER, TO THE GREAT GODS

The only Philip and Alexander to rule coevally are the successors of Alexander the Great, his half-brother Philip III Arrhidaios and his posthumous son, Alexander IV. This elegant building with its confident inscription is one of the few physical manifestations of their brief reign between 323 and 317 B.C.E. The building consisted of a Pentelic marble temple front façade before a broad, shallow chamber constructed of Thasian marble. Although signaling a sacred space, the building did not constitute a propylon. The interior was open like a stoa, and because it was not secured by either a door wall or metal grille, it could

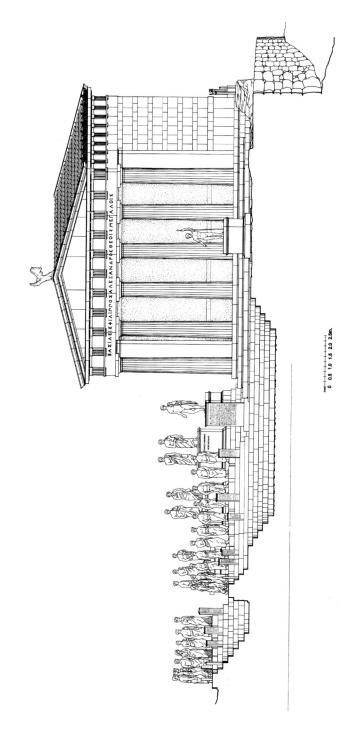

3.4. Samothrace, Sanctuary of the Great Gods, section through the reconstructed Theatral Complex, Sanctuary of the Great Gods, Samothrace. Drawing Mathew Grant, Reagan Ruedig, Albert Hopper, and Nathaniel Zuelzke, Samothrace Excavations.

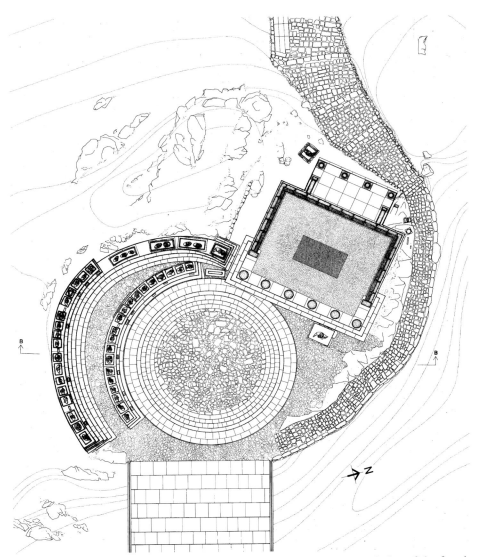

3.5. Samothrace, Sanctuary of the Great Gods, Theatral Complex, restored plan of the fourth phase of development. Drawing Andrea Day, Albert Hopper, Reagan B. Ruedig, and Yong K. Kim, Samothrace Excavations.

not have held precious objects or cult paraphernalia. While dozens of statue bases and built monuments have been unearthed on the Eastern Hill, none were found in clear proximity to this building, and the mosaic floor bears no evidence that it supported large orthostate monuments. The orientation toward the processional way, a clear divergence from the orientation of its predecessor, suggests that the Dedication of Philip

3.6. Samothrace, Sanctuary of the Great Gods, reconstruction of the Propylon of Ptolemy II and the Theatral Complex, from the north. Digital model Kyle Thayer and J. Matthew Harrington, Samothrace Excavations.

III and Alexander IV served as a kind of pavilion or large exedra, providing shelter and a place of reception. Although not a canonical dining facility, the Dedication could easily have served as a place for refreshment as well.[19]

Once in place, the Dedication of Philip III and Alexander IV was rapidly followed by a series of platforms supporting life-size bronze statues, built serially but eventually forming a continuous sweep framing the southwestern side of the Theatral Circle (Figs. 3.3 bottom, 3.4, 3.6, 3.21). Some twenty-two statue bases survive, made both of imported Thasian marble and local soft gray limestone. Most of the bases have either a pair of foot-shaped cuttings or one foot-shaped cutting and a rectangular socket; both arrangements supported standing male figures with slightly different distribution of weight. A few bases, however, have a different arrangement, with two sockets, one set close to the front of the block, and additional cuttings toward the back of the block; these may have secured statues of women in long dress. Of the statues themselves precious little survives: eyelashes, toes, a drapery tassel, and many rectangular patches – in short the kind of parts that might snap off when the bronze was salvaged.

The configuration of statues is unusual. The platforms suggest group monuments, but each statue is set on an individual base. To complicate matters, not one of these bases is inscribed. I doubt the statues were mythological in nature. Although we hear of two ithyphallic bronze statues erected "before the doors" in the Sanctuary, the texts specifically note two, not twenty-two or more such statues.[20] Beyond these two ithyphallic statues, there is not a known tradition in the Sanctuary of dedicating monumental generic types.[21] Group compositions such as royal families would resonate with the several royal architectural dedications found in the Sanctuary, but they are equally unlikely, for group statues are invariably set on a continuous base.[22] The statues that encircle the Theatral Circle can best be described as individual dedications erected in groups. While we cannot know with certainty, the use of different materials for the bases on the different platforms suggests that each platform accommodated a roughly contemporary set of commissions. In the instances of the smaller Platforms II, III, V and the infilled space between Platforms III and IV, which could only accommodate two to three statues, the commissions were surely established at the time the platform was constructed. The essentially individual aspect of each statue suggests that they probably honor benefactors. There are cuttings for stelai, not one per statue but several per platform, and it is possible that the names of the honored were inscribed on these stelai.[23]

The pilgrims' experience of the Eastern Hill changed dramatically with the construction of the Propylon of Ptolemy II in the 280s B.C.E. (Figs. 3.2 no. 26, 3.6). The course of the torrent was redirected to the east so that this time-honored natural boundary might pass beneath the new Propylon. The massive foundation of the Propylon projected well into the original eastern ravine, raising the Sacred Way circa 4.9 meters above the top step of the Theatral Circle while narrowing the distance between the two structures to a mere 18.5 meters. The 12 meters wide causeway connecting the two structures descended at a precipitous slope of one in four, about fourteen degrees.[24] The steep descent and plunging perspective view into the Theatral Complex, coupled with the concentrically framing statues and Doric pavilion, would have had a strong affect on the perceived scale of the Theatral Circle, giving it the feeling of a more intimate, tightly bounded space. The circular orchestra and surrounding steps formed a cul-de-sac that no longer shaped the threshold of the Sanctuary. Instead of a point of entry, the Complex became the first destination within the Sanctuary, where prospective initiates gathered to prepare for the rites they would experience in the heart of the Sanctuary.

In the late Hellenistic period, an additional outer, stepped retaining wall and platform, potentially supporting up to one hundred more pilgrims and many more statues on individual bases and large orthostate monuments, was cut back into the hillside in a nonconcentric sweep behind the first set of statues (Figs. 3.4–3.5). It met the southern balustrade of the causeway from the Propylon to frame and close the space, thus tightening the connection between the Propylon and the Theatral Complex and sharpening the focus on the two buildings: the east façade of the Dedication and the western façade of the Propylon. In this respect the expanded Complex approaches the great Western tradition of architectonically framed façades, such as the western side of Mnesikles's Propylaia on the Athenian Acropolis, or Bernini's great colonnade before Carlo Maderna's façade of St. Peters. This focusing of space, as I argue below, proves especially important to the experience of leaving the Sanctuary.

At its height, the density of the sculptural dedications framing the Theatral Circle rivaled that of the great panhellenic sanctuaries of Greece.[25] The statues, however, are not set in the opportunistic profusion we often witness, even along such controlled passages as the Sacred Way at Delphi, where diversity and distinction are clear aims. Rather, they tightly frame the theatral space and, by extension, the participants in the rituals that took place there. The configuration is not precisely akin to statue groups set on semicircular bases, but some of the same effects are achieved, including apprehending the series of figures as a unified group.[26] In terms of disposition, we find a striking parallel in the archaic precinct on the Sacred Way from Miletos to Didyma, where twelve enthroned figures placed on a semicircular base, circa 13.30 meters in diameter, frame an outdoor cultic space (Fig. 3.7).[27] The statues not only help define the space but also metaphorically preside over the events accomplished there. Freestanding exedrae with statues arranged on a hemispheric base that includes a bench for passersby, develop this concept more informally, while the arrangement of statues in the circular precinct of Demeter in the Agora at Cyrene explores the relationship on a more intimate scale.[28] At Samothrace, the statues form a dense congregation that simultaneously greets the

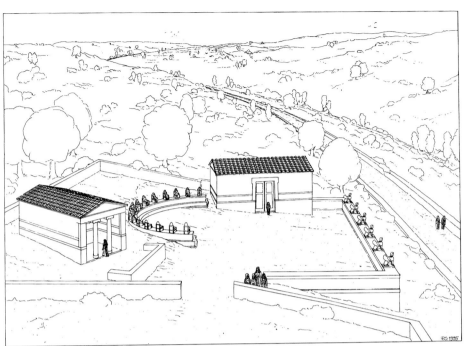

3.7. Didyma, archaic shrine along the Sacred Way from Miletos to Didyma. K. Tuchelt, P. Schneider, and C. Cortessis, *Ein Kultbezirk an der Heiligen Straße von Milet nach Didyma, Didyma* 3.1, Mainz 1996, fig. 32. Courtesy of the Deutsches Archäologisches Institut.

pilgrim while physically and visually shielding his or her view of the main cult buildings in the central valley of the Sanctuary. During the daylight hours they would have formed a dignified gathering enframing the theatral space. During the night ceremonies of initiation, the flickering play of torchlight on the statues would have given them a powerful, uncanny animation.[29]

In sum, the Theatral Complex stands within the sacred temenos defined by the natural boundary of the eastern torrent (in contrast, for example, to the gathering spaces outside the manmade boundary of the Eleusinian walls and gateways).[30] It is clearly not in the heart of the Sanctuary in the valley below and to the west, and its outward-facing configuration and exposed location make it unsuitable for any kind of secret or secluded action. In fact, its position in the landscape and the configuration of built structures serve to shield from view the cult buildings beyond. While at first the Theatral Circle was conceived as part of the flow of the sacred procession, it was very soon drawn off that course to become a prominent, independent locus. Experience may have generated the change; once the pierced circle was in place, the superior potential of the closed circle to shape the rites became obvious. In both arrangements, the Theatral Circle provides a transitional, transformative space. Everything about its location and organization suggests that the Theatral Circle served as a primary gathering place in the prospective initiates' progress through the sanctuary, and that the actions that took place there prepared them for the central experience in the main cult buildings below. Relatively large numbers of people could be accommodated (between 240 and 435), but the strength of the space would not be diminished if smaller groups gathered around the lowest steps; the space may well have served both festival crowds and smaller groups of initiates.

Components of the Design and Architectural Resonance

The basic design of this complex, a circular pavement surrounded by stands, seems both straightforward and commonplace, given that places of performance and watching are central features of Greek sanctuaries.[31] However, the precise configuration turns out to be less common than one might suspect. What kinds of architectural associations would have affected the pilgrims entering such a space?

A circular space brings to our mind the orchestra of a theater, but the Theatral Circle antedates the earliest such circular orchestra (that of the theater at Epidauros Fig. 3.8) by at least half a century.[32] The diameter circumscribed by the lowest step, circa 9.15 meters, is a good deal smaller than that of the typical orchestra of the civic theater, which runs between 20 and 30 meters.[33] The orchestras of theaters designed for cultic performances, including the theater on the western slope of the Sanctuary of the Great Gods, could be a great deal smaller, but again, they are rarely as cleanly circular.[34] Moreover, the Theatral Circle was paved. The floor of a theater's orchestra, at this stage in its history, was composed of beaten earth.[35] Not only does the original conception of the shape have little to do with the orchestra of the theater, but also the experience of the space in the Theatral Circle appears to have been entirely different, given the intimacy of size and proximity of the encircling witnesses.

Potentially closer to the idea explored in the Theatral Circle is the generic type of space identified as a χορός (*khoros*), possibly circular

3.8. Epidauros, orchestra of the theater. Photo William Bruce.

and surely for singing and dancing. The *khoros* is well known in ancient Greek literature, not only as the shape of actions but also as a formal space.[36] *Khoroi* are attested to epigraphically in Crete, at the Sanctuary of Asklepios at Lebena (recording the relocation of the *khoros*), in the city of Eltynia (a law protecting young people when at the *khoros*), and in a dedication found at Istron but associated with Lato (recording the construction of a *khoros* in the Sanctuary of Ares and Aphrodite).[37] Another inscription records the construction of a *khoros* for the nymphs at Vari by Archedemos the Nympholept.[38] Charalambos Kritzas has discussed the connection of these structures with Homeric descriptions of the fine dancing floors of the nymphs (*Od.* 12.315–318), as well as Ariadne's dancing floor (*Il.* 18.590–592). Daidalos is named the architect of the latter, which surely signifies that a structure, and not just a place, was imagined. Peter Warren identifies Minoan *khoroi* in the circular platforms outside the Palace of Knossos.[39] A *khoros* could be as simple as a level area of beaten earth, and indeed, neither the texts nor the inscriptions explicitly specify a circular design. However, the discovery in the agora at Argos of the remains of a late-fifth or early-fourth century B.C.E framed, nearly circular space, circa 28 meters in diameter, suggests what the more formally crafted versions may have looked like (Figs. 3.9–3.10).[40] The circular space is surrounded by a stone border of two steps

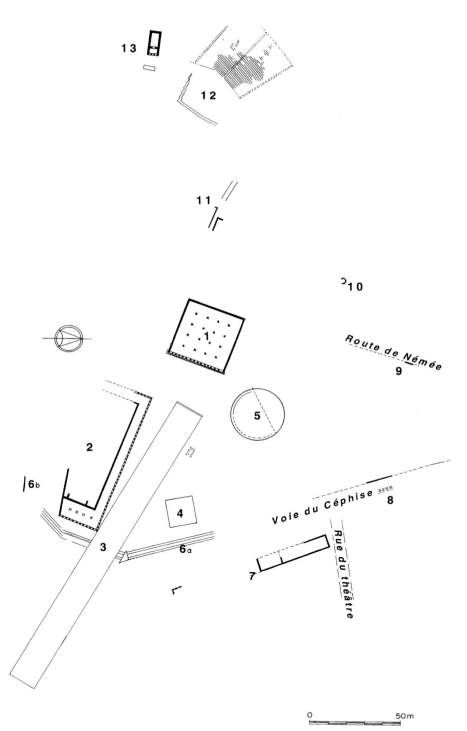

3.9. Argos, plan of the agora, with circular structure, no. 5. Courtesy of the École française d'Athènes, Y. Rizakis.

3.10. Argos, circular structure in the agora. Photo Bonna D. Wescoat.

(the lower one accessible from both sides), wide enough to support a seated audience with perhaps additional standing spectators behind.[41] The combination of a designated circular space with an area for witnessing in this contemporary structure resonates with the Theatral Circle at Samothrace, with one important difference – the floor of the *khoros* was beaten earth, not paving.

The discovery of the Argive structure gives greater credence to the claim that the large circular structure uncovered on the southern side of the Palaiokastro acropolis should be connected with the region of the agora of Sparta that Pausanias (3.11.9) called *khoros* and that Herodotos (6.67) and Lucian (*Anach.* 38) identify as a theatron; the terms emphasize aspects of both performance and watching.[42] The preserved monument, circa 43.3 meters in diameter, consists of a stepped platform supporting orthostates that serve as a retaining wall; of the superstructure we know little.

Closer still to the Theatral Circle's floor is the ἄλως (halos), or threshing floor. Earlier in the twentieth century scholars believed that the orchestra of the theater descended from the threshing floor, where the harvest, both of grain and grapes, was accompanied by celebration (Figs. 3.11).[43] While that idea is now unpopular, the connection is intriguing in our case.[44] For one, our structure has more in common

3.11. Naxos, threshing floor. Photo Margaret M. Miles.

with a threshing floor than does the orchestra of the theater or even
the *khoros*. Like the threshing floor, it is set on a ridge, has a paved floor,
and is framed. Most threshing floors range between 12 and 18 meters
in diameter, which is only slightly greater than the internal diameter
of the Theatral Circle. Although essentially an agrarian structure, in
advance of formal civic structures such as bouleuteria and theaters, the
threshing floor would have been the largest communal gathering space
and by far the most familiar round structure within the topography of
ancient Greece (evidenced even in its vestigial appearance in the landscape today).[45]

Threshing floors figure prominently in sacred contexts. The Eleusinian
accounts of 329/8 B.C.E. (*IGII* [2] 1672, line 233) mention a sacred threshing floor, which Eugene Vanderpool places on the raised terrace in front
of the Telesterion.[46] Within the fill beneath the later Telesterion, there is
in fact a curved wall of the Geometric period that describes a diameter
too large for an apsidal temple, as it is often identified. It is not out of
place for an earlier threshing floor on this site.[47]

The case of Delphi is even more suggestive. The open area below
the terrace supporting the temple of Apollo was known as the *Halos* or

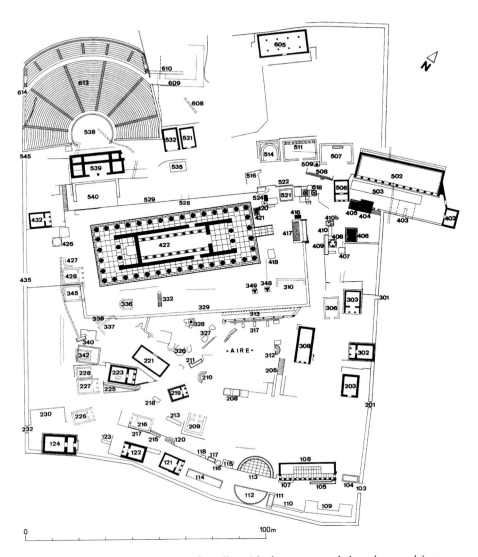

3.12. Delphi, plan of the Sanctuary of Apollo, with the open area below the temple's terrace, which was called the Halos ("Aire"). Courtesy of the École française d'Athènes, D. Laroche.

threshing floor (Fig. 3.12).[48] Monuments and viewing platforms such as the Stoa of the Athenians loosely framed the space; the Sacred Way passed right through it. Here, every eight or nine years, the pageant called the Stepterion was performed, reenacting perhaps the death of Python, and certainly the burning of a palace and the flight of the child Apollo from Delphi to the Vale of Tempe.[49] The performance was not professional or sponsored theater but rather the dramatization of sacred events and stories; the lead performer, a male child whose parents were both living, played the role of Apollo. Although the places for watching the events was not as formalized as it was at Samothrace, the location was not without opportunity, especially from the vantage of the Stoa of the Athenians and the many exedrai in the region, or more remotely from the temple terrace itself.

At Delphi, the *Halos* was also the designated gathering place for processions, at least in the Hellenistic period, as we know from decrees connected with the Eumenaia and Attaleia, festivals of the second century B.C.E.[50] In fact, the topography and configuration of monuments within the Sanctuary makes the *Halos* the only viable place for large assemblies to gather before approaching the altar of Apollo.

Threshing floors were clearly places of gathering, encounter, witness, and transformation, not only in the Greek world but across the ancient Mediterranean. Although further afield, it is worth noting their significance in the Old Testament. In Chronicles (1.21.15–28), the threshing floor of Ornan is a charged place, with epiphany, encounter, sacrifice, and memorial, for here the angel of Yahweh appears; Yahweh answers David; David buys the threshing floor and sacrifices. Later Solomon builds the Temple on the place of this threshing floor, where David had sacrificed.[51]

Ch. Kritzas has proposed that the word *halos*, threshing floor, could also take on the sense of *khoros*, dancing floor. Certainly a level circular space brings to mind circle dancing, and at Samothrace the ritual reenactment of the search for Harmonia, her safe return and joyous wedding to Kadmos, suggests that dancing formed an important part of the celebration.[52] The splendid frieze of dancers that wraps around the central cultic building of the Sanctuary, the Hall of Choral Dancers, makes dancing a prominent visual motif in the Sanctuary.[53] The recurring references to Korybantic dancing in the ancient testimonia suggest a role for this very different form of dance within the cult as well.[54] Steven Lonsdale has underscored the volatility of the dance floor, which he describes as "a locus with the magnetic power to attract a divinity or lover, to experience union, to dismember, to reconstitute, in short a theatron for recreating and manipulating the natural and supernatural worlds."[55]

3.13. Oropos, Sanctuary of Amphiaraos, view from the temple toward the curved steps (center) that face the altar (right). Photo Bonna D. Wescoat.

Although less consistent, the shape of the altar precinct also belongs within our architectural typology of the circular spaces, for it, too, occasionally takes circular form. Circumambulation of the altar, while purifying it with water, or singing to honor the god, or gathering to witness sacrifice, forms an important part of the ritual of sacrifice.[56] When space is specifically engineered for sacrificial witness at monumental altars, the area designated for the crowd is generally to one side, for example, the zone between the altar and temple. Or, as in the case of the altar in the Sanctuary of Amphiaraios at Oropos, the audience gathered on curved stands to one side of the altar (Fig. 3.13).[57] Few theaters have permanent altars in the orchestra; the one at Thorikos is set to the side.[58] So, too, is the altar in the ekklesiasterion at Poseidonia[59] (Fig. 3.14). But altars are occasionally set within an encircling space, especially on nearby Thasos. The late archaic altar in the Sanctuary of Demeter at Arkouda on Thasos was framed by a pavement circa 9.35–9.5 meters in radius that was at least semicircular and may have circumscribed the rectangular altar.[60] Sacrificial areas could also be enclosed in circular precincts, as in the Altar of Zeus Agoraios on Thasos, in which a circular peribolos wall with two entrances frames a rectangular altar with a precinct about 9 meters

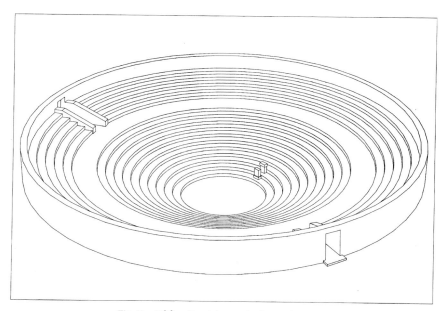

Fig. 31 – Edifice Circulaire, restitution, variante A.

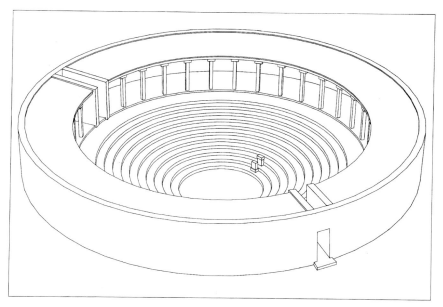

3.14. Poseidonia/Paestum, two possible reconstructions for the Ekklesiasterion, with the altar set within the lower seats. After E. Greco and D. Theodorescu, *Poseidonia – Paestum II. L'Agora*. Collection de l'École française de Rome 42, Rome 1983, figs. 31–2. Courtesy of the École française de Rome.

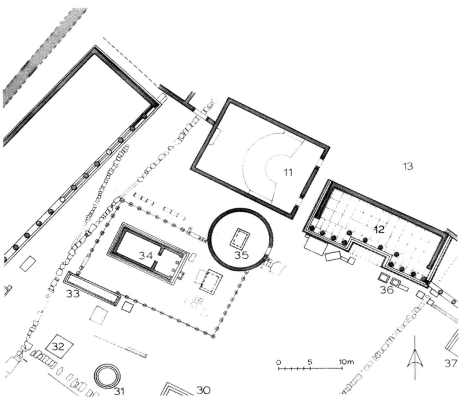

3.15. Thasos, plan of the agora, with the circular precinct of the altar of Zeus Agoraios (center). Courtesy of the École française d'Athènes, M. Worch-Kozelj.

in diameter (Fig. 3.15).[61] While this precinct is later than the Theatral Circle, earlier constructions apparently preceded it. Broadly speaking, it too could be a form of *khoros*, with circular actions taking place around the altar. We find a similar arrangement although on a much smaller scale on the island of Paros.[62] The archaic circular structure to the east of the archaic temple of Apollo at Didyma has long been understood as a peribolos wall encircling the archaic altar of Apollo, although recently other functions have been proposed.[63] James McCredie has proposed that the cylindrical, molded block found on the Eastern Hill was an altar originally placed in the center of the Theatral Circle.[64] The association remains a possibility, but not a certainty, given the scale of the block and some of its features.[65]

For the pilgrim entering the Sanctuary of the Great Gods, the orchestra of the Theatral Circle would have resonated with at least some of these associated forms encountered in other contexts. The association of forms may also have triggered association of actions and emotions, for nearly all the spaces are gathering places for festive occasions. And what of the way in which the participants stood around this circular space, on tiers of stands that circumscribe the entire performance area? This configuration represents the most remarkable aspect of the Theatral Circle. Of course, banks of stairs, stands, or seats designed for witnessing events are legion within Greek sanctuaries.[66] A few examples may stand for the many: the seats facing the side door of the Temple of Despoina at Lykosoura or the altar in the Sanctuary of Demeter at Pergamon; the curved stairs facing the altar at the Sanctuary of Amphiaraos at Oropos; the L-shaped stands, cut into bedrock, that face onto the Sacred Way just inside the Lesser Propylaia at the Sanctuary of Demeter and Kore at Eleusis; the L-shaped bank of steps to the north of the Erechtheion; or the later theater facing the temple in the Kaberion at Thebes and a similar configuration in the Sanctuary of Artemis Ortheia at Sparta (Fig. 3.16).[67] Mary Hollinshead has explored several highly evocative examples of steps serving as places of witness in her chapter in this volume. All of these configurations, however, differ from the theatron at Samothrace in their appositional arrangement, with the viewers on one side, and those performing the actions on the other.

Structurally more akin to the Theatral Circle are the ekklesiasteria (meeting places for the Ekklesia) found in the western Greek cities of Metapontion, Poseidonia, and Akragas, which consist of a theatron composed of continuous seats encircling a central area. These buildings are, however, far larger in scale and are designed for a seated audience: the structure at Metapontion accommodated some seventy-five hundred to eight thousand; that of Poseidonia, fourteen hundred (Fig. 3.14).[68] The structures at Poseidonia and Akragas surround a circular orchestra, but the ekklesiasterion at Metapontion had a rectangular central area (the term orchestra might still apply); the whole structure was bisected by a pathway circa 8 meters wide.[69] At basis, the design of these buildings may ultimately reflect the idea of the ἱερὸς κύκλος (hieros kyklos, sacred circle) used by Homer on the shield of Achilles to describe the configuration of

3.16. Thebes, theater facing the temple (foreground) in the Kaberion. Photo Tsimas, Deutsches Archäologisches Institut Athen Neg. No. ATH-1969/1590.

the judges who, seated in a sacred circle on smoothed stones, adjudicate an argument in the agora, as the onlookers gather around (*Il.* 18.497–508).[70] The context in Homer and in western Greece is decidedly civic.[71] Moreover, the fundamentally different act of sitting has none of the tension and transience of standing.

Two additional structures that have important design connections deserve mention, even though their contexts make them unlikely matches for the Theatral Complex. The theatron at Ayioi Theodoroi near the Isthmus resembles ours in having a sunken "orchestra" surrounded by steps, although on a smaller scale.[72] Roughly half of the structure survives, consisting of an orchestra roughly 7.4 meters in diameter, with at least twelve low, shallow steps. The surviving section forms only half of a full circle, but from the design it seems likely to have been a full circle. Closer in design, but decidedly different in context, is the Hellenistic structure located on the narrow strip of land behind the market stoa at Aigai in Asia Minor.[73] It consists of a sunken, paved circular area, circa 8.5 meters in diameter, framed by at least two steps. As it stands, this structure is, in fact, the one most physically similar to our Theatral Circle. However, its context in connection with the market stoa is worlds apart.

In short, the circular stands we find at Samothrace are atypical. They generate a very specific outcome by organizing the participants into a circular relationship with one another (and whatever actually transpired in terms of cult practice), an essential relationship that reconstituted itself with each initiation. The closed form stops directional movement, focusing the participants inward to the shared experience that began their initiation within the sacred grounds. Cultic actions performed here – possibly a purification rite such as sacrifice or libation, possibly the delivery of sacred instructions, possibly the witnessing of some dance or sacred pageant – would have prepared the pilgrim for his or her initiation. In fact, we have seen that all of these actions – sacrifice, dance, ritual theater, and judgment – are the actions most directly associated with circular space in ancient Greece. But here, the participants look not only at the actions performed, but also across the space of performance to their fellow participants.[74] The shape of the space dissolves the distinction between the actions and the witnesses. In this way strangers who had journeyed a great distance here become intimates and everyone is equally liable.

Circular Associations

It is not only the geometry of the circle in relation to architecture but also the associations the circle conjures that are paramount here.[75] The strength and potential motion of the circle trigger associations that range from the mundane to the cosmic. In the ancient Greek context, we find the form noticed in material artifacts (the bowl, the ring, the shield, the coin, the stephane, the tambourine, and the wheel);[76] in the body (the eye);[77] in the natural world (the trunk of a tree, the configuration of islands [e.g., the Cyclades], the circumference of the ocean, the sun, the moon, and the planets, the vault of the sky, the dome of heaven, the orbit of a planet, path of the sun, and the imagined shape of the cosmos);[78] in metaphysical contexts (the wheel of one's fortune, the cyclical life force);[79] and, in human actions (dancers in chorus, ritual cleansers around the altar, parents around the hearth with a newborn, or hunters around prey).[80] And there are the social circles: the circle of defenders, the circle of chieftains, the council of elders, the circle of witnesses, the circle of friends, the circle of the family,[81] even the circle of gods.[82]

To describe human relations, the Greeks used the term circle much as we do to signal a close-knit community of friends, followers, leaders, or fellow believers; in other words, a community of the like-minded or like-purposed. The axiom of the circle involves the seamless definition of what is included and what is excluded, while maintaining all points on its circumference equidistant from the center. Gathering in a circle creates insiders who are equal, at least in a structural sense and at least for the brief time that the circle rules.[83] In the Sanctuary, the Theatral Circle established the parameters of the shared experience, both physically and psychologically. Consider the effect of such a configuration on pilgrims who gathered from all over the Greek world whose initial experience in the Sanctuary required that they stand as "formal" equals among strangers before they moved forward together into the simultaneously collective and deeply personal process of initiation. Ultimately, this spontaneous *communitas* (as defined by Victor Turner) created in the Theatral Circle would lead to longer-lasting and widespread community – *koinonia*, in the larger Greek and Roman world, as the many Samothrakeia across the Aegean attest.[84]

Leaving the Circle

I have thus far concentrated on the Eastern Hill as the threshold of sacred experience. Acknowledging and marking the end of worship or celebration is also a fundamental human concern.[85] We lack literary or epigraphic evidence for actions that might have brought closure to the experience of initiation at Samothrace.[86] However, there are some good reasons to suspect that the Theatral Circle on the Eastern Hill served as the final, as well as the initial, place of assembly for the *mysteria*. This possibility underscores and helps to explain the significance of the western Corinthian façade of the Propylon of Ptolemy II.

Following initiation in the heart of the Sanctuary and celebratory dining on the slopes of the Western Hill, the newly initiated could simply drift away from the Sanctuary (as noted above, the precinct is not walled). The topography, however, offers several impediments, and the prospect of finding one's way to the sea by clambering down one of the ravines was presumably as awkward in antiquity as it is today.[87] The primary route *into* the Sanctuary offered the only convenient way *back* to the ancient city: up the Sacred Way, past the Theatral Circle, and up the ramp leading to the Propylon of Ptolemy II.

We find possible material evidence that the initiates not only followed this route but also may have reentered the Theatral Circle on their way out in the thousands of sherds of Samothracian conical bowls, a humble but distinctive courseware ritual vessel, left behind on the Eastern Hill (Fig. 3.17).[88] Although the advent of this vessel, its shape, and its precise function are not our subject here, the bowl appears some time in the second half of the third century B.C.E. and remains the vessel of choice within the Sanctuary through the early Imperial period.[89] Its shape, roughly 0.16 meters in diameter, with conically raised sides and a thick rim, makes it unwieldy for drinking or eating. It does, however, make a convenient libation vessel. While Samothracian conical bowls have been unearthed throughout the Sanctuary, the vast majority was found to the southeast of the Dedication of Philip III and Alexander IV, in the terrace fill, over the collapsed terrace wall, and spilled across the area of the robbed-out steps of the outer retaining wall. The overwhelming quantity of conical bowls, the state of their preservation, and the fact that they were mixed with very little earth argue in favor of a primary deposit.[90] The bowls were not carefully stacked in a kind of ritual interment. Nor can we claim with any certainty that they were ritually smashed, although most were broken in large fragments, frequently just in half. It is clear, however, that they were intentionally discarded – while in good condition – just on the perimeter of the Circle. Two possible explanations suggest themselves. First, the bowls might have played a role in some aspect of the rites performed upon entering on the Eastern Hill. Having served their purpose, they were discarded before the prospective initiate descended to the heart of the Sanctuary. However, the discovery of these bowls elsewhere (including the central Sanctuary and the Western Hill) suggests that they were also the vessel of choice within the Sanctuary proper. In this case, the second possibility seems more likely – on leaving the Sanctuary, the pilgrims discarded their bowl, which (as property of the gods) remained within the Sanctuary. Possibly, the act of discarding was accomplished formally, through reassembly in the circular Theatral Complex on the Eastern Hill. Although they left behind their bowls, the initiates departed the Sanctuary securely encircled by the more valuable tokens they took

3.17. Samothracian conical bowl, 66.37. Photo Samothrace Excavations.

away: the magnetized iron ring worn on their finger and the purple taenia wrapped around their waist. These tokens not only signified membership but also served as special talismans that afforded protection at
sea (Fig. 3.18).[91]

Leaving the Sanctuary in the light of day from the vantage of the
Theatral Circle, the initiates could appreciate fully the Corinthian order
of the western façade of the Propylon of Ptolemy II. Passing through the
Propylon on their way into the Sanctuary during their original entrance
(probably at nightfall),[92] the prospective initiates had little opportunity

3.18. Samothracian iron rings, 65.1026 (left); 70.0860 (right). Photo Craig Mauzy, Samothrace Excavations.

to notice the change in order from Ionic on the east to Corinthian on the west. Shrouded in darkness, the Corinthian façade was soon left behind as the prospective initiates focused their attention and energy on the steeply descending ramp into the Theatral Circle and the events that would take them from there to the heart of the Sanctuary. The entire procession from the Propylon to the center of the Sanctuary was one of continuous descent into the secluded cleft in the earth where the *mysteria* were performed. The chthonic overtones are explicit. Leaving the Sanctuary, by contrast, involved a steady ascent toward the east. Anticipation of the rites themselves gave way to the growing awareness of the changed life that initiation promised: divine protection and a sense of moral improvement. Samothracian initiates in particular were known as "pious" (*mystai eusebeis* or *mystae pii*).[93] The Corinthian order on the western façade of the Propylon of Ptolemy II was intended for this audience, in this state of mind.

The Propylon of Ptolemy II finds an important place in the history of Greek architecture as among the first monumental building in Greek architecture to use the Corinthian as a structural exterior order (Figs. 3.19–3.20).[94] Significantly, that order appears *only* on the western

3.19. Samothrace, Sanctuary of the Great Gods, restored Corinthian column from the western facade of the Propylon of Ptolemy II. Photo Bonna D. Wescoat.

façade. The eastern façade, which faces toward the ancient city and through which the prospective initiate entered the sanctuary, is purely Ionic. Alfred Frazer recognized the overt distinction between the façades of this bilingual building, and he argued for the revolutionary change in architectural thinking represented here: from an architecture conceived independently of its surroundings to one that derived form and meaning from its location and environment. For Frazer, this change suggested the distinction between the secular world to the east and the sacred precinct of the Sanctuary to the west.[95] In effect, the Corinthian order finds its characteristic place on the "inside," as it had since its first appearance in the late fifth century, although in this instance it appears on the inside of a temenos rather than the interior of a structure.[96] We can, I think, elaborate on both these points.

3.20. Samothrace, Sanctuary of the Great Gods, leaving the Theatral Circle: view to the reconstructed Corinthian façade of the Propylon of Ptolemy II. 3-D model Kyle Thayer and J. Matthew Harrington, Samothrace Excavations.

The Corinthian order is the interior order *par excellence*, particularly in round buildings, including the tholoi at Delphi and Epidauros, the Philippeion at Olympia, and the Rotunda of Arsinoe on Samothrace.[97] These Corinthian colonnades encircle the interior, framing the space and any congregants. In the tholos at Delphi, the Corinthian columns are set on a high socle; in the Philippeion they appear engaged within the wall upon an even higher socle; while on the Rotunda, they form a gallery high above floor level. In other words, the Corinthian interiors of round buildings often were situated well above ground level. The association of the Corinthian façade of the Propylon of Ptolemy II with the circular space of the Theatral Circle, while hardly identical to, nevertheless has some broad points of comparison with these Corinthian interiors, both in the higher elevation of the Corinthian order and in the proximity to circular space. The architect of the Propylon, whom Alfred Frazer believes also designed the Rotunda of Arsinoe, may have had this relationship of circular space to Corinthian order in mind when he designed the Propylon.[98]

But a more important reason accounts for the appearance of the Corinthian order in this elevated position and on this side of the boundary of the Sanctuary. The akanthos that forms the foliage of the Corinthian capital has intimate connections in the ancient world with the idea of cyclical death and rebirth. According to Vitruvius (1.2.4), the Corinthian capital took its inspiration from the vision of akanthos growing up around a basket placed on the grave of a Corinthian maiden of marriageable age. The appearance on many Attic white-ground lekythoi of a stele bearing an akanthos crown or having akanthos leaves sprout from its base confirms the strong association of the plant with the grave at least by the second half of the fifth century B.C.E.[99] The nature of the plant – a weed the dies back in the fall and regenerates irrepressibly in the spring – speaks to the cyclical force of nature,[100] a key part of Vitruvius' story. The akanthos becomes the visual embodiment of a lush, regenerative life force, "the most significant vegetal motif in history."[101]

Among the blessings that accrued to initiates in the *mysteria*, including salvation at sea and perhaps even the hope of a blessed afterlife,[102] Diodorus (5.48.4–50.1, noted above) tells us that initiates became "both more pious and more just and better in every respect than they were before." While no one knows what the personal experience of initiation at Samothrace was like, the initiates seem to have gained a new awareness of the prospects before them. In the light of the day following the rites, the initiates ascended from the deep cleft of the valley floor. They again arrived at the Theatral Circle, where to the east, the Corinthian façade of the Propylon rose up before them, now the threshold to a new life (Fig. 3.20). Viewed from within the geometric of the circle, immanent with its notions of cosmos, continuity, and community, the splendid order, replete with it own associations of regenerative life force, would have had a meaningful resonance.

Notes

1. Versions of this paper were delivered in the session, "Circular Space and Performance," at the 2006 meeting of the Archaeological Institute of America in Montreal (Wescoat 2006b) and at the American School of Classical Studies in Athens in 2007. I am grateful to Professor James R. McCredie and to Dimitris Matsas of the 19th Ephorate of Prehistoric and Classical Antiquities, Komotini, for their continued support of my research on Samothrace, as well as to Rush Rehm, also a speaker in the colloquium, "Circular Space and Performance," whose valuable suggestions have helped to sharpen the focus of this paper. Conversations with Bronwen Wickkiser and Peter Schultz, who both spoke at the colloquium, also contributed to my understanding. I am grateful to Nora Dimitrova for her advice on epigraphic matters, to John Camp and William Aylward for discussing the circular structure at Aigai in Asia Minor, to Jenifer Neils for discussing the circle of gods on the Parthenon frieze and to

my colleagues Cynthia and Richard Patterson for thoughtful perspective. My thanks also go to Maggie L. Popkin, Susan Ludi Blevins, and Amy Sowder for their helpful discussion and editorial comments. Part of the research for this work was generously funded by the Institute for Comparative and International Studies of Emory University.

2. In general, Jones 2000.

3. E.g., Kolb 1981; Polacco 1998; Rehm 2002, 2006.

4. Ure 1955, for the origins of Greek theater in the grape harvest on the threshing floor; tracing the roots of Greek drama in the agrarian cycle (ideas central to the Cambridge School) still hold allure today, for an overview, see Rehm 2002, pp. 39–40 and n. 22. Against the original circular orchestra, see below.

5. Translation *Samothrace* 1, pp. 65–66, no. 142.

6. Burkert 1993, p. 180, places the Theatral Complex outside "the sanctuary proper." However, the explicit shifting of the eastern torrent to run beneath the Propylon of Ptolemy II demonstrates that the eastern ravine was clearly understood to be the earlier boundary of the Sanctuary.

7. There are indications of earlier architecture in the Sanctuary, for example a fragmentary geison block, *Samothrace* 5, pp. 17–19, fig. 17 (possibly belonging to the predecessor of the Hall of Choral Dancers), and some of the architectural elements that were cut up to form the rubble walls of the so-called Hall of Votive Gifts, *Samothrace* 4.1, fig. 22 (but not fig. 23). However, several buildings once thought to be archaic are not. The Orthostate Structure belongs to the first half of the 4th century, probably the second quarter. The Hall of Votive Gifts is early Hellenistic; the Anaktoron is early Imperial. The archaic phases of the Hieron must also be eliminated. For the Anaktoron and Orthostate Structure, McCredie 1979, pp. 28–35; Hieron, Cole 1984, pp. 13–16. Evidence for the date of the Hall of Votive Gifts has not yet been published, but for a revision of its function, see Roux 1973, p. 554. For earlier studies on the Eastern Hill, see McCredie 1965, pp. 118, 122–4, fig. 4, pl. 39; McCredie 1968, pp. 216–34, pls. 64–72; McCredie 1979, pp. 6–8, pl. 3; Wescoat 2003, 2006.

8. With the exception of the generic monuments on the western side of the Sanctuary, including the theater, dining rooms, and stoa, the problem is endemic. For the main buildings in the heart of the Sanctuary, only the inscriptions prohibiting the entry of the uninitiated give some indication of the place(s) of initiation, which the Lehmanns identified in the buildings named by them the Anaktoron and the Hieron. K. Clinton (2003, p. 65), however, interprets the prohibitions as referring to the entire central temenos and does not connect these buildings with rites associated with the *mysteria*. For the prohibition inscriptions, see *Samothrace* 2.I, pp. 117–20, nos. 62–63.

9. McCredie (1968, p. 219) suggests that the low, round altar found in the area in 1939 may have belonged in the center of the Theatral Circle; Burkert 1993, p. 180.

10. Cole 1984, p. 26. She also suggests the *praefatio sacrorum* may have been delivered here, but Kevin Clinton has pointed out to me this event would have to happen in advance of entering the Sanctuary. For the *praefatio sacrorum*, see Livy 45.5.1–6.11, *Samothrace* 1, pp. 48–50, no. 116.

11. Clinton 2003, pp. 63–65. For the rite, Pl. *Euthydem.* 277de; Dio Chrys. *Or.* 2.33–34; Sibylline oracles. 8.43–9. The rite involves ecstatic dancing with much noise-making around the seated (enthroned) and blindfolded initiand, in order to induce a state of wonder, amazement, and disorientation. While thronosis

is not explicitly attested to at Samothrace, the numerous ancient references connecting the Korybantes and Korybantic dancing with the island make it an attractive hypothesis; see *Samothrace* 1, pp. 97–100, nos. 214–20. Multiple venues have been suggested. A. D. Nock (1941) first placed the rite in the Anaktoron; Burkert (1993, pp. 185–6) suggests it may have taken place in the Rotunda of Arsinoe.

12. The design of late Classical and Hellenistic Greek theaters broaches this idea by having a theatron that wraps around more than half the orchestra, but the impact affects only a portion of the audience; it does not hold for the actions performed on the skene.

13. See below, n. 32.

14. Calculated with four steps, including a single row of participants on the top step.

15. Burkert 1993, pp. 180–1, elides the several phases of development. The Theatral Circle does not, in its initial construction, block access, but the further development of the region does work toward screening the central Sanctuary.

16. For a full discussion of the Fieldstone Building, see *Samothrace* 9, forthcoming.

17. McCredie 1968, pp. 221–2, pl. 67e, and *Samothrace* 9, forthcoming.

18. McCredie 1968, pp. 222–9, pls. 64–65, 66b, 68–69; Wescoat 2003.

19. The main celebratory dining took place on the western side of the Sanctuary; see McCredie 1979, pp. 12–22, figs. 3–4, pls. 5–7; Lehmann 1998, pp. 109–15. I appreciate discussing these ideas with Sheila Dillon.

20. Varro, *Ling.* 5.10.57–58 (*Samothrace* 1, pp. 80–81, no. 175); Serv. *in Aeneidem* 3.12 (*Samothrace* 1, pp. 82–83, no. 179); Hippol. *Haer.* 5.8.9–10, from a sermon by the Naassene, a Gnostic author (*Samothrace* 1, p. 68, no. 147). Herodotos 2.51–52 (*Samothrace* 1, pp. 63–64, no. 140) notes the cultic connection with ithyphallic Hermes, but does not mention specific statues in the Sanctuary. The texts diverge on the precise location of these statues; see Clinton 2003, n. 62.

21. We lack evidence for votive images of a god, such as the many statues of Demeter dedicated in the sanctuary at Eleusis, or, although very different, the Zanes at Olympia; Pausanias 5.21.2–9. Some smaller scale herm statues have been found (60.526; 76.11; 87.1119a-c), but they clearly bear no relation to the statues erected on the Eastern Hill.

22. Royal votives include the Dedication of Philip III and Alexander IV, the Propylon of Ptolemy II, and the Rotunda of Arsinoe. Note also the column monument dedicated by the Macedonians to Philip V (68.1): McCredie 1979, p. 16, pl. 8a; Lehmann 1998, p. 163, fig. 80. For bronze statue groups on a single base, note, e.g., the Eponymous Heroes Monument in Athens, Mattusch 1994; Achaian Dedication at Olympia, Ajootian 2003; Base of the Arkadians, Monument of the Epigonoi and Heroes, or Monument of the Argive Kings, Delphi, Bommelaer and Laroche 1991, pp. 104–15, nos. 105, 112, and 113; Freifrau von Thüngen 1994, p. 183 with further bibliography; Philetairos Monument or Progonoi Monument on Delos, Bruneau and Ducat 2005, p. 182, no. 10, p. 196, no. 31, with further bibliography. On Hellenistic family groups, Hintzen-Bohlen 1990, 1991; Freifrau von Thüngen, pp. 41–43.

23. E.g., *IGII*² 682, 983, 1223, 1299; *IGXII.*9 236; *IDélos* 1497bis (one stele for two statues); *IPergamon* 160 (one stele set up next to several statues of King Antiochos).

24. *Samothrace* 10, p. 138. Calculations based on the 2008 topographical survey confirm the drop in elevation. Elevation of the euthynteria of the Propylon, 48.95

m.; calculated elevation of the stylobate of the Propylon, 49.76 m.; elevation of the top step of the Theatral Circle, 44.86–44.94 m; difference, 4.82 to 4.90 m.

25. Delos: Bruneau and Ducat 2005, pp. 101–11; Delphi: Bommelaer and Laroche 1991. Also Oropos: Löhr 1993; Petrakos 1997. Generally, Hintzen-Bohlen 1991, catalogue.

26. Jacob-Felsch 1969, pp. 184–6; Borbein 1973, pp. 60–72; Freifrau von Thüngen 1994; Ajootian 2003, in consideration of the Achaian dedication at Olympia.

27. *Didyma* 3.1, pp. 49–51, 139–62, 232–4, fig. 32.

28. For exedra monuments, see especially Freifrau von Thüngen 1994 Schmidt 1995, pp. 111–23. For an especially large example, note the exedra on the middle terrace of the Sanctuary of Asklepios on Kos, Schmidt, pp. 477–8, figs. 132–3. For the circular precinct of Demeter in the agora at Cyrene, see Luni 2001, p. 1549, figs. 19–20.

29. For evidence that the rites took place at night, see below, n. 92.

30. For Eleusis, see Miles, this volume, and Palinkas 2008.

31. See Hollinshead, this volume.

32. The theater at Epidauros belongs to the last third of the fourth century; Ciancio Rossetto and Pisani Sartorio 1994–1996, vol. 2, pp. 209–10. The archaeological evidence for the orchestra of the fifth century B.C.E. Theater of Dionysos in Athens is meager and highly contested. The orchestras of the early deme theaters of Attica were not circular. Many scholars are willing to understand the classical orchestra as a variably shaped space in front of the sloping seats of the cavea, while others uphold the idea of a circular orchestra in the early Theater of Dionysos in Athens. Against an early history for a circular orchestra generally and in the Theater of Dionysos specifically, see Anti 1947, pp. 55–82; Gebhard 1974, pp. 428–40; Anti and Polacco 1969, pp. 129–59; Polacco 1990, pp. 101–4, 160–74, figs. 39–40; Polacco 1998, pp. 90–97; Goette 1995, pp. 9–30; Rehm 1988, pp. 276–83; Rehm 2002, pp. 39–41 and especially n. 17; Rehm 2006. For a review of the early evidence, concluding in favor of the circular orchestra for the Theater of Dionysos originally proposed by W. Dörpfeld, see Wiles 1997, pp. 23–54, who emphasizes the place of dithyramb in the Dionsysia and argues (p. 50) that the appearance of the circular orchestra outside Attica relies on its invention in Athens at the Theater of Dionysos. H. P. Isler, in Ciancio Rossetto and Pisani Sartorio 1994–1996, vol. 1, p. 96, follows a similar logic. While the Theater at Epidauros has the earliest certain circular orchestra, it is possible that slightly earlier examples may have been planned with a circular orchestra. These include the theater at Megalopolis, dated to the 360s B.C.E. and the theater attached to the palace at Aigai, assigned to the mid- to second half of the fourth century B.C.E., both, in any case, well after the construction of the Theatral Circle on Samothrace. Ciancio Rossetto and Pisani Sartorio 1994–96, vol. 2, p. 317 (Aigai); pp. 262–3 (Megalopolis).

33. More than thirty-five surviving theaters from the Late Classical and Hellenistic periods have an orchestra whose diameter is between 19.5 and 30 m. In general, see Ciancio Rossetto and Pisani Sartorio 1994–1996.

34. For the diameter of smaller scale orchestras of cultic theaters, see Neilsen 2002, Table, pp. 340–1. Examples include theaters in the Sanctuary of Asklepios, Messene, diameter: 9.7 m., Hellenistic/Early Roman period, Ciancio Rossetto and Pisani Sartorio 1994–1996, vol. 2, p. 261; Sanctuary of the Great Gods, Samothrace, diameter: c. 10 m., second century B.C.E.?, Ciancio Rossetto and Pisani Sartorio 1994–1996, vol. 2, p. 288; Sanctuary of Syrian Gods, Delos,

diameter: 10.16 m, late second century B.C.E., Ciancio Rossetto and Pisani Sartorio 1994–1996, vol. 2, p. 195; Sanctuary of Amphiaraos, Oropos, diameter: 11.1 m., fourth century B.C.E., Ciancio Rossetto and Pisani Sartorio 1994–1996, vol. 2, 227. Of comparable scale is the urban theater at Thera, diameter: 9.58 m., second century B.C.E.(?), Ciancio Rossetto and Pisani Sartorio 1994–1996, vol 2, p. 289–90.

35. Wycherley 1962, p. 165; Rehm 1988, p. 277n.58; Rehm 2002, p. 39.

36. Polacco 1998, pp. 105–16, argues that the term alludes more often to the shape of actions than to the shape of space, but there are many instances, enumerated below, in which a space is meant.

37. Kritzas 1998. In papers delivered at the Annual Meeting of the Archaeological Institute of America, Montreal 2006, both C. Kritzas, whose paper, "Choroi. The dancing floors of Greek Sanctuaries," was delivered as the response, and I advanced many of the same parallels drawn here.

38. IG 1³ 977B; Kritzas 1998, p. 287.

39. Warren 1984.

40. Pariente 1988, pp. 697–705, figs.1, 4–10; Marchetti and Rizakis 1995, pp. 455–456, figs. 1, 12; Nielsen 2002, p. 103, fig. 37.

41. Pariente (1988 p. 702) calculates roughly eighty people (given two feet of room each), could be accommodated on the projected 49 m. of bench available if the structure was not completely circular, but instead was set against the "krepis" that now forms one of its sides. She then proposes the possibility that magistrates named the Eighty (Ὀγδοήκοντα) could meet here, to witness dances in addition to sacrifice. The idea is intriguing, but Marchetti and Rizakis (1995 p. 455) argue the structure was originally a completely circular one and that the top step has been recut when the "krepis" was built. If so, the circumference of c. 88 m. would allow a seating capacity of around 150.

42. Kourinou 2000, p. 114–27, 280–281, figs. 2–4, pls. 22–6, with references to earlier work; Nielson 2002, pp. 91–93. The structure has also been identified as the Skias (σκιάς, object providing shade such as a canopy, pavilion, or parasol) mentioned by Pausanias (3.12.10–3.13.1), next to which was a tholos. The latter was certainly circular, and the Skias likely was as well, given the fact that the tholos in the Athenian Agora was also known by this name, *Agora* III, pp. 179–184. The name implies a roof, which would have been a challenge for such a large structure. For a discussion of the literary evidence for circular spaces, building (overly rigid, in my opinion) physical connections between the ἱερὸς κύκλος, χορός, ὀρχήστρα, and ἀγορά, see Kolb 1981, pp. 5–19. Against the connection, perhaps too strongly, see Polacco 1998, pp. 105–16. At Corinth, a curved platform surrounded by a sidewalk that also approximates a *khoros*, see Nielson 2002, p. 96, fig. 32.

43. Ure 1955.

44. The position against the orchestra's origins in the threshing floor is summarized by Rehm 2002, pp. 39–40 and n. 23.

45. Some of the best ancient evidence for threshing floors is preserved in South Attica, e.g. Princess Tower Farm, Young 1956, pp. 122–4, fig. 1; Goette 2000, p. 83, figs. 178–9; Cliff Tower Farm, Young 1956, pp. 124–6, fig. 2; Langdon and Watrous 1977, fig. 1, pp. 173–5; Goette 2000, pp. 81–82, figs. 169–70; Souriza Farm, Goette 2000, p. 80–81, fig. 166. See also Lohmann 1992, p. 44 n.316, for threshing floors in South Attica.

46. Vanderpool 1982.

47. Mylonas 1961, wall E3, pp. 67–69, figs. 13, 20, 23. It has been identified both as the wall of an apsidal structure or as a retaining wall; for the latter, see most recently A. Mazarakis Ainian 1997, pp. 147–50, figs. 169–71. Discussed in Palinkas 2008.

48. *GDI* 2101, 2642; Plutarch, *Quaest. Graec.* 203c; *De def. or.* 418A (for the Doloneia); *De mus.* 1136; Aelian, *VH* 3.1.

49. Bourguet 1914, pp. 124–6; Harrison 1962, pp. 425–9; Roux 1976, pp. 166–168; Bommelaer and Laroche 1991, pp. 146–7.

50. Inscribed on the base of a statue of Eumenes II dedicated by the Aetolians; *FdD* III.3 pp. 207–13, nos. 237–9; Daux 1936, pp. 686–98.

51. The story is also told in 2 Samuel 24.16–24.

52. References to the wedding of Kadmos and Harmonia, in which Harmonia is explicitly identified as the daughter of Elektra and not Aphrodite, include scholia to Euripides *Phoinissai* 7 (*Samothrace* 1, pp. 74–75, no. 75); Diodorus 5.48.4–50.1 (*Samothrace* 1, pp. 65–66, no. 142); scholia, Laurentiana to Ap. Rhod. *Argon* 1.916 (*Samothrace* 1, p. 33, no. 70); scholia, Parisina to Ap. Rhod. *Argon.* 1.915–16 (*Samothrace* 1, pp. 33–34, no. 70a); Nonnus *Dionysiaca* 3.38–51, 77–96; 3.373–81 (*Samothrace* 1, pp. 34–35, nos. 73–74).

53. For the idea that the frieze on the Hall of Choral Dancers represents the celebration of the wedding of Kadmos and Harmonia, *Samothrace* 5, pp. 230–3. Against this idea and in favor of choral groups, see Marconi 2010.

54. *Samothrace* 1, nos. 214–27, 219–20 (Korybantic dancing); 190–2 (cultic dance in arms of the Salii introduced by Soan or Dardanos of Samothrace).

55. Lonsdale 1995, p. 281.

56. Burkert 1985, pp. 87–88. Purifying: Ar. *Pax* 956; *Av.* 955; Eur. *IA* 1569. Dancing and singing: Kallim. *Hymn* 4 (*Delos*) 310; *CA* 140 (inscription from Erythrai calling for a paean sung to Apollo while circling three times round the altar). My thanks to Bronwen Wickkiser for the last reference.

57. See Hollinshead, this volume, for places for witnessing sacrifice. See Rehm 2002, p. 41, against participants gathered in a circle to witness sacrifice.

58. Rehm 1988, pp. 264–74; Rehm 2002, p. 41.

59. Greco and Theodorescu 1983, vol. 2, pp. 34–49, figs. 21–32.

60. Most recently Ohnesorg 2005, pp. 110–13, fig. 51; Grandjean and Salviat 2000, pp. 129, 217, no. 72.

61. Grandjean and Salviat 2000, p. 76, figs. 31–32, no. 35.

62. Ohnesorg 1991, p. 122, pl. XXVIb; Ohnesorg 2005, pp. 48–50, pl. 19.

63. Interpreted by H. Knackfuß as a peribolos wall encircling an altar, an identification maintained by most scholars. F. Cooper and S. Morris argue, on the basis of evidence put forth by B. Fehr, that the structure was a circular dining room with a temporary tentlike roof; *Didyma* 1, pp. 136–9, pls. 14, 15, 227; Fehr 1971–72, pp. 29–34; Cooper and Morris 1990, pp. 69–71. Ohnesorg 2005, p. 49 n. 252, pl. 46.8 (aerial photograph).

64. McCredie 1968, p. 219.

65. See also Clinton 2003, n. 49. It stands 0.64 m. high, is cylindrical (diameter across the body, 0.744 m.), and has a molded base and crown. Empolia cut in the top and bottom surfaces, as well as two lateral dowels with pour channels, indicate the block was part of a larger composition that included an additional base and crown. Usually round altars on this scale are made in a single block, but the arrangement is also somewhat unusual for a statue base. The carved moldings are more indicative of an altar. Compare round bases, Schmidt 1995, pp. 30–38, 69–79, to round altars, Berges, Patsiada and Nollé 1996. Note also

the similar (but smaller) cylindrical tripod base from Samothrace, Matsas and Dimitrova 2006, pp. 131–2, no 5. Figs. 10–11.

66. See Hollinshead, this volume, as well as Nielsen 2002, who discusses a wide range of theatra across the Mediterranean that may have served a cultic purpose.

67. Sanctuary of Despoina, Lykosoura: Leonardos 1896, pp. 101–26; Nielson 2002, pp. 106–8, fig. 42, pl. 27; Sanctuary of Demeter, Pergamon: *Pergamon* XIII, pp. 36–38; Neilson 2002, pp. 137–8; Sanctuary of Amphiaraos at Oropos: Anti and Polacco 1969, pp. 163–71; Ginouvès 1972, pp. 66–69; Nielsen 2002, p. 128, fig. 57, pl. 35; Sanctuary of Demeter and Kore at Eleusis: Mylonas 1961, pp. 143–6, fig. 4. no. 21 (there are cuttings for statue bases at the top of these steps, although they are not set out with the same regularity as those at Samothrace); Erechtheion: Paton and Stevens 1927, pls. 1–2; Ginouvès 1972, pp. 70–71; Kaberion at Thebes: *Kabirenheiligtum* II, pp. 30–32, pl. 2a; Nielsen 2002, p. 133, fig. 61; Schachter 2003, pp. 114–20; Sanctuary of Artemis Ortheia at Sparta: Nielsen 2002, p. 88–91, figs. 27–28, pl. 19.

68. Metapontion: Mertens 2006, pp. 334–7, figs. 597–603; Poseidonia: Greco and Theodorescu. 1983, vol. 2, pp. 44 n. 25; Mertens 2006, pp. 337–9, figs. 604–7 (fewer persons could be accommodated if the structure consisted only of the sunken theatron around the 7.5 m. diameter orchestra); Akragas: Mertens 2006, p. 318, figs. 576–8.

69. Mertens 2006, p. 335 and fig. 598 (Metapontion).

70. For this passage in relation to the formation of the Greek agora, see n. 42.

71. We should not rule out the possibility that the Theatral Circle served the polis of Samothrace at times when it was not being used for functions connected with the Sanctuary. The steps could serve as seats if every other one was used. This function would not, however, have been the primary purpose for which the Theatral Circle was erected.

72. My thanks to Professor Elizabeth Gebhard and Fritz Hemans for bringing this structure to my attention.

73. Seiler 1986, p. 157, fig. 75. The Hellenistic date is suggested on the basis of the mason's marks. The area is now under excavation by Ersin Doğer.

74. While this situation has been connected to the theater, Wiles 1998, pp. 209–10, the architecture does not bear it out with the same intensity. Only a part of the spectators in a Greek theater witnesses the actions in the orchestra against the backdrop of the audience.

75. For the mathematical aspects in relation to architecture, Polacco 1998.

76. For textual references, note, e.g., the shield: *Il.*11.33; 20.280; Aesch. *Sept.*489; 496, 591. Chariot wheel: *Il.*6.42, 23.340, 23.394; Aesch. *Sept.* 203. Potter's wheel: *Il.*18.600, Ar. *Eccl.* 1. Wheel of torture: Andok. *De mysteriis* 43; Ar. *Plut.* 850; Apollod. E. 1.20; Antiph. repeatedly. Wreath or stephane: Pind.*Ol.* 14.24, *Nem.* 11.21; Pl. *Lg.* 12.943c, 12.946b; Aeschin. *On the Embassy* 2.46. Tambourine: Eur. *Bacch.* 120.

77. Soph. *OT* 1270, *Phil.* 1354, *Ant* 974, *OC* 704–706.

78. Cyclades as a chorus of islands around Delos, Kallim. *Hymn 4 (Delos)* 300; also 28 for songs circling Delos. Circumference of the ocean and shape of the world: Herod. 4.36.2 (against the simplicity of in maps). Shape of the sun or moon: Aesch. *Pr.V* 91, *Pers.* 504; Soph. *Ant* 416; Eur. *Ion* 1155; Herod. 6.106. Vault of the sky/heaven: Herod. 1.131; Eur. *Ion* 1147; Soph. *Ph.* 815; Soph. *Aj.*672; Arist. *Mete.* 345a25. Cosmos and Soul: Pl. *Tim.* 34, 36. Orbit of celestial bodies: *h.Hom.* 8.6; Procl. *Hypotyp.* 2.17.

79. Wheel of fortune: Arist. *Eth. Nic.* 1100b; *Poet.* 1452a. Regenerative life force: Plato *Phaedo* 72b. Life cycle: Plato, *Republic* 8.546.

80. Dancing: Hom. *Il.* 18.599; Eur. *Tro.* 330; Ar. *Thesm.* 968. Purifying the altar: Ar. *Pax* 956; *Av.* 955; Eur. *IA* 1569. Circling the hearth with a newborn: Amphidromeia. Hunters circling their game: Hom. *Od.* 4.792; *Il.* 5.476; Herod. 1.43.1.

81. Circle of armed men: Soph. *Ichneutae Fr.*210.9; Eur. *Andr.*1089; Eur. *IT* 330; Xen. *An.* 5.7.2. Circle of defenders: Thuc. 2.83.5; 3.78.1 (ships); Xen. *Cyr.* 7.1.40; 7.5.41 (men). Circle of chieftains: Hom. *Il.* 4.208; Soph. *Aj.* 748–49. Council of elders: Hom. *Il.* 18.502. Circle of the like-minded (or of acquaintances): Plato *Prot.* 316c; Arist. *Eth. Eud.* 7.1245b. Circle of witnesses: Aesch. *Cho.* 980. Circle of friends: Arist. *Eth. Nic.* 1170b; 1171a; Plato *Prot.* 317d. Family circle: Arist. *Poet.* 1453b19.

82. Pind. *Nem.* 4.60. For gods in a circle on the Parthenon frieze, Neils 2001, pp. 61–66.

83. Gathering in a circle as a means to create a community of equals remains fundamental in some of our own earliest experiences, such as the morning circle in kindergarten or the campfire gathering for scouts; most western children know well the story of King Arthur's Round Table. There is, of course, the potential to differentiate, with more important participants on the first step and those of lesser status behind. I also do not mean to imply that there is confusion of status or an erasure of difference between the masters and their slaves who participated.

84. Turner 1969, pp. 94–165; Turner 1974. Turner's model remains a useful tool for understanding the Samothracian experience, despite criticisms expressed by scholars studying modern Christian pilgrimage, such as Eade and Sallinow 1991, pp. 1–5. *Koinonia* can have the sense of association, partnership, fellowship, Liddell and Scott. For Samothrakeia, Cole 1984, pp. 57–86; note especially the Samothrakeion on Delos, *EAD* XVI. See also Kowalzig 2003, pp. 60–72, for performances of *theoria* in the formation of *communitas* at Samothrace.

85. To draw on modern examples, the closing ceremony of the Olympic Games or the benediction at the end of the Sunday service in Christian worship.

86. While in the Eleusinian Mysteries there was no final group departure from the Sanctuary, the completion of the sacred rites was marked by changing clothes and offering libations for the dead using *plemochoai*; Mylonas 1961, pp. 279–80, with references. Clothing also seems to be involved in concretizing the Andanian Mysteries; Gawlinski 2006, pp. 24, 109–28.

87. The alignment of the three late Hellenistic buildings on the Western Hill (Fig. 2.1–3) suggests that a road or some kind of formal boundary ran along the western side of the site, but excavations revealed neither. McCredie 1968, pp. 210–11; McCredie 1979, p. 24.

88. For conical bowls, see *Samothrace* 9, forthcoming.

89. There are no conical bowls in the sealed fill of the Rotunda of Arsinoe, *Samothrace* 7, pp. 277–326; or in the fill of the Stoa. Although these bowls exhibition several forms of rim, the only decisive change in the profile that is chronologically significant is the shift from ring-base to string cut bases, which occurs possibly as early as the first century B.C.E., and certainly by the early first century C.E., where bowls with strong-cut bases appear in the fill of the Anaktoron, the date of which is discussed in McCredie 1979, pp. 33–35.

90. The finds include many thousands of large sherds, dozens of bowls reassembled from large fragments, and many more that could be. Dozens more fragments continue every year to wash out of the scarp.

91. For the ring, Isid. *Origines* 19.32.5; Lucr. 6.1044–7, Plin.(E) *NH*, 33.1.23; *Samothrace* 1, pp. 11, 96–7, nos. 30, 212, 213; *Samothrace* 5, pp. 403–404; Burkert

1993, pp. 187–8. For the taenia, Schol. Ap.Rhod. *Argon.* 1.917–18; *Samothrace 1*, pp. 107–8, nos. 229g–h. Roux, *Samothrace 7*, pp. 174–6, figs. 115–16, suggests that the taenia given to initiates is represented in the exterior parapet frieze of the Rotunda of Arsinoe.

92. The literary references to torches (indicating a nocturnal ceremony) come chiefly from Nonnos, *Dionysiaca* 3.124–79, 4.4–15, (*Samothrace 1*, no. 67), 13.393–407 (*Samothrace 1*, no. 69), 3.38–51, 77–96 (*Samothrace 1*, no. 73), 4.183–5 (*Samothrace 1*, no. 151), 14.17–22 (*Samothrace 1*, no. 166), 29.193–6, 213–14 (*Samothrace 1*, no. 167). A night ceremony is also suggested by the evocation of "nuptial fire" in the account of Philip and Olympias' encounter, Himer. *Or.* 9.12 (*Samothrace 1*, no. 194). The several lamps found on or near the floor of the Theatral Circle are strong indicators that the Theatral Circle was also used at night. For the lamps, see McCredie 1968, pp. 232–233, pl. 69e; *Samothrace 9*, forthcoming.

93. For protection at sea: Schol. Aristid. *Or.* 13, *Samothrace 1*, p. 73, no. 158; Orphic Hymn 38, *Samothrace 1*, p. 98, no. 217; Ar. *Pax* 277–8, *Samothrace 1*, pp. 102–103, nos. 226, 226a; Theophr. *Char.* 25.2, *Samothrace 1*, p. 103, no. 227; Kallim. *Epigr.* 47, *Samothrace 1*, p. 104, no. 228; Ap.Rhod. *Argon.* 1.915–21, *Samothrace 1*, pp. 104, 107, nos. 229, 229g, 229h; Diod.Sic. 4.42.1, 4.43.1–2, 4.48.5–7, *Samothrace 1*, pp. 104–5, nos. 229b–c; "Orpheus" *Argonautica* 467–72, *Samothrace 1*, p. 106, no. 229f; Cic. *Nat. D* 3.37.89, *Samothrace 1*, p. 108, no. 230; Diog. Laërt. 6.2.59, *Samothrace 1*, p. 108, no. 231; Anon. *Comoedia nova* frg., *Samothrace 1*, p. 109, no. 233; Luc. *Epigram* 15, *Samothrace 1*, p. 110, no. 237. Moral betterment: Diod. Sic. 5.48.4–50.1, *Samothrace 1*, p. 66, no. 142; Ar. *Pax* 276–86, *Samothrace 1*, pp. 102–3, nos. 226, 226a; Valerius Flaccus, *Argonautica* 2.431–42, *Samothrace 1*, p. 106, no. 229e. The title, *mystai eusebeis* or *mystae pii* on initiate lists, Cole 1984, pp. 39–57 and Appendix III; Dimitrova 2008, pp. 5–6.

94. The Lysikrates Monument of 335/4 B.C.E. has exterior Corinthian columns, but it is a monument, not a full-scale building. The Mausoleum at Belevi is roughly contemporary. The Temple of Zeus Olbios at Diocaesarea is now thought to be early second century B.C.E. See Frazer's discussion, *Samothrace 10*, pp. 218–233.

95. *Samothrace 10*, p. 226.

96. As pointed out by James R. McCredie in conversation. For the appearance of the Corinthian order and the development of its capital, see Bauer 1973; Börker 1972; *Apollo Bassitas* I, pp. 305–24; Lawrence 1996, pp. 137–41; Winter 2006, p. 221–4.

97. For the design of tholoi, Seiler 1986; Roux in *Samothrace 7*, pp. 177–230.

98. *Samothrace 10*, pp. 227–33. Scholars debate whether the Rotunda was built before or after the Propylon of Ptolemy II. A. Frazer and J. R. McCredie place the Rotunda first, while G. Roux believes the Rotunda follows the Propylon; both opinions are expressed in *Samothrace 7*, pp. 228, 231–9.

99. Wesenberg 1996, pp. 2–5, figs. 2–3, for white ground lekythoi Athens NM1938 and 1800, which depict akanthos leaves emerging from the base of a stele or column; Rykwert 1996, pp. 317–27. Earlier, Yates 1846, on the term *akanthos* in ancient sources; Hauglid 1947, pp. 112–16, on the prophylactic aspect of spiky things associated with the grave; Kempker 1954, pp. 71–94, esp. 81–89, on the connection of the Corinthian story of the maiden and akanthos not just with the grave but with the afterlife as revealed in the Eleusinian mysteries. Note also Kallimachos's other great invention, a golden lamp with a flue in the form of a palm tree, for the Erechtheion in Athens (Pausanias 1.26.6–7). Surviving bronze lamps and candelabra are decorated with akanthos, thus forming a further association between that plant and light.

100. On the visual symbolism of the akanthos in later Hellenistic and Augustan art, see Pollini 1993, especially pp. 183–5, with bibliography, n. 12; and, Castriota 1995, pp. 124–38, who both associate the motif with the concept of ἀνακύκλωσις (anakyklosis) or "circling about," connected with the eternal return, which in Roman usage has political meanings. As I am chiefly interested in the experience of the initiate, I leave for future research the issue of whether Ptolemy II, or his architect, used the Corinthian order to signal an ascendant cosmic cycle associated with his reign. His grand procession (Ath. *Deip* 197C–203B) indicates that he was deeply interested in such ideas. See Castriota 1995, p. 127; Rice 1983.

101. Riegl 1992, pp. 187–207, esp. p. 190. Whether or not the impetus for the appearance of the akanthos motif lies in the direct observation of nature or the development of preexisting vegetal motifs is irrelevant to the significance the plant rapidly acquired in the visual tradition. The akanthos motif found its way onto simas, antefixes, and mosaics, but it is most animate in its capacity as a columnar crown.

102. Concerning a blessed afterlife, which had not been previously attested, note, the epitaph on a stele now in the Archaeological Museum of Kavalla (inv. No. Λ 70, provenance unknown) in which a mime, initiated into both the Eleusinian and Samothracian mysteries, feels promised an afterlife. Dimitrova argues that the Land of the Blessed, here called the region of the reverent (χῶρος εὐσεβέων) relates to the Samothracian initiates' title, μύσται εὐσεβεῖς, and therefore that promise of an afterlife is connected with the Samothracian initiation. See Karadima-Matsa and Dimitrova 2003, especially pp. 342–4; Dimitrova 2008, pp. 83–90, no. 29.

Works Cited

Agora III = R. E. Wycherley, *The Athenian Agora,* Vol. III: *Literary and Epigraphical Testimonia,* Princeton 1957.

Ajootian, A. 2003. "Homeric Time, Space and the Viewer at Olympia," in *The Enduring Instant. Time and the spectator in the Visual Arts,* ed. A. Roesler-Friedenthal and J. Nathan, Berlin, pp. 136–63.

Anti, C. 1947. *Teatri greci arcaici da Minosse a Pericle,* Padua.

Anti, C. and L. Polacco 1969. *Nuove ricerche sui teatri greci arcaici,* Padua.

Apollo Bassitas I = Cooper. F. *The Temple of Apollo Bassitas. I. The Architecture,* Princeton 1996.

Bauer, H. 1973. *Korinthische Kapitelle des 4. und 3. Jahrhunderts vor Chr. Ath.Mitt. Beiheft* 3, Berlin.

Berges, D. V. Patsiada, and J. Nollé, 1996. *Rundaltäre aus Kos und Rhodos,* Berlin.

Bommelaer, J.-F. and D. Laroche. 1991. *Guide de Delphes: Le Site,* Paris.

Borbein, A. H. 1973. "Die griechische Statue des 4. Jahrhunderts v. Chr. " *JdI* 88, pp. 43–212.

Börker, C. 1972. "Die Datierung des Zeus-Tempel von Olbia-Diokaisereia in Kilikien," *AA,* pp. 37–54.

Bourguet, É. 1914. *Les Ruines de Delphes,* Paris.

Bruneau, P. and J. Ducat 2005. *Guide de Délos,* 4th ed. Paris.

Burkert, W. 1985. *Greek Religion,* Cambridge, MA.

Burkert, W. 1993. "*Concordia discours*: the literary and the archaeological evidence on the sanctuary of Samothrace," in *Greek Sanctuaries, New Approaches*, ed. N. Marinatos and R. Hägg, London, pp. 178–91.

Camp, J. M. 1986. *The Athenian Agora. Excavations in the Heart of Classical Athens*, London.

Castriota, D. 1995. *The Ara Pacis Augustae and the Imagery of Abundance in Later Greek and Early Roman Imperial Art*, Princeton.

Ciancio Rossetto, P. and G. Pisani Sartorio, 1994–96. *Teatri greci e romani: alle origini del linguaggio rappresentato: censimento analitico*, 3 vols. Rome.

Clinton, K. 2003. "Stages of initiation in the Eleusinian and Samothracian Mysteries," in Cosmopoulos 2003, pp. 50–78.

Cole, S. 1984. *Theoi Megaloi: The Cult of the Great Gods at Samothrace*, Leiden.

Cosmopoulos, M. ed. 2003. *Greek Mysteries: The Archaeology and Ritual of Ancient Greek Secret Cults*, New York.

Cooper. F. and S. Morris 1990. "Dining in Round Buildings," in *Sympotica; a Symposium on the Symposion*, ed. O. Murray, Oxford, pp. 66–85.

Daux, G. 1936. *Delphes au IIe et au Ier siècle, depuis l'abaissement de l'Étolie jusqu'à la paix romaine, 191–31 av. J. C.*, Paris.

Didyma 1 = H. Knackfuß, *Didyma*, Vol. 1, *Die Baubeschreibung*, Berlin 1941.

Didyma 3.1 = K. Tuchelt, P. Schneider and C. Cortessis, *Didyma*, vol. 3.1, *Ein Kultbezirk an der Heiligen Straße von Milet nach Didyma*, Mainz 1996.

Dimitrova, N. 2008. *Theoroi and Initiates in Samothrace: The Epigraphic Evidence* (Hesperia Supplement 37), Princeton.

Eade, J. and M. Sallnow, eds. 1991. *Contesting the Sacred: The Anthropology of Christian Pilgrimage*, New York.

EAD XVI = F. Chapouthier, *Exploration archéologique de Délos*, Vol. XVI, *Le Sanctuaire des dieux de Samothrace*, Paris 1935.

Étienne, R. and M.-T. Le Dinahet, eds 1991. *L'espace sacrificiel dans les civilisations méditerranéennes de l'antiquité: actes du colloque tenu à la Maison de l'Orient, Lyon, 4–6 juin 1988*, Paris.

FdD III.3 = G. Daux and A. Salač, *Fouilles de Delphes, École française d'Athènes*, vol. III.3, *Inscriptions depuis le trosir des Atheniens jusqu'aux bases de Gélon*, Paris 1932.

Fehr, B. 1971–1972. "Zur Geschichte des Apollonheiligtums von Didyma, ii: Tholos," *Marburger Winckelmannsprogramm*, Marburg, pp. 29–34.

Freifrau von Thüngen, S. 1994. *Die Frei Stehende griechische Exedra*, Mainz.

Gawlinski, L. 2006. "The Sacred Law of Andania: Sanctuary and Cult," Diss., Cornell, Ithaca, NY.

Gebhard, E. 1974. "The Form of the Orchestra in the Early Greek Theatre," *Hesperia* 43, pp. 429–40.

Ginouvès, R. 1972. *Le théâtron a gradins droits et l'odéon d'Argos. Études Péloponnésiennes* VI, Paris.

Goette, H. R. 1995. "Griechische Theaterbauten der Klassik – Forschungsstand und Fragestellungen," in *Studien zur Bühnendichtung und zum Theaterbau der Antike. Studien zur klassischen Philologie*, ed. E. Pöhlmann, R. Bees, and H. R. Goette, vol. 93, Frankfurt, pp. 9–48.

Goette, H. R. 2000. Ο αξιόλογος δήμος Σούνιον. Landeskundliche Studien in Südost-Attika, Rahden.

Grandjean, Y. and F. Salviat 2000. *Guide de Thasos*, Athens.

Greco, E. and D. Theodorescu. 1983. *Poseidonia – Paestum* II. *L'Agora. Collection de L'Ecole française de Rome* 42, Rome.

Hauglid, R. 1947. "The Greek Acanthus: Problems of Origin," *Acta Archaeologica* 18, pp. 93–116.

Harrison, J. E. 1962. *Epilegomena to the Study of Greek Religion* and *Themis*, New York.

Hintzen-Bohlen, B. 1990. "Die Familiengruppe – Ein Mittel zur Selbstdarstellung hellenistischer Herrscher," *JdI* 105, pp.129–54.

Hintzen-Bohlen, B. 1992. *Herrscherrepräsentation im Hellenismus: Untersuchungen zu Weihgeschenken, Stiftungen und Ehrenmonumenten in den mutter ländischen Heiligtümern Delphi, Olympia, Delos und Dodona*, Cologne.

Jacob-Felsch, M. 1969. *Die Entwicklung griechischer Statuenbasen und die Aufstellung der Statuen*, Waldsassen.

Jones, L. 2000. *The Hermeneutics of Sacred Architecture. Experience, Interpretation, Comparison*. Vols. 1–2, Cambridge, MA.

Kabirenheiligtum II = W. Heyder and A. Mallwitz, *Das Kabirenheiligtum bei Theben*, Vol. II, *Die Bauten im Kabirenheiligtum bei Theben*, Berlin 1978.

Karadima-Matsa, C. and N. Dimitrova 2003. "Epitaph for an Initiate at Samothrace and Eleusis," *Chiron* 33, pp. 335–45.

Kempter, F. 1954. *Akanthus: Die Entstehung eines Ornamentmotives*, Leipzig.

Kolb, F. 1981. *Agora und Theater, Volks- und Festversammlung*, Berlin.

Kourinou, E. 2000. Σπάρτη. Συμβολή στη μνημειακή τοπογραφία της, Athens.

Kowalzig, B. 2003. "Mapping out Communitas: Performaces of Theoria in their Sacred and Politcal Context," in *Pilgrimage in graeco-Roman and Early Christian Antiquity: Seeing the Gods*, ed. J. Elsner, and I. Rutherford, Oxford, pp.41–72.

Kritzas, C.B. 1998. "Nouvelle inscription provenant de l'Asclépiéion de Lebena (Crète)," *ASAtene* 70–71 (1992–93), pp. 275–290.

Langdon, M. and L.V. Watrous, 1977. "The Farm of Timesios: Rock-cut Inscriptions in South Attica," *Hesperia* 46, pp. 162–177.

Lauter, H. 1986. *Die Architektur des Hellenismus*, Darmstadt.

Lehmann, K. 1998. *Samothrace A Guide to the Excavations and Museum*. 6th ed., rev. J. R. McCredie, Thessaloniki.

Leonardos, B. 1896. "Ανασκαφαί του εν Λυκοσούρα; Ιέρου της Δεσποίνης," *Praktika*, pp. 93–126.

Lohmann, H. 1992. *Atene: Forschungen zu Siedlungs- und Wirtschaftsstruktur des klassischen Attika*, 2 vols., Cologne.

Löhr, C. 1993. "Die Statuenbasen im Amphiareion von Oropos," *AthMitt* 108, pp. 183–212.

Lonsdale, S. H. 1993. *Dance and Ritual Play in Greek Religion*, Baltimore.

Lonsdale, S. H. 1995. "A Dancing floor for Ariadne (*Iliad* 18.590 – 592): Aspects of Ritual Movement in Homer and Minoan Religion," in *The Ages of Homer:*

A Tribute to Emily Townsend Vermeule, ed. J. B. Carter and S. P. Morris, Austin, pp. 273–284.

Luni, M. 2001. "Le temple dorique hexastyle dans le sanctuaire découvert hors de la porte sud à Cyrène," *CRAI*, pp. 1533–1552.

Marchetti, P. and Y. Rizakis, 1995. "Recherches sur les mythes et la topographie d'Argos. IV. L'Agora revisitée, " *BCH* 119, pp. 437–472.

Marconi, C. 2010. "*Choroi, Theōriai* and International Ambitions: The Hall of Choral Dancers and Its Frieze," in *Samothracian Connections, Essays in Honor of James R. McCredie*, ed. O. Palagia and B. Wescoat, Oxford, pp. 107–136.

Matsas, D. and N. Dimitrova 2006. "New Samothracian Inscriptions Found Outside the Sanctuary of the Great Gods," *ZPE* 155, pp. 127–136.

Mattusch, C. 1994. "The Eponymous Heroes: The idea of Sculptural Groups," in *The Archaeology of Athens and Attica under the Democracy. Proceedings of an International Conference Celebrating 2500 years since the Brith of Democracy in Greece, Held at the American School of Classical Studies at Athens, December 4–6,1992*, ed. W. D. E. Coulson, Oxford, pp. 73–81.

Mazarakis Ainian, A. 1997. *From Rulers' Dwellings to Temples Architecture: Religion and Society in Early Iron Age Greece (1100–700 B.C.)*, Jonsered.

McCredie, J. R. 1965. "Samothrace: Preliminary Report on the Campaigns of 1962–1964," *Hesperia*, 34, pp. 100–24.

McCredie, J. R. 1968. "Samothrace: Preliminary Report on the Campaigns of 1965–1967," *Hesperia* 37, pp. 200–34.

McCredie, J. R. 1979. "Samothrace: Supplementary Investigations, 1968–1977," *Hesperia* 48, pp. 1–44.

Mertens, D. 2006. *Städte und Bauten der Westgriechen*, Munich.

Mylonas, G. 1961. *Eleusis and the Eleusinian mysteries*, Princeton.

Neils, J. 2001. *The Parthenon Frieze*, New York.

Nielsen. I. 2002. *Cultic Theatres and Ritual Drama*, Aarhus.

Nock, A. D. 1941. "A Cabiric rite," *AJA* 45, pp. 377–81.

Ohnesorg, A. 1991. "Altäre auf Paros," in Etienne and Le Dinahet 1991, pp. 121–6.

Ohnesorg, A. 2005. *Ionische Altäre. Formen und Varianten einer Architekturgattung aus Insel- und Ostionien*, Berlin.

Palinkas, J. 2008. "The Walls and Gates of Eleusis," Diss. Emory University, Atlanta, GA.

Pariente, A. 1988. "Rapport sur les traveaux de l'École française en Grèce en 1987, Argos 2. Terrain Karmoyannis," *BCH* 112, pp. 697–709.

Paton, J. M. and G. P. Stevens 1927. *The Erechtheum: Measured, Drawn and Restored*, Cambridge, MA.

Pergamon XIII = C. H. Bohtz, *Altertümer von Pergamon*, Vol. XIII, *Das Demeter-Heiligtum*, Berlin 1981.

Pedley, J. 2005. *Sanctuaries and the Sacred in the Ancient Greek World*, Cambridge.

Petrakos, V. C. 1997. Οι επιγραφές του Ωρωπού. Βιβλιοθήκη της εν Αθήναις Αρχαιολογικής Εταιρείας vol. 170, Athens.

Polacco, L. 1990. *Il teatro di Dioniso Eleutereo ad Atene. Mongrafia della Scuola Archeologica di Atene 4*, Rome.

Polacco, L. 1998. *Kyklos. La fenomenologia del cerchio nel pensiero e nell'arte die greci,* Venice.

Pollini, J. 1993. "The Acanthus of the Ara Pacis as an Apolline and Dionysiac Symbol of *Anamorphosis, Anakyklosis,* and *Numen Mixtum,*" in *Von der Bauforschung zur Denkmalpflege; Festschrift für Alois Machatschek zum 65. Geburtstag,* ed. M. Kubelík and M. Schwarz, Vienna, pp. 181–217.

Rehm, M. P. 1988. "The Staging of Suppliant Plays," *GRBS* 29, pp. 263–307.

Rehm, R. 2002. *The Play of Space,* Princeton.

Rehm, R. 2006. "Going in Circles: Speculations on the Introduction of the Circular Orchestra in Greek Theaters," http://www.archaeological.org/webinfo.php?page=10248&searchtype=abstract&ytable=2006&sessionid=4D&paperid=774 (accessed December 2010).

Rice, E. E. 1983. *The Grand Procession of Ptolemy Philadelphus,* Oxford.

Riegl, A. 1992 *Problems of Style. Foundations for a History of Ornament,* trans. E. Kain, Princeton.

Roux, G. 1973. "Salles de banquets à Délos," in *Études déliennes publiées à l'occasion du centième anniversaire du début des fouilles de l'École française d'Athènes à Délos,* ed. A. Plassart, Athens, pp. 525–554.

Roux, G. 1976. *Delphes. Son oracle et ses dieux,* Paris.

Rykwert, J. 1996. *The Dancing Column,* Cambridge, MA.

Samothrace 2.I = P. M. Fraser, *Samothrace: Excavations Conducted by the Institute of Fine Arts of New York University,* Vol 2.I, *The Inscriptions on Stone,* London 1960.

Samothrace 3 = P. W. Lehmann, *Samothrace: Excavations Conducted by the Institute of Fine Arts of New York University,* Vol. 3, *The Hieron,* Princeton 1969.

Samothrace 5 = P. W. Lehmann and D. Spittle, *Samothrace: Excavations Conducted by the Institute of Fine Arts of New York University,* Vol. 5, *The Temenos,* Princeton 1982.

Samothrace 7 = J. R. McCredie, et al. *Samothrace. Excavations Conducted by the Institute of Fine Arts of New York University,* Vol. 7, *The Rotunda of Arsinoe,* Princeton 1992.

Samothrace 10 = A. K. Frazer, *Samothrace: Excavations Conducted by the Institute of Fine Arts of New York University,* Vol. 10, *The Propylon of Ptolemy II,* Princeton 1990.

Schachter, A. 2003. "Evolutions of a Mystery Cult: The Theban Kabiroi," in *Cosmopoulos* 2003, pp. 112–42.

Schmidt, I. 1995. *Hellenistische Statuenbasen. Archäologische Studien* vol. 9., Frankfurt.

Seiler, F. 1986. *Die Griechische Tholos,* Mainz am Rhein.

Turner, V. 1969. *The Ritual Process: Structure and Anti-Structure,* Chicago.

Turner, V. 1974. "Pilgrimage and communitas," *Studia Missionalia* 23, pp. 305–27.

Ure, A. D. 1955. "Threshing Floor or Vineyard," *CQ* V, pp. 225–30.

Vanderpool, E. 1982. "ΕΠΙ ΠΡΟΥΧΟΝΤΙ ΚΟΛΩΝΩΙ, The Sacred Threshing Floor at Eleusis," in *Studies in Athenian Architecture, Sculpture and Topography; Presented to Homer A. Thompson,* (Hesperia Supplement 20), Princeton, pp. 172–4.

Warren, P. 1984. "Circular Platforms at Minoan Knossos," *BSA* 79, pp. 307–23.

Wescoat, B. D. 2003. "Athens and Macedonian Royalty on Samothrace: the Pentelic Connection," in *Macedonians in Athens, 323–229 B.C.*, ed. O. Palagia and S. Tracy, Oxford, 2003, pp. 102–16.

Wescoat, B. D. 2006a. "Recent Work on the Eastern Hill of the Sanctuary of the Great Gods, Samothrace," in *Proceedings of the XVI International Congress of Classical Archaeology, Boston, August 23–26, 2003. Common Ground: Archaeology, Art, Science, and Humanities*, ed. C. Mattusch, A. Donahue, and A. Brauer, Boston, 2006, pp. 79–83.

Wescoat, B. D. 2006b. "Gathering in the Sanctuary of the Great Gods, Samothrace," http://www.archaeological.org/webinfo.php?page=10248& searchtype=abstract&ytable=2006&sessionid=4D&paperid=778 (accessed December 2010).

Wesenberg, B. 1996. "Die Entstehung der griechischen Säulen- und Gebälkformen in der literarischen Überlieferung der Antike," in *Säule und Gebälk*, ed. E.-L. Schwandner, Mainz, pp. 1–15.

Wiles, D. 1997. *Tragedy in Athens: Performance Space and Theatrical Meanings*, Cambridge.

Winter, F. E. 2006. *Studies in Hellenistic Architecture*, Toronto.

Wycherley, R. E. 1962. *How the Greeks Built Cities*, 2nd ed., London.

Yates, J. 1846. "On the Use of the Terms Acanthus, Acanthion, etc. in the ancient Classics," *The Classical Museum*, 3, pp. 1–21.

Young, J. H. 1956. "Studies in South Attica: Country Estates at Sounion," *Hesperia* 25, 122–46.

CHAPTER FOUR

ENTERING DEMETER'S GATEWAY: THE ROMAN PROPYLON IN THE CITY ELEUSINION

Margaret M. Miles

Recent anthropological and sociological studies of processions in the early modern and modern periods have emphasized their binding nature: formal movement through cities, whether in Baroque Rome or nineteenth-century Philadelphia, linked the topography of the city and created an intense sense of community between the processors, the observers, and the setting. Processions are said to reenact a cognitive map of a given territory and assert spatial dominance. In some periods and places, such as twentieth-century Belfast, such processions acted as aggressive statements about contested territorial and historical claims.[1] Classical scholars also have long recognized the central importance of processions in Greek religion: together with sacrifice, processions are key rituals that recalled interactions with gods in the past and marked space and time. In ancient Athens, festival processions also linked the countryside with the urban sanctuaries and enhanced civic identity and unity.

The significance of processing in antiquity, and of entering and leaving a sanctuary, is marked by the prominence in Greek architecture of entrance gates.[2] They served as *termini* for processions, less formal pilgrimages and individual visits, and framed their beginning and end. In this chapter, I examine the distinctive entrances built in the Roman period that connected the famous Eleusinian processions. The gateways (*propyla*) to the sanctuary at Eleusis are well preserved, while in the City Eleusinion in downtown Athens, fragmentary remains suggest at least one similar, corresponding gateway into the innermost part of the sanctuary. I discuss the reconstruction of this entrance, the symbolic significance of the entrances to Demeter's sanctuaries, and the social climate of the Second Sophistic that encouraged a retrospective, nostalgic ordering and commemoration of the famous old rituals.

The Eleusinian Procession

In a well-known passage, Herodotos uses the imagery of the procession of the Eleusinian Mysteries as a divine omen of the Persian defeat in 480/79 B.C.E.: two Greek exiles, on the side of the Persian forces in Attica, witness a huge cloud of dust, as if cast up by 30,000 people (8.65). As they observe the cloud, soon they hear emanating from it the cries of "Iakche," a sight and sounds characteristic of the Athenian ritual. The cloud of dust then drifts toward the island Salamis, opposite Eleusis, and the observers believe it must presage the destruction of Xerxes' fleet. The procession of the Eleusinian Mysteries was the most public part of the sanctuary's annual ceremony and in Herodotos' text it represents the Goddesses themselves, who implicitly defend Greece.[3]

In the Athenian celebration each year in late September, the priestesses of Demeter and Kore set out from Eleusis near the western border of Attica, carrying Sacred Objects (*ta hiera*) in cylindrical boxes some 21 kilometers along the Sacred Way to central Athens. After passing along the Panathenaic Way through the Agora, the priestesses deposited the Sacred Objects for safekeeping in the City Eleusinion, the branch sanctuary of Demeter and Kore on the north shoulder of the Akropolis. After several days of preliminary rituals in Athens, first the new, prospective initiates and then those about to undertake a second step of initiation would process the 21 kilometers from the City Eleusinion back to Eleusis.[4] Unusually for Greek sanctuaries, a public gathering area in a forecourt is found in both the City Eleusinion and at Eleusis, and is attested as a feature in other Eleusinia in Attica: the rituals and the secrecy surrounding them required a place in front of the sanctuary that could be accessible.[5] The propyla demarcated the boundary between gathering areas and the sanctuary proper. Although the ceremony began and ended with events so private and secrecy so mandatory that death was the penalty for divulging them, in contrast, the processions formed an assertive, highly public event that was carefully choreographed and followed a prescribed sequence along a fixed trajectory, with memorable topographical landmarks and bridges that were maintained over centuries.

During some years of the Peloponnesian War, the processional route had to be circumvented because the Spartan occupation of Dekeleia, a fortification on Mt. Parnes that dominated the plain of Athens, made it unsafe. Xenophon states that during these years the festival continued, but the annual procession had to go by boat from Piraeus to Eleusis (I.4.20). In a brilliant move that showed defiance of the occupying Spartans and his improved relationship with the hierarchy at Eleusis, Alkibiades personally arranged for the army to escort a solemn procession on its usual route on the Sacred Way (Xen. I.4.20). The fullest description of this event is provided by Plutarch, in his account of Alkibiades' return from exile. After giving a highly moving speech in his own defense, and consulting the Kerykes and Eumolpidai, Alkibiades' first act in Athens was the staging of the procession, in its full array. Plutarch notes that for some years, sacrifices, choral dances, and other rituals that were customarily performed on the Sacred Way (as a part of the celebration of the Mysteries) had had to be suspended (*Alc.* 34.4–7).[6]

Although the exact procedure of initiation is unknown, because the secret was well kept, some details about accompanying rituals are known. Symbols of the rituals, including representations of vessels and equipment, were displayed on the façades of the entrance gates of the two sanctuaries in central Athens and at Eleusis. Thus advertised even to an uninitiated public, the symbols stood not just for the secret rituals carried out within the gates, but also for the whole ceremony, including the public procession. The last day of the festival before participants returned to Athens was named *Plemochoai*, because of a ritual that involved overturning vessels of a distinctive shape, called plemochoai, onto the ground in a form of direct libation to the underworld. Such vessels have been found both at Eleusis and in the City Eleusinion, and despite general ancient reticence on the subject, they seem to have been used in rituals for Plouton and other chthonic deities within the Eleusinian pantheon.[7]

The shape of the plemochoe changed over time, but retained a flared pedestal base, a wider basin with out-turning lip, and either a fenestrated or solid lid. They are meant to be overturned rather than poured. The fabric is typically a slightly coarse clay, sometimes with a slip or added paint, with representations of myrtle.[8] Many examples of bottoms and lids have small holes on the sides, perhaps to tie them together, and hold small sprigs of myrtle. The symbolic importance of this vessel is reflected in the dedication of marble plemochoai (at Eleusis) and a very large marble plemochoe, with fenestrated lid, used as sanctuary furniture in the City Eleusinion.[9] Plemochoai are among the symbols of the Eleusinian Mysteries represented on the entrance gates to the sanctuaries, but also in other Eleusian contexts.

The one well-preserved image we have of an Eleusinian procession is enigmatic and difficult to decipher, not surprising given the prevailing indirection in communicating Eleusinian events. This red-figured terracotta plaque was dedicated in the first half of the fourth century B.C.E. by a woman named Ninnion, and was found at Eleusis and published by A. Skias in 1901. Since then, scholarly exegesis of this imagery has continued, most recently by Kevin Clinton, who sees the arrival of the Eleusinian procession in the bottom register of figures, with Iakchos presenting Ninnion to Demeter, and the end of the festival along the upper register, with Ninnion now presented by Kore to Demeter. In both registers and in the pedimental area the figure Clinton identifies as Ninnion is depicted wearing a plemochoe on her head, tied with string and decorated with myrtle sprigs (Fig. 4.1). This seems the most persuasive interpretation so far, and if correct, this plaque highlights the importance of the plemochoe as a ritual vessel, used not just at the end of the festival but also in arrival at Eleusis, as a culmination of the procession.

This more extensive use of the plemochoe is corroborated by the many vessels found in the City Eleusinion in central Athens, used in rituals there. Possibly some participants carried plemochoai with them as they processed from Athens to Eleusis, along with bundled rods or wreaths of myrtle, which are also represented on the public façades of the entrance gates. The plemochoe as a ritual vessel was significant enough to be depicted on both propyla of the Roman period (in Athens and in Eleusis), discussed further later in this chapter.

The Sacred Way

The *hiera hodos* in Attica is hardly unique, as sacred ways may be found leading to many Greek sanctuaries. A less common characteristic is

4.1. Detail of Ninnion pinax (Athens, National Museum 11036). Photo M. M. Miles.

that the Athenian Sacred Way had overlapping portions designated as primary for two major festivals (the Eleusinian Mysteries and the Panathenaia) and also continued on westward outside of Attica across the territories of neighboring poleis to Delphi, as a sort of "international" Sacred Way. This route was followed by Athenian Pythaistai, a *theoria* sent to Delphi at appropriate intervals (when lightning was sited over a particular spot on Mt. Parnes).[10] The Sacred Way as the processional road to Eleusis was designated with boundary markers, of which three have been found that read *"horos* of the road to Eleusis" (*IG* I³ 1095, earlier fifth century B.C.E.; *IG* I³ 1096, c. 420 B.C.E.; *IG* II² 2624, fourth century B.C.E.). Two other inscriptions attest further to the care taken to maintain the processional route to Eleusis: a decree for the bridge over the Rheitoi salt-springs (*IG* I³ 79, 422/1 B.C.E.) – it specifies that the construction provide a safe passage for the priestesses carrying *ta hiera* – and an honorary decree awarded to Xenokles in part for paying for the upkeep of a bridge over the Kephisos river close to Eleusis that benefited both the annual procession and local Eleusinians (*IG* II² 1191, 321/20? B.C.E.).[11]

By far the fullest ancient account of the Sacred Way that linked Athens and Eleusis is found in Pausanias (1.36.3–38.6), who might have read Polemon of Ilion's book on the Sacred Way (now lost) before or after his own visit.[12] Pausanias begins his description of the Sacred Way where it emerges from the city near the Dipylon Gate. Earlier in his account he describes the publicly accessible part of the City Eleusinion, and states that a dream forbade a full description of its interior (1.14.3–4).[13] He also mentions a Temple of Demeter located near the Dipylon on the inside of the gate, beside the Pompeion; in it were statues by Praxiteles of Demeter, Kore, and Iakchos, who was depicted holding a torch (1.2.4).[14] Now at the Kerameikos, Pausanias picks up the Eleusinian theme and continues it methodically (without digression) until he reaches the forecourt of the sanctuary at Eleusis. His procedure is to describe the monuments "worth seeing" along the road itself, with commentary, so that in effect the reader can reenact the public passage vicariously.[15] Pausanias makes no attempt to recall the private ceremony of initiation: on the contrary, he brings the reader to the forecourt at Eleusis but declines to describe the sanctuary, confining his remarks only to the outer, public areas in the forecourt that precedes the sanctuary. As he reminds the reader once his account reaches Eleusis, he was warned in a dream not to include descriptions of areas accessible only to the initiated.[16] Rather, the Sacred Way and its monuments were worthy of notice in and of themselves, and by the time of Pausanias's visit (c. 165 C.E.) this stretch of road was dense with historical and religious associations.

Pausanias selects the most outstanding tombs: those notable for the circumstance of death of the deceased, or the prominence of the deceased, including the tomb of the best harpist, the best tragic actor, and, the very best tomb of all ancient tombs in Greece. Harpalos, the sometime treasurer of Alexander the Great, built this very best tomb for his wife Pythionike.[17] Because she was a former courtesan, this spectacular marble monument became a cause célèbre as a conspicuous transgression against "normal" commemoration and is frequently mentioned by ancient authors, especially those decrying Macedonian political control and attacking their excessive consumption.[18] Surely Pausanias included it as a much-discussed, conspicuous landmark, but also because of its high quality and its position, just at the crest of the pass over Mt. Aigaleos. Here, for those coming from Eleusis, the plain below with the Athenian Acropolis and Parthenon suddenly comes into view, a famous sight often remarked by early modern travelers.

There are shrines of several heroes, some of them obscure even to Pausanias, and altars and temples to various deities. But the whole narrative and Pausanias's selection of what to include is punctuated with landmarks associated with Demeter and Kore and other Eleusinian figures, a stream of signs that this is the Sacred Way to Eleusis, with a steady buildup of Eleusinian reminders. Skiros, a soothsayer from Dodona, was buried by Eleusinians. The tomb of Akestion is noted, and he remarks on her several male relatives who were prominent officials in the Mysteries (*Dadouchoi*, their names epigraphically attested).[19] There is a sanctuary of Demeter, Kore, Athena, and Poseidon near an altar of Zephyr and the place where Demeter gave the sacred fig-tree to Phytalos. Another tomb commemorates a doctor, Mnesitheos, who dedicated an image of Iakchos. In a sanctuary of Apollo (under the present monastery at Daphne) were images of the Two Goddesses. At the Rheitoi salt-springs, Pausanias notes that only priests at Eleusis were allowed to fish there.[20] Nearby was the tomb of Eumolpos, the first Hierophant in the Mysteries, and near the river Kephisos Pausanias comments on the place where Pluto descended into the underworld after abducting Persephone. Even after leaving the forecourt at Eleusis, and moving onward toward Megara, Pausanias continues to remark on landmarks associated with Demeter, such as the Flowered Well, where she sat in disguise, mourning her daughter, and was found by the daughters of the king Keleos and invited to Eleusis.

Such landmarks doubtless became resting places on the long journey for those walking in the annual procession from Athens or journeying to the sanctuary from other directions. Thus the reader acquires a detailed picture of the sacred geography of the road and the region around Eleusis, with Eleusis itself as the focal point, but left as a blank for the uninitiated. Pausanias's immediate audience in the later second century C.E. could witness vicariously the ancient passage along the Sacred Way.

Links between the City Eleusinion and the Sanctuary at Eleusis

Besides the physical link of the Sacred Way, the ritual link between the City Eleusinion in central Athens and the sanctuary at Eleusis resulted in administrative and architectural links. The two sanctuaries were administered by the same Eleusinian officials throughout their history, so that in effect the branch in Athens "belonged" to Eleusis, and preserved financial accounts (where expenditures in both places are sometimes recorded in one account) and many other inscriptions attest to their close relationship. In some instances, two copies of important inscriptions were made, one to be set up at Eleusis and the other in the City Eleusinion; this is attested in the inscriptions themselves.[21]

In *Agora* XXXI, I described what has been uncovered so far of the City Eleusinion, excavated mostly in the 1930s and 1950s. A series of successive walls and doors set apart the forecourt of the sanctuary from the Panathenaic Way. In the center of the forecourt area is an Ionic Temple of Triptolemos, built in the first half of the fifth century B.C.E. On the south side was a Hellenistic stoa, perhaps a gift from a devotee in the second century B.C.E. When that stoa was constructed a new, modest propylon from the Panathenaic Way into the forecourt was also constructed. The main part of the sanctuary extends to the east under modern Plaka and remains unexcavated, although its eastern limit was found in recent excavations of the Street of the Tripods.[22] The forecourt area was publicly accessible and a place where inscriptions were posted, and some dedications set up.

What I have concluded from studying the excavated remains in Athens is that the history of architectural construction in one of the sanctuaries is often mirrored in the other, since the prosperity or donation that allowed embellishment of one often naturally extended to the other. After the fifth century B.C.E., only in the period of Roman domination of Greece did the sanctuaries at Eleusis and Athens receive such concentrated embellishment and new architectural features. Such appreciation of the by then very old and venerable shrines and traditional ceremonies shows a heightened sense of respect and desired connection with the distant classical past in a period marked by cultural nostalgia for the fifth century B.C.E.

The ornamental propyla built in the Roman period at each end of the route for the Eleusinian procession functioned as marked transitional zones, from the freely accessible (public roads) to the highly limited inner sanctuaries. While all propyla in Greek sanctuaries perform this function to some degree, because of the intense secrecy and security surrounding the Eleusinian sanctuaries, the propyla for the City Eleusinion and Eleusis took on heightened functions of control. As in other propyla, the timing of the flow of visitors and devotees was controlled, and the entrance gate reminded them of the transition into the deity's property, along with necessary restrictions on behavior. In addition, the Eleusinian propyla barred many people, since only those initiated or about to be initiated could pass through, on pain of death.[23] The two propyla of the Roman period were decorated on their outer, publicly visible faces with items emblematic of the Mysteries that were used in rituals and carried in the procession, and hence could be shown.

The Fifth Century B.C.E. Propylon at Eleusis

More than a century of excavation and study at Eleusis has uncovered the main features of the sanctuary.[24] The Anaktoron or Telesterion which served as the hall of initiation dominates the center, while a series of heavy fortification walls enclosed the whole sanctuary, and gateways were inserted through them in various periods. In an example of excellent architectural detective work, D. Giraud identified the earliest preserved propylon to the sanctuary with remains substantial enough to provide a confident reconstruction, located on the east side of the sanctuary where its high wall opened out toward the Sacred Way. Built originally circa 430 B.C.E., the propylon had a simple plan with the outside in the form of two Doric columns between two projecting antae (distyle in antis), probably surmounted by a Doric frieze and gabled pediment. On the interior, Giraud reconstructs two free-standing columns under a porch; the doorway itself was a narrow 2.01 meters. His reconstruction is based on blocks from the stylobate and crepidoma that were reused in a Roman building (traditionally referred to as the "Mithraion"), and an anta capital he found on the site.[25] This marble propylon, modest in scale but handsome in design, is thus another addition to propyla in sanctuaries constructed in the 420s: the sanctuary of Poseidon at Sounion (a parallel discussed by Giraud), and the sanctuary of Demeter Malophoros at Selinous, which might have been partly inspired by the new propylon at Eleusis.[26] Giraud's reconstructed marble propylon at Eleusis was still fairly new when it framed the elaborate and well-protected staging of the Eleusinian procession by Alkibiades in 407 B.C.E.

The Propylon of Appius Claudius Pulcher at Eleusis

Appius Claudius Pulcher was consul of Rome in 54 B.C.E. and a correspondent of Cicero. One of the colorful and ambitious men who vied for power in the late Republic, Claudius Pulcher was an enthusiast for esoteric aspects of religious ritual: he is cited by Cicero as an authority on augury, and he is known to have consulted the Delphic Oracle during one of his visits to Greece. Like many educated upper-class Romans who traveled abroad, he was initiated into the Eleusinian Mysteries, probably in 61 B.C.E., when he was in Greece collecting statues to take back to Rome. In the year of Claudius Pulcher's consulship, the Tiber River flooded Rome catastrophically.[27] Cicero wrote about the flood to his brother Quintus in a preserved letter, describing the extensive damage along the Via Appia, and commenting that the standing water was still remaining (*Ad Quint. fr.* 3.7.1). Most dire was the destruction of the city's grain supply, so severely damaged that Pompey was sent out on an emergency expedition to buy grain abroad; Cassius Dio reports public opinion that the gods had something to do with this terrible flood (39.61.1–3, 63.3).

4.2. Eleusis, view of propylon of Appius Claudius Pulcher, from the west. Photo M. M. Miles.

K. Clinton offers the persuasive suggestion that the devastating flood of 54 and the resulting loss of the city's grain supply (when App. Claudius Pulcher was consul and therefore charged with overall responsibility for the city's welfare) may have been the occasion on which he vowed to Ceres and Proserpina a sumptuous gift.[28] The inscription on the architrave of this propylon at Eleusis (the only inscription in Latin among over one hundred found there) tells us that he vowed it to the Goddesses, and that it was completed after his death by his two nephews.[29]

The marble gateway was started about 50 B.C.E. and finished within a decade (Fig. 4.2). The Propylon has been reconstructed on paper several times, and that of Hörmann published in 1932 is still probably the most accurate, although some of its details have been questioned.[30] The plan, style, and decoration of Appius's propylon reflect the eclecticism of the first century B.C.E. in both sculpture and architectural ornament. On the outer side, a Doric frieze decorated with Eleusinian symbols faced the entering initiates, above an Ionic architrave and Corinthian

4.3. Eleusis, Doric frieze from propylon of Appius Claudius Pulcher. Photo M. M. Miles.

capitals with winged griffons at the corners (Fig. 4.3).[31] The frieze with Eleusinian symbols (a sheaf of wheat, phiales, a kiste, and boukranion) recalls the elaborately decorated propyla at Epidauros and the entrance to the sanctuary of the Great Gods at Samothrace, donated by Ptolemy II. Those friezes, however, are continuous Ionic friezes, while this one is Doric; unusual here are the carvings of Eleusinian symbols over the triglyphs, in addition to those in the metopes.[32]

Especially striking in its design are the pair of caryatids that framed the inner part of the gateway, bearing the sacred kistai on their heads, with their arms raised up to secure them. One of the first monuments at Eleusis to be noted by early modern travelers was one of these colossal caryatids, at first thought to be a statue of Demeter or Kore.[33] Today the better preserved of the caryatids is in the museum at Eleusis (Fig. 4.4), and her transported sister is in Cambridge in the Fitzwilliam Museum, having been taken off from Eleusis in 1803 despite local opposition.[34] On the kistai are representations of items sacred to the Eleusinian goddesses, with a plemochoe featured prominently on each front alongside poppies, sheaves of wheat, and rods made of myrtle (Fig. 4.5). The caryatids, carved more than twice life-size in a retrospective style that recalls the Severe period of the earlier fifth century, represent majestic Eleusinian priestesses returning to Eleusis from the City Eleusinion in Athens, with the Sacred Objects (*ta hiera*) in the kistai on their heads, leading the processing devotees into the sanctuary.

4.4. Eleusis, caryatid from propylon of Appius Claudius Pulcher (Eleusis Museum 5104). Photo M. M. Miles.

The handsome propylon was a stunning addition to the venerable sanctuary, and together with the Tower of the Winds represents the finest of architectural gifts to Athens in the later Republican period. Elizabeth Rawson has identified the Roman enthusiasm for religion and the history of religious ritual as a new intellectual development that

4.5. Eleusis, detail of kiste carried by caryatid (Eleusis Museum 5104). Photo M. M. Miles.

marks the late Republic, interests that were shared by App. Claudius Pulcher, Cicero, Varro, and others.[35] Cicero in particular was moved by his experience of the Eleusinian Mysteries. He alludes to them several times in both published essays and in private letters, and states that "Athens has given nothing to the world more excellent or divine than the Eleusinian Mysteries," and that through initiation "not only do we learn a way of living in happiness but also a way of dying with greater hope"(*Leg.* 2.36).

The Eleusinian caryatids also recall the famous Korai or Maidens on the south porch of the Temple of Athena Polias (the Erechtheion), who also represent priestesses in procession, originally bearing phiales for libations, and are perhaps also shown on the east frieze of the Parthenon. The caryatids on the Acropolis stand for the primary female participants in the festivals, and not punished, imprisoned widows as

Vitruvius would later suggest, writing from an Augustan perspective in a library and without having seen these buildings (Vitr. 1.1.5–6). The Eleusinian caryatids from Appius' propylon commemorate and model the Eleusinian procession, just as the Erechtheion caryatids model the Panathenaia. Implicitly they link Eleusis and Athens.

The Greater Propylaia at Eleusis

The propylon at Eleusis only became the "Lesser" propylon some two hundred years later in the second century C.E., when Hadrian invigorated Athens and Eleusis with generous benefactions, new organizations, and started the construction of a handsome new "Greater" propylaia, a direct copy of the central building of Mnesikles' fifth-century propylaia to the Acropolis. The new propylaia were part of a general refurbishing of the whole entrance area to the sanctuary at Eleusis: the courtyard was paved, and a small Doric temple was added (this is usually identified as the Temple of Artemis Propylaia but it could well be the Temple of Triptolemos). Hadrian was himself honored along with the Two Goddesses by two arches set up by members of a civic organization he founded, the Panhellenion, who took a special interest in Eleusinian matters.[36] These arches were exact copies of the Arch of Hadrian near the Olympieion in Athens. They frame the entrance court in a manner similar to the omitted wings of Mnesikles' Propylaia, in effect, bringing a contemporary Roman aspect into the overall design while paying homage to Classical Athens. This is specifically the import of the twin inscriptions on the arches that read "the Panhellenes [dedicate this] to the Two Goddesses and the emperor" (*I.G.* II² 2958).[37]

Recent studies by Demetrios Giraud have shown almost conclusively that the Greater Propylaia were started by Hadrian, even though the building was not completed until the reign of Marcus Aurelius, whose portrait was set within one of the tympana.[38] Construction had been interrupted, and delayed further by invasion of the Costobocs in 170. As a visual link between Eleusis and the Akropolis of Athens, the Propylaia of Eleusis are an impressive statement of classicism in the second century. A direct emulation of a fifth-century B.C.E. building would not be constructed again until the late eighteenth century.

A Hadrianic Propylon in the City Eleusinion

The visual connections between the two sanctuaries, already made kinetically each year by the processions, were made even more emphatic with the addition of a new propylon to the City Eleusinion, which in my study of the City Eleusinion I suggested should be dated to the reign of Hadrian.[39] This propylon is now represented only by pieces of its superstructure, but enough are preserved to suggest a reconstruction, which I discuss in greater detail here. The propylon would have been set into a wall that divided the publicly accessible area of the City Eleusinion (the area already excavated) from the inner area that included the Temple of Demeter and Persephone mentioned by Pausanias (but which he could not describe, because of a warning in a dream, I.14.3–4). The probable location of the wall, and the propylon, is indicated in Figure 4.6. No foundations for the propylon have yet been uncovered (as its likely location is under modern Plaka), hence this reconstruction is necessarily provisional.

Numerous pieces of two caryatids that were used as architectural supports provide evidence for part of the propylon. So far, all known fragments have been found in or very near the City Eleusinion.[40] Most important among them are the two heads found in the area of the Eleusinian in 1859 by K. Pittakys, and studied further in 1985 by Eliana Raftopoulou. For her reconstruction she added fragments of feet, a plinth, and drapery also found by Pittakys in the area of the Eleusinion and stored in the National Museum.[41] Raftopoulou associated the two slightly over life-size korai with a type of Severizing caryatid represented in other Roman versions such as the Tralleis/Cherchel type.[42] To those pieces in the National Museum are now added three new fragments, recently identified and published by George Despinis, that were found during cleaning by the Ephoreia around Tower W 2 of the late Roman fortification wall, just to the north of the City Eleusinion on the Panathenaic Way.[43] The newly found fragments include part of the plinth, the left foot, and lower legs of caryatid B, which joins the plinth and right foot published by Raftopoulou, part of the left breast and locks of hair of caryatid A (Figs. 4.7, 4.8, and 4.9), and a small fragment of drapery. Figure 4.10 shows the largest piece, with the left foot and lower legs, added to Raftopoulou's reconstruction of caryatid B.

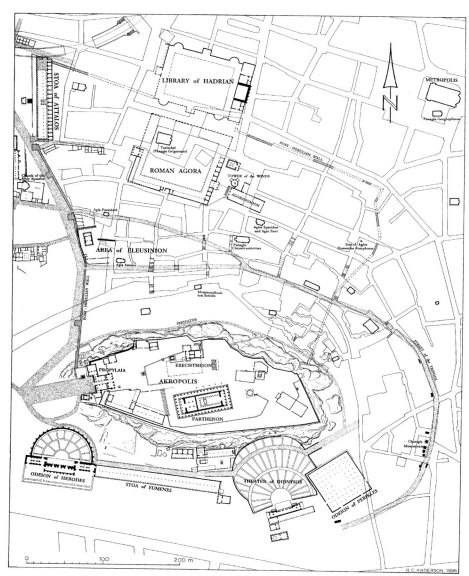

4.6. Athens, plan of area around Eleusinion. Drawing American School of Classical Studies: Agora Excavations, R. Anderson.

In Figure 4.11 is a suggested reconstruction, with the two caryatids distyle prostyle in a simple, façade-like gateway facing east into the inner side of the sanctuary. They do not carry kistai, but instead kalathoi with an upward-curving rim. Since the Sacred Objects (*ta hiera*) were brought to the City Eleusinion for safekeeping while the festival began,

4.7. Athens, fragment of caryatid A from City Eleusinion, Agora S 3517. Photo American School of Classical Studies at Athens: Agora Excavations.

presumably a kalathos was substituted for the official kistai. This type of design directly (and deliberately) mirrors the propylon at Eleusis. In the proposed reconstruction presented here, a hypothetical Ionic frieze runs above the caryatids, featuring items relevant to the Eleusinian cult; this is drawn from an extant Ionic architrave of Roman imperial date at Eleusis (Fig. 4.12).[44]

4.8. Athens, fragment of caryatid B from City Eleusinion, front view, Agora S 3519. Photo American School of Classical Studies at Athens: Agora Excavations.

The entablature of the outer, west side of the gateway, again on the analogy of Appius Claudius Pulcher's earlier propylon at Eleusis, may be represented by the Doric frieze block with Eleusinian symbols now built into south side of the Church of the Panagia Gorgoepikoos ("Little Metropolitan") in Athens (Fig. 4.13).[45] The frieze block is one of a very large number of reused ancient and medieval *spolia* built into the church; in fact, most of the fabric of the church consists of re-used

4.9. Athens, fragment of caryatid B from City Eleusinion, side view, Agora S 3519. Photo American School of Classical Studies at Athens: Agora Excavations.

ancient and medieval figured or structural blocks. In a recent reevaluation of the church, B. Kiilerich has suggested a date for it early in the period of Ottoman control of Athens, and sees a deliberate planning in the placement of the blocks, which then took on new meanings.[46]

The Doric frieze block consists of two triglyphs and two metopes carved onto one piece, each element bearing a cultic symbol appropriate to the Eleusinian Mysteries (Fig. 4.14). The block is 0.589 meter high, and 1.578 meters long.[47] The frieze is framed in its current position

4.10. Reconstruction of caryatid B with Agora S 3519 added. Drawing R. Leonardis, after E. G. Raftopoulou, "Neue Zeugnisse archaistischer Plastik im Athener Nationalmuseum," *AM* 100, 1985, fig. 1.

4.11. Athens, reconstruction of façade of propylon to City Eleusinion, east side. Drawing R. Leonardis.

4.12. Eleusis, Ionic frieze. Photo M. M. Miles.

4.13. Athens, view of south side of the Church of Panagia Gorgoepikoos (Little Metropolitan Church). Photo M. M. Miles.

4.14. Athens, frieze block from City Eleusinion, now in the Church of Panagia Gorgoepikoos. Photo M. M. Miles.

by other marble blocks, including an additional piece of white marble that gives the appearance of a continuing triglyph on the right. From left, carved over the two triglyphs of the frieze are two crossed bundled rods of myrtle over three poppies (Fig. 4.15), and a plemochoe (Fig. 4.16), and in the metopes, a phiale and a boukranion. Although

4.15. Athens, detail of frieze block from City Eleusinion: myrtle and poppies. Photo M. M. Miles.

in an earlier era the frieze would require Doric columns as support, by the time of the second century order mixing had become quite common, and the Corinthian order was favored by Romans in general and Hadrianic architects in particular.[48] Hence I suggest the outer side of

4.16. Athens, detail of frieze block from City Eleusinion: plemochoe. Photo M. M. Miles.

the propylon might have had Corinthian columns, shown here in the simplest plan possible, distyle prostyle. This seems to work best with a doorway that would allow two persons to enter or leave together, about 2.30 meters wide.[49]

Notable on this preserved Doric frieze block is the plemochoe, carved on a projecting support to make it even more prominent (Fig. 4.17). As I mentioned above, this distinctive vessel was used both at Eleusis,

4.17. Athens, detail of frieze block from City Eleusinion. Photo M. M. Miles.

toward the end of the ceremonies, and at the City Eleusinion, in connection with rituals for Plouton and other chthonic deities. Typically such
vessels found in the excavations in the City Eleusinion and at Eleusis
are made of a somewhat coarse fabric, but the sculpted representation
of a plemochoe on the frieze, with a ribbed design on the body of the
vessel, may represent a metal plemochoe (gold, silver, or bronze). A
plemochoe is also represented on silver and bronze Attic coinage, and

bronze and lead tokens from Athens, dating from the mid-fourth century B.C.E. to the first century B.C.E.; these were likely minted as a "festival coinage" to facilitate visitors' commercial transactions during the annual influx of participants into the city.[50] The plemochoe and its use in the Mysteries clearly was not a secret, but rather it was a public symbol of the Mysteries, one that was deemed suitable to represent the city itself on coinage, along with the head of Athena and her owls, and other (public) Eleusinian symbols such as Triptolemos, piglets, and myrtle rods. The plemochoe is also represented on the faces of the kistai carried by the caryatids at Eleusis, and thus its prominent representation provides yet another link between the two sanctuaries.

The reconstruction of the propylon is necessarily tentative in the absence of foundations, hence the simplicity of the proposed plan (Fig. 4.18). The proposed façades of the propylon thus would directly recall the elegant propylon of Appius Claudius Pulcher at Eleusis. The propylon served as a corresponding bracket for the grand entrances at Eleusis: the Eleusinian symbols on the outside hinted at the future ceremony, while the caryatids model the procession to come. Since a Hadrianic date for the start of the new outer propylaia for Eleusis seems likely (although it was not completed until the reign of Marcus Aurelius), with it the intended correspondences were made even more emphatic between the City Eleusinion, located on the north slope of the Acropolis just below the Mnesiklean Propylaia, and Eleusis, with its two monumental Roman entrance gates, one with caryatids and the other a direct copy of the Mnesiklean Propylaia.

The Second Sophistic

The second-century context of the new features in both sanctuaries deserves closer consideration. The construction, together with a strong epigraphical record that indicates continuing local participation, is not simply a matter of whimsical imperial beneficence, or even simply testimony to the continuing prestige of the Eleusinian Mysteries. The first-century B.C.E. propylon given by Appius Claudius Pulcher illustrates the scope for individual, private donations from foreigners to what had been the realm of publicly funded architecture in "state" sanctuaries. In the

4.18. Reconstruction of façade of propylon to City Eleusinion, west side. Drawing R. Leonardis.

second century, the complete refurbishing of the forecourt to Eleusis, and the new propylon in the City Eleusinion, have as their counterpart the completion of the Temple of Zeus Olympios in Athens: much of this was financed through Hadrian's generosity, but why these choices? I suggest that what we have here in the realm of sanctuary architecture is the monumental manifestation of the cultural impetus of the Second Sophistic.

A label borrowed from Philostratos to describe a literary movement from about 50 to 250 C.E., but focused especially on the second century, the Second Sophistic has been much analyzed in recent scholarship.[51] The Greek authors of this period are thought to convey a set of attitudes and cultural ambitions that allowed them to cope with the realities of Roman dominance, while still aspiring to the cultural ideals of the past that enshrined independence and democracy. Simon Swain's *Hellenism and Empire* articulates useful definitions of this period, which I summarize here. The male Greek elite living in the cities of Old Greece and Asia Minor had no genuine political independence or even representation, but they could channel their ambitions into cultural evocations of Greece's illustrious past. Their cultural confidence came from their perceived close connection to the classical Greeks, an idealized view of their forebears some five and six centuries earlier. As Swain has pointed out, this idealization manifests itself in the literary world with an obsessive movement for purity in language, with Atticism as a form of emulation of classical authors, and both general and specific nostalgia for the past, before Rome was on the scene. The works of Plutarch and Pausanias, for example, clearly illustrate the period's preoccupation with the sacred and its realia, but with a strong preference for the Archaic and Classical varieties and an interest in mythic origins.[52]

The architectural embellishments for the Eleusinian Mysteries, and much of the epigraphical record for the Roman period, reflect the choices and patronage of the elite who found great value in the continuity with the distant past. The choices of style and architectural features, even the creation of direct copies, are examples of selective nostalgia, and although financed from afar, were accomplished by locals. The reiterations of "classical" types such as caryatids, and the mixture of antecedent sculptural styles may be seen in the caryatids of both propyla. The elegant and technically skillful rendering of the Doric frieze is notable on the block from the City Eleusinion.

This cultural preoccupation of the Greek elite with its own distant past remained vital until the insecurities and the invasions of the third century so weakened the civic fabric that it could not last. An inscription dated to circa 220 C.E. (*IG* II² 1078, 1079) was made in three copies, one set up in the City Eleusinion and found nearby; it prescribes the arrangements for the Eleusinian procession, and it illustrates the persistence of the procession as an essential part of the ritual.[53] The role of ephebes is an important part of the decree, and it provides specifications for the timing of their escort of *ta hiera* from Eleusis to the Eleusinion in the city, apparently reiterating or restoring the procedure in exact detail. The ephebes are to wear full armor and wreaths of myrtle, and they are allowed to participate in sacrifices, libations and (the singing of) paeans on the way to Eleusis as they traverse the Sacred Way (lines 25–31). This reiteration of traditional detail may well have been impelled by the persistent requirements of ritual, but one that had lasted more than eight hundred years, now into an era with very different social and political circumstances.

Even a generation later, after the Herulian sack of Athens in 267, the Eleusinian Mysteries were still celebrated and would continue for more than a hundred years. The last known legitimate Hierophant was Nestorius, active until around 375, so somehow the festival did continue tenaciously. The processions, the crowds, and their talking, joking, chanting and singing, the young men on horses, and the pilgrims carrying myrtle or plemochoai were an enduring feature of a seemingly age-old, annual ritual from one elegant Athenian gateway to another, the liminal frames which themselves became part of the sacred landscape of Athens and Attica. But after the invasion of Alaric and the Visigoths in 396 the Eleusinian Mysteries could not be revived, and the Classical era ended. The buildings of the sanctuaries, including the elegant propyla, were dispersed and recycled.

Notes

1. Davis 1986; Boyer 1994; Çelik, Favro, and Ingersoll 1994; Cosgrove 1998. I thank Bonna Wescoat and Robert Ousterhout for inviting me to participate in the panel on "Ritual and Sacred Space in Premodern architecture" for the College Art Association annual meeting, 2005, in which I gave an earlier version of this paper. I am very grateful to the Byzantine Ephoreia of Athens for permission to measure and photograph the block from the City Eleusinion now embedded in the Church of the Panagia Gorgoepikoos ("Little Metropolitan"), to the staff of the Athenian Agora for their assistance, and to Rocco Leonardis, who made the drawings in Figures 4.11 and 4.18.

2. On Greek processions, with a selection of literary and epigraphical testimonia, *ThesCRA* 1, 2004, pp.1–20 (M. True et al.); on propyla, Carpenter 1970; Hellman 1992, pp. 350–4; Hagn 1999; *ThesCRA* IV, 2005, pp. 70–75 (U. Sinn).

3. For discussion of Eleusinian Demeter's role in the defense of Greece, see Boedeker 2007; on the Eleusinian procession(s), Graf 1996, Robertson 1998; on Iakchos, Clinton 1992, pp. 64–71.

4. For details of the chronology and arrangement of devotees, Robertson 1998.

5. Discussion of the need for a forecourt in Parker 2005, pp. 332–3; topography of the City Eleusinion, *Agora* XXXI, pp. 11–12.

6. As part of his reconciliation with Athens, Alkibiades had restored to him the value of his confiscated household property, and the curses upon him (cast by some of the Eleusinian priesthood after he was found guilty of profaning the Mysteries) revoked. For details and sources, see Ellis 1989, pp. 89–90; Furley 1996, pp. 31–48; *Agora* XXXI, pp. 65–66, 203–5 (nos. 46–57); on rewards given to him by the demos, Gygax 2006.

7. For the vessels and their terminology, *Agora* XXXI, pp. 95–103.

8. Myrtle (a type of evergreen shrub with edible berries) was used in bundled rods, in wreaths, and in sprigs, and was carried or worn by the people in the processions, and therefore became symbolic of the processions and of the whole phenomenon of the Eleusinian Mysteries.

9. *Agora* XXXI, p. 100, fig. 13 and pl. 18, 19.

10. Daverio Rocchi (2002) collects and discusses the evidence, provided by a several inscriptions including boundary markers, and literary testimonia. Continuation to Delphi: *Agora* XIX H34 ("Boundary of the Sacred Street by which the Pythais proceeds to Delphi"); for its beginning in Athens, Parsons 1943, p. 238. Panathenaia: *Agora* III.729, inscription cut into north face of Mnesiklean bastion, west of the Propylaia; for discussion, *Agora* XIV, pp. 193–4, testimonia, *Agora* III, pp. 224; Camp 1986, pp. 45–46; for Greek roads in general, see Pritchett 1980, 143–96; in Attica, Lohmann 2002.

11. Discussion of the Sacred Way and illustrations in Travlos 1988, 177–90; Camp 2001, 129–31. The Sacred Way used for the Eleusinian Mysteries should be the stretch between the sanctuary at Eleusis and the City Eleusinion, but in their plans they show it as ending at the Altar of the 12 Gods, presumably because Herodotos states that the Altar was considered the starting point for measuring distances. The stretch near Eleusis is illustrated in Alexandris 1969, pp. 324–5; a summary of excavations of the Third Ephoreia, with bibliography, is given in Karagiorga-Stathakopoulou 1988. For the section around the Kerameikos, see Knigge 1991, 57–59, 64–65, 66–67, 95–96, 148–50, passim; Costaki 2006, pp. 230–9, 492–8, 603–8.

12. Polemon of Ilion's book is attested in several sources (collected by Frazer 1898, II, p. 484), the most complete are Dicaearchus, apud Athenaeus, 13.594f. *Peri tes hieras hodou biblion* (*FGH* III, 111, 119) and Harpokration, s.v. *hiera hodos*.

13. He mentions the dream again at 1.38.6–7, and a third time in his description of the sanctuary of Demeter and Persephone at Andania (4.33.5).

14. Iakchos was a personification of the mystic cry "Iakche!" called out by initiates during the procession. He was viewed as an escorting figure, and a wooden image of him was likely carried or accompanied in procession by an official referred to in several preserved inscriptions as the *Iakchagogos* (see further Clinton 1974, pp. 96–97; Clinton 1992, pp. 64–71).

15. Elsner has remarked that the design of Pausanias's work as a whole is intended to allow the reader a vicarious journey through Greece (Elsner 2001, pp. 4–8).

16. For further discussion of this point, with references to scholarship on Pausanias's secrecy, see *Agora* XXXI, pp. 50–51; thorough analysis of Pausanias's reticence in Foccardi 1987. Even a parody of the mysteries could lead to great trouble, as in the episode of the mutilation of the herms and the investigation of Alkibiades on the eve of the Athenian invasion of Sicily (Thuc. 6.27–28).

17. For Pythionike, *DNP* 10, col. 667 (E. Badian); *RE* XXIV, col. 564–6 [1963] (K. Ziegler); McClure 2003, pp. 146–8. Foundations of the monument were

excavated in the late nineteenth century and small fragments of marble found in the fill indicate the position of her monument (Travlos 1988, p. 177, 181; discussed fully by Scholl 1994, pp. 254–261). Harpalos himself was buried nearby.

18. McClure 2003, pp. 43, 52–53.
19. Clinton 1974, pp. 54–58, with stemma of the family on p. 58.
20. Frazer notes that in the nineteenth century flying fish (small and succulent) were observed there (Frazer 1898, II, p. 486).
21. E.g., a record of the Epistatai for Eleusis and the Eleusinion, *IG* I³ 32, whose text states a copy is to be set up in the City Eleusinion (found at Eleusis, copy in Eleusinion posited) and in (an Eleusinion) in Phaleron, and *IG* II² 1672 (found at Eleusis), which lists expenses at both sanctuaries. The close administrative relationship begins at least as early as the mid-fifth century B.C.E.: see further *Agora* XXXI, p. 64–65; Parker 2005, pp. 332–4.
22. *Agora* XXXI, pp. 11–12; for the Street of the Tripods, see Choremi-Spetsieri 1994.
23. Slaves who worked in the sanctuaries underwent initiation at public expense.
24. Overviews in Mylonas 1961; Travlos 1988; Giraud 1991.
25. Giraud 1991, pp. 57–85. Giraud finds a close parallel for the anta capital in the Temple of Nemesis at Rhamnous, to which he assigns an early date in the 430s (p. 82, and footnote 273, p. 293); the temple should be dated to the 420s B.C.E.: see Miles 1989, pp. 226–35. K. Clinton points out that the Roman building in which blocks of the propylon were re-used, dated by Giraud to the Augustan period, cannot be a Mithraion at that date and is more likely to have been used for the imperial cult (Clinton 1997, p. 171).
26. Sounion: Travlos 1988, pp. 406–407, 415; Giraud 1991, p. 72 and ill. 30; Goette 2000, pp. 24–25; Selinous: Miles 1998, pp. 43–44, 52–53.
27. Aldrete 2007, pp. 20–21, on the effects of the flood on the food supply, including dangers posed by molds and ergot, pp. 131–41.
28. Clinton 1997, pp. 164–5.
29. *CIL* I² 775=*ILLRP* 401.
30. Dinsmoor ([1975]1950, p. 286, n. 4) wishes to insert Ionic columns on the eastern side, but the evidence is very slight and rightly rejected by Hörmann 1932 and Giraud 1991. Dinsmoor is surely correct in suggesting that the caryatids supported an entablature and pediment as a distyle porch, corresponding to the outer side with Corinthian columns.
31. Hörmann 1932; discussion and further bibliography in Giraud 1991, pp. 107–14; Ridgway 2002, pp. 3–8, 164–6. On the possible significance of the ornamentation, Sauron 2001.
32. Epidauros: Roux 1961, pp. 253–74; Samothrace: *Samothrace* 10. One antecedent for the figured triglyphs is the Stoa of Antigonos Gonatas (mid-third century B.C.E.) in the Sanctuary of Apollo on Delos, where alternating triglyphs are carved with a bull's head in high relief (Webb 1986, pp. 136–7; Schmidt-Dounas 1994).
33. Palagia 1997, pp. 84–85, with references to earlier comments by travelers.
34. Cambridge, Fitzwilliam Museum GR.I.1865, Budde and Nicholls, 1964, pp. 46–49, no. 81; Eleusis Museum 5104, Preka-Alexandri 1991, p. 19; on the sculptural style, Palagia 1997, pp. 82–91, and Ridgway (2002, pp. 5–8, 164–9), who also discusses the evidence for related types.

35. Rawson 1985, p. 93, 302. Cicero himself considered building a propylon for the Academy, in emulation of Claudius Pulcher (*Att.* 6.1.26; 6.6.2).

36. On Hadrian's interest in Eleusis and building activities there, see Clinton 1989, 1997; on Athens and the Panhellenion, Spawforth and Walker 1985, Boatwright 1994.

37. Greater Propylaia: Giraud 1991, pp. 131–276; Hadrianic revisions to forecourt, Giraud 1991, pp. 115–29; Clinton 1989; Clinton 1997, pp. 174–6.

38. Giraud 1991, pp. 268–72.

39. *Agora* XXXI, pp. 89–91.

40. Among all the catalogued sculptural pieces in the Agora collection, I was able to identify only one additional fragment that possibly could belong (on the basis of the worked surface, marble, style and scale), but it was found on the north side of the Agora (S 3427, a fragment of drapery).

41. Raftopoulou 1985. One the two heads, NM 1682, preserves part of the top surface of the polos, with a dowel hole indicating that it supported a course above.

42. This type, represented by well-preserved versions from Tralleis in Turkey and Cherchel in Algeria, and all associated versions, and views about their dates, are discussed by Ridgway 2002, pp. 164–9; see also Schmidt 1982, pp. 92–95; Landwehr 1993, pp. 72–74, p. 72, 73; Palagia 1997.

43. Despinis 2001. These fragments are catalogued in the Athenian Agora as S 3517, S 3519, and S 3542. Their dimensions are as follows: S 3517 p.H. 0.304 m, p.W. 0.154 m, p.Th. 0.157 m. Fragment preserves part of left side and breast of Caryatid A, with locks of hair falling over breast. S 3519 p.H. 0.355 m, p.W. 0.312 m, p.D. 0.314 m. Piece preserves part of plinth (H. 0.041 m at front – 0.43 m at back) with left sandaled foot of Caryatid B and part of lower legs covered with drapery (crinkly chiton); joins fragment with right foot illustrated by Raftopoulou (1985, pl. 73, 1–2), and Despinis (2001, p. 9, fig. 8), as shown in Figure 4.10. S3542 p.H. 0.057 m, p.W. 0.079 m, p.Th. 0.028 m. Fragment preserves part of two parallel folds, likely part of himation of one of the figures (as suggested by Despinis 2001, p. 7).

44. The Ionic architrave at Eleusis with cultic symbols (kistai, myrtle rods, boukranion, phiale and choe, sheaves of wheat) bears the inscription *IG* II² 5209 (Clinton 2005, no. 363), of the first or second century C.E. It might have been part of an honorary monument for an emperor dedicated by a high priest of the imperial cult, as Clinton suggests (Clinton 2008), or possibly another propylon at Eleusis, and requires further study. I thank K. Clinton for the references.

45. This block has been illustrated repeatedly since the seventeenth century (*Agora* XXXI, p. 90, n. 10). The architectural spolia built into the Panagia Gorgoepikoos ("Little Metropolitan") are discussed by Steiner 1906 and Kiilerich 2005. Ohnesorg (2005, p. 207), lists this block among a collection of examples possibly from an altar (following the suggestion of Boetticher 1866); she also apparently confuses this block with an illustration (in Durm 1910, ill. 238b on p. 267) of the frieze from the propylon of Appius Claudius Pulcher at Eleusis. The unusual character of the block, with decorated triglyphs, and its similarity to the frieze of the propylon at Eleusis and to Ionic friezes of other propyla, make the assignment to a propylon seem more likely than an altar with a Doric frieze (more typically found in western Greece), for which there are no parallels in Athens or Attica.

46. Kiilerich argues persuasively for a date after 1456 (rather than more widely assumed date in the late twelfth or early thirteenth century), and sees the construction of the unusual church as both an effort to preserve *spolia* and to assert Christian themes: the Eleusinian block, with poppies and myrtle rods (interpreted as torches), may have suggested death and resurrection (2005, esp. 108–11).

47. H. of triglyphs, 0.477 m; H. of metopes, 0.423 m; W. of triglyphs, from left, 0.342 m, 0.359 m; W. of metopes, from left, 0.406 m, 0.471 m. The face of the upper left corner of the block is battered, and cement obscures the upper right corner.

48. This particular combination of Corinthian columns below a Doric frieze (with an Ionic architrave) may be seen already in a series of Hellenistic grave stelai from Delos, *Délos* XXX: no. 107, pl. 26; no. 109, 118, pl. 27; no. 124, pl. 29 (end second cencury B.C.E.); no. 127, pl. 31 (second half second century B.C.E.); no. 159, pl. 37 (end second century B.C.E.). I thank Olga Palagia for this reference.

49. The reconstructed doorway is the same width and height in the two drawings, but the heavy Doric frieze block requires a taller façade overall. Presumably a wall ran between them. This reconstruction is necessarily tentative since the foundations have not yet been excavated.

50. As Kroll has argued, this use of convenient bronze coins for the Eleusinian Mysteries led to general acceptance of regular bronze issues in Athens: see *Agora* XXVI, especially pp. 27–32; plemochoe as a type in bronze coinage: catalogue nos. 61, 72–75, 102–4, 299; as an adjunct symbol, nos. 39, 45, 70, 91, 116, 117, 120, 146; on silver coinage: Pollitt 1979, p. 233.

51. Conveniently summarized in Whitmarsh 2005.

52. The scholarship on the Second Sophistic is now extensive; see esp. Swain 1996, Goldhill 2001, Borg 2004, Whitmarsh 2005; on Plutarch, Pausanias and religious identities, Lamberton 1997, Preston 2001, Alcock, Cherry and Elsner 2001, Galli 2004, 2005.

53. *IG* II² 1078, 1079; *SEG* XLII 1776 (= *Agora* XXXI, 78A, 78B); Clinton 2005, no. 638; see discussion in Graf 1996; Robertson 1998. The preserved text states that three copies were to be set up at Eleusis, in the City Eleusinion, and in the Diogeneion; the two from Athens are partly preserved.

Works Cited

Agora III = R. E. Wycherley, *The Athenian Agora*, III: *Literary and Epigraphical Testimonia*, Princeton 1957.

Agora XIV = H. A. Thompson, and R. E. Wycherley, *The Athenian Agora*, XIV: *The Agora of Athens*, Princeton 1972.

Agora XXVI = J. H. Kroll, *The Athenian Agora*, XXVI: *Greek Coins*, Princeton 1993.

Agora XXXI = M. M. Miles, *The Athenian Agora*, XXXI: *The City Eleusinion*, Princeton 1998.

Alcock, S. E., J. F. Cherry and J. Elsner, eds. 2001. *Pausanias. Travel and Memory in Ancient Greece*, Oxford and New York.

Alexandris, O. 1969. "Eleusis," *Analekta* 2, pp. 323–9.

Boatwright, M. T. 1994. "Hadrian, Athens and the Panhellion," *JRA* 7, pp. 426–31.

Boedeker, D. 2007. "The View from Eleusis: Demeter in the Persian Wars," in Bridges, Hall, and Rhodes 2007, pp. 65–82.

Borg, B. E. 2004. Paideia: the World of the Second Sophistic, Berlin.

Boyer, M. C. 1994. *The City of Collective Memory*, Cambridge, MA, and London.

Bridges, E, E. Hall, and P. J. Rhodes, eds. 2007. Cultural Responses to the Persian Wars. Antiquity to the Third Millennium, Oxford.

Budde, L. and R. Nichols. 1964. A Catalogue of the Greek and Roman Sculpture in the Fitzwilliam Museum Cambridge, Cambridge.

Camp, J. M. 1986. *The Athenian Agora*, London.

Camp, J. M. 2001. *The Archaeology of Athens*, New Haven.

Carpenter, J. R. 1970. "The Propylon in Greek and Hellenistic Architecture," Diss. Univ. of Pennsylvania.

Çelik, Z., D. Favro, and R. Ingersoll, eds. 1994. *Streets. Critical Perspectives on Public Sphere*, Berkeley, London.

Choremi-Spetsieri, A. 1994. "Η οδός των Τριπόδων και χορηγικά μνημεία στην αρχαία Αθήνα," in *The Archaeology of Athens and Attica under the Democracy*, ed. W. D. E. Coulson, et al. Oxbow Monograph 37, pp. 31–42.

Clinton, K. 1974. *The Sacred Officials of the Eleusinian Mysteries* (*TransAmPhilS* 64), Philadelphia.

Clinton, K. 1989. "Hadrian's Contribution to the Renaissance of Eleusis," in Walker and Cameron 1989, pp. 56–68.

Clinton, K. 1992. Myth and Cult. The Iconography of the Eleusinian Mysteries, Stockholm.

Clinton, K. 1997. "Eleusis and the Romans: Late Republic to Marcus Aurelius," in Hoff and Rotroff 1997, pp. 161–181.

Clinton, K. 2005, 2008. *Eleusis. The Inscriptions on Stone: Documents of the Sanctuary of the Two Goddesses and Public Documents of the Deme*, vols. 1-2, Athens.

Connor, W. R. 1987. "Tribes, Festivals and Processions: Civic Ceremonial and Political Manipulation in Archaic Greece," *JHS* 107, pp. 40–50.

Cosgrove, D. E. 1998. *Social Formation and Symbolic Landscape*, Madison, WI.

Cosmopoulos, M. B., ed. 2003. *Greek Mysteries. The Archaeology and Ritual of Ancient Greek Secret Cults*, London and New York.

Costaki, L. 2006. "The *intra muros* road system of ancient Athens," Diss. University of Toronto.

Daverio Rocchi, G. 2002. "Topografia dello spazio internazionale. La *hierà hodós* da Atene a Delfi," in *Stuttgarter Kolloquium zur historischen Geographie des Altertums* 7, 1999, ed. E. Olshausen and H. Sonnabend, Stuttgart, pp. 148–159.

Davis, S. G. 1986. *Parades and Power. Street Theatre in Nineteenth-Century Philadelphia*, Philadelphia.

Délos XXX = M.-T. Couilloud, *Les monuments funéraires de Rhénèe*, (*Exploration archéologique de Délos*, XXX), Paris 1974.

Dillon, M. 1997. *Pilgrims and pilgrimage in ancient Greece*, London.

Dinsmoor, W. B. [1950] 1975. *The Architecture of Ancient Greece*. 3rd edition, New York.

Durm, J. 1910. *Die Baukunst der Griechen*[3], Leipzig.

Elsner, J. 2001. "Structuring 'Greece': Pausanias's *Periegesis* as a Literary Construct," in Alcock, Cherry, Elsner 2001, pp. 3–20.

Elsner, J. and I. Rutherford. 2005. *Pilgrimage in Graeco-Roman and Early Christian Antiquity: Seeing the Gods*, Oxford.

Foccardi, D. 1987. "Religious Silence and Reticence in Pausanias," in *Regions of Silence: Studies on the Difficulty of Communicating*, ed. M. G. Ciani, [London Studies in Classical Philology 17] Amsterdam, pp. 69–113.

Frazer, J. G. 1898. *Pausanias's Description of Greece*, London. 6 vol.

Fullerton, M. D. 1990. *The Archaistic Style in Roman Statuary* (Mnemosyne Supp. 110), Leiden.

Galli, M. 2004. "'Creating religious identities': *Paideia* e religione nella Seconda Sofistica," in Borg 2004, pp. 315–356.

Galli, M. 2005. "Pilgrimage as Elite *Habitus*: Educated Pilgrims in Sacred Landscape During the Second Sophistic," in Elsner and Rutherford 2005, pp. 253–90.

Giraud, D. 1991. Η Κυρία Είσοδος του ιερού της Ελευσίνος, Athens.

Goette, H. R. 2000. Ο αξιόλογος δῆμος Σούνιον: *Landeskundliche Studien in Sudost-Attika*, (Internationale Archäologie, 59), Rahden/Westf.

Goldhill, S. 2001. *Being Greek under Rome. Cultural Identity, the Second Sophistic and the Development of Empire*, Cambridge.

Graf, F. 1996. "*Pompai* in Greece: Some Considerations about Space and Ritual in the Greek Polis," in *The Role of Religion in the Early Greek Polis*, ed. R. Hägg, Stockholm, pp. 55–65.

Gygax, M. D. 2006. "Plutarch on Alcibiades' Return to Athens," *Mnemosyne* 59, pp. 481–500.

Hagn, T. 1999. "Das griechische Propylon: Definition und Dokumentation einer Denkmälergruppe," in *Proc. XVth International Congress of Classical Archaeology, Amsterdam, July 12–17, 1998*, ed. R. F. Docter and E. M. Moormann, Amsterdam, pp. 184–6.

Hellmann, M.-C. 1992. *Recherches sur le vocabulaire de l'architecture grecque, d'après les inscriptions de Délos* (BEFAR 278), Paris.

Hoff, M. C. and S. I. Rotroff, eds. 1997. *The Romanization of Athens* (Oxbow monograph 94), Oxford.

Karagiorga-Stathakopoulou, T. 1988. "Δημόσια έργα και ανασαφές στην Αθήνα τα τελευταία πέντε χρόνια," *Horos* 6, pp. 87–108.

Kiilerich, B. 2005. "Making Sense of the *Spolia* in the Little Metropolis in Athens." *Arte medievale* 4, pp. 95–114.

Knigge, U. 1991. *The Athenian Kerameikos. History, Monuments, Excavations*, Berlin.

Köhler, J. 1996. *Pompai. Untersuchungen zur hellenistischen Festkultur*, Frankfurt am Main.

Lamberton, R. 1997. "Plutarch and the Romanizations of Athens," in Hoff and Rotroff 1997, pp. 151–60.

Lenormant, F. 1862. *Recherches archéologiques a Éleusis. Recueil des inscriptions*, Paris.

Lippolis, E. 2006. *Mysteria. Archeologia e culto del santuario di Demetra a Eleusi,* [Milan].

Lohmann, H. 2002. "Ancient Roads in Attica and the Megaris," in *Ancient Roads in Greece (Antiquitates* 21), ed. Hans R. Goette, Hamburg.

McClure, L. K. 2003. *Courtesans at Table. Gender and Greek Literary Culture in Athenaeus,* New York and London.

Miles, M. M. 1998. "The Propylon to the Sanctuary of Demeter Malophoros at Selinous," *AJA* 102, pp. 38–57.

Miles, M. M. 1989. "A Reconstruction of the Temple of Nemesis at Rhamnous," *Hesperia* 58, pp. 138–249.

Ohnesorg, A. 2005. *Ionische Altäre. Formen und Varianten einer Architekturgattung aus Insel- und Ostionien (Archäologische Forschungen* 21), Berlin.

Palagia, O. 1997. "Classical Encounters: Attic Sculpture after Sulla," in Hoff and Rotroff 1997, pp. 81–95.

Palagia, O. and W. Coulson, eds. 1998. *Regional Schools in Hellenistic Sculpture* (Oxbow monograph 90), Oxford.

Parker, R. 2005. *Polytheism and Society at Athens,* Oxford.

Parsons, A. W. 1943. "Klepsydra and the Paved Court of the Pythion," *Hesperia* 12, pp. 237–8.

Pollitt, J. J. 1979. "Kernoi from the Athenian Agora," *Hesperia* 48, pp. 205–33.

Preka-Alexandri, K. 1991. *Eleusina,* Athens.

Preston, R. 2001. "Roman Questions, Greek Answers: Plutarch and the Construction of Identity," in Goldhill 2001, pp. 86–119.

Pritchett, W. K. P. 1980. *Studies in Ancient Greek Topography,* III, Berkeley and Los Angeles.

Raftopoulou, E. G. 1985. "Neue Zeugnisse archaistischer Plastik im Athener Nationalmuseum," *AM* 100, pp. 355–365.

Rawson, E. 1985. *Intellectual Life in the Late Roman Republic,* London.

Ridgway, B. S. 2002. *Hellenistic Sculpture III: The Styles of ca. 100–31 B.C.* Madison, WI.

Robertson, N. D. 1998. "The Two Processions to Eleusis and the Program of the Mysteries," *AJP* 119, pp. 547–575.

Roux, G. 1961. *L'architecture de l'Argolide aux IVe et IIIe siècles avant J.-C.* (BEFAR 199), Paris.

Samothrace 10 = A. Frazer, *Samothrace. Excavations Conducted by the Institute of Fine Arts of New York University,* vol. 10, *The Propylon of Ptolemy II,* Princeton 1990.

Sauron, G. 2001. "Les propylées d'Appius Claudius Pulcher à Éleusis: l'art néo-attique dans les contraditions idéologiques de la noblesse romaine à la fin de la République," in *Constructions publiques et programmes édilitaires en Grèce entre le IIe siècle av. J.-C. et le Ier siècle ap. J.-C.,* ed. J.-Y. Marc and J.-C. Moretti (*BCH* Supp. 39), pp. 267–83.

Schmidt, E. 1982. *Geschichte der Caryatide,* Würzburg.

Schmidt-Dounas, B. 1994. "Der dorische Fries der Stoa des Antigonos Gonatas aus Delos," *AM* 109, pp. 227–42.

Scholl, A. 1994. "*Polytalanta Mnemeia.* Zur Literarischen und monumentalen Überlieferung aufwendiger Grabmäler im spätklassischen Athen," *JdAI* 109, pp. 239–71.

Spawforth, A. and S. Walker. 1985. "The world of the Panhellenion, I: Athens and Eleusis," *JRS* 75, pp. 78–104.

Swain, S. 1996. *Hellenism and Empire: Language, Classicism and Power in the Greek World, AD 50–250,* Oxford.

Townsend, R. F. 1987. "The Roman Rebuilding of Philon's porch and the Telesterion at Eleusis," *Boreas* 10, pp. 97–106.

Travlos, J. 1988. *Bildlexicon zur Topographie des antiken Attika,* Tübingen.

Walker, S. and A. Cameron, eds. 1989. *The Greek Renaissance in the Roman Empire* (*BICS* Supp. 55), London.

Webb, P. A. 1986. *Hellenistic Architectural Sculpture: Figural Motifs in Western Anatolia and the Aegean Islands,* Madison, WI.

Whitmarsh, T. 2005. *The Second Sophistic,* Oxford.

Willers, D. 1990. *Hadrians panhellenisches Programm* (*Antike Kunst,* Beiheft 16), Basel.

Willers, D. 1996. "Der Vorplatz des Heiligtums um Eleusis – Überlegungen zur Neugestaltung im 2.Jahrhundert n. Chr," in *Retrospektive. Konzepte von Vergangenheit in der griechisch-römischen Antike,* ed. M. Flashar, H.-J. Gehrke, E. Heinrich, Munich, pp. 179–225.

CHAPTER FIVE

ARCHITECTURE AND RITUAL IN ILION, ATHENS, AND ROME

C. Brian Rose

Most citizens of a state, whether ancient or modern, consistently look for visual and verbal signs that evoke and justify the foundations of that state. Such signs typically feature or are framed by sacred components that build on the collective memory of a past more heroic than the present, and they are habitually incorporated into political or religious rituals designed to promote community identity.[1] Mussolini, for example, framed his new parade route with the Colosseum, the temples of Mars Ultor and Venus Genetrix, and the monument to King Victor Emmanuel II, thereby highlighting the Imperial foundations of his new regime, while Romans of the Republic staged their *Lupercalia* festival at the Palatine cave where the she-wolf allegedly suckled Romulus and Remus.[2]

The site of Ilion in northwestern Turkey differs from the aforementioned examples in that its entire identity, and much of its economy, were tied to the Homeric tradition (Figs. 5.1, 5.2).[3] In an attempt to reinforce that identification, the residents continually shaped their architecture and rituals so that they functioned as mutually reinforcing components of a new sacred topography. Two of those rituals – the Penance of the Lokrian Maidens and the Panathenaia – succinctly illustrate the ways in which memory of the Trojan War could be exploited for the political benefit of both sides of the Aegean. In this chapter I reconstruct both traditions within the context of Ilion's built and natural environment, and then extend the analysis to Athens and Rome, focusing in particular on the context of rituals rooted in Trojan tradition.

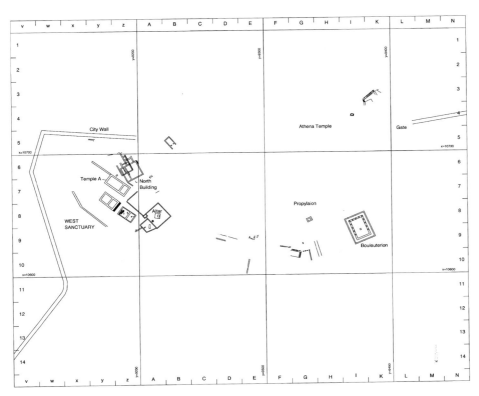

5.1. Ilion, plan of Troy VIII. Troy Excavations.

Ilion is located at one of the easiest crossing points between continental Europe and Asia, near the mouth of the Dardanelles or Hellespont. Consequently, the residents of Ilion essentially controlled the maritime entrance to the Black Sea, which is one of the reasons it was a locus for armed conflict throughout much of its history. Fear of conquest prompted the residents to erect an enormous limestone fortification wall around their citadel, nearly 10 meters high and 3 meters wide, which still serves as the site's most prominent landmark. The citadel wall and a fortification ditch that encircled the Lower City were, nevertheless, insufficient protection against attackers, and much of the settlement was damaged during a battle in the early twelfth century B.C.E.[4]

The settlement's population decreased dramatically after the conflict, but the site appears never to have been abandoned, and its strength began to return during the Geometric period. In the eighth century B.C.E., on the southwest side of the citadel, a damaged late Bronze Age building was reconstructed with benches inside and out, an interior apsidal altar,

5.2. Ilion, aerial view of Trojan mound. Troy Excavations.

and a stone base, presumably for some sort of image. The structure was subsequently flanked by at least twenty-eight stone paved circles with an average diameter of 2 meters; each was clearly the locus of a fire, and the associated ceramic assemblages suggest feasting (cups, dinoi, kraters, etc.).[5] All of these structures lay within the shadow of the late Bronze Age citadel wall, which was still preserved to a height of nearly 5 meters, and it seems very likely that they were intended for hero cult.[6]

The following century witnessed the establishment in Ilion of a new custom that effectively solidified the Homeric credentials of the site. At least on a superficial level, the custom involved the territory of Lokris in central Greece, from which two aristocratic maidens were sent annually to Ilion. Their mission was to clean the Sanctuary of Athena Ilias, the principal goddess of the site, thereby atoning for the crime of their legendary ancestor Ajax, who raped Kassandra in Athena's temple during the Trojan War.[7]

It seems strange, to say the least, that the Lokrians would allow two of their aristocratic children to be subjected to such humiliation on an annual basis on the opposite side of the Aegean, especially since Ilion was hardly a power center at this time. The only sensible explanation is that Lokris was simultaneously attempting to establish a link to their local hero, Ajax, and to the Homeric tradition that Troy now embodied, by making the custom a permanent component of their civic identity.

Lokris was not the only site in mainland Greece attempting to co-opt and ritualize the Homeric tradition by exploiting the Trojan land-scape. Around 620 B.C.E. Athens established its first overseas colony at Sigeion, approximately six kilometers from Ilion; another colony at Elaious, opposite Ilion on the northern side of the Dardanelles, fol-lowed shortly thereafter.[8] Adjacent to these new colonies were monu-mental tumuli identified as the tombs of Achilles (Fig. 5.7), Patroklos, Ajax, and Protesilaos.[9] It seems likely that Athens was attempting to incorporate both Sigeion and Elaious into the well-established leg-endary framework that encompassed Ilion and the surrounding area, thereby increasing her own status vis-à-vis the other major powers of the Aegean whose ancestral links to the Homeric heroes were far stron-ger.[10] Less than a century later, the newly inaugurated Panathenaic fes-tival in Athens featured *rhapsodes* singing sections of the *Iliad*, thereby reinforcing the Homeric links that had first been established by the city's Troad colonies.[11]

The Archaic period closed with the first of a series of high-profile vis-its to Ilion prompted by the site's legendary associations.[12] When Xerxes' arrived during his march to Greece in 480, he ascended the acropolis and made offerings to the Homeric heroes, reportedly sacrificing one thousand cattle to Athena in the process.[13] Alexander arrived at the site in 334 and continued the same general pattern of homage – depositing his own armor in the temple as a dedication to Athena and removing the finest armor remaining from the Trojan War, which he subsequently wore into battle. The lyre of Paris was also apparently kept in the tem-ple, which must have housed a treasury of relics linked to the Homeric legends.[14]

At this point the Athenaion appears to have been a small and plain structure, judging by Strabo's description of it, but the temple was transformed into the largest Doric temple in northwestern Asia Minor during a major building program between ca. 240 and 160 B.C.E. The new structure was hexastyle peripteral, measuring approximately 50 x 100 Doric feet, and featured metopes depicting the Gigantomachy, Amazonomachy, Centauromachy, and Ilioupersis (Figs. 5.2–5.5).[15]

5.3. Ilion, proposed restoration of the Athenaion. Troy Excavations.

To build the complex, an enormous terrace measuring nearly 100 meters square had to be constructed, and the eastern side of the temenos was probably extended by about 20 meters (Fig. 5.3). The platform was bordered by porticoes at the east, south, and west, with the northern side left open so that the expansive view of the Dardanelles and the plains of Troy was not blocked. One of the most unique features of the renovated precinct was a new well axially aligned with the cult statue and the altar (Figs. 5.3, 5.4). The well-cut ashlar stones lining the well are bonded to those of the new temenos pavement, so the two are clearly contemporary.

Directly above the well was a decorative marble enclosure that featured a three-stepped podium with a circular wall articulated by six pilasters, above which was a marble lattice and possibly a conical roof.[16] The well-head completely encircled the shaft and was at least 1.5 meters in height, which was just high enough to prevent easy access to the water. It would

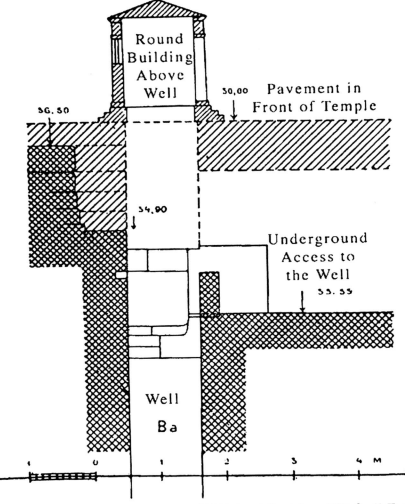

Round
Building
Above
Well

Pavement in
Front of Temple

30,00

36,50

34,90

Underground
Access to
the Well

33,33

Well

Ba

5.4. Ilion, section of Well Ba. After W. Dörpfeld, *Troia und Ilion*, Athens, 1902, fig. 68, Troy
Excavations.

also have been difficult to climb the steps to reach a higher point since
their tread was only 0.10 meters. In other words, the marble enclosure
was intended both to monumentalize the well and to prevent the water
from being collected.[17] The only access lay in a subterranean tunnel constructed of large ashlar blocks that extended at least ten meters toward
the north, in the direction of a series of steps by the Northeast Bastion
(Figs. 5.3, 5.5). The tunnel measured 2.05 meters in width by 2.3 meters
in height, and it was clearly an original component of the new design.[18]

5.5. Ilion, underground passage leading to the Athenaion's well, looking north. Troy Excavations.

At first glance, none of this makes sense: the designers created a new water source and situated it on primary axis of the sanctuary, monumentalizing the opening while simultaneously restricting public access. The only logical explanation for such an idiosyncratic topography is that it was designed to highlight the custom of the Lokrian maidens, and thereby strengthen the site's Homeric associations. The custom appears to have begun by the seventh century B.C.E.; it was revived circa 350 B.C.E. following a hiatus of more than a century, and probably continued up to the Mithridatic Wars, and possibly even longer. In any event, the tribute of the Lokrian maidens seems to have been in operation at Ilion for at least five hundred years.[19]

The ancient historians comment on the ways in which these maidens were subjected to humiliation and risk of death at the hands of the Ilians. They could enter and leave the Sanctuary only by night because the residents were reportedly entitled to kill them if they were found outside the borders of the temenos.[20] The maidens were also required to stay out of the line of sight of the cult statue, which meant avoiding any activity on the central axis of the precinct.

The Lokrian tribute was revived at approximately the same time in which plans for the new Athenaion were being prepared, and the unusual configuration of well and subterranean corridor must have been designed with this custom in mind. The new design aligned the wellhead with the temple and allowed only for subterranean access to the water – on the same axis as the cult statue but over two meters below it. Such an unorthodox arrangement would have allowed the site's tour guides to link the circuitous paths of the Maidens with Ajax's rape of Kassandra in the same locale. It was, in essence, a museum exhibit, and the link between ritual and architecture in this case seems certain.

The Sanctuary's layout was clearly part of a coordinated visual network designed to exploit the Homeric associations of the site – in essence, to materialize memory.[21] The ancient accounts mention Hellenistic tour guides pointing to sites in the surrounding landscape where Anchises and Aphrodite made love, or from which Zeus carried off Ganymede.[22] Within the temple, in addition to the relics from the Trojan War, visitors would have seen a reproduction of the Palladion, the archaic cult statue of Athena that was allegedly stolen by Odysseus and Diomedes prior to the sack of Troy.[23] Tourists standing on the open (north) side of the precinct would have seen a series of burial mounds identified as tombs of the Homeric heroes, including Ajax, Patroklos, and Protesilaos.[24] None of these tumuli actually contained a Bronze Age burial, from what we can tell, but the rhetoric of the guides, coupled with the images on and around the acropolis, conferred upon them a level of sanctity they had never possessed.

Needless to say, the size of each mound was expected to match the stature of its alleged occupant, and in most cases there was no problem. But the mound attributed to Achilles (modern Sivritepe) was a rather diminutive mound that held the remains of a Neolithic settlement, and it was much smaller than the other "Homeric" tumuli

(Fig. 5.7).[25] Consequently, around the middle of the third century B.C.E., the city added over ten meters of earth and stone to the upper section of the tumulus so that its size would equal that of the others. Like the Lokrian-influenced design of the Athena Sanctuary, whose construction dates to the same time, the tumulus enlargement was an attempt to co-opt the legendary Trojan past in order to strengthen its current status. In other words, the ritual activities of the Lokrian maidens were framed by a series of complementary narratives, encompassing the Athenaion's architecture, the legendary landscapes, and the rhetoric of the tour guides, all of which attested to Ilion's legendary heritage.

There was a second ritual activity that played upon the same network of imagery. At the end of the fourth century B.C.E., Antigonos I had designated Ilion as the capital of a new Koinon or league of Troad cities, centered on the Sanctuary of Athena Ilias, and the primary ritual manifestation of the Koinon's public identity was the Panathenaic festival, apparently modeled on the one in Athens.[26] In addition to games, parades, and dramatic events, *rhapsodes* would have sung sections of the *Iliad* in Ilion's agora, which lay in front of the still-visible late Bronze Age fortification wall (Fig. 5.6).[27] That wall was no doubt presented as a remnant of Priam's citadel, and sections of it were repaired and exhibited to spectators near the Bouleuterion and on the road to the theater (Fig. 5.8). Here again, the ritual reinforced the Homeric heritage of the surrounding architecture, which, in turn, lent historical validity to the Homeric epics.

The backdrop of the Panathenaia was the precinct of the Athenaion, which, like the Parthenon, featured carved metopes on all four sides with the identical decorative cycles. The Troad Koinon was clearly looking to Athens in their search for models of civic identity, although all of this is rather ironic: the Greek-speaking residents of Ilion were building a framework that tied them to the defeated Trojans of the Homeric epics, but they used Athenian models to frame these legendary connections.[28]

Functionally, the custom of the Lokrian maidens nearly parallels the office of the *arrhephoroi* on the Athenian Acropolis, which is especially noteworthy in light of the connections between Athens and Ilion noted

5.6. Ilion, aerial view of the agora at Ilion, looking west, with the reconstructed Late Bronze Age fortification wall (Troy VI) running behind the Odeion. Troy Excavations.

5.7. Troad, the "tumulus of Achilles" or "Sivritepe." Troy Excavations.

earlier.[29] At both Athens and Ilion, two young maidens would have lived on the Acropolis for a year in the service of the goddess Athena, using subterranean passageways to exit the sanctuary by night (Fig. 5.9).[30] There is, of course, no evidence that the two institutions were inaugurated at the same time, or that one influenced the other; but visitors to both sanctuaries, at least during the Hellenistic period, would undoubtedly have been struck by the similarities between the two customs.

They would also have been struck by the related design strategies employed for the monumental entrances to each acropolis. The ramp leading to Ilion's Athenaion propylon led the visitor past the monumental late Bronze Age fortifications, and the same was true for the Propylaia on the Athenian Acropolis, which was built against – and showcased – the remnants of a Bronze Age citadel wall (Fig. 5.10).[31] Both designs immediately engaged the viewer and advertised the illustrious ancestry of the city in question. In the case of Athens, such a proclamation camouflaged the relatively insignificant role played by the city in the Homeric epics, as did the foundation of their first overseas colony at Sigeion, built in the shadow of Achilles' tumulus.

The links between the two cities went even further than that: as one entered the precinct of the Athenian Acropolis during the Panathenaia,

5.8. Ilion, view of the late Bronze Age remains of the Northeast Bastion at Troy. Photo C. Brian Rose.

one of the most dazzling images would have been a colossal bronze horse in the sanctuary of Artemis Brauronia, adjacent to the Parthenon.[32] Constructed during the Peloponnesian War, this horse was reportedly 6 meters tall – nearly two-thirds the height of the Parthenon's columns; and among the warriors positioned in the trap doors of the horse's

5.9. Athens, view of the Acropolis. After R. V. Schroder, *Ancient Greece from the Air*, London, 1974, p. 33.

body were two of the sons of Theseus. Such an arrangement would have highlighted Athens' role in the Trojan conquest while adding a new layer of meaning to the *rhapsodes* performance of the *Iliad* during the Panathenaia – in effect providing a footnote to the epic.

Rome enjoyed the same kind of symbiotic relationship with Ilion as had Athens, although the ancestral links were far stronger in the latter case in that they claimed a common ancestry. That ancestry was expressed in figural decoration throughout the city, beginning with the mid-Republic, but it was encapsulated in only one ritual: the *lusus Troiae*, or Trojan Games.[33] The *lusus Troiae* was an equestrian parade and mock battle staged by Rome's patrician youths, generally between the ages of eight and fourteen, which probably involved between two hundred and three hundred boys during the early empire.[34] The date at which the ritual was introduced is unclear, but its Trojan links were fixed by the time Sulla revived it in the early first century B.C.E. Not surprisingly, it developed into an especially popular custom under Augustus and his Julio-Claudian successors, since this was a dynasty that traced its origins to Troy and Aeneas.[35]

The most elaborate description of the *lusus Troiae* is provided in *Aeneid* V, in the context of the funeral games of Anchises, and Vergil's

5.10. Athens, Propylaia, with remains of late Bronze Age fortification wall. Photo Jeffrey Hurwit, *The Athenian Acropolis: History, Mythology, and Archaeology from the Neolithic Era to the Present*, New York, 1999, fig. 54, reproduced with his permission.

description of the pageant probably reproduces its format during the reign of Augustus.[36] The two most distinctive features of the boys' costume were a twisted metal torque, worn low, and a *"tonsa corona,"* which is usually regarded as a garland of cut leaves.[37] The first attribute merits special attention. Torques often served as a sign of eastern status, such as those worn by the Persians in the Alexander mosaic, by Attis, the consort of Cybele, and by Cybele's priests (Figs. 5.12).[38] At first glance, then, a torque would seem a logical component of the boys' costume, since Troy was also located in the east. A survey of ancient Mediterranean imagery, however, reveals that the Trojans were never shown with torques, which means that its use in the *lusus Troiae* cannot have been stimulated by Trojan iconography *per se*.

Here one needs to examine the context of the ritual, for that holds the key to its visual configuration. The *lusus Troiae* always took place in the Circus Maximus, directly below the temple of Cybele on the Palatine Hill, where her priests also lived (Fig. 5.11).[39] As noted earlier, torques formed part of the costume of both Attis and the priests, and a connection between the cult of Cybele and the *lusus Troiae* would therefore have been readily apparent.[40] One would, in fact, expect such a link in light of

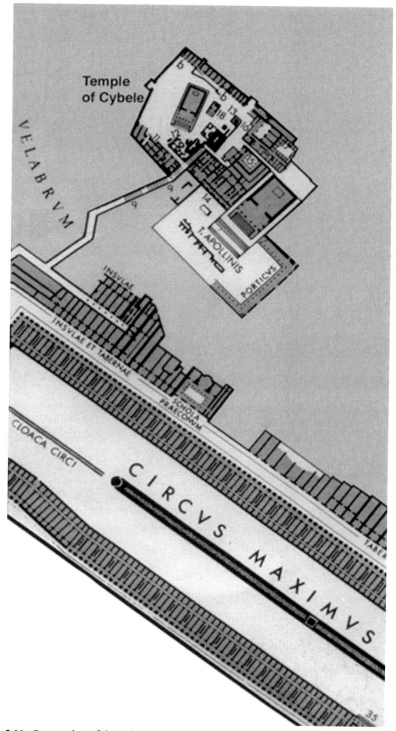

5.11. Rome, plan of the Palatine hill, showing the Temple of Cybele and Circus Maximus below. Plan prepared by John Wallrodt.

5.12. Silver plate with a bust of Attis from Hildesheim. Antikensammlung, Staatliche Museen zu Berlin-Preussischer Kulturbesitz, Inv. Misc. 3779, 4. Photo Johannes Laurentius.

the legendary and historical interactions that had existed among Troy, Cybele, and Rome. The cult was brought from Asia Minor to Rome in 205 B.C.E., toward the end of the Second Punic War, and enshrined in a large new temple on the southwest corner of the Palatine hill, which held more legendary associations than any other part of the city.[41]

By this point in time, the cult had become closely entwined with the Trojan tradition, and that association would grow even stronger in early imperial literature: Aeneas reportedly used Phrygian pine sacred to Cybele to build his fleet, which was adorned with an image of the goddess, and in the *Fasti* Cybele almost follows the ships of Aeneas from Asia Minor to Italy, but decides that fate has not yet called for the transfer of her cult.[42] It seems likely that the Romans transferred the cult from Asia Minor as a means of highlighting their Trojan ancestry more emphatically than they had done in the past, and the inauguration of the *lusus Troiae* may have been a by-product of that decision.[43] If viewed in this light, the Trojan festival was structured so as to forge a bond with the temple that towered over the festivities, thereby creating yet another network of symbiotic relationships: the cult's Trojan origins were emphasized, as was Rome's Trojan ancestry, and Cybele's temple was pulled into the same legendary framework as the Palatine cave where the *Lupercalia* was staged.

Festivals such as these that enlisted memories of the past to elevate the status of the present never lost their popularity, and are still a prominent feature of modern ritual. We now label them Sound and Light shows, set against such backdrops as the Pyramids of Giza, the Taj Mahal, or the Blue Mosque in Istanbul, but their function is really no different from what one would have found in antiquity.[44] Some of the architectural contexts exploited in ancient festivals still form the centerpiece of modern ritual, although the meaning of those contexts depends on the political/religious priorities of the sponsoring society, and a new ritual can completely alter one's perception of the old imagery.

Once again, Ilion and Athens are excellent cases in point. During the Panathenaia the Athenian Acropolis served as a stage where Athena's victory in the Gigantomachy was celebrated; and although the Acropolis remains the focus of the city's current Sound and Light show, it is used primarily to illustrate armed conflict with the east, such as Persians and Ottomans.

Similarly, visitors who travel to Ilion for the Troy festival can still hear the *Iliad* recited in front of the late Bronze Age fortification wall, and watch the restaging of the Judgment of Paris on the site where it allegedly occurred. The costumes, architectural contexts, and activities are not significantly different from their ancient counterparts. What has changed is the interpretation of the rituals, and the role that they now play in political discourse. One of the arguments for Turkey's membership in the European Union is that Troy is located within the country's borders, and the accounts of the citadel's destruction, as preserved in the *Iliad* and *Odyssey*, constitute the foundations of the Western literary tradition. When viewed in this context, the Troy festival and its scenery become a diachronic chart of East-West interaction, not unlike the Athenian Sound and Light show, and both testify eloquently to the transitory meaning of any structure embraced by ritual.

Notes

1. Alcock 2002.
2. Manacorda and Tamassia 1985, pp. 170–171; Insolera and Perego 1983, p. 178; Ulf 1982.
3. Rose 2006.
4. Klinkott 2004; Latacz 2004, pp. 283–287.
5. *Troy* VI, pp. 274–279; Basedow 2006, pp. 19–20; Rose 1997, p. 89. Feasting also occurred in the vicinity of similar stone circles at Mycenae.
6. The application of sanctity to a citadel destroyed and/or abandoned at the end of the Bronze Age was not restricted to Ilion – one finds evidence for the same phenomenon at Bronze Age palaces on the other side of the Aegean, such as Knossos, Mycenae, and Tiryns, all of which received new cult buildings in the early Iron Age, even though the citadels were abandoned: Wallace 2003, pp. 267–8 (Knossos); Klein 1997, 297 (Mycenae); Foley 1988, pp. 145–7; Antonaccio 1994, pp. 86–90.
7. The rather large number of ancient historians who comment on the custom agree in general on the basic form of the tribute, but disagree on the date when it originated, with some placing it shortly after the Trojan War, and others to the period of Persian domination. According to Polybius, whose account is usually regarded as the most authoritative, the custom had begun before 673 B.C.E., when the colony of Lokri Epizephyroi in southern Italy was founded (Polyb. 12.5.7; Lycoph. *Alex.* 1141–1173; Aen. Tact. 31.24; Strabo 13.1.40). For modern assessments of the custom of the Lokrian Maidens, see Hughes, 1991, pp. 166–84; Graf 1978; Walbank 1967, pp. 335–6; Leaf 1923, pp. 191–193; Redfield 2003, pp. 85–150. Bonnechere (1994, pp. 159–60) has argued that the maidens traveled only as far as the temple of Athena Ilias in Lokris, but all of the ancient accounts indicate that they traveled to Ilion itself.
8. Cook 1973, pp. 178–88; Aigner 1978; Tenger 1999, pp. 121–6.
9. Some of these were Bronze Age hüyüks; others were tumuli containing a single tomb. For a summary see Rose 1999, pp. 61–63; Rose 2000, pp. 65–66.
10. One finds further evidence for the incorporation of Troy in Athenian propaganda in the fifth century, which witnessed a revision of the deeds of Akamas, son of Erechtheus, and the geneology of Ion in an attempt to jusitfy Athens' political and military presence in the Troad and Ionia: Erskine 2001, pp. 107–8; Hall 1997, pp. 42–44.

11. Shapiro 1992.
12. Most of the visits are summarized in Vermeule 1995.
13. Herodotos 7.43.
14. Arrian 1.11.7–8; Diodorus 17.17.6–7; 17.18.1; Strabo 13.1.26; Plutarch *Alexander* 15.7.
15. Rose 2003; Rose 2006; Goethert-Schleif 1962.
16. Dörpfeld 1902, p. 228. Most of the pieces of the wellhead were found in the shaft, and although no sections of a roof were unearthed, there must have been a covering of some sort to keep the water clean.
17. Dörpfeld (1902) originally assumed that one part of the well was left open to facilitate access to the water, but there is evidence for vertical slabs on each of the base stones (Leaf 1912, pp. 126–127), which means that the well-head completely blocked direct access to the water.
18. The ceiling would have been one meter below the level of the temenos pavement. The only subterranean corridors in sanctuaries that I have been able to find are linked to divine epiphanies, e.g., the Asklepieion and the Sanctuary of the Egyptian Gods at Pergamon: Radt 1988, pp. 228–39, 250–71, esp. 268–70.
19. Richard Catling (1998, 164) has identified Protogeometric amphorae from Ilion that seem to have been imported from central Greece, and he proposed that the Lokrian custom may be related to their transport. If so, then the custom can be pushed back to the early first millennium B.C.E.
20. Somewhere around the Athenaion, possibly within one of the porticoes, there must have been sleeping quarters for the maidens.
21. Joyce 2000; Van Dyke *and* Alcock 2003.
22. Lucan *Pharsalia* 9. 970–3.
23. Rose 2003, pp. 59–60.
24. Cook 1973, pp. 159–65.
25. Rose 1999, pp. 61–3; Rose 2000, pp. 55–6.
26. Frisch 1975, nos. 2, 5, 6, 10, 12, 13, 15–17, 32. Dörpfeld 1902, pp. 577–82 (Brückner); Bellinger 1957; Bellinger 1961, p. 3; Robert 1966, pp. 18, 20, 29, 30, 36, 37, 40, 90, 93.
27. Kanephoroi: Frisch 1975, nos. 15–17; crowning of Athena: Frisch 1975, no. 32. See now Shear 2001, pp. 45–46, 130, 195.
28. The overwhelming influence of Attica is especially apparent in a fourth-century B.C.E. votive deposit in quadrat D9, southwest of the Athena Sanctuary. Most, and possibly all of the lamps are Attic imports; approximately one-third of the fine tableware has also been imported from Athens, and the remainder is Atticizing: Berlin 2002; Berlin-Lynch 2002.
29. For the *arrhephoroi* see also Pausanias 1.27.3; Burkert 2001, pp. 37–63; Hurwit 1999, pp. 42–43, 199–200; Boulé 1987, pp. 83–123; Simon 1983, pp. 38–46.
30. For the subterranean passage see Broneer 1933; Travlos pp. 72–75, 228–32.
31. Hurwit 1999, pp. 75–76, 158–9, 194.
32. Pausanias 1.23.7–8; *IG* I.3, 895; Hamdorf 1980, pp. 231–5; Higbie 1997, p. 291; Hurwit 1999, pp. 198, 229.
33. For the *lusus Troiae*, see Schneider 1927; Mehl 1956; Williams 1960, pp. 145–57; Weinstock 1971, p. 88; Fuchs 1990.
34. Boys of nobility in *lusus Troiae*: Dio 49.43.3; 48.20.2.
35. Suetonius *Caesar* 39.2; *Augustus* 43.2; *Tiberius* 6.4; *Claudius* 21.3; Dio 54.26.1, 55.10.6–7, 59.11.2; Pliny 8.65. The *lusus Troiae* was held in conjunction with Caesar's triumph in 46 B.C., the dedications of the Theater of Marcellus, the

temples of Mars Ultor, Divus Julius Caesar, and Divus Augustus, the funeral of Drusilla, and the Saecular Games of C.E. 47.

36. *Aeneid* 5.545–603.
37. Williams 1960, p. 148. Augustus awarded a gold torque to one of the boys who was injured in the *lusus Troiae*: Suetonius *Augustus* 43.
38. Herodotos 8.113.3 (as Persian marks of distinction); King Darius: Pfrommer 1998, pls. 6 and 8; generic Persians: Boardman 2000, p. 215, figs. 5.93c–d; Xenophon *Anabasis* 1.5.8 (gifts to foreign princes by Persians). For Attis: *LIMC* III, 1986, nos. 345, 361, s.v. Attis (M. Vermaseren and M. DeBoer); priests of Cybele: Vermaseren 1977B, no. 250; Roller 1998; Roller 1999, pp. 290–1, 297–303. In general, see Schuppe 1937.
39. Wiseman 1982.
40. In the *Aeneid*, Aeneas and the Trojans were actually compared with the priests of Cybele: *Aeneid* 4.215, 9.617–20, 12.97–100; Roller 1999, pp. 302–4.
41. Pensabene 1996; Roller 1999, pp. 263–85; Tagliamonte 1999; Vermaseren 1977A, pp. 41–43; Wiseman 1984, p. 126.
42. *Aeneid* 9.77–83, 107–22; 10.156–8; *Fasti* 4. 251–4, 273–4.
43. Gruen 1990, pp. 5–33; Gruen 1992, p. 47; Roller 1999, pp. 269–71; Rose 2002.
44. Rituals with political/religious overtones have experienced something of a revival during the last half century, as indicators of revived empires (the Shah's neo-Persian festival in the ruins of Persepolis), or as evocations of resurgent religious traditions (the Shahbaniyah festival at the holy shrines of Iraqi Karbala).

Works Cited

Aigner, H. 1978. "Sigeion und die Peisistradische Homerförderung," *RhM* 121, pp. 204–9.

Alcock, S. 2002. *Archaeologies of the Greek Past: Landscape, Monuments, and Memories*, Cambridge.

Antonaccio, C. M. 1994. "Placing the Past: The Bronze Age in the Cultic Topography of Early Greece," in *Placing the Gods: Sanctuaries and Sacred Space in Ancient Greece*, ed. S. Alcock and R. Osborne, Oxford, pp. 79–104.

Basedow, M. 2006. "What the Blind Man Saw: New Information from the Iron Age at Troy," in *Common Ground: Archaeology, Art, Science, and Humanities. Acta of the XVIth International Congress of Classical Archaeology (August 2003)*, ed. C. Mattusch, A. Brauer, and A. A. Donohue, Oxford, pp. 88–92.

Bellinger, A. R. 1957. "The Earliest Coins of Ilium," *ANSMN* 7, pp. 43–49.

Bellinger, A. R. 1961. *Troy. The Coins. (Troy Supplement 2)*, Princeton.

Berlin, A., and K. Lynch. 2002. "Going Greek: Atticizing Pottery in the Achaemenid World," *Studia Troica* 12, pp. 167–78.

Boardman, J. 2000. *Persia and the West: An Archaeological Investigation of the Genesis of Achaemenid Persian Art*, London.

Bonnechere, P. 1994. *Le sacrifice humain en Grèce ancienne*, Athens.

Boulé, P. 1987. *La fille d'Athènes: La religion des filles à Athènes à l'epoque classique. Mythes, cultes, et societé*, Paris.

Broneer, O. 1933. "Excavations on the North Slope of the Acropolis in Athens," *Hesperia* 2, pp. 329–417.

Burkert, W. 2001. *Savage Energies: Lessons of Myth and Ritual in Ancient Greece*, Chicago and London.

Catling, R. W. V. 1998. "The Typology of the Protogeometric and Sub-protogeometric Pottery from Troia and its Aegean Context," *Studia Troica* 8, pp. 151–87.

Cook, J. M. 1973. *The Troad: An Archaeological and Topographical Study*, Oxford.

Dörpfeld, W. 1902. *Troia und Ilion: Ergebnisse der Ausgrabungen in den vorhistorischen und historischen Schichten von Ilion, 1870–1894*, Athens.

Erskine, A. 2001. *Troy Between Greece and Rome: Local Tradition and Imperial Power*, Oxford.

Foley, A. 1988. *The Argolid 800–600 B.C.: An Archaeological Survey, Together with an Index of Sites from the Neolithic to the Roman Period*, Goteborg.

Frisch, P. 1975. *Die Inschriften von Ilion.* (Inschriften griechischer Städte aus Kleinasien 3), Bonn.

Fuchs, H. 1990. "Lusus Troiae," Diss. Universität Köln.

Goethert, F., and H. Schleif. 1962. *Der Athenatempel von Ilion.* (Denkmäler antiker Architektur 10), Berlin.

Gruen, E. 1990. *Studies in Greek Culture and Roman Policy*, Leiden.

Gruen, E. 1992. *Culture and National Identity in Republican Rome*, Ithaca.

Pensabene, P. 1996. "Magna Mater Aedes," *LTUR* 3, pp. 206–8.

Hall, J. M. 1997. *Ethnic Identity in Greek Antiquity*, New York.

Hamdorf, F. W. 1980. "Zur Weihung des Chairodemos auf der Akropolis von Athens," in: Στήλη. Τόμος εις μνήμην Νικολάου Κοντολέοντος, Athens, pp. 231–5.

Higbie, C. 1997. "The Bones of a Hero, the Ashes of a Politician: Athens, Salamis, and the Usable Past," *ClAnt* 16, pp. 278–307.

Hughes, D. D. 1991. *Human Sacrifice in Ancient Greece*, London and New York.

Hurwit, J. 1999. *The Athenian Acropolis: History, Mythology, and Archaeology from the Neolithic Era to the Present*, New York.

Insolera, I., and F. Perego. 1983. *Archeologia e città: Storia moderna dei fori di Roma*, Rome.

Joyce, R. 2000. "Heirlooms and Houses: Materiality and Social Memory," in *Beyond Kinship. Social and Material Reproduction in House Societies*, ed. R. Joyce and S. Gillespie, Philadelphia, pp. 177–88.

Klein, N. L. 1997. "Excavation of the Greek Temples at Mycenae by the British School at Athens," *BSA* 92, pp. 247–322.

Klinkott, M. 2004. "Die Wehrmauern von Troia VI – Bauaufnahme und Auswertung," *Studia Troica* 14, pp. 33–85.

Latacz, J. 2004. *Troy and Homer: Towards a Solution of an Old Mystery*, Oxford.

Leaf, W. 1912. *Troy. A Study in Homeric Geography*, London.

Leaf, W. 1923. *Strabo on the Troad; Book XIII, Cap. I*, Cambridge.

Manacorda, D., and R. Tamassia, 1985. *Il picone del regime*, Rome.

Mehl, E. 1956. "Troiaspiel," in: *RE* Suppl. VIII, 888–905.

Palagia, O., and A. Choremi-Spetsieri. eds. 2007. The Panathenaic Games: proceedings of an international conference held at the University of Athens, May 11–12, 2004, Oxford.

Pfrommer, M. 1998. *Untersuchungen zur Chronologie und Komposition des Alexandermosaiks auf antiquarischer Grundlage*, Mainz.

Radt, W. 1988. *Pergamon. Geschichte und Bauten, Funde und Erforschung einer antiken Metropole*, Cologne.

Redfield, J. M. 2003. *The Locrian Maidens: Love and Death in Greek Italy*, Princeton.

Robert, L. 1966. *Monnaies antiques en Troade*, Geneva.

Roller, L. 1998. "The Ideology of the Eunuch Priest," in *Gender and the Body in the Ancient Mediterranean*, ed. M. Wycke, Oxford, pp. 118–35.

Roller, L. 1999. *In Search of God the Mother: the cult of Anatolian Cybele*, Berkeley.

Rose, C. B. 1995. "The 1994 Post-Bronze Age Research and Excavation at Troia," *Studia Troica* 5, pp. 81–105.

Rose, C. B. 1997. "The 1996 Post-Bronze Age Excavations at Troia," *Studia Troica* 7, pp. 73–110.

Rose, C. B. 1998. "The 1997 Post-Bronze Age Excavations at Troia," *Studia Troica* 8, pp. 71–113.

Rose, C. B. 1999. "The 1998 Post-Bronze Age Excavations at Troy," *Studia Troica* 9, pp. 35–71.

Rose, C. B. 2000. "Post-Bronze Age Research at Troia, 1999," *Studia Troica* 10, pp. 53–71.

Rose, C. B. 2002. "Bilingual Trojan Iconography," in *Mauerschau. Festschrift für Manfred Korfmann*, ed. R. Aslan S. Blom, G. Kastl, and D. Thumm, Remshalden-Grünbach, pp. 329–350.

Rose, C. B. 2003. "The Temple of Athena at Ilion," *Studia Troica* 13, pp. 27–88.

Rose, C. B. 2006A. "Ilion," in *Stadtgrabungen und Stadtforschung im westlichen Kleinasien*, ed. W. Radt, Istanbul, pp. 135–158.

Rose, C. B. 2006B. "The Temple of Athena at Ilion: Recent Excavations and Research," in: *Common Ground: Archaeology, Art, Science, and Humanities: Acta of the XVIth International Congress of Classical Archaeology (August 2003)*, ed. C. Mattusch, A. Brauer, and A. A. Donohue, Oxford, pp. 88–92.

Shapiro, A. 1992. "Mousikoi Agones: Music and Poetry at the Panathenaia," in *Goddess and Polis. The Panathenaic Festival in Ancient Athens*, ed, J. Neils, Princeton, pp. 53–75.

Schneider, K. 1927. Lusus Troiae, in: *RE* XIII, 2059–2067.

Schroder, Raymond V. 1974. *Ancient Greece from the Air*, London.

Schuppe, Erwin. 1937. Torques, *RE* ² VI: 1800–1805.

Simon, E. 1983. *Festivals of Attica: An Archaeological Commentary*, Madison, WI.

Tagliamonte, G. 1999. "Palatium, Palatinus Mons (fino alla prima età repub-blicana), in *Lexicon Topographicum Urbis Romae* IV: 14–22.

Tenger, B. 1999. "Zur Geographie und Geschichte der Troas," in *Die Troas: Neue Forschungen 3*, ed. E. Schwertheim, Bonn, pp. 103–180.

Travlos, J. 1971. *Pictorial Dictionary of Ancient Athens*, New York.

Troy VI = C. W. Blegen, C. Boulter, J. Caskey, and M. Rawson. *Troy IV: Settlements VIIa, VIIb and VIII*, 1958, Princeton.

Ulf, C. 1982. *Das Römische Lupercalienfest. Ein Modellfall für Methodprobleme in der Altertumswissenschaft*, Darmstadt.

Van Dyke, R. and S. Alcock. 2003. *Archaeologies of Memory*, Malden, MA.

Vermaseren, M. 1977A. *Cybele and Attis: the Myth and the Cult*, London.

Vermaseren, M. 1977B. *Corpus Cultus Cybele Attidisque 3, Italia-Latium*, Leiden.

Vermeule, C. 1995. "Neon Ilion and Ilium Novum: Kings, Soldiers, Citizens, and Tourists at Classical Troy," in *The Ages of Homer. A Tribute to Emily Townsend Vermeule*, ed. J. Carter and S. Morris, Austin, pp. 467–82.

Walbank, F. W. 1967. *Historical Commetary on Polybius II*, Oxford.

Wallace, S. 2003. "The Perpetuated Past: Re-Use or Continuity in Material Culture and the Structuring of Identity in Early Iron Age Crete," *BSA* 98, pp. 251–77.

Weinstock, S. 1971. *Divus Julius*, Oxford.

Williams, R. D., ed. 1960. *Virgil. Aeneis. Liber 5*, Oxford.

Wiseman, T.P. 1982. "Philodemus 26.3 G-P." *CQ* 32, pp. 475–6.

Wiseman, T.P. 1984. "Cybele, Virgil, and Augustus," in *Poetry and Politics in the Age of Augustus*, ed. T. Woodman and D. West, Cambridge, pp. 117–28.

CHAPTER SIX

THE SAME, BUT DIFFERENT: THE TEMPLE OF JUPITER OPTIMUS MAXIMUS THROUGH TIME

Ellen Perry

It is difficult to overestimate the importance of the Capitoline Temple of Jupiter Optimus Maximus in the lives of the people of Rome.[1] Most famously, triumphing generals sacrificed here at the end of the triumphal processions that followed victorious military campaigns, and the temple stored war spoils that had been dedicated by victorious generals.[2] This temple was also where consuls and praetors sacrificed and made vows to the gods on their first day of office (Ov. *Pont.* 4.4). During the Republic, consuls and praetors who were departing for their provinces, or to go to war, also made their vows here (so, for example, Livy 12.63.7–9 and 45.39.12).[3] And the Capitoline Temple also came to be the starting point for the procession associated with the *Ludi Romani* (*Ludi Magni*), an annual cycle of competitions (equestrian, chariot, boxing, wrestling, theatrical, etc.) in honor of Jupiter Optimus Maximus. These games expanded in scope from a one-day event (13 September, the foundation date of the temple) in the fourth century B.C.E. to something like half the month by the reign of Augustus.[4] The religious procession that kicked off the games followed a route that seems to have been a portion of the triumphal procession in reverse: from the Capitoline Temple down through the Forum and to the Circus Maximus. It consisted of young men of military age on horseback and foot, charioteers, athletes, dancers (serious and satyric – the latter literally, since they were dressed as satyrs), musicians (flute and lyre players), men with incense, carrying vessels of gold and silver and, finally, men carrying statues of the gods (D.H. 7.72.1–13). As one scholar has written, "Successive rituals and ceremonies repeatedly brought Roman society into contact with this sacred vessel of cultural and religious values."[5] Moreover, this repeated contact was sustained for some nine hundred years, from the construction of the building at the end of the sixth century B.C.E. to sometime before it was quarried for materials in the fourth century C.E.

The Temple

The Capitoline Temple also has great potential for illuminating our understanding of Roman ideas about imitation and emulation. There are several reasons for this – most famously, perhaps, the fact that, when it burned down, as it did in 83 B.C.E. and in 69 C.E. – there was a clear imperative to rebuild it closely following the model of the original.[6] This imperative may have derived, in part, from the conservatism of Roman religion. This was a religion, for example, that took elaborate steps to assure that the formula of a particular prayer was precisely followed (Plin. *HN* 28.10–11). For centuries, when a new ritual or foreign cult was introduced to Rome, a carefully delineated procedure involving the Sibylline Books had to be followed in order to render the innovation acceptable. Yet religious conservatism can only be a part of the explanation for the perception that the Capitoline Temple needed to remain "the same" throughout the ages. To judge from our sources, the need to reproduce the structure and contents of this particular temple was felt to an extraordinary degree. Other Roman temples that burned down and had to be rebuilt do not appear to have been under the same stricture. They underwent design changes that seem radical by comparison, the Pantheon being, perhaps, the most famous example.[7] Indeed, the very fact that ancient sources comment on the faithfulness of the Capitoline Temple reconstructions suggests that this was an exceptional structure. A similar place appears to have been reserved in the Roman imagination for the Hut of Romulus, which was also repeatedly restored to its former condition. (The Hut of Romulus, however, was restored without *any* improvements, as we learn from Dionysios of Halikarnassos, D.H. 1.79.) The fact that it was these two structures that were restored and reconstructed so conservatively suggests that it was, perhaps, the patriotic and legendary resonances of the temple that made accurate reproduction, or at least the perception of accurate reproduction, a priority.

Our sources make it clear that some changes to the Capitoline Temple were, in fact, permitted – and even deemed necessary or praiseworthy. One purpose of this chapter is to track how faithfully the Capitoline Temple, its contents and the contents of the Area Capitolina (the open area in front of the temple) were reproduced after successive destructions. Another is to determine the degree and kinds of changes that were permissible, and to consider what we know about the justifications and rituals that rendered those changes acceptable. For, to the Romans, a people who took elaborate steps to ensure that they did not deviate from the precise wording of a prayer, repetition was an essential mechanism in the construction of sanctity.

Individual restorations and improvements were, of course, made to the temple throughout its history. For example, the thresholds were replaced with bronze in 296/5 B.C.E., and a terracotta quadriga on the roof was replaced at the same time and with the same funding as the thresholds (Plin. *HN* 28.16 and 35.157). The new quadriga may also have been of bronze, though the evidence is not clear on this point. Gilded shields were affixed to the pediment of the temple in 193 B.C.E.; in 179 B.C.E. the columns were whitened – probably with stucco; and inlaid pavement was put down at about the time of the Third Punic War in 149–146 B.C.E. (respectively Livy 35.10, Livy 40.51 and Plin. *HN* 36). Still, it is the instances of complete destruction and subsequent reconstruction that allow us to detect an ideology; therefore, these moments will be the object of the present investigation.

We turn first to the destruction of the temple in 83 B.C.E. and its subsequent reconstruction by Sulla and Q. Lutatius Catulus. Dionysios tells us that Sulla's temple was built "on the same foundations" (ἐπὶ τοῖς αὐτοῖς θεμελίοις) as its predecessor, which is not terribly surprising because the reuse of original foundations will have been both practical and commonplace. More remarkable, though, is his assertion that the new temple differed from the old one only in the extravagance of the materials (τῇ πολυτελείᾳ τῆς ὕλης μόνον διαλλάττων τοῦ ἀρχαίου, D.H. 4.61). In other words, Dionysios seems confident that the temple of his day was identical in plan to the original temple (Fig. 6.1). Both the original and the first reconstruction had, as he describes, three rows of columns on the south front and one row on each of the flanks, and there were three contiguous cellas for the three gods housed here (D.H. 4.61).

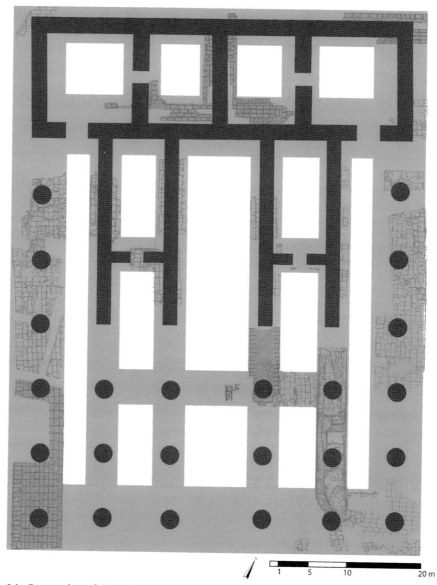

6.1. Rome, plan of the archaic Capitoline Temple. Drawing John North Hopkins, with his permission (after Mura Sommella 1998, Fig. 6).

From Livy we also know that Jupiter was in the center cella, Minerva in the right cella, and Juno in the left (Livy 7.3.5).

But if the temple was reconstructed "the same" after the fire of 83 B.C.E. it was, "the same but better." For example, the material upgrades to which Dionysios refers included gilded bronze rooftiles (Plin. *HN* 33.57).[8] In addition, a very good case can be made that the columns were replaced with marble.[9] At any rate, we read in Pliny the Elder that Sulla brought columns from the Athenian Olympieion "for the Capitoline shrine" (*ex quo Sulla Capitolinis aedibus advexerat columnas*: Plin. *HN* 36.45). Admittedly, there has been a great deal of debate about how precisely to interpret these seven words. Some have suggested that the columns came from the second century B.C.E. Olympieion – that is, from the reconstruction designed by the Roman architect Cossutius under the patronage of Antiochos IV, and that they were in some way incorporated into this first major reconstruction of the Temple of Jupiter Optimus Maximus.[10] Others, believing that it would have been too difficult for Sulla to dismantle columns that were already in place, have suggested that he only brought to Rome columns that had not yet been incorporated into the Olympieion. In a third alternative, scholars suggest that only the capitals were taken, and that these ultimately served as the paradigm for the Roman Corinthian order, which indeed closely follows a type exemplified by the Olympieion columns.[11]

However, R. Tölle-Kastenbein and the authors of the topographical dictionaries have even argued that the temple that was reconstructed after the fire of 83 B.C.E. cannot have incorporated the Olympieion columns because it was clearly a Tuscano-Doric structure. Their chief evidence comes from denarii from 43 B.C.E. depicting the temple with columns that do not appear to be Corinthian (Fig. 6.2). Starting from this numismatic evidence, they then suggest one of two explanations for the seeming contradiction of the textual and numismatic evidence. The first is that Sulla actually brought limestone columns from the original, Peisistratid Doric temple.[12] This, however, seems unlikely: The material from these columns had been cut up to go into the defensive wall that runs across the precinct of the Olympieion. Moreover, the surviving column drums are unfinished; presumably the capitals were also.[13] The archaic limestone columns will, in other words, have offered poor construction material, particularly considering that this iteration of the Capitoline Temple was afterwards famous for its lavishness. These same scholars have also suggested that perhaps the marble columns of the Olympieion were brought over by Sulla, who had every intention of

6.2. Denarius from 43 B.C.E. © The Trustees of the British Museum.

using them *capitolinis aedibus*, but that in the end they were never actually used.[14]

However, die cutters – and relief sculptors, as we shall see later – were largely interested depicting buildings so as to make them identifiable; neither had much interest in depicting them with complete accuracy. Therefore, "on many numismatic representations [sc. of buildings] the column style is indistinct."[15] The allegedly Tuscano-Doric columns on the denarius of 43 B.C.E. might well, therefore, simply be columns of indistinct order.

Perhaps, however, the most important evidence to adduce for the present argument is that Pliny's comment occurs in a passage of the *Natural History* devoted to the subject of marble. The temple Pliny describes, the one built by Catulus, was the one that Pliny himself would have seen up close during many of the rituals listed at the beginning of this chapter. He would have had many opportunities to examine the building up close and in person right up until it burned down again in 69 C.E. Under these circumstances, the chances are slim that he will have been mistaken about the material of the columns. Even if he was incorrect about the story of their origin – and I do not believe he was – he is unlikely to have been incorrect about the fact that these columns were made of marble.

One can easily imagine why Sulla would have wanted to use columns from the Olympieion in spite of any logistical difficulties posed by their transportation. Having seized and sacked Athens only a few years before, he may have seen the transfer of building materials to Rome as an opportunity to incorporate a symbol of his conquest directly into the fabric of the Capitoline Temple. The message will have been fitting for two reasons. First, columns from Athens's largest temple, dedicated to Zeus, will have become the columns of Rome's largest temple, dedicated to Jupiter. Second, this transfer of columns will have suited perfectly the temple's function as a symbol of Rome's leading role in the world. That the Capitoline Temple served as a vivid representative of Rome's imperial ambitions and patriotic pride requires little proof, since perhaps the best known function of the Temple was as the end point of triumphal processions. However, the archives and collections of the temple reiterated this triumphal and hegemonic message. Either on or near the temple were posted bronze tablets recording treaties between the Romans and foreign powers (Plb. 3.26; Suet. *Ves.* 8). Perhaps because they were the location for such treaties, the Capitoline Temple and the Area Capitolina were hotspots both for spoils of war and for dedications made by foreign cities and dignitaries.[16] The foreign dedications included statues depicting Roma and the Genius of the Roman People (for which, see below), extravagant objects such as bejeweled candelabra, and golden crowns of a size and weight that would have made them impossible for mere mortals to wear (Cic. *Ver.* 2.4. 28–32; Livy 2.22.6 and 43.6.6).[17] These massive gold crowns were dedicated during the Republic, but centuries later, upon the occasion of the Armenian King Tiridates' visit to Rome and submission to Nero, the emperor dedicated a laurel wreath to Jupiter. The message was clearly the same in the Empire as it had been during the Republic: Rome was and continued to be the acknowledged *caput mundi* (Suet. *Nero* 12).[18] After the fire of 83 B.C.E., therefore, an incorporation of the

Olympieion columns into the reconstructed Capitoline Temple will have allowed Sulla to make his own, impressive contribution to the message of Roman hegemony that was inextricably woven into the story of the Temple.

If the columns of the new temple were marble, however, the temple's epistyle continued to be constructed of wood. This is logical, given the temple's proportions, and it is attested in Vitruvius (Vitr. 3.3.5) who, writing in the late first century B.C.E., lists the Capitoline Temple among his examples of *araeostyle* structures, that is, structures whose intercolumniations are too broad to support a stone architrave.

The archaeological evidence suggests that, in the strictest sense, the changes after 83 B.C.E. were not only in the extravagance of the construction materials. At the very least, it seems that the podium of the building was raised by the addition of several courses of cappellaccio tufa.[19] We also have one literary testimonium to an attempt at improving the proportions of the temple after the fire of 83 B.C.E. Aulus Gellius reports that Catulus wanted to lower the ground level beneath the Area Capitolina, the open space in front of the temple, in order to make the podium higher and the proportions of the building more "correct." He was hindered, however, by the existence of certain storage chambers (*favisae*) beneath the area. These chambers, he tells us, were used to store statues that had fallen off of the temple, as well as other votive objects (Gell. 2.10).

Whatever the precise truth about substantive changes to the elevation of the temple, the crucial point is that the story the Romans told themselves was the one that we find in Dionysios, namely, that the only changes to the temple after the fire of 83 B.C.E. were enhancements to the lavishness of its materials. In the Verrine Orations, which were contemporary with this first rebuilding of the temple, Cicero addresses Catulus in an apostrophe that expresses approval for these material enhancements, even casting them as the reason why the gods allowed the temple to burn down in the first place:

> tibi haec cura suscipienda, tibi haec opera sumenda est, ut Capitolium, quem ad modum magnificentius est restitutum, sic copiosus ornatum sit quam fuit, ut illa flamma divinitus extitisse videatur, non quae deleret Iovis Optimi Maximi templum, sed quae praeclarius magnificentiusque deposceret.

> You must take pains to ensure that, just as the Capitolium itself was
> restored more lavishly, so it may be adorned more abundantly. In this
> way, the fire may seem to have had a divine origin, intended not to
> destroy the temple of Jupiter Optimus Maximus, but rather to require
> a more brilliant and splendid one. (Cic. *Ver.* 2.4.31)

This characterization of the new temple is, admittedly, colored by the
fact that Cicero's goal is to construct the most effective attack he can
on the rapacious governor Verres, who had intercepted for himself
a lavish candelabrum that a Syrian prince had intended to dedicate
to Jupiter Optimus Maximus. Still, the passage suggests that, at least
among some of Catulus' contemporaries, the material enhancements
to the temple were received positively. Not everyone saw them this way,
though – perhaps not even at the outset, and certainly not as time went
on. Pliny diplomatically tells us that the decision to gild the rooftiles
after the fire of 83, was "judged variously" [*varie existimaverit*] by Catulus'
contemporaries. This remark reflects the common Roman feeling that
the increase of *luxuria* in the late Republic was to Rome's moral detri-
ment. Imperial writers clearly included the Capitoline Temple in this
narrative: Seneca the Elder explicitly says that "As paupers, we had qui-
eter times. When the Capitol was gilded, we fought civil wars" (Sen. *Con.*
2.1.1). And Ovid opines that, in the good old days, Jupiter barely stood
in a narrow shrine (*angusta vix totus stabat in aede*) that he held a clay thunderbolt in his hand, and that the temple itself was decorated with leaves
(*frondibus*), rather than the gems (*gemmis*) of his day (Ov. *Fast.* 1.201–203).
From this imperial, moralizing point of view, the materially more magnificent second Capitoline Temple was not "the same, but better;" it was
actually "the same, but worse."

The Capitoline Temple burned down again in the civil strife between
the Flavians and the Vitellians in 69 C.E. Once again, the historical evidence reveals a sense of the imperative to rebuild the temple in some
way "the same" as before. Yet this narrative differs from the earlier one
in interesting ways. Tacitus tells us that the *haruspices*, soothsayers of
Etruscan descent who were brought in for the occasion, decreed that
the new temple should be constructed "in the same tracks" (*isdem ves-
tigiis*, Tac. *Hist.* 4.53). The *vestigia* of the temple embraced more than
just what we might call the footprint – indeed, in contexts where literary imitation is the topic, the term often means something like

"exemplum" or "model." So the *haruspices* were likely suggesting not just that the temple be rebuilt with a podium of the same dimensions, but that it be rebuilt in all respects following the previous temple as a model. That this meaning is intended by Tacitus seems to be confirmed by his subsequent clarification. The gods, he tells us, did not want the previous appearance (*veterem formam*) to be altered (*mutari*). This passage seems positively to argue against any change to this second reconstruction of the temple – even a change in the lavishness of the construction materials. Although piety will have required that the Flavian temple be as opulent as its predecessor, it is possible that decades of censorious reactions to the excessive *luxuria* of Catulus' upgrades made it, for the time being, impossible to construct a building that was still more extravagant.

Tacitus does modify his initial statements about the sameness of the Flavian temple, however, and he does so in ways that might give us material with which to think: "Height was added to the temple" (*altitudo aedibus adiecta*), he admits, because religious scruples permitted this alteration alone, and it was the feature deemed most to be missing from the grandeur of the earlier temple (Tac. *Hist.* 4.53). This weakness had evidently troubled the Romans for at least a couple of centuries, since Catulus was already trying to address it after the fire of 83. Evidently, then, in spite of the imperative to rebuild the temple as much like its predecessor as possible, this reconstruction was also "the same, but different." In this case, however, the salient difference permitted to the structure was thought to require an explicit exception, probably from the *haruspices* themselves.

The temple burned down yet again in 80 C.E. Unfortunately, we have no clear textual evidence that Domitian had it rebuilt on the same plan yet again, although it seems probable that he did. Plutarch, interestingly, saw the Pentelic marble columns of this last reconstruction before they ever left Athens – presumably while they were still in the quarry or while they were about to be shipped. He thought they were of fine proportion, but was subsequently surprised at how thin they looked when they were actually on the Capitoline Temple, a feature that he attributed to oversmoothing (Plu. *Publ.* 15.1–4). It is not impossible, however, that it was the enormous dimensions of the temple and the wide spacings between the columns that made the columns look so thin *in situ*.

6.3. Copy of a relief representing a religious ceremony in front of the Temple of Jupiter Optimus Maximus. American Academy in Rome, FU 13211, FU.Roma.IUPO.19.

In this third reconstruction, increased material extravagance was apparently, once again, permissible, since Plutarch tells us that Domitian spared no expense in the gilding of the temple. The wealthiest citizen of Rome could not afford that gilding, which Plutarch reckoned at more than 12,000 talents.

Some of the best preserved depictions of the Capitoline Temple in relief sculpture represent the Domitianic reconstruction. Figure 6.3 is a Trajanic relief depicting sacrifice in front of the temple; Figure 6.4 is the well known panel relief of Marcus Aurelius, probably from a triumphal arch, also depicting a sacrifice in front of the temple. We know that these reliefs depict the Capitoline Temple because on both of them the columns are recognizably Corinthian and the building has triple cella doors. In addition, the temple's pediment is preserved on the relief of Marcus Aurelius and includes, in the center, sculptures of Jupiter, Juno, and Minerva. Such depictions, therefore, offer a general notion of the building's appearance. M. D. Grunow has reminded us, however, of the pitfalls of using such reliefs to propose architectural reconstructions. The variations of detail even between these two reliefs include the number of columns, the spacing of the columns, the height of the podium, and the size of the architrave relative to the rest of the building.[20] The

6.4. Panel relief of Marcus Aurelius sacrificing before the Capitoline Temple, Musei Capitolini, Rome, Italy. © Erich Lessing / Art Resource, NY.

sculptors of these reliefs clearly had goals – like aesthetics and legibility – that were more important than mere photographic accuracy. In fact, because the Capitoline Temple was so well documented in textual sources, it is easier, at least in this one case, to recover some sense of the dimensions and proportions of the building from the textual sources than from the visual representations. From textual sources, we have a fairly precise notion of the temple's footprint – a notion that, incidentally, is largely supported by the evidence on the ground. We also know that Romans generally felt that, before the fire of 69 C.E, the temple was too squat for that footprint; and we know that, even after the Vespasianic reconstruction, the columns appeared overly skinny to some viewers.

Temple Contents

This fixed interest in reproducing the essential elements of the temple "the same" actually extended to the contents and decoration of the sanctuary. The Sibylline oracles offer perhaps the most famous example of temple contents that were lost in a fire and subsequently reconstituted. The original oracles were utterly destroyed in the fire of 83 B.C.E. along with Vulca's terracotta statue of Jupiter (Plut. *Mor* 379D). The Sibylline Books which, in legend, had been sold to Tarquinius Priscus and in history had been consulted in times of civic crisis, perished despite their being stored underground in a stone box.

After this event, Dionysios of Halikarnassos and Tacitus both inform us that Sibylline oracles were collected from many places – from Italy, Sicily, Ilion, Samos, Africa, Erythrai, and Asia. Dionysios informs us that an embassy was sent to Erythrai to make copies of their oracles. He also informs us that oracles were collected from elsewhere, when private citizens sent them in. Naturally, all of this oracle-gathering occasioned anxiety about the authenticity of the newly gathered texts. The priests – presumably the *quindecemviri*, since they were in charge of the Sibylline Books – were given the task of identifying which oracles were real, as Tacitus says "to the extent that they were able by human means." In this phrase, the sense of doubt about the results is palpable. Dionysios tells us that some of the verses were deemed unacceptable because they did not take the form of acrostics – a feature that was commonly taken as a sign of authenticity (D.H. 4.62, Tac. *Hist.* 6.12).[21] Ironically, acrostic oracles do not seem to pre-date the Hellenistic period, so none of the oracles that were judged authentic could have dated back to the sixth century B.C.E., when the original Sybilline Books are legendarily supposed to have been transferred to Tarquinius.[22] As E. M. Orlin has asserted, "There is no hint in our sources that the Senatorial commission was trying to find exact duplicates of the oracles which had been lost; rather it was searching for genuine Sibylline utterances. By the first century it was the divine source, the Sibyl, which gave the scrolls their legitimacy, and not the particular hand of the old woman who had visited Tarquinius Superbus. That set could be, and was, supplemented or replaced by any set of oracles which the Senate deemed to be authentically Sibylline."[23] Thus the oracles were replaced but, as a matter of necessity, not reproduced, and a body of religious officials had to be granted to authority to declare particular oracles authentic or inauthentic.

Epigraphic evidence provides another probable instance of reproduction, this time of the sanctuary's contents after the fire of 83 B.C.E. That fire must have destroyed, or at least badly damaged, many of the prestigious foreign dedications that had been made to Jupiter Optimus Maximus. These included a number of statues of the goddess Roma and of the Genius of the Roman People, which had been dedicated in the Area Capitolina, the open space in front of the Capitoline Temple, by various cities of Asia. In the nineteenth century, T. Mommsen gathered together a number of inscriptions attesting to these dedications, recognized that they belonged together as a group, and dated the inscriptions to the Sullan period.[24] A sample inscription reads

[- -POPVLVM R]OMANVM, COGNATVM, AMICVM, SOCIV[M]
[VIRTUTIS ET BENIVOLENT]IAEI BENEFICIQVE ERGA LVCIOS IN COMV[NE]

In fact, the physical similarities of the stone on which all of these dedications were inscribed (size, material, moldings, and lettering) later led A. DeGrassi to conclude that the inscriptions all belonged to a single monument, a large travertine structure that stood in the Area Capitolina and that may have served as a statue base for all of the dedications.[25] Finally, R. Mellor, who agreed with his predecessors about everything except the date of the dedications, argued convincingly that, although the inscriptions are Sullan in date, the contents actually refer to significantly earlier events. Some of the statues mentioned in the inscriptions were originally dedicated in the *second* century B.C.E., in gratitude for Roman benefactions of that period. This, in turn, means that although some of the first-century B.C.E. dedicatory inscriptions on this monument memorialize contemporary events, others are *re*-inscriptions, copies of dedicatory inscriptions from the previous century. It is, therefore, not at all unreasonable to suggest that the original dedications were destroyed or seriously damaged in the fire of 83 B.C.E., and that Sulla or Catulus undertook to reproduce the dedicatory inscriptions on a new, replacement monument that was erected near the new Capitoline Temple.[26] This, in turn, raises the intriguing question – which may never be answered – of whether Sulla or Catulus also undertook to reproduce the statues, the actual depictions of Roma and of the Genius of the Roman People, that are referred to in the inscriptions, or whether they were satisfied with reproducing the texts that had once accompanied those statues. Whether or not the statues themselves were replaced, the recreation of the inscriptions is consistent with the other evidence considered here and supports the assertion that the Romans felt a particular need to reproduce the contents of this sanctuary whenever they were damaged or destroyed.

The extreme lengths to which the Romans went to reproduce various contents of the Capitoline temple is further attested to after the fire of 69 C.E. Suetonius tells us that Vespasian undertook to replace the three thousand bronze tablets that recorded decrees of the Senate and information concerning alliances and treaties from throughout the history of the city (Suet. *Ves.* 8.5). As with the Sibylline Books over a century and a half earlier, the Romans undertook a search for the original texts in other locations [*undique investigatis exemplaribus*] before they attempted to reconstitute the lost texts. One wonders whether some senatorial decrees and foreign treaties may have been invented anew through the accident of poor memory.

So, the Romans clearly went to some effort to replace the Sibylline oracles, the statues to Roma and the Genius of the Roman People (or at least their inscriptions), and the bronze tablets that recorded treaties, alliances, and senatorial decrees. There is even some evidence, admittedly circumstantial, that the *imago,* or wax ancestor mask, of Scipio Africanus was replaced, with the blessing and aid of his descendants, after the major fires. Oddly enough, Jupiter's cella in the Capitoline Temple was also the location of this *imago* of Scipio, the great general of the Second Punic War. Most prominent families usually kept their ancestor masks in the atrium of the home, so Valerius Maximus interprets the presence of Scipio's imago in the Capitoline Temple as evidence that, in life, Scipio had considered the sanctuary to be a second home (V. Max. 8.15.1).[27] If we consider that the Sibylline Books perished in 83 B.C.E. – although they were in a stone box, under ground and under guard – and that the original cult statue of Jupiter made by Vulca also perished in that fire, what chance is there, then, that a wax mask would have survived this fire, or any of the subsequent fires? After all, the cult statue of Jupiter was in the very same room as Scipio's mask. Yet Appian, writing in the second century C.E., says that it is still the case (καὶ νῦν ἔτι) that the image of Scipio is carried from the Capitoline Temple in funeral processions (App. *Hisp.* 89)! This is not as inexplicable as it might at first seem: H. Flower, in her recent book on ancestor masks, asserts that, "Any relative, either by marriage or by blood, would normally be entitled to keep Africanus' *imago* in his or her atrium."[28] There must, therefore, have been a number of copies of Scipio's ancestor mask to hand, and it would not have been difficult to replace, even to replace repeatedly, the one that was in Jupiter's cella of the Capitoline Temple.

The Statue of Jupiter Optimus Maximus

The cult statue of Jupiter is a striking exception to the general rule that every attempt was made to replace the contents of the sanctuary with the greatest possible accuracy. For, in this case, the Romans seem to have been happy to replace the original schema with a type that had the greatest possible recognition around the Mediterranean world, namely, the Olympian Zeus by Pheidias. Not much is known about the appearance of the original, sixth-century B.C.E. statue of Jupiter Optimus Maximus. What we do know is that the original was made by the workshop of the Etruscan Vulca of Veii, that it carried a thunderbolt, and that on festival days it was painted red with cinnabar or *minium* (Ov. *Fast.* 1.201–203; Pliny *HN* 35.157).[29]

After one of the fires, probably that of 83 B.C.E., Vulca's terracotta cult statue was replaced with a work that imitated the Olympian Zeus: it was enthroned, and held a scepter in its left hand, and its upper body was largely nude except for a mantle draped over the left shoulder. Also like the Olympian Zeus, this statue was chryselephantine.[30] The evidence is fragmentary but ultimately persuasive that the fire of 83 B.C.E. was the occasion for the adoption of the new type. First, a few ancient sources may hint at the possibility.[31] Second, in this period the master sculptor, Pasiteles, produced an ivory statue of Jupiter for the Temple of Jupiter Stator in the Porticus Metelli (Plin. *HN* 36.40). Apparently, some contemporary Romans had a taste for such statues, and the technical expertise was available. In addition, because the fire of 83 B.C.E. was seen as an opportunity to use more extravagant materials for the temple itself, this seems the most likely occasion to abandon terracotta in favor of ivory and gold.

Two kinds of evidence are, however, particularly persuasive on the question of when the statue of Jupiter became Pheidian in its appearance. One is a denarius from Gaul, minted in 69 C.E. but before the fire that destroyed the Capitoline Temple in Jupiter of that year (Fig. 6.5). The denarius gives evidence of the Pheidian disposition, with Jupiter depicted according to the Olympian formula, and the legend reads, "I(uppiter) O(ptimus) MAX(imus) CAPITOLINUS."[32] Second, Pliny's discussion of the use of *minium* on the cult statue suggests that the statue was already chryselephantine when he was writing the *Natural History*. In two passages, he mentions that the face of the terracotta Jupiter was painted on festival days. Citing Varro, Pliny makes it clear with the word *ideo* that the ritual of painting the statue's face was logically connected to the fact that the figure was made of terracotta, *fictilem eum fuisse et ideo miniari solitum* (Plin. *HN* 35.157). Elsewhere, he relies on Verrius' quotation of earlier authors "whom one must believe" (*quibus credere necesse sit*) for the fact that the censors undertook to have the statue colored (Plin. *HN* 33.111). Pliny's citation of earlier authorities, along with the assertion that one must believe them, suggests that there is a great deal of chronological distance between him and the terracotta statue that was painted red on festival days.[33] He would surely not have cited Varro, or a list of authors in Verrius, for a ritual that he could have witnessed himself, had the statue still been terracotta right up until the fire of 69 C.E. Instead, it seems most logical to argue that the first-century B.C.E. statue was already Pheidian in style and material, and that the change of material had occasioned a change in ritual: neither the first chryselephantine statue nor its successors were painted on festival days, for the obvious reason that this will have been an inappropriate way of treating a material as precious as ivory.

6.5. Silver denarius from Gaul, 69 C.E. Reverse legend: I O MAX CAPITOLINUS. © The Trustees of the British Museum.

It appears, therefore, that one feature of the original, archaic temple that was *not* reproduced with fidelity after the fire of 83 B.C.E. was the terracotta statue by Vulca. The impulse to abandon the old type and follow Pheidias' example surely derived, in part, from the near-universal consensus that the Zeus at Olympia was a pinnacle of aesthetic achievement. A passage in Chalcidius' fifth-century C.E. commentary on Plato's *Timaeus* is striking for what it reveals about how a chryselephantine Jupiter was interpreted by later generations. Perhaps it can even give us some insight into the initial rationale for the adoption of the new type:

Ut enim in simulacro Capitolini Iovis est una species eboris, est item alia, quam Apollonius artifex hausit animo, ad quam directa mentis acie speciem eboris poliebat–harum autem duarum specierum altera erit antiquior altera: sic etiam species, quae silvam exornavit, secundae dignitatis est. illa vero alia, iuxta quam secunda species absoluta est, principalis est species, de qua sermo habetur ad praesens.

For, just as in the image of Capitoline Jupiter there is one Form which is made of ivory, there is another, corresponding one which the artisan, Apollonius, imbibed with his soul, and with reference to which, by the direct vision of his mind, he gave finish to the ivory Form. Moreover, of these two Forms the one will be antecedent to the other: the Form which beautified matter is of lesser honor. That other one, concerning which we currently speak, truly is the original one. (Chalcidius, commentary on Plato's *Timaeus* 338 C, p. 361, ed. Wrobel).

We do not know for certain if Chalcidius was describing the first-century B.C.E. statue, as some believe, or if he was describing its Domitianic replacement, the one he would have been able to see. Chalcidius's language and thinking in this passage reflect the ancient theory of *phantasia*.[34] This theory held that particularly gifted artists created their works after their visions or visualizations, which were divinely inspired and, in some fundamental sense, even true.[35] In many ancient texts, it was the Pheidian Zeus that served to illustrate this theory. Cicero, for example, had claimed that Pheidias, when he was creating his statue, "did not look at something from which he might trace a likeness; instead a vision of exceeding beauty settled in his mind. Examining this and remaining focused on it he guided his skill and hand" (Cic. *Orat.* 9).[36]

It was essential to *phantasia* theory that the artist's vision be divinely inspired. If it was, and if the subject matter was a god, the result would necessarily be a beautiful work of art that inspired reverence.[37] We therefore find Quintilian asserting that the beauty (*pulchritudo*) of the Olympian Zeus actually added something to traditional religious feeling (*adiecisse aliquid etiam receptae religioni videtur*, Quint. *Inst.* 12.10.9). Therefore, Catulus was not simply engaging in conspicuous consumption when he commissioned a chryselephantine Jupiter; nor was his desire for a Pheidian type likely to have been "merely" aesthetic. Rather, the theories that associated beauty with divinity suggest that reverence was also a genuine motivation for adopting the new statue type.

The choice to follow a Pheidian model was clearly considered a happy one. After Vulca's type was abandoned, subsequent replacements seem to have adhered to the Pheidian type. The evidence for the appearance of the cult statue after 69 C.E. is secured by a sestertius of Vespasian

6.6. Sestertius depicting the Temple of Jupiter Optimus Maximus, reign of Vespasian. American Academy in Rome, FU 4265 F, FU.Roma.IUPO.15.

(Fig. 6.6) which depicts the Capitoline Jupiter in the basic, Pheidian schema described above, although with his right hand he holds a thunderbolt in his lap instead of the Nike that was in the hand of the Pheidian Zeus. Again, it is quite clear from the numismatic evidence that the cult statue after the fire of 80 C.E., presumably a replacement, generally followed the schema of the Olympian Zeus. Once the Romans discovered the ideal formula for depicting their best and greatest god, they did not abandon it.

Emulation and the Construction of Sanctity

A detailed examination of the textual, numismatic, and art historical evidence clearly demonstrates that, although the Romans felt strongly

about the imperative to rebuild the Capitoline Temple in some significant way "the same" as it was before, what this actually meant in practice turns out to have been quite complicated. After the fire of 83 C.E.,
the plan remained the same but Catulus undertook to reconstruct the
building in more lavish materials. By contrast, after the fire of 69 C.E. and
in the wake of decades of discourse concerning the unfortunate *luxuria*
of the first reconstruction, the *haruspices* allowed no alterations except
to the one feature that had long been deemed lacking, the height of the
building. After the fire of 80 C.E., Domitian seems to have reconstructed
the temple for the third and final time in a manner that was even more
lavish than its predecessors.

After each of these fires, it was not just the temple itself that the
Romans reproduced: many of its contents, and the contents of the
Area Capitolina, were also piously replaced. Once again, some of these
replacements were fairly "exact," as was the case for the inscriptions
from the Area Capitolina and probably for at least some of the bronze
treaties. Sometimes, however, the replacements necessarily deviated
almost completely from the originals. This must have been the case for
the Sibylline Books: once these were lost, the imperative was to ensure
that Rome's ancient rituals could continue; and for this to happen, the
ideal of replacing the books with exact duplicates had to be abandoned
in favor of a looser policy that accepted any oracles that were deemed
authentically Sibylline.

All of this repetition – of architecture, cult furniture, and even, we
should remember, of the annual and occasional rituals associated with
the temple – goes to the heart of Roman identity. Repetition is, of course,
a way of establishing and reinforcing shared identity in any culture. But
it was a particularly important feature of Roman self-definition. It is no
accident that, in the city of Rome, it was precisely the Capitoline Temple
and the Hut of Romulus that were legendary for the scrupulousness
with which they were repeatedly restored. The rituals that took place at
the Capitoline temple – for example, the annual vows of office – under-
line the site's central importance to Roman identity. A similar employment of repetition to express and reinforce traditional values can also
been seen in Roman attitudes to family and ancestors. Rome, after all,
was a civilization in which an appeal to the *mos maiorum* functioned as a
sort of rhetorical trump card.

The essence of *aemulatio* was to repeat praiseworthy models, while admitting those few changes that could be staunchly defended as improvements. In this light, the few dramatic alterations that were willingly and wittingly introduced to the Capitoline Temple are particularly interesting, since these help to give us some idea of how change was rendered acceptable in a context where sameness was so essential to Roman identity. The lavishness of the temple materials after the fire of 83 B.C.E. clearly occasioned discomfort and disapproval, apparently among contemporaries and certainly among later generations. By contrast, the Romans seem to have been relatively comfortable with the fact that Vulca's original terracotta statue of Jupiter was not replicated at all after it was destroyed. Instead, from the first century B.C.E. on the statue in Jupiter's cella followed the model of the Olympian Zeus. The widespread acceptance of the new schema surely derives from the fact that Pheidias' statue was, by the middle of the first century B.C.E., already widely considered to be an exemplum of beauty, and therefore of religious piety. Similarly, the height of the temple was increased after the fire of 69 C.E., but only after a century and a half – at least – of discussion concerning the squat proportions of the building – and only after the *haruspices* approved of the change, specifying that it was the one feature of the building that might be altered. While the rhetoric of the Vespasianic reconstruction was all about how everything was reconstructed the same, this particular change will have reinvented the building rather dramatically, rendering it even more dominant than it had been in the overall landscape of the city. Such changes underscore the fact that even a location as conservative as the Capitoline Temple and a religion as conservative as Rome's allowed deviation from an original if that deviation was widely acknowledged as improvement.

Notes

1. I am grateful to all of the friends and colleagues who listened to or read early versions of these ideas and responded generously with their own suggestions. These include especially Bettina Bergmann, Mary Ebbott, Elaine Gazda, Caroline Johnson Hodge, David Karmon, Barbara Kellum, Michael Koortbojian, Eugenia Lao, Miranda Marvin, Bill Mierse, and Bonna Wescoat. Thanks, too, to colleagues who responded to specific inquiries of mine, including Ken Harl, John Hopkins and Tom Martin. The following article came to my attention too late for me to take it into consideration: M. G. Sobocinski, "Visualizing

Architecture Then and Now: Mimesis and the Capitaloine Temple of Jupiter Optimius Maximus," forthcoming in *A Companion to Roman Architecture*, ed. R. Ulrich and C. Quenemoen.

2. For a recent and comprehensive treatment of triumphal processions, see Beard 2007.

3. Orlin (1997, pp. 39–40) considers the question of whether the vows on the first day of office are different from those taken before departing for war or for a province. He concludes that they are.

4. Beard, North, and Price, 1998, p.137.

5. Stamper 2005, p. 83.

6. The temple also burned in 80 C.E., but after this fire our sources are less clear about the imperative to rebuild the temple along previous lines.

7. There has been, admittedly, a great deal of debate about the precise plan of the Agrippan Pantheon, which makes it difficult to measure the degree of innovation in the extant structure. For example, recent work strongly suggests that the Agrippan building had, like its successor, a north-facing façade, and that the columns of the *pronaos* had the same diameter and interaxial spacing as those of the later temple. Recent reconstructions have even suggested a round courtyard on the site of the later rotunda, but posit that this courtyard was open to the sky and encircled by something that might have been an ambulatory. There are other clear differences with the later structure, including evidence of a projection towards the south and, – as we know from textual sources – bronze capitals and a series of caryatids by Diogenes the Athenian that may have decorated the attic. For sources and a convenient summary of the evidence, see Haselberger and Romano 2002, p. 188.

8. This same passage informs us both that the interior ceilings were gilded after the fall of Carthage (146 B.C.E.), and that Catulus was responsible for gilding the rooftiles.

9. For the evidence in favor of stone columns on the archaic temple, see Hopkins (forthcoming).

10. See, most recently, Coarelli 2007, p. 34.

11. Wycherley 1964, p. 171. Winter 2006, p. 26, also appears to prefer the suggestion that only capitals were brought over. For a description of the particular features shared by the Olympieion capitals and by the Roman Corinthian order, see Winter 2006, p. 224.

12. Tölle-Kastenbein 1994, p. 152, Platner-Ashby 1929, s.v. "Iuppiter Optimus Maximus Capitolinus, Aedes;" *NTADAR*, s.v. "Iuppiter Optimus Maximus." *LTUR*, s.v. "Iuppiter Optimus Maximus Capitolinus Aedes (Fasi Tardo-Republicane e di Età Imperiale)" (S. De Angeli). G. Lugli (1946, p. 23) even describes the columns on the denarius simply as "Doric" which, strictly speaking, cannot be true, since they are clearly rendered with separately carved bases.

13. I thank B. Wescoat (pers. corr.) for these observations.

14. Indeed, there has been skepticism about whether the peristyle columns of the Hellenistic Olympieion were too large even for the Capitoline Temple. This has, in turn, led to speculation that perhaps smaller columns from the cella of the Olympieion were used. But at 1.92 meters in diameter, the peristyle columns of the Hellenistic Olympeion will actually have been a good fit with current estimations of the Capitoline column diameters. Hopkins (forthcoming) suggests

that the columns of the archaic temple were between 1.5 and 2.0 m. thick. And although it is tempting to try to make something of the plural *capitolinis aedibus*, and to suggest that perhaps the Athenian columns were intended for use on other buildings, it is difficult to imagine any *other* Roman temple of that time, whether on the Capitoline Hill or anywhere else in the city of Rome, that would have been large enough to incorporate the columns of the Olympieion.

15. Grunow 2002, p. 21.
16. Indeed, the clutter of military dedications was such that, in 179 B.C.E. a number of them, including shields that had been affixed to the temple's columns, had to be removed (Livy 40.51).
17. The bejeweled candelabrum mentioned in Cicero was, of course, intercepted by Verres, and we do not know if it ever ultimately found its way to the Capitoline Temple. Cicero (*Ver.* 2.4.30) makes it clear, however, that that candelabrum was just one of many foreign dedications that adorned the sanctuary "as the majesty of the temple and the reputation of Rome require" (*ut templi dignitas imperiique nostri nomen desiderat*).
18. On the symbolism of the Capitoline Hill as the head of Rome and therefore the *caput mundi*, see Gowers 1995.
19. Gjerstad 1960, pp. 176–7; Gjerstad 1962, pp. 174–7.
20. Grunow 2002, p. 26.
21. Dionysios tells us that the new Sibylline oracles were obtained from Italy, Erythrai and "private persons." Tacitus also mentions Italy and Erythrai, and adds that the search encompassed Samos, Ilion, Africa and Sicily.
22. Orlin 1997, p. 80.
23. Orlin 1997, p. 80.
24. Mommsen 1858, p. 206.
25. Degrassi 1962, pp. 433–8.
26. Mellor 1978.
27. For a consideration of the evidence, see Flower 1996, pp. 48–52.
28. Flower 1996, p. 48.
29. For a consideration of all the evidence for the appearance and treatment of the original statue, see O.-W. v. Vacano 1973, pp. 531–3. Even less is known about the appearance of the original statues of Juno and Minerva.
30. For evidence in favor of this suggestion, see Maderna 1988, p. 27–28; Lapatin 2001, pp. 123–4.
31. For a summary of these, see Lapatin 2001, pp. 123–4.
32. RIC I, revised edition (1984) pp. 213–14, nos. 127–129. Illustrations: RIC pl. 24.126 and BMCRE I, no. 70.
33. It also indicates that the ritual of painting the bodies or faces of triumphing generals, mentioned in Plin. *HN* 33.111, is in the far past. This has caused Beard (2007, pp. 232–4) to wonder about the accuracy of this passage as a source for the ritual of painting the triumphing general.
34. Lapatin 2001, p. 123.
35. For detailed descriptions of *phantasia* theory see Birmelin 1933a, Birmelin 1933b, Cocking 1991, and Perry 2005, pp. 150–71.
36. For another, even more detailed ancient example of the Pheidian Zeus as an illustration of *phantasia* theory, see Dio Chrys. *Or.* 12.
37. From the Hellenistic period on, many writers held that beauty in general, and the beauty of art specifically, symbolized the divine. See Rouveret 1989, pp. 402–5.

Works Cited

Beard, M. 2007. *The Roman Triumph*, Cambridge, MA.

Beard, M., J. North and S. Price. 1998. *Religions of Rome, Volume 2: A Sourcebook*, Cambridge University Press, 1998.

Birmelin, E. 1933a. "Die kunsttheoretischen Gedanken in Philostrats Apollonios," *Philologus* 88, pp. 149–80.

Birmelin, E. 1933b. "Die kunsttheoretischen Gedanken in Philostrats Apollonios (Fortsetzung und Schluss)," *Philologus* 88, pp. 392–414.

Coarelli, F. 2007. *Rome and Environs*, trans. J. J., Clauss and D. P. Harmon, Berkeley, CA.

Cocking, J. 1991. *Imagination: A Study in the History of Ideas*, London and New York.

DeGrassi, A. 1962. "Le Dediche di Popoli e Re Asiatici al Popolo Romano e a Giove Capitolino," in *Scritti Vari di Antichità*, Vol. 2, Rome, pp. 415–44.

Flower, H. 1996. *Ancestor Masks and Aristocratic Power in Roman Culture*, Oxford.

Gowers, E. 1995. "The Anatomy of Rome from Capitol to Cloaca," *JRS* 85, pp. 23–32.

Gjerstad, E. 1960. *Early Rome: Fortifications, Domestic Architecture, Sanctuaries, Stratigraphic Excavations*, Vol. 3. Lund.

Gjerstad, E. 1962. "The Etruscans and Rome in Archaic Times," in *Etruscan Culture: Land and People*, trans. Nils G. Sahlin, New York.

Grunow, M. D. 2002. "Architectural Images in Roman State Reliefs, Coins, and Medallions: Imperial Ritual, Ideology, and the Topography of Rome," Diss. The University of Michigan, Ann Arbor.

Haselberger, L. and D. G. Romano. 2002. *Mapping Augustan Rome, Journal of Roman Archaeology* Supplementary Series No. 50, Portsmouth, RI.

Hopkins, J. N. (forthcoming). "The Colossal Temple of Jupiter Optimus Maximus in Archaic Rome," in *Arqueologia della construzione, 2.I cantieri edili nel mondo romano: Italia e province orientali*, ed. S. Camporeale, H. Dessales, and A. Pizzo, Mérida.

Lapatin, K. 2001. *Chrystelephantine Statuary in the Ancient Mediterranean*, Oxford.

Lugli, G. 1946. *Roma Antica: Il Centro Monumentale*, Rome.

Maderna, C. 1988. *Iuppiter, Diomedes und Merkur als Vorbilder für Römische Bildnisstatuen*, Heidelberg.

Mellor, R. 1978. "The Dedications on the Capitoline Hill," *Chiron* 8, pp. 319–30.

Mommsen, T. 1858. *Annali del Istituto di corrispondenza archeologica* 30, 1858.

Mura Sommella, A. 1998. "Le recenti scoperte sul Campidoglio e la fondazione del Tempio di Giove Capitolino," *RendPontAc* 70, pp. 57–79.

Orlin, E. M. 1997. *Temples, Religion, and Politics in the Roman Republic*, Leiden and New York.

Perry, E. 2005. *The Aesthetics of Emulation in the Visual Arts of Ancient Rome*, Cambridge and New York.

Rouveret, A. 1989. *Histoire et imaginaire de la peinture ancienne*, Rome.

Stamper, J. W. 2005. *The Architecture of Roman Temples: The Republic to the Middle Empire*, Cambridge and New York.

Tölle-Kastenbein, R. 1994. *Das Olympieion in Athen*, Cologne, Weimar, and Vienna.

v. Vacano, O.-W. 1973. "Vulca, Rom and die Wölfin: Untersuchungen zur Kunst des frühen Rome," *ANRW* 1, 4.

Winter, F. E. 2006. *Studies in Hellenistic Architecture*, Toronto.

Wycherley, R. E. 1964. "The Olympieion at Athens," *GRBS*, Vol. 5, pp. 161–79.

CHAPTER SEVEN

MAPPING SACRIFICE ON BODIES AND SPACES IN LATE-ANTIQUE JUDAISM AND EARLY CHRISTIANITY

Joan R. Branham

The concept of "sacred space" has become a focal point for interdisciplinary inquiry in recent years, attracting the attention of historians of art, religion, gender, and ritual theory. A construct ripe for analysis, sacred space raises questions about the agency of architecture in choreographing ritualized bodies and the power of iconography in the formation of religious identities. Within the study of late-antique Judaism and Christianity, a number of scholars have shown that sanctity is constructed by no single process, but rather through a complex constellation and convergence of elements depending on geographical location, time period, and tradition. The presence of holy texts and images, the physical remains of revered individuals, the practice of healing or magic, and the performance of sacred words and actions all act as variable vehicles, both discursive and nondiscursive, toward establishing sanctity.[1]

In this inquiry, I would like to suggest an approach to the construction of sanctity by identifying one particular strategy operative and recurrent in late-antique Judaism and Christianity, and that is the textual and visual mapping of sacrifice from one sacred model to another distinct and disparate entity. I will argue that mapping, or theological cartography, reconstitutes spatial and corporeal entities by creating new legends and guides for viewers, readers, and liturgical participants, thus enabling them to interpret reconfigured spaces, bodies, and objects through alternative lenses. Late-antique Judaism and Christianity both draw upon formulations of sanctity, and more specifically sacrifice, that derive from ancient biblical and Jewish prototypes, namely, the Jerusalem Temple(s) and the Israelite Tabernacle, with the latter acting as an inherently portable and movable map particularly suited for mapping/colonizing new territories wherever it lands. While scholars in recent years have addressed examples of Tabernacle and Temple evocation in late antiquity and beyond, three enigmatic and understudied examples drive this paper's investigation of mapping sacrifice in these traditions.[2]

Mosaics of a late-sixth-century ecclesiastical structure, the Theotokos Chapel at Mt. Nebo in Jordan (Figs. 7.4–7.7), juxtapose *representations* of sacrificial space from the Jerusalem Temple with *actual* sacrificial space in the Christian altar area. Such typological associations between ancient Jewish sanctuaries and early Christian institutions are a common iconographical and literary trope, particularly in Patristic literature, rendering the church as the New Temple that displaces, eclipses, or fulfills the mission of its Jewish forerunners. How, in this example, does the sacrificial map of the Jerusalem Temple act as an orientation key or code for interpreting Christian sacrificial territory? And in turn, how does Christian sacrificial ritual and space recreate and revise the Jewish map?

In the second example, early Christian typology takes on a perplexing twist when texts describe certain groups of women – virgins and widows in particular – as accoutrements from Jewish and Israelite sacrificial stage sets. A number of Patristic writings from roughly the second through fourth centuries interpret women's bodies as Israelite sacrificial furniture or props, referring to women as "altars," "altars of gold," "altars of bronze," or "incense on the altar." What is at stake when sacrificial accoutrements from the Israelite Tabernacle are superimposed onto female Christian bodies, correlating Christian women and sacrificial paraphernalia?

Finally, and perhaps the main interpretative goal of this study, is the intriguing fifth-century Sepphoris synagogue (Figs. 7.8–7.13), excavated by Zeev Weiss and recently published in the final 2005 excavation report. The structure's mosaics explicitly depict Tabernacle sacrifice in the decidedly *nonsacrificial*, liturgical space of the synagogue. What strategies are at play when the sacrificial map of the Tabernacle is superimposed on the nonsacrificial territory of the synagogue?

While at first take, these three examples may seem somewhat disparate and unrelated in nature, they are in fact linked by their explicit reference to a common authoritative map – the sacrificial arena of ancient Judaism. In all of these examples, we must ask how evocations of sacrifice from Israelite and Jewish prototypes work performatively and cartographically to redefine late-antique spaces and bodies. What creative overlaps, as well as disjunctures and lacunae, emerge when incongruous mappings take place?[3]

Mapping. To introduce the notion of mapping, I begin in 1931 with the Polish-born mathematician Alfred Korzybski, who coined the phrase "the map is not the territory."[4] For Korzybski, founder of the discipline of General Semantics, this phrase expressed a fundamental premise that the word is not the thing it defines, the symbol is not the thing it symbolizes, and the map is not the territory for which it stands. Our access to reality – or territory – is through a set of perceptions – or maps – that only provide legends and keys to those territories. They are not the territories themselves.

This hermeneutical approach resonated with an array of contemporary thinkers and artists who were also working out representational systems, such as René Magritte in his painting *La Trahison des Images* (Fig. 7.1) of just two years earlier. Magritte's famous titulus, *Ceci n'est pas une pipe,* boldly reminds the viewer that the image of a pipe is not the object itself, but a visual map to the territory or reality it represents. One might speculate that much of art, at least representational art, operates in this way. Image is to object as map is to territory. Representational art, in many cases, functions as map.

Korzybski's thesis more directly influenced a number of historians of religion, most notably Jonathan Z. Smith in his 1978 groundbreaking book, *Map is Not Territory,* named after Korzybski's contribution. Integrating the map/territory dichotomy into the study of ancient cultures, Smith asserts, "We need to reflect on and play with the necessary incongruity of our maps before we set out on a voyage of discovery to chart the worlds of other men. For the dictum of Alfred Korzybski is inescapable: 'Map is not territory' – but maps are all we possess."[5] Here, Smith acknowledges the limits of the historian working with textual and material data – the maps – which function as intermediaries between the historian and the societies she examines – the territories.

7.1. René Magritte, La Trahison des Images (1929), oil on canvas. Los Angeles County Museum of Art. Digital Image © 2009 Museum Associates / LACMA / Art Resource, NY.

The following year, and in homage to Smith, Jacob Neusner in turn published his article, "Map without Territory: Mishnah's System of Sacrifice and Sanctuary" in *History of Religions* (1979).[6] In it, he sets up the Mishnah – a set of Jewish writings redacted in the second to third centuries C.E. – as a highly defined spatial and ritual road map to a territory now absent, the destroyed Jerusalem Temple. Neusner writes: "Mishnah maps out nonsense ... a territory wholly of the imagination, a realm of the unreal: *Not only is map not territory. Map is all one has, for now there is no territory*.... Our task now is to ask what it means to make maps of a forbidden city, to reflect upon an unattainable sanctuary, and to make rules on a sacrificial system none can carry out."[7] In other words, why even make a map to a nonextent territory unless that territory is acting with some sort of authority?

It is within this discourse of mapping that I would like to offer a related yet distinct approach to map and territory. I suggest that late-antique Jewish and Christian traditions construct sanctity through acts of textual and visual mapping that occur at subtle, multiple, and overlapping levels. At one level, mapping indicates the use of a sacred model – the map – as a guide or legend to another disparate entity – the territory – in order to read, understand, and interpret that secondary territory. At another level, mapping superimposes a particular map on a distinct territory in order to transform and radically reconstitute that territory. And finally, what I call reverse or boomerang mapping emerges when, in the process of superimposing an authoritative map on a territory, the original map itself undergoes reformulation in terms of the territory it occupies. Admittedly, these paradigms may seem quite complex and opaque at first, so I will try to unpack them in the following discussion. But the key here is that mapping is relational; the mapping of one entity by means of another redefines and reformulates spaces as well as the participants acting within them. Let us turn briefly to the Tabernacle and Temple maps first, and then to instances of iconographical and textual mapping manifested within territories of late-antique Christianity and Judaism.

The Tabernacle/Temple Map. Biblical and rabbinic texts describe both the Tabernacle in the Wilderness, or Hebrew *mishkan*, and the various Temple structures located in Jerusalem – the Temple of Solomon in particular – as consecrated spaces with a number of characteristics in common.[8] They are defined by physical dividers that do a number of things: detach these sacred structures from surrounding profane space, create courtyards with gradational sanctity, and mark the location of an ultimate sacred chamber – the Holy of Holies – endowed with the divine presence of the Shekhinah.[9] Exodus 25–28 and 35–40 are primary passages that describe the Tabernacle, while additional texts portray the Tabernacle as a model for other constructions, such as the Temple of Solomon (1 Kgs 6:2 and Chron. 3,4) and the temple vision of Ezekiel (Eze. 40–42).[10] These textual traditions construct the Tabernacle as an inherently movable map, functioning as "the house of Israel at each stage of their journey" (Ex. 40:38), able to define new territories wherever it drops anchor. The portability and sanctity of the Tabernacle allow the Israelites to place it anywhere, thus transforming and reconstituting preexisting territories into a new, Israelite sacred space. The intrinsic mapability of sanctity associated with the Tabernacle renders it, in many ways, as an ideal protomap for late-antique mapping strategies.

In both the portable map of the Tabernacle and the stationary Jerusalem Temple versions, a clan of priests, male gendered and

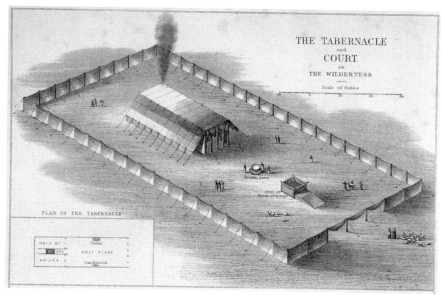

7.2a. Nineteenth-century lithograph of the Biblical Tabernacle in the Wilderness.
©Bridgeman Art Library.

THE TABERNACLE OF MOSES

All dimensions are in cubits. 1 cubit = 1 royal cubit = 20.67 inches.

7.2b. Diagram of Tabernacle and sacrificial accoutrements. ©Arnold vander Nat.

hierarchical, governs liturgical systems, administering the primary ritual of animal sacrifice.[11] The inventory of sacred objects populating the Jewish sanctuaries supports the practice of sacrifice, including a four-horned altar for burnt offerings, a golden altar for incense, a brazen water laver, a table of showbread, a golden menorah, a veil, and the Ark of the Covenant. A number of these elements have been represented

7.3a. Reconstruction of Herod's Jerusalem Temple. Model by Alec Garrard. © 2010 Tim Dowley Associates, London, England.

in visual sources, such as the nineteenth-century lithograph of the Tabernacle and the more recent reconstruction of the Tabernacle plan (Figs. 7.2a and 7.2b), as well as three-dimensional models and plans of the Herodian Temple in Jerusalem (Figs. 7.3a and 7.3b). As we will see in the three examples set forth for this study, these accoutrements emerge

Plan of Herod's Temple

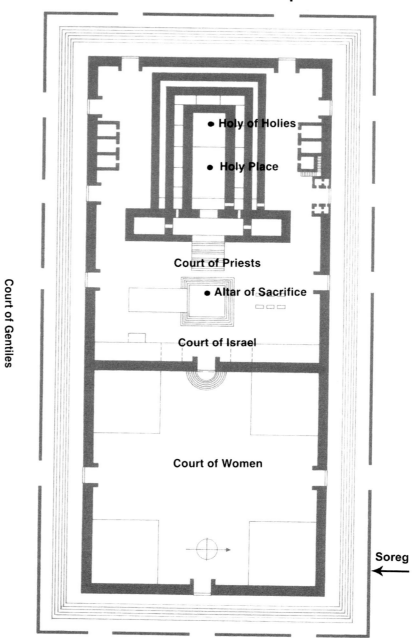

7.3b. Jerusalem, plan of the Temple. Adapted from A. Edersheim, *The Temple*, 1997.
©2010 Tim Dowley Associates, London, England.

as important indices of sacrality in late-antique strategies of mapping spaces and bodies within Judaism and Christianity.

Ecclesiastical Mapping. Typological strategies developed within Christianity act to appropriate, reinterpret, and reconstitute theological prototypes from the Hebrew Bible in Christianity's own key figures and stories. David the King prefigures Christ the King, Solomon the Judge anticipates Christ the Judge, Mary serves as an antidote to Eve, for some authors, and the whale that swallows Jonah and spits him up after three days predicts Christ's tomb, spewing him up for resurrection.[12] Typological readings take on particular power when they draw from sacrificial imagery. Isaac the sacrificial son foreshadows Christ the sacrificial son[13] and the High Priest who enters the Holy of Holies with animal blood heralds Christ the High Priest who offers his very own blood (Hebrews 9:7–12) – both of these latter examples serving as typologies of contrast and superiority, in the words of Harold Attridge.[14]

In addition to the rich tradition of viewing Hebrew Bible personages as archetypal models for New Testament figures, a hallmark of early Christianity is the typological association of early church edifices with the Tabernacle and Jerusalem Temple(s), rendering ecclesiastical space as a New Temple that alternately dethrones and supplants Jewish archetypes of sacred space. One such example appears in the late-sixth-century floor mosaics of the Chapel of Theotokos at Mount Nebo in Jordan (Figs. 7.4–7.6).[15]

Positioned in the apse in front of the altar and behind chancel screens, is the outline of an architectural complex approached by bulls and gazelles. In his 1941 excavation report, S. J. Saller interprets the building as a successor to the Israelite Tabernacle, the "temple of Yahweh in Jerusalem" destroyed in 70 C.E.[16] Comparing it to a ground plan taken from Francis X. Kortleitner's 1906 monograph on archaeology, Saller identifies the large fire as the Temple altar area set within a number of courtyards that also accommodate an inner edifice signifying the Holy of Holies (Fig. 7.7).[17] A Greek inscription in the mosaics draws from Psalm 51, "Then they shall lay calves upon your altar," and serves as a header for the entire composition, confirming the sacrificial content of the scene.[18] These images of Jewish sacrificial offerings, priestly courtyard, altar, and Holy of Holies, now embedded within a new Christian architectural context, function as interpretive maps or legends for

7.4. Mt. Nebo, Theotokos Chapel, detail of Jerusalem Temple in apse mosaic, late sixth century. By permission Franciscan Press.

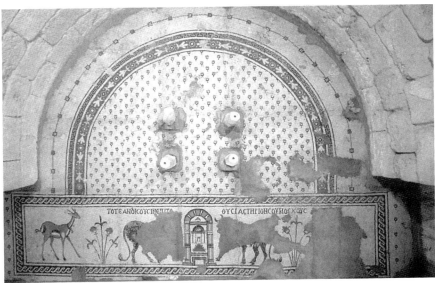

7.5. Mt. Nebo, Theotokos Chapel, apse mosaic, late sixth century. Courtesy of ACOR.

7.6. Mt. Nebo, Theotokos Chapel, apse mosaic, late sixth century. Courtesy of Evelyn Bazalgette.

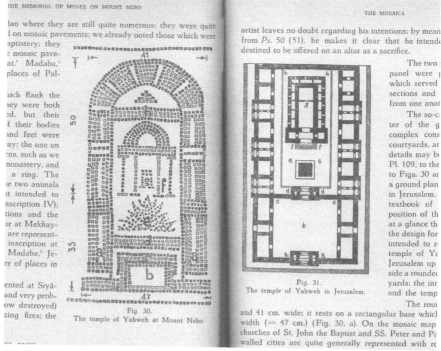

THE MEMORIAL OF MOSES ON MOUNT NEBO

lan where they are still quite numerous; they were quite
l on mosaic pavements; we already noted those which were
aptistery; they
: mosaic pave-
at,' Madaba,'
places of Pal-

iich flank the
iey were both
ed, but their
f their bodies
and feet were
ay; the one on
rns, such as we
nonastery, and
a ring. The
ie two animals
it intended to
nscription IV);
tions and the
ir at Mekhay-
are represent-
inscription at
Madaba,' Je-
er of places in

ented at Siyâ-
and very prob-
ow destroyed)
zing fires; the

Fig. 30.
The temple of Yahweh at Mount Nebo.

THE MOSAICS

artist leaves no doubt regarding his intentions; by mean
from Ps. 50 (51), he makes it clear that he intend
destined to be offered on an altar as a sacrifice.

The two :
panel were ;
which served
sections and
from one anot
The so-c.
ter of the g
complex cons
courtyards, ar
details may be
Pl. 109, to the
to Figs. 30 ar
a ground plan
in Jerusalem,
textbook of
position of th
at a glance th
the design for
intended to r
temple of Ya
Jerusalem up
side a roundec
yards; the inr
and the temp
The rour

Fig. 31.
The temple of Yahweh in Jerusalem.

and 41 cm. wide; it rests on a rectangular base whic
width (= 47 cm.) (Fig. 30, a). On the mosaic map
churches of St. John the Baptist and SS. Peter and Pa
walled cities are quite generally represented with rc

7.7. Saller's excavation report of Mt. Nebo comparing mosaic outline with Kortleitner's plan
of the Jerusalem Temple. By permission Franciscan Press.

deciphering the territory of the Christian altar and endow the Christian
edifice with an ancient, legitimate, and sacred pedigree. Moreover, the
strategic positioning of the Temple mosaic – behind the chancel screens
in Christian priestly space and underfoot as one enters the apse to stand
at the altar – literally constructs an iconographical and theological platform upon which the priest performs the Christian sacrifice.

Finally, reverse or boomerang mapping occurs, I would argue, in
the mosaic's depiction of Temple architecture. The Temple's rectangular courtyards are presented to the viewer through a rounded Roman
arch, thus morphing the outer framework and form of the Jewish map
to echo, mimic, and cohere to the curvilinear shape of the Christian
apse in which the Temple diagram appears. In this case, Mt. Nebo both
appropriates and transforms the pre-existent map, recreating it in its
own image.

While Mt. Nebo's use of imagery to relate one sacrificial space to
another provides us with what one might call relatively congruent

mapping – correlating object to object and space to space – some early Christian strategies take a more incongruous approach, as evidenced in written sources. Texts, like iconography, also function as guides to ritual and space, providing the religious participant with an alternative experience of religious architecture. In some cases, the same fundamental imagery of the Temple, altar, and sacrifice conveyed through visual means is also mediated via texts to serve as interpretative guides and maps for how human bodies can be read, moved, and understood in early Christian spaces. In this essay examining the construction of sanctity through the mapping of sacrifice from one entity to another, I now turn to the second case study, to texts from late antiquity that identify women's bodies – particularly widows and virgins – as sacrificial appurtenances and equipment from the ancient Israelite Tabernacle.

Christian texts from the second to the fourth centuries show varying degrees of association between women and sacrificial objects.[19] For example, the *Didascalia Apostolorum* recounts a detailed map of the Tabernacle sacrificial system from Numbers and then states, "widows shall be reckoned by you in the likeness of the altar,"[20] and widows "are the holy altar of God, of Jesus Christ."[21] The *Didascalia* also attempts to correlate the placement of the Tabernacle altar and the location of women's altar-bodies within Christian social space by instructing widows not to go from one domestic setting to another: "Let a widow know she is the altar of God … the altar of God does not go wandering about everywhere, but it is fixed in a single place."[22] Ironically here, the *Didascalia* subverts the Tabernacle altar arrangement, which *did* wander about in an itinerant system, thereby revising one of the defining characteristics of Israelite cult.

The *Apostolic Constitutions* depict widows and virgins as typological realizations of the Levitical priesthood,[23] but specify that widows represent "types" of the bronze altar that existed for burnt sacrifices in the Tabernacle, while virgins represent "types" of the golden altar for incense. Furthermore, the text expands the inventory of sacrificial accoutrements stating, "consider the virgins as a type of censer (*thymiatērion*) and the incense,"[24] thus portraying virgins as both the material vessel that accommodates the incense offering and the offering itself.

Finally, Methodius of Olympus (d. 311) reports one of the most explicit mappings of widows and virgins in relation to Israelite altars:

> Since the Tabernacle was a symbol of the Church ... it is fitting that the altars should signify some of the things in the Church ... the brazen altar to the company and circuit of widows; for they are a living altar of God ... but the golden altar within the Holy of Holies, before the presence of the testimony, on which it is forbidden to offer sacrifice and libation, has reference to those in a state of virginity, as those who have their bodies preserved pure, like unalloyed gold, from carnal intercourse.... Therefore, also, it stands nearer to God within the Holy of Holies, and before the veil, with undefiled hands, like incense, offering up prayers to the Lord, acceptable as a sweet savour.[25]

In this text a number of rhetorical strategies are at work. First, Methodius co-opts the sacred lineage of the Tabernacle by mapping it onto Christian entities. But unlike the Mt. Nebo mosaics – which correlate Israelite altar with Christian altar – Methodius creates an incongruous map, super-imposing sacrificial spaces and objects onto the territory of women's bodies. Second, this type of mapping reconstitutes and recreates women's bodies, in this case establishing a female taxonomy by likening widows to the bronze or brass altar, but virgins to pure, unmitigated metal used in the golden altar (mistakenly located by Methodius) within the Tabernacle's most sacred chamber, the Holy of Holies – which also happens to wear a veil. Third, a simultaneous and reverse mapping occurs as Methodius actually genders the Tabernacle altars by associating Christian women's bodies with these objects. Finally, in all these texts, the metaphoric pairing of Christian women and sacrificial space stands in ironic opposition to the developing relationship of women's *actual proximity* to literal spaces used for Eucharistic sacrifice – a relationship defined by growing exclusion and marginalization.[26] The texts set up an analogy between church altars, controlled increasingly by male bishops and presbyters, to widows and virgins, who – as symbolic altars – may be interpreted to fall under the same control and dominion as their inanimate counterparts.[27]

Synagogue Mapping. While early Christian authors and church builders stake out sacred ancestry through the appropriation and mapping of Hebrew Bible prototypes, the recapitulation of Tabernacle and Temple traditions in late-antique synagogues is a somewhat more complicated endeavor. The late-antique synagogue has been interpreted by many scholars as a radical shift in ancient Jewish worship, leaving behind the hierarchical and sacrificial system of the destroyed Temple for a more communal, nonsacrificial one. Instead of highly defined courtyards governed by purity regulations, gender, and priestly status, early synagogue architecture is often characterized as common assembly space in a single hall where the reading of scripture, recitation of prayers, and delivery of sermons take place.[28] In the synagogue of late antiquity there is no priesthood, no altar, and no sacrifice. So what is at work when the sacrificial map of the Tabernacle is superimposed upon the nonsacrificial territory of the synagogue? How does the "memory" of sacrificial images work in the self-definition and identity formation of late-antique Judaism?[29]

The fifth-century Sepphoris synagogue (Fig. 7.8) located in the Galilee provides us with a thought-provoking example. In 1993 a bulldozer clearing a parking lot for a national park dug into the wall of the synagogue's upper northeast section and revealed a rectangular synagogue with a long congregational gathering space flanked by an eastern side aisle. Participants would have entered through a door in the southwest corner of the building (Fig. 7.9–7.10) and moved in a longitudinal direction toward the focal part of the building, the bema, or raised platform where the reading of Torah took place.[30] The discovery also uncovered extensive floor mosaics with figural representations, including the Akedah or Binding of Isaac, a sun disk in the center of a zodiac, lions, menorot flanking a, and – in an unprecedented manner – detailed sacrificial images from the Tabernacle tradition (Figs. 7.11–7.12a–c). Prominently displayed in two large panels located close to the bema, Aaron, the High Priest, officiates at a four-horned altar with various sacrificial accoutrements including a water basin, incense shovels, flour, oil, showbread table, and basket of first fruits. Inscriptions cite textual passages from the book of Numbers identifying the animals as the first and second sacrifices of the day within a narrative that consecrates the Tabernacle and priesthood of Aaron and his sons.[31]

The discovery of these elaborate synagogue mosaics has evoked commentary from a number of scholars. The excavator Zeev Weiss argues that all the panels make up a single and unified iconographic theme of "God's promise to Abraham." He states,

> The ... combination (of scenes) represents man's basic needs – bread, fruit, and meat – and within the context of this structured iconographic

7.8. Sepphoris, synagogue, view of excavated floor mosaic, fifth century. Courtesy of Prof. Zeev Weiss, The Sepphoris Excavations, The Hebrew University of Jerusalem. Photo Gabi Laron.

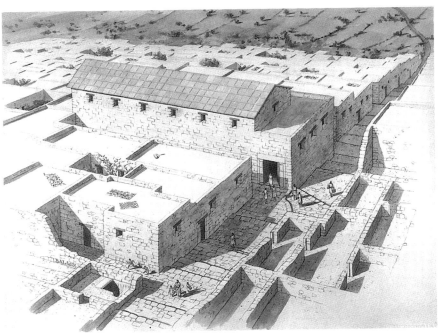

7.9. Sepphoris, synagogue, view of reconstructed exterior and entrance, fifth century. Courtesy of Prof. Zeev Weiss, The Sepphoris Excavations, The Hebrew University of Jerusalem. Drawing Balag.

scheme, conveys a clear eschatological message. These elements were selected ... to express the hope that just as God had filled the world with abundance in the past, by virtue of the Temple cult, so would He redeem His people in the future ..., rebuild the Temple, cause the Shekhina to dwell there, and return prosperity to the world. This eschatological message, which expresses the world view and religious aspirations of the Jews of the Land of Israel, is a theme that runs throughout the rich fabric of the entire mosaic.[32]

Alternatively, Lee Levine has suggested that no one overall program governs the floor, but that diverse registers may represent "a different sequence of ideas (covenant, creation, and redemption), a series of separate and independent themes, or certain liturgical motifs."[33] Steven Fine brings texts and images together and relates certain parts of the synagogue floor to liturgical poetry, piyyutim, but does not pursue the question of the sacrificial imagery.[34] Moreover, Fine writes in 2005 of the Sepphoris mosaics, "We would barely notice the pavement below, covered with furniture and perhaps with reed mats," literally sweeping the mosaics under the rug.[35]

7.10. Sepphoris, synagogue, view of reconstructed interior, fifth century. Courtesy of Prof. Zeev Weiss, The Sepphoris Excavations, The Hebrew University of Jerusalem. Drawing Balag.

Most treatments of the Sepphoris synagogue have surprisingly side stepped or neglected any in-depth inquiry into the function of explicit sacrificial imagery and its impact on synagogue space, or its relationship to contemporary Christian practices of depicting Temple and Tabernacle sacrifice within liturgical spaces. Here I would like to offer an

7.11. Sepphoris, synagogue plan with highlighted sacrificial panels, fifth century. Courtesy of Prof. Zeev Weiss, The Sepphoris Excavations, The Hebrew University of Jerusalem. Drawing Pnina Arad.

7.12a. Sepphoris, synagogue, detailed drawing of central, sacrificial mosaic panels, fifth century. Courtesy of Prof. Zeev Weiss, The Sepphoris Excavations, The Hebrew University of Jerusalem. Drawing Pnina Arad.

examination of Sepphoris's Tabernacle motifs within the larger theoretical framework of mapping, as we have witnessed in other late-antique settings, to open a new set of questions for consideration.

The Sepphoris mosaics employ discursive and nondiscursive elements – images juxtaposed with scriptural quotations – to map out the Tabernacle's sacrificial system and priesthood of Aaron. At one level, these prominent depictions might be interpreted as giving a seal of authority to ancient Tabernacle traditions and priestly hierarchy, as well as their continued legitimacy into the late-antique period. A growing number of scholars – Jodi Magness, Paul Flesher, Beverly Mortensen,

7.12b. Sepphoris, synagogue mosaics, sacrificial panel with Aaron, altar, water basin, and sacrificial animals, fifth century. Courtesy of Prof. Zeev Weiss, The Sepphoris Excavations, The Hebrew University of Jerusalem. Photo Gabi Laron.

and others – have recently suggested that priestly influence was more extensive than thought before, especially after Julian the Apostate's promise to rebuild the Temple in the fourth century C.E.[36] They have shown that priests used visual art and Targumim to establish their historic and future status in the local Jewish communities of ancient Palestine and in the Diaspora. Indeed, a dedicatory inscription that significantly appears directly beside the Tabernacle panel in the side aisle at Sepphoris cites a priestly family, "Remembered be for good Yudan son of Isaac the Priest and Parigri his daughter. Amen. Amen," lending weight to priestly presence in this community (Fig. 7.13).[37] This interpretation of the Tabernacle map would posit the Sepphoris mosaics as a territory partially defined by priestly patrons and power in late-antique Galilee. A performative-art theory approach would further nuance the ways in which images work and suggest that the *representation* of priestly

7.12c. Sepphoris, synagogue, sacrificial animal and objects (incense shovels, flour, oil, showbread table, basket of first fruits), fifth century. Courtesy of Prof. Zeev Weiss, The Sepphoris Excavations, The Hebrew University of Jerusalem. Photo Gabi Laron.

sacrifice actually acts to *perform* priestly sacrifice in this space, which otherwise would be void of explicit sacrificial ritual. Actual sacrifice is absent, yet still made present iconographically. Tabernacle sacrifice is, one might say, under erasure, visually asserted, yet liturgically denied.[38] This dichotomy of simultaneous affirmation and absence could be seen as operating in a similar manner to Magritte's representation of a pipe. The image of sacrifice evokes sacrifice, but is not sacrifice, it is a map to another sacrificial territory and reality. *Ceci n'est pas sacrifice.*

Examining the Sepphoris mosaics within a comparative framework to contemporaneous Christian settings provides us with yet another reading of the iconography.[39] The Christian chapel at Mt. Nebo and the

7.13. Sepphoris, synagogue, dedicatory priestly panel of Yudan and Parigri, fifth century.
Courtesy of Prof. Zeev Weiss, The Sepphoris Excavations The Hebrew University of Jerusalem.
Photo Gabi Laron.

synagogue at Sepphoris – located just seventy-five miles apart and dated
to within a century of each other – both harness Temple/Tabernacle
sacrificial iconography, but to new and distinct ends. First, there is a
significant difference in the placement or *mise-en-scène* of Tabernacle
iconography in these buildings. In the Christian sacrificial space,
Temple iconography is set behind chancel screens where only priests
tread, mutually reinforcing the exclusive character of both Jewish and
Christian sacrificial space, further legitimating the hierarchy of the
priesthood in the church. At Sepphoris, however, priestly and sacrificial iconography extends into the wider, communal, and altar-less space
of the congregation. In this sense, the Tabernacle map lends its sacred
memory and presence to the larger space of the late-antique synagogue
itself. Mapping Tabernacle imagery in the synagogue does not merely
provide a seal of approval to priestly heritage and power, it supplies a
stamp of authority and sanctity to the emergent institution of the synagogue, its space, liturgy, and nonpriestly officiants. The Tabernacle map
provides a key for legitimizing and endorsing synagogue territory.[40]

Unlike Christian Nebo, then, we imagine crowds of synagogue participants accessing and standing on the foundational images of the Tabernacle and its priesthood, as well as other images from the Bible and liturgical texts, forging a new association among synagogue participants, sacrificial iconography, liturgical space, and sacred scripture. Drawing from ritual theorists, like Catherine Bell, we can interpret such sacrificial imagery as producing ritualized bodies "through the interaction of the body with a structured and structuring environment."[41] As synagogue participants without priestly origins occupy the image of Aaron, they figuratively fill the shoes of the old hierarchical priesthood, replacing them with more communal-oriented synagogue systems. In the words of Shaye Cohen, Temple "sacrificial cult could be supplemented or replaced by democratic alternatives" in the synagogue.[42] Such occupation might also be read as reverse mapping, transforming and reworking ancient, elite Israelite models of worship by visually synthesizing/working them into the more communal, non-hierarchical liturgy and structure of the synagogue. The strategic mapping of Tabernacle sacrificial imagery in communal, congregational space is theological cartography in action, that is to say, the actual organizing, defining, laying out, and identity-making of late-antique synagogue territory.

回圙圙

In this essay, I have attempted to tease out textual and visual strategies of mapping as one method, among many, of constructing sanctity within late-antique Judaism and Christianity. The two examples from Christianity presented here reveal the employment and deployment of Tabernacle/Temple sacrificial motifs in an effort to interpret, reconstitute, and forge new spaces and bodies within Christian communities in terms of sacred prototypes. Likewise, the Tabernacle sacrificial map also emerges in late-antique Judaism, reformulated through synagogue space, liturgical actions, texts, and prayers. Post-Temple Judaism, i.e., postsacrificial Judaism, deliberately utilizes sacrificial imagery for a variety of purposes as it struggles to define itself in terms of its own sacred and sacrificial past, as well as its relationship to Christian neighbors who maintain sacrificial systems based on Hebrew Bible prototypes – priesthood, altar, sacrifice – in nearby ecclesiastical struc-tures. Synagogue imagery of Tabernacle sacrifice works to construct and reclaim its own sacred heritage by use of preexistent maps. Finally, we have seen that while mapping involves the identification with and recapitulation of sacred histories, late-antique traditions employ reverse mapping by revising the original Tabernacle and Temple maps they are evoking in order to imprint them with new theological interpretations and realities.

Notes

1. I am indebted to the Women's Studies in Religion Program at Harvard Divinity School for support while writing this essay in 2007–2008, and to the Research Associates for their feedback on initial drafts. I also thank the following for pro-viding further critical feedback: Jonathan Brumberg-Kraus, Michael Anthony Fowler, David Frankfurter, Sean Freyne, Andrew McGowan, Laura Nasrallah, Mariah Proctor-Tiffany, and Lawrence Wills.
2. A number of scholars have addressed late-antique and medieval typological rep-resentations of the Tabernacle and Temple within the visual arts. For example, see Lundquist 2008; Kessler 1990–1991; Ousterhout 1990; Kühnel 1986–1987; Rosenau 1979; Comay 1975; Krinsky 1970.
3. This appropriation and reclaiming of ancient sacred histories might alterna-tively be thought of, in the words of Eric Gruen, as "ancient identity theft." Gruen comments, "… ancient societies reconstructed their past or conceived their cultural identity … by associating themselves with the history, achieve-ments, and legends of other societies…. It discloses not how they distinguished themselves from other cultures and peoples but how they transformed or rei-magined them in their own terms. The "Other" takes on quite a different shape. This is not rejection, denigration, or distancing, but rather appropriation. It represents a more ingenious, creative, and complex mode of fashioning a col-lective image," Gruen, 2007, pp. 6–8.
4. Korzybski's paper, "A Non-Aristotelian System and its Necessity for Rigour in Mathematics and Physics," was initially presented on 28 December 1931 for the American Mathematical Society meeting at the larger American Association for the Advancement of Science, and then later printed in Korzybski 1933, p. 750.
5. Smith 1978, p. 309.
6. Neusner 1979.
7. Neusner 1979, pp. 110–12, emphasis is Neusner's.
8. See Hamblin and Seely 2007; Levenson 1986; Ritmeyer 2006; Goldhill 2005; Eliav 2005; Roitman 2003.
9. Branham 2006a.
10. For a review of scholarly debates about the literary or historical basis for the Tabernacle, see Friedman 1980, pp. 241–8; also Strong 1987, pp. 8–10.
11. See Wegner (1999) on spatial limits of women in the Tabernacle.
12. On Christian typology and supersessionism, see, for example, Goppelt 1982; Skarsaune 2002; Charity 1987; Klawans 2005.
13. Levenson 1995, p. 200.
14. See Attridge 1989, p. 36; also Salevao 2002, p. 345; Coloe 2001.

15. For earlier treatments of this mosaic, its relationship to chancel screens, and the employment of Tabernacle/Temple iconography, see Branham 1992. For subsequent discussions, see Kessler 2000; Branham 2002.

16. Saller 1941, p. 235. Also see Piccirillo 1993, p. 151.

17. Saller takes the plan from Kortleitner 1906, p. 36. Kortleitner labels this plan the Temple of Solomon. But Saller identifies it as the Jerusalem Temple destroyed in 70 C.E.

18. Saller also traces these words to a fourth-century Greek liturgical text of Jerusalem. Saller 1941, pp. 235–8, 254–5. See my discussion of this mosaic in the larger context of early Christian sacred spaces in Branham 1992, pp. 381–2.

19. I have discussed these and other texts in relation to early Christian women and ecclesiastical space in Branham 2006b. A few relevant texts include: Polycarp: "Our widows must be sober-minded … making intercession without ceasing for all men … abstaining from … every evil thing, knowing that *they are God's altar, and that all sacrifices are carefully inspected*" (my emphasis). See *Epistle to the Philippians* 4.3; Lightfoot 1885, I, p. 585 and Camelot 1951, pp. 208–9, n.3. Polycarp echoes 1 Timothy's description of widows who offer supplications night and day, framing contemporary widows as intermediary agents between God and people, as sacrificial tables, and as offerings to be carefully examined for blemishes. See Gryson and Daniélou on widows who receive alms and offerings, like an altar, and send uninterrupted prayers to God just as smoke rises from sacrifice; Gryson 1976, p. 13, Daniélou 1961, p. 18. Also see Tertullian's third-century comparison of ordained widows to the purity of sacrificial altars and dissuasion of widows from second marriages: "it behooves God's altar to be set forth pure." *Ad Uxorem*, 1.7.4 (*CCSL* 1.381); Coxe 1994, IV, p. 43, also quoted in Gryson 1976, p. 21.

20. *Didascalia Apostolorum* 2.26.8 (Syr. 9); Funk 1905, p. 104; Connolly 1929, p. 88.

21. *Didascalia Apostolorum*, 3.10.7 (Syr. 15); Funk 1905, p. 204, Connolly 1929, p. 143.

22. *Didascalia Apostolorum* 3.6.3 (Syr. 15); Funk 1905, p. 190, Connolly 1929, p. 133. See also Gryson 1976, p. 58.

23. Gryson 1976, p. 58.

24. *Apostolic Constitutions*, 2.26.8; Funk 1905, pp. 104–5; Gryson 1976, p. 59.

25. *Apostolic Constitutions*, 5.8.

26. See Branham 2006b, pp. 373–82.

27. See work of Cardman 1999; also see Osiek 1983.

28. Levine 2000, p. 169.

29. For an art historical approach to the ways in which self-definition and cultural identity are formed in the communities of Dura Europos, see Elsner 2007, pp. 254–88.

30. Weiss 2005, pp. 40–3.

31. Weiss 2005, p. 55.

32. Weiss and Netzer 1998, p. 38. Also see a similar interpretation in Weiss 2005, p. 255.

33. Levine 2000, 610.

34. Fine 1999.

35. Fine 2005, pp. 188–9.

36. See Levine's discussion (2000) of current scholarship on the priestly class and dominance, p. 520. Mortensen and Flesher argue that the priests came into

prominence because of Julian the Apostate, and that they wrote the fourth-century Targum Pseudo-Jonathan as a handbook for their own profession. See for example, Mortensen 2006; Flesher 2003, pp. 467–508; also see Magness' work in connection with the Dura synagogue in this volume.

37. At Sepphoris, of the twenty dedicatory inscriptions preserved, a priest and a Levite are mentioned once. See Weiss 1998, pp. 203–4.

38. For a full discussion of erasure and its usefulness in reading synagogue images and spaces, see Branham, 1992.

39. Some Christian remains have been discovered in Sepphoris, see Freyne 2000; also see Netzer and Weiss 1995, pp. 164–76; Netzer and Weiss 1996, pp. 29–38.

40. I have tried to show elsewhere that the endeavor to work out the relationship of synagogue space to ancient Tabernacle and Temple space involves a certain amount of anxiety and ambivalence, as manifested in rabbinic sources and synagogue iconography. See Branham 1992, 1995.

41. Bell 1992, p. 98.

42. Cohen 1999, pp. 162, 163, 168, 170.

Works Cited

Attridge, H. W. 1989. *Hebrews: A Commentary on the Epistle to the Hebrews* (Hermeneia), Philadelphia.

Bell, C. 1992. *Ritual Theory, Ritual Practice*, New York.

Branham, J. R. 2006a. "Penetrating the Sacred: Breaches and Barriers in the Jerusalem Temple," in *Thresholds of the Sacred: Architectural, Art Historical, Liturgical, and Theological Perspectives on Religious Screens, East and West*, ed. S. Gerstel, Cambridge, MA, pp. 6–24.

Branham, J. R. 2006b. "Women as Objects of Sacrifice? An Early Christian 'Chancel of the Virgins'," in *La Cuisine et l'Autel: Les Sacrifices en Questions dans les Sociétés de la Méditerranée Ancienne*, ed. S. Georgoudi, R. K. Piettre, and F. Schmidt, Turnhout, pp. 371–86.

Branham, J. R. 2002. "Bloody Women and Bloody Spaces: Menses and the Eucharist in Late Antiquity and the Early Middle Ages," *Harvard Divinity Bulletin* 30, pp. 15–22.

Branham, J. R. 1995. "Vicarious Sacrality: Temple Space in Ancient Synagogues," in *Ancient Synagogues: Historical Analysis and Archaeological Discovery*, vol. 2, ed. D. Urman and P. V. M. Flesher, Leiden, pp. 319–45.

Branham, J. R. 1992. "Sacred Space Under Erasure in Ancient Synagogues and Early Churches," *The Art Bulletin* 74, pp. 375–94.

Camelot, P. Th. 1951. *Ignace d'Antioche, Polycarpe de Smyrne: Lettres, Martyre de Polycarpe*, SC 10/2, Paris.

Cardman, F. 1999. "Women, Ministry and Church Order in Early Christianity," in *Women and Christian Origins*, ed. R. S. Kraemer and M. R. D'Angelo, New York, pp. 300–29.

Charity, A. C. 1987. *Events and Their Afterlife: The Dialectics of Christian Typology in the Bible and Dante*, Cambridge, pp. 83–102.

Cohen, S. 1999. "The Temple and the Synagogue," in *The Cambridge History of Judaism*, vol. 3, The Early Roman Period, ed. W. Horbury, W. D. Davies, and J. Sturdy, Cambridge, pp. 922–90.

Coloe, M. L. 2001. *God Dwells with Us: Temple Symbolism in the Fourth Gospel*, Collegeville, MN.

Connolly, R. H. 1929. *Didascalia Apostolorum: The Syriac Version Translated and Accompanied by the Verona Latin Fragments*, Oxford.

Comay, J. 1975. *The Temple of Jerusalem*, New York.

Coxe, C. (ed.). 1994. *Ante-Nicene Fathers*, Peabody, MA.

Daniélou, J. 1961. *The Ministry of Women in the Early Church*, New York.

Eliav, Y. 2005. *God's Mountain: The Temple Mount in Time, Space, and Memory*, Baltimore.

Elsner, J. 2007. *Roman Eyes: Visuality and Subjectivity in Art and Text*, Princeton.

Fine, S. 2005. *Art and Judaism in the Greco-Roman World*, Cambridge.

Fine, S. 1999. "Art and the Liturgical Context of the Sepphoris Synagogue Mosaic," in *Galilee Through the Centuries: Confluence of Cultures*, ed. E. M. Meyers, Winona Lake, IN, pp. 227–238.

Flesher, P. V. M. 2003. "The Literary Legacy of the Priests? The Pentateuchal Targums of Israel in their Social and Linguistic Context," in *The Ancient Synagogue from its Origins Until 200* C.E., ed. B. Olsson and M. Zetterholm, Stockholm, pp. 467–508.

Freyne, S. 2000. "Christianity in Sepphoris and in Galilee," in *Galilee and Gospel* (Wissenschaftliche Untersuchungen zum Neuen Testament 125), ed. M. Hengel, Tübingen, pp. 299–307.

Friedman, R. E. 1980. "The Tabernacle in the Temple," *Biblical Archaeologist* 43, pp. 241–8.

Funk, F. X. 1905. *Didascalia et Constitutiones Apostolorum*, Paderborn.

Goldhill, S. 2005. *The Temple in Jerusalem*, Cambridge, MA.

Goppelt, L. 1982. *Typos: The Typological Interpretation of the Old Testament in the New*, trans. D. H. Madgiv, Grand Rapids, MI.

Gruen, E. S. 2007. "Ancient 'Identity Theft': Cultural Identity and the Peoples of the Ancient Mediterranean," *First Draft: Newsletter of the Getty Research Institute*, pp, 4–9.

Hamblin, W. J. and D. Seely. 2007. *Solomon's Temple: Myth and History*, New York.

Kessler, H. 2000. "The Sepphoris Mosaic and Christian Art," in *From Dura to Sepphoris: Studies in Jewish Art and Society in Late Antiquity*, ed. L. I. Levine and Z. Weiss (Journal of Roman Archaeology supp. no. 40), pp. 65–72.

Kessler, H. L. 1990–1991. "Through the Temple Veil: the Holy Image in Judaism and Christianity," *Kairos* 32–33, pp. 53–77.

Klawans, J. 2005. *Purity, Sacrifice, and the Temple: Symbolism and Supersessionism in the Study of Ancient Judaism*, New York.

Kortleitner, F. X. 1906. *Archaeologiae Biblicae Summarium*, Innsbruck.

Korzybski, A. 1933. "A non-aristotelian system and its necessity for rigour in mathematics and physics," in *Science and santiy: an introduction to non-aristotelian systems and general semantics* (1st ed.); 1948, 3rd ed., Lakeville, CT, pp. 747–61.

Krinsky, C. H. 1970. "Representations of the Temple of Jerusalem before 1500," *Journal of the Warburg and Courtauld Institutes* 33, pp. 1–19.

Kühnel, B. 1986–1987. "Jewish Symbolism of the Temple and the Tabernacle and Christian Symbolism of the Holy Sepulchre and the Heavenly Jerusalem," *Jewish Art* 12–13, pp. 147–68.

Levenson, J. D. 1995. *The Death and Resurrection of the Beloved Son: The Transformation of Child Sacrifice in Judaism and Christianity*, New Haven.

Levenson, J. D. 1986. "The Jerusalem Temple in Devotional and Visionary Experience," in *Jewish Spirituality: From the Bible through the Middle Ages*, vol. 1, ed. A. Green, New York, pp. 32–61.

Levine, L. I. 2000. *The Ancient Synagogue: The First Thousand Years*, New Haven.

Lundquist, J. M. 2008. *The Temple of Jerusalem: Past, Present, and Future*, Westport, CT.

Mortensen, B. P. 2006. *The Priesthood in Targum Pseudo-Jonathan: Renewing the Profession*, 2 vols., Boston.

Netzer, E. and Z. Weiss. 1996. "Hellenistic and Roman Sepphoris: The Historical Evidence," in *Sepphoris in Galilee: Crosscurrents of Culture*, ed. R. M. Nagy et al., Raleigh, pp. 29–38.

Netzer, E. and Z. Weiss. 1995. "New Evidence for Late-Roman and Byzantine Sepphoris," in *The Roman and Byzaninte Near East: Some Recent Archaeological Evidence* (JRA Supplementary Series 14), ed. J. Humphreys, Ann Arbor, pp. 164–76.

Neusner, J. 1979. "Map without Territory: Mishnah's System of Sacrifice and Sanctuary," *History of Religions* 19, pp. 103–27.

Ousterhout, R. 1990. "The Temple, the Sepulchre and the Martyrion of the Savior," *Gesta* 30, pp. 44–53.

Osiek, C. 1983. "The Widow As Altar: The Rise and Fall of a Symbol," *The Second Century* 3, pp. 159–69.

Piccirillo, M. 1993. *The Mosaics of Jordan*, Amman.

Ritmeyer, L. 2006. *The Quest Revealing the Temple Mount in Jerusalem*, Jerusalem.

Roitman, A. 2003. *Envisioning the Temple: Scrolls, Stones, and Symbols*, Jerusalem.

Rosenau, H. 1979. *Vision of the Temple: The Image of the Temple of Jerusalem in Judaism and Christianity*, London.

Salevao, I. 2002. "The Superiority of Christianity and the Inferiority of Judaism," in *Legitimation in the Letter to the Hebrews: The Construction and Maintenance of a Symbolic Universe*, London, pp. 345–82.

Saller, S. J. 1941. *The Memorial of Moses on Mount Nebo*, Jerusalem.

Lightfoot, J. B. 1885. *The Apostolic Fathers*, vol. 2.2; *St. Ignatius and St. Polycarp*, London.

Skarsaune, O. 2002. *In the Shadow of the Temple: Jewish Influences on Early Christianity*, Downers Grove, IL.

Smith, J. Z. 1978. *Map is Not Territory: Studies in the History of Religions*, Chicago.

Strong, J. 1987. *The Tabernacle of Israel: Its Structure and Symbolism*, Grand Rapids, MI.

Wegner, J. R. 1999. "'Coming before the LORD'": *lpny yhwh* and the Exclusion of Women from the Divine Presence," in *Hesed ve-Emet: Studies in Honor of Ernest S. Frerichs*, ed. J. Magness and S. Gitin, Atlanta, pp. 81–91.

Weiss, Z. 2005. *The Sepphoris Synagogue: Deciphering an Ancient Message through its Archaeological and Social-Historical Contexts*, Jerusalem.

Weiss, Z. and E. Netzer. 1998. *Promise and Redemption: A Synagogue Mosaic from Sepphoris*, Jerusalem.

CHAPTER EIGHT

THE "FOUNDATION DEPOSIT" FROM THE DURA EUROPOS SYNAGOGUE RECONSIDERED

Jodi Magness

Introduction

In the year 70 the Romans destroyed the Second Jewish Temple in Jerusalem.[1] In the centuries that followed, Judaism was transformed from a religion centered on a temple building where a sacrificial cult was conducted by a priestly caste to a religion consisting of community worship and prayer in synagogues. Although Jewish society after 70 was presumably no less diverse than it had been previously, nearly all of the evidence we have for this period relates to the rabbinic class.[2] The rabbis (or sages) preserved and codified a mass of legal rulings on Judaism – most prominently the Mishnah and Talmud – that remain authoritative until today.[3]

Although most of the existing literary and archaeological evidence for Judaism after 70 relates to Palestine, Diaspora communities flourished around the Mediterranean, including in Egypt and North Africa, Asia Minor, Greece, and Italy.[4] Perhaps the most important Diaspora population was in Babylonia, descended in part from the Judean exiles of the late seventh and early sixth centuries B.C.E. The illustrious rabbis and academies in Babylonia produced the Babylonian Talmud, which is considered more authoritative than the Palestinian Talmud.[5]

Aside from the Babylonian Talmud, little evidence of Babylonian Jewry in the first five centuries of the Common Era has survived. However, in the early 1930s an ancient synagogue decorated with a stunning cycle of wall paintings was discovered at Dura Europos in modern Syria.[6] The paintings are preserved thanks to an earthen embankment piled along the inner face of the city wall, which buried the synagogue during the Sasanian siege in 256, when Dura was destroyed and abandoned.[7] The synagogue is located in a residential block next to the western wall of the town. It was originally a private dwelling that was converted for use as a synagogue, probably between 165 and 200.[8] In 244/245 the building was remodeled and decorated with a new set of paintings.[9] The paintings on the west wall are preserved to their full height. On the north and south walls fewer than half of the paintings are preserved, and on the east wall only parts of the lowest registers are preserved.[10]

The main hall or hall of assembly consists of a single room lined with benches and a Torah Shrine in the center of the west (Jerusalem-oriented) wall (Fig. 8.1). The synagogue was accessed through an open courtyard surrounded by additional rooms that presumably served the Jewish community. The building had a flat roof with wooden ceiling beams forming a framework for ceiling tiles.[11]

The Dura synagogue provides important archaeological evidence for Diaspora Judaism in the third century. Furthermore, in my opinion it is the earliest surviving synagogue building with permanent liturgical furniture (a built Torah Shrine) and distinctive Jewish iconography.[12] However, because Dura is located in Mesopotamia, far from the major Babylonian and Palestinian centers, scholars have long recognized the problems inherent in understanding the Dura synagogue and its community in light of rabbinic writings.[13] We simply do not know to what extent the Jews of Dura were familiar with or observed rabbinic law (*halakhah*) or whether the rabbis exercised any authority at Dura.[14]

The extent to which rabbinic law (*halakhah*) was followed by the Jews of Dura has been an important factor in discussions of the synagogue and its paintings. In this paper I consider a find that has also been viewed through the lens of rabbinic Judaism but has received much less attention than the paintings: a deposit of human bones buried under the threshold of the main doorway to the synagogue. Contrary to scholarly consensus, these bones would not have conveyed ritual impurity to those entering the building even if rabbinic law was followed at Dura. I

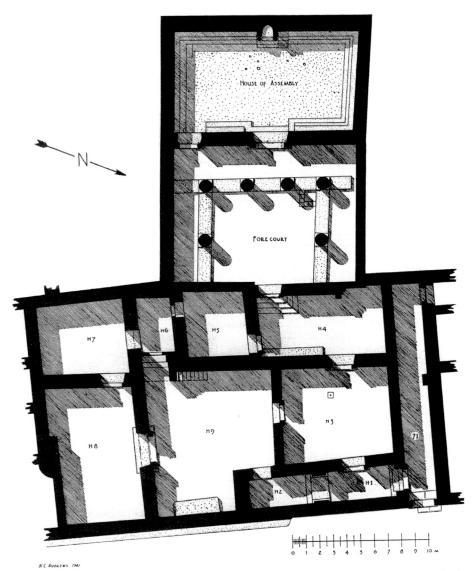

8.1. Dura, plan of the synagogue. Kraeling 1956, Plan VI; reproduced with permission of Yale University Press.

propose that this deposit represents the remains of someone who the congregation hoped would intercede with God on their behalf, perhaps a priestly leader. To conclude, I review evidence for the prominence of priests in the Dura synagogue and consider the possibility that apocalyptic expectations circulated among the Jews of Dura.

The Bone Deposit

Carl Kraeling, the excavator of the Dura synagogue, described the bone deposit as follows:

> The doorpost [of the main doorway into the hall or House of Assembly] pivoted in the hollowed block and rested on the iron plate. Toward the east the cavity housing the socket had a noticeable extension. This lay under the doorsill itself, being gouged out of the rubble bedding upon which the sill was set. In the pocket of the cavity was found a collection of bones that are reported to have been parts of two human fingers. Their presence at this point cannot have been the result of an accident, because of the genuine inaccessibility of the pocket and because of the discovery of analogous remains in the socket of the south doorway. The bones, whatever their character, must therefore represent a foundation deposit of the kind known to us also at Dura from pagan structures.[15]

According to Kraeling, these bones would have rendered the site and people approaching it impure.[16] Other scholars have made the same assumption. For example, Christopher Beall recently suggested that the bones were deposited secretly by non-Jewish builders at the time of construction, in an attempt to curse or render impure those entering the building.[17] This suggestion is problematic because it assumes that non-Jews participated in the construction of the synagogue and that they understood Jewish purity laws. More problematic, however, is the more widespread assumption that these bones would have rendered those entering the synagogue ritually impure. In fact, the Mishnah and Talmud stipulate that individual human bones without flesh convey impurity only through direct contact:

> Two hundred forty-eight limbs [are] in man: thirty in the foot, six in each toe; ten in the ankle; two in the shin; five in the knee; and one in the thigh; three in the hip; eleven ribs; thirty in the hand; six in each finger; two in the forearm; two in the elbow; one in the upper arm; four in the shoulder – one hundred one on one side, one hundred one on the other. Eighteen vertebrae are in the spine; nine in the head; eight in the neck; six in the breast; five in the genitals. Each one conveys uncleanness through contact, and through carrying, and through the Tent. When? When there is on them an appropriate amount of flesh. But if there is not on them an appropriate amount of flesh, they convey

uncleanness through contact and through carrying but do not convey uncleanness in the Tent. (Mishnah Oholot 1.8)[18]

The Babylonian Talmud states: "For we have learnt: 'A bone the size of a barley grain causes defilement by contact and carrying, but not by cover'" (Tractate 'Erubin 4a).[19] The Tosefta discusses this passage as follows: "Is it possible that the flesh should render unclean through contact, carrying, and Tent, while the limb should be clean? Said R. Simeon, 'I should be surprised if [under all circumstances] R. Eliezer declared it unclean. He declared it unclean only when there is on the limb appropriate flesh, so that this and this should render unclean through contact, carrying, and Tent'" (Ahilot 2:7).[20]

These passages indicate that even according to rabbinic *halakhah* (which may or may not have been followed at Dura), the human bones buried beneath the synagogue's threshold would not have conveyed impurity.

An Apotropaic Deposit?

Kraeling interpreted the buried bones as a foundation deposit, a common phenomenon in the ancient Near East.[21] However, he noted that the parallels for this practice come from pagan, not Jewish contexts.[22] Near Eastern foundation and building deposits were generally built into the walls or placed under the floors of buildings (usually palaces and temples), and most of them are much earlier in date than the Dura synagogue. Human remains are rare and consist mostly of infants, and the burial of individual human bones is unparalleled in Near Eastern foundation deposits.[23]

The placement of human bones under the threshold of the main doorway leading into the synagogue suggests apotropaic motivations.[24] Richard Ellis noted that the reasons for ancient Near Eastern foundation and building deposits included sanctification and a desire to protect the building against hostile powers.[25] Similar practices are evident in the Jewish necropolis at Beth Shearim in Israel's Galilee, which is contemporary with the Dura synagogue. Symbols and inscriptions with apotropaic value were placed on the archways of passages between rooms in the burial halls: an abecedary in Catacomb 1, Hall N;[26] two winged figures in Catacomb 1, Hall G;[27] and an Eis theos boethei inscription in Catacomb 7, Hall A.[28] Similarly, in the Christian baptistery at Dura an Eis theos inscription was written on a doorjamb leading from the court-yard and several abecedaries were written on the walls near doorways in the Christian building.[29]

The possibility that the bones were buried for apotropaic reasons does not explain why such a deposit occurs in the Dura synagogue alone. Why would human finger bones protect the entrance to the building from evil or sanctify it? A passage from the Babylonian Talmud may shed light on this phenomenon:

> Why do they go to the cemetery? With regard to this there is a difference of opinion between R. Levi b. Haman and R. Hanina. One says: [To signify thereby], we are as the dead before Thee; and the other says: In order that the dead should intercede for mercy on our behalf. (Tractate Ta'anith 16a)

This passage indicates that the dead were considered intercessors for the living.[30] Perhaps the bones buried under the threshold of the Dura synagogue represent the remains of someone who the congregation hoped would intercede with God on their behalf.[31] In this regard the Christian cult of the relics of saints might provide a better analogy than ancient Near Eastern foundation deposits.[32] Could it be that the buried bones belonged to a priest, who in this capacity acted as an intercessor for the congregation? Although this is admittedly spec-ulative, it is interesting to note that there are depictions of priests elsewhere in the synagogue and that this congregation's leader was a priest, as we shall see.

Evidence for Priests and Priestly Influence in the Dura Synagogue

Oded Irshai has noted that the Babylonian priesthood preserved its status and occupied a leadership position that was recognized even by the Palestinian sages.[33] The Dura synagogue provides evidence for the prominence of priests (both past and contemporary), only a few exam-ples of which I cite here. The most important paintings in the synagogue are concentrated on and around the Torah Shrine, which was the focal

8.2. Dura, paintings on the north half of the west wall of the synagogue. Kraeling 1956, Pl. XIX; reproduced with permission of Yale University Press.

point of the building. A large figure of Aaron – labeled with his name in Greek – is prominently represented in connection with the consecration of the Tabernacle and its priests, above and to the left of the Torah Shrine (Panel WB2). Aaron is clothed as a high priest and stands next to an altar in front of the Tabernacle, inside which the Ark of the Covenant can be seen. Kraeling identified the scene with the episode described in Exodus 40 and Numbers 7, when the Tabernacle was erected and Aaron, the high priests, and the Levites were installed in office.[34]

Kraeling noted horizontal thematic connections between the panel depicting the consecration of the Tabernacle and the panel on the other side of the Torah Shrine, which shows a building that he identified as the Jerusalem Temple (Panel WB3) (Fig. 8.2): "What the Encampment and the Wilderness Tabernacle inaugurated only foreshadowed, from the later point of view, what Jerusalem and its Temple brought to monumental and perfect expression."[35]

There are also vertical thematic connections between the anointing of David to the right of the Torah Shrine and the panel above the Torah Shrine showing David as king over all Israel.[36] The panel immediately

8.3. Dura, original painting on the central area of the west wall of the synagogue (panel above the Torah Shrine). Kraeling 1956, Pl. XVII; reproduced with permission of Yale University Press.

above the Torah Shrine initially depicted a vine flanked by a table and an empty throne, which Kurt Weitzmann and Herbert Kessler identified as a celestial throne that is the seat of the future king (Fig. 8.3).[37] This panel was repainted with an enthroned man representing David at the top center of the vine (Fig. 8.4). He is flanked by two togate figures and a lion (referring to David's ancestral tribe of Judah and by way of extension the

8.4. Dura, the Torah Shrine in the synagogue. Kraeling 1956, Pl. XXIV; reproduced with permission of Yale University Press.

genealogy of the messiah) underneath.[38] Kraeling and others have identified the two togate figures as David's priests Zadok and Abiathar, who represent the tribe of Levi.[39] Weitzmann and Kessler believe the figures are the priest Joshua ben Jehozadak and Zerubbabbel, who rebuilt the Second Temple after the return from the Babylonian exile.[40] Both possibilities emphasize the centrality of the Zadokite priests. Weitzmann and Kessler suggested that the repainting of the panels above the Torah Shrine strengthened an eschatological message regarding the future arrival of a messianic king who would rebuild the Jerusalem Temple, countering Christian claims that the messiah had already come.[41]

Not only do the Dura paintings emphasize the prominent role played by priests in the history of Israel, but Aramaic dedicatory inscriptions painted on ceiling tiles leave no doubt about the leadership role of priests in the Dura congregation. One inscription reads: "This house was built in the year 556, this corresponding to the second year of Philip Julius Caesar; in the eldership of the priest Samuel son of Yeda'ya, the Archon. Now those who stood in charge of this work were: Abram the Treasurer, and Samuel son of Sapharah, and ... the proselyte ... "[42]

A similar inscription on another ceiling tile (C) apparently referred to Abram the Treasurer and Samuel bar-Sapharah as priests.[43] Kraeling noted that the priest Samuel son of Yeda'ya "more than anyone else represents the community, and in his official capacity as well as in his personal dignity gives expression to its character and purpose.... He is a man of high religious station, being proudly referred to as priest in all three Aramaic texts."[44] Samuel's family might be the same one known from the books of Chronicles, Ezra, and Nehemiah.[45] He held the offices of presbyter (Aramaic *kashish*; Hebrew *zaken*) and archon.[46] According to Kraeling, "Samuel's eldership is of such import for the historical and chronological life of the community that it is in effect eponymous, Samuel as Elder being mentioned in one breath, so to speak, with the Emperor Philip Julius Caesar."[47]

Irshai has suggested that apocalyptic and eschatological expectations increased among the Jews of Palestine and Babylonia during late antiquity, especially after the failed attempt to rebuild the Jerusalem Temple under Julian the Apostate.[48] Jewish expectations were paralleled by similar apocalyptic anxiety among the Christian population, who anticipated the Parousia.[49] Jewish priestly circles apparently supported and perhaps promoted apocalyptic and eschatological expectations, as the rebuilding of the Temple would have bolstered their leadership position.[50] The rabbis may have been ambivalent about such expectations, which if fulfilled would have resulted in the loss of their status (as reflected in their silence about the rebuilding of the Temple under Julian the Apostate and their opposition to mystical practices).[51]

The possibility that apocalyptic expectations circulated among the Jews at Dura finds support in a passage in the Babylonian Talmud (Tractate Sanhedrin 97a–97b), which lists dates and calculations of an eschatological nature:

> A. After the four hundredth year of the destruction of the Temple if someone offers you a field worth a thousand dinars for just one do not buy it. B. After the four hundredth year of the destruction of the Temple if someone offers you a field worth a thousand dinars for just one do not buy it after the year 4231 A.M. C. Elijah said to R. Judah, the brother of R. Salla the Pious: "The world shall not exist less than eighty-five jubilees and in the last jubilee the son of David will come." He asked him at the beginning or at the end (of the jubilee)? He replied: "I do not know." Shall this period be completed or not? "I do not know" he answered. R. Ashi said: "He spoke thus to him." Before that do not expect him, afterwards thou mayest await him.[52]

To conclude, the bone deposit might indicate that Jews at Dura believed the dead could act as intercessors for the living. In light of the evidence for priestly prominence in the Dura synagogue, I tentatively suggest identifying these bones as belonging to a priest. The presence of this deposit in a synagogue is surprising since according to Jewish law corpses are a source of ritual impurity.[53] In this regard Judaism stands in direct opposition to Christianity, which venerates saints and holy people by burying their remains inside churches.[54] In other words, whereas in Christianity human burials consecrate sacred space, in Judaism they pollute it. No bone deposits have been found in other ancient synagogues, making the Dura find exceptional. Although this deposit might reflect localized beliefs and practices among the Dura Jews, these bones did not convey ritual impurity even according to rabbinic Jewish law.

Notes

1. All dates refer to the Common Era unless otherwise indicated.
2. See, for example, Levine 1992, p. 126: "Many of the Jewish sects that had played a central role in Jewish religious life during the first century disappeared [after 70]." On the other hand, Goodman 1994, pp. 348, 355, has observed,

"The standard assumption that these Jewish groups disappeared soon after 70 is therefore no more than an assumption. Furthermore, the presuppositions which have encouraged the assumption are so theologically loaded that historians' suspicions should be instinctive... My hypothesis is that groups and philosophies known from pre-70 Judaism continued for years, perhaps centuries, after the destruction of the Temple." Goodman's observation may be supported by evidence for third century Galilean Jewish-Christians (Christians who were apparently ethnic Jews) with Pharisaic leanings; see Boyarin 1999, p. 29; Baumgarten 1992, pp. 39–50. Also see Swartz 1996, p. 11, "Recently, though, there has been increased recognition that ancient Palestinian and Babylonian Jewish societies were complex ones, encompassing tensions between circles within the rabbinic estate, and between the academy and other sectors of the population." Even if Jewish groups changed or were reconfigured after 70, the fact remains that rabbinic norms were just one of many and that different Jewish groups were in dialogue and tension with each other.

3. For introductions see Cohen 1992, pp. 216–23; Gafni 1992, pp. 251–5.
4. For surveys with bibliography see Levine 2000, pp. 232–87; Barclay 1996.
5. See Gafni 1992, pp. 226–7, 261–5.
6. Kraeling 1956 remains the definitive study of the building and wall paintings.
7. For the possibility that Dura Europos was occupied by the Sasanians in 253, see Kraeling 1956, p. 337; Rostovtzeff 1943, p. 53; Grenet 1988.
8. Kraeling 1956, p. 327.
9. Kraeling 1956, p. 6.
10. Kraeling 1956, p. 39.
11. Kraeling 1956, pp. 12–15.
12. Earlier synagogue buildings such as those at Masada and Gamala lack these features, and instead are simply Jewish congregational buildings in the most basic sense; for these synagogue buildings see Foerster 1981; Gutman 1981; Ma`oz 1981; Levine 2000, pp. 42–73. Even if we assume that the building at Ostia functioned as a synagogue already in the first or second centuries (an unfounded assumption, in my opinion), there is no evidence for the installation of permanent liturgical furniture (such as the Torah Shrine) and Jewish symbols before the fourth century. For the Ostia synagogue, see White 1997; Runesson 2001.
13. For example, Goodenough 1988, p. 184: "We may question, however, that the Judaism of Dura ever resembled at all closely the Judaism of the Babylonian communities."
14. Fine 2005b, pp. 174–7, argues that a prayer (apparently related to the blessing after meals) found on a parchment fragment outside the Dura synagogue that displays similarities to rabbinic texts from late antiquity attests to rabbinic influence at Dura. However, he ignores the fact that rabbinic literature is our only source of information for Judaism (at least, for the interpretation of Jewish law) in this period. The practices of groups other than the rabbis are not preserved. In other words, although this fragment could indicate rabbinic influence at Dura, Fine's argument is based on circular reasoning; he associates the prayer (which was found outside the synagogue) with rabbinic Judaism, and by way of extension the paintings inside the synagogue with rabbinic Judaism. However, nonrabbinic Jews presumably also pronounced blessings in connection with meals. In fact, many of the sectarian prayers and liturgies from Qumran display similarities and parallels with rabbinic tradition; see Schiffman 1994, pp. 294–5.

15. Kraeling 1956, p. 19.
16. Kraeling 1956, p. 19, n. 86.
17. Beall 2005.
18. All translations of the Mishnah are from Neusner 1988.
19. Unless otherwise noted all translations of the Talmud are from the Soncino Talmud; see Simon 1960–. The Soncino Talmud's note to this passage states that "only a backbone, a skull, and the like cause the defilement of a person in the same tent or under the same roof or cover"; Simon 1960–, p. 19, n. 10.
20. Translation from Neusner 1977, p. 84.
21. Kraeling 1956, p. 19.
22. In addition to the references cited by Kraeling 1956, p. 19, n. 86, see Ellis 1968.
23. See Ellis 1968, pp. 35–42.
24. In fact, Kraeling 1956, p. 361 suggested they were buried for magical purposes.
25. Ellis 1968, pp. 165–166.
26. Mazar 1973, p. 122.
27. Mazar 1973, pp. 80–81.
28. Schwabe and Lifshitz 1974, p. 89.
29. Welles 1967, pp. 95, 125; on p. 126 he discusses how this inscription and other elements in the Christian building attest to magical and apotropaic practices. For the abecedaries in the Christian building see Welles 1967, pp. 90–92, nos. 2, 3, 4, 5, 8. For abecedaries on the walls of the temples of Bel, Gadde, and Azzanathkona at Dura, see Welles 1967, p. 89; on p. 90 he lists examples from secular contexts at Dura.
30. Brown 1981, p. 3 cites Midrash Tehillim (Midrash to Psalms) 16.2 to show that veneration of tombs or relics of saints existed also among late antique Jews (in this case, the Tombs of the Patriarchs in Palestine); also see p. 10.
31. For this concept in late-antique Christianity, see Brown 1981, p. 66.
32. Brown 1981, p. 4, notes that "the Christian cult of saints rapidly came to involve the digging up, the moving, the dismemberment – quite apart from the avid touching and kissing – of the bones of the dead, and, frequently, the placing of these in areas from which the dead had once been excluded." By contrast, Sukenik 1947, p. 187, n. 2 says there is no support for the suggestion that the Dura bones belonged to a saint who was buried there in order to sanctify the spot. I thank Hanan Eshel z"l for bringing this reference to my attention.
33. Irshai 2004, p. 81. Not all scholars accept the claims of priestly prominence or agree on the extent of priestly influence; see, for example, Fine 2005a.
34. Kraeling 1956, p. 130. This event took place on the first day of the month of Nisan. Kraeling based his identification of this scene on the fact that one bull and two lambs are included in the scene, animals which were sacrificed as part of the consecration of the priests as described in Exodus 29:1. The animal in the left foreground is a red heifer (Num. 19:1–13), the ashes of which were used to make the water of purification necessary for the sprinkling of the Levites; see Kraeling 1956, pp. 130–1. The first day of Nisan was also the beginning of the year according to the solar calendar falling on the vernal equinox and on a Wednesday, the day the heavenly luminaries were created (as expressed in the book of Jubilees); see Elior 2004, pp. 46–48, including n. 48.
35. Kraeling 1956, p. 131. The building in Panel WB3 likely represents the seven heavenly temples described in Jewish mystical literature; see Elior 2004, p. 79, n. 77: "a wall painting on the western wall of the ancient synagogue at Dura Europos portrays a heavenly Temple with seven walls, each behind another,

surrounding a central sanctuary; perhaps there is some connection between this 3rd-century depiction and priestly traditions of septuples in the style of Heikhalot literature."

36. Kraeling 1956, pp. 168, 225. Only seven (rather than eight) of Jesse's sons are depicted in the anointing of David scene; Kraeling 1956, p. 168. The highly charged symbolism of the number seven counters the claim by Weitzmann and Kessler 1990, p. 81 that "there was simply not enough space for an additional figure." Kraeling 1956, pp. 168, 220 noted that the depiction of David in these panels is not just historical but expresses eschatological or messianic hopes. In contrast, Flesher 1995 argues against messianic and eschatological messages in the Dura synagogue paintings, mainly on the basis of his claim that David in the central panel above the Torah is not depicted as Orpheus.

37. Weitzmann and Kessler 1990, p. 160; on p. 158 they suggest that the fruitless vine must refer to the eschatological idea that the tree will bear fruit only when the Messiah comes. Also see Kraeling 1956, p. 65, where he discusses the original paintings in the panel immediately above the Torah Shrine and identifies a possible theme of a messianic banquet. The repainting of this panel strengthened its eschatological message; see Revel-Neher 2004, p. 74.

38. Weitzmann and Kessler 1990, p. 164. For the lions as a symbol of Judah and David's ancestry, see also Kuhnel 1986/87, p. 148. Flesher 1995, p. 363 argues that the vine was painted over in the second phase.

39. See Flesher 1995, p. 362.

40. Weitzmann and Kessler 1990, pp. 165–6.

41. Weitzmann and Kessler 1990, p. 169.

42. On Tile A, see Kraeling 1956, p. 263.

43. Kraeling 1956, p. 268.

44. Kraeling 1956, p. 331.

45. Kraeling 1956, p. 331; for dedicatory inscriptions by priests in Palestinian synagogues, see Amit 2004, pp. 148–9.

46. Kraeling 1956, p. 331.

47. Kraeling 1956, p. 331.

48. Irshai 2000, p.142.

49. Irshai 2000, p. 151.

50. See Irshai 2004, p. 97; see also Goodblatt 1996. Rajak 2002 argues against widespread apocalyptic expectations among Jews in the late Second Temple period.

51. See Irshai 2004, pp. 97–98, n. 77; Irshai 2000, p. 143. Irshai 2000, pp. 128–9, notes that some rabbis engaged in eschatological computations, though after the Bar Kokhba revolt (132–135 C.E.) they attempted to tone down the messianic fervor. A passage in the Babylonian Talmud cautions: 'Rabbi Shmuel ben Nahmani declared in the name of Rabbi Jonathan 'blasted be the bones of those who calculate the End, for they used to say since the time of his arrival has arrived and he has not come he will never come" (Tractate Sanhedrin 97b); from Rajak 2002, p. 166. On p. 167 Rajak suggests that the rabbis may have disapproved of apocalyptic expectations because of the relationship to mystical speculation, which they tried to limit. Elior 2004 and Irshai 2004, p. 105, believe that the priestly apocalypticism of late antiquity (as expressed for example in Hekhalot literature) is related to the apocalypticism of the sectarian literature from Qumran.

52. From Irshai 2000, pp. 148–9, who notes that J. Neusner identified the probable Babylonian messianic context of these statements.

53. For example, Leviticus 22:4.
54. See, for example, Brown 1981.

Works Cited

Amit, D. 2004. "Priests and Remembrance of the Temple in the Synagogues of Southern Judea," in *Continuity and Renewal, Jews and Judaism in Byzantine-Christian Palestine*, ed. L. I. Levine, Jerusalem, pp. 143–54 (in Hebrew).

Barclay, J. M. G. 1996. *Jews in the Mediterranean Diaspora, From Alexander to Trajan (323 BCE – 117 CE)*, Berkeley.

Baumgarten, A. I. 1992. "Literary Evidence for Jewish Christianity in the Galilee," in *The Galilee in Late Antiquity*, ed. L. I. Levine, New York, pp. 39–50.

Beall, C. 2005. "A Bone of Contention: Foundation Deposits from the Dura Synagogue," *Abstracts of the Annual Meeting of the Society of Biblical Literature in Philadelphia, PA, 19–22 November 2005*, p. 18.

Boyarin, D. 1999. *Dying for God: Martyrdom and the Making of Christianity and Judaism*, Stanford.

Brown, P. 1981. *The Cult of the Saints, Its Rise and Function in Latin Christianity*, Chicago.

Cohen, S. J. D. 1992. "Judaism to the Mishnah: 135–220 C.E.," in *Christianity and Rabbinic Judaism, A Parallel History of Their Origins and Early Development*, ed. H. Shanks, Washington DC, pp. 195–223.

Elior, R. 2004. *The Three Temples, On the Emergence of Jewish Mysticism*, Oxford.

Ellis, R. S. 1968. *Foundation Deposits in Ancient Mesopotamia*, New Haven.

Fine, S. 2005a. "Between Liturgy and Social History: Priestly Power in Late Antique Palestinian Synagogues?" *Journal of Jewish Studies* 56.1, pp. 1–9.

Fine, S. 2005b. *Art & Judaism in the Greco-Roman World. Toward a New Jewish Archaeology*, Cambridge.

Flesher, P. V. M. 1995. "Rereading the Reredos: David, Orpheus, and Messianism in the Dura Europos Synagogue," in *Ancient Synagogues, Historical Analysis and Archaeological Discovery*, ed. D. Urman and P. V. M. Flesher, New York, pp. 346–66.

Foerster, G. 1981. "The Synagogues at Masada and Herodium," in *Ancient Synagogues Revealed*, ed. L. I. Levine, Jerusalem, pp. 24–9.

Gafni, I. M. 1992. "The World of the Talmud: From the Mishnah to the Arab Conquest," in *Christianity and Rabbinic Judaism, A Parallel History of Their Origins and Early Development*, ed. H. Shanks, Washington DC, pp. 225–65.

Goodblatt, D. 1996. "Priestly Ideologies of the Judean Resistance," *Jewish Studies Quarterly* 3 (1996) 225–49.

Goodenough, E. R. 1988. *Jewish Symbols in the Greco-Roman Period, Abridged Edition*, ed. J. Neusner, Princeton.

Goodman, M. 1994. "Sadducees and Essenes after 70 CE," in *Crossing the Boundaries, Essays in Biblical Interpretation in Honour of Michael D. Goulder*, ed. S. E. Porter, P. Joyce and D. E. Orton, Leiden, pp. 347–56.

Grenet, F. 1988. "Les sassanides a Doura-Europos (253 ap. J.-C.), Réexamen du matériel épigraphique iranien du site," in *Geographie historique au Proche-Orient*

(Syrie, Phénicie, Arabie, grecques, romains, Byzantines), Actes de la Table Ronde de Valbonne, 16–18 septembre 1985, ed. P.-L. Gatier, B. Helly, and J.-P. Rey-Coquais, Paris, pp. 133–58.

Gutman, S. 1981. "The Synagogue at Gamla," in *Ancient Synagogues Revealed*, ed. L. I. Levine, Jerusalem, pp. 30–34.

Himmelfarb, M. 2001. "'A Kingdom of Priests': the Democratization of the Priesthood in the Literature of Second Temple Judaism," *Journal of Jewish Thought and Philosophy* 6, pp. 89–104.

Irshai, O. 2000. "Dating the Eschaton: Jewish and Christian Apocalyptic Calculations in Late Antiquity," in *Apocalyptic Time*, ed. A. I. Baumgarten, Leiden, pp. 113–53.

Irshai, O. 2004. "The Priesthood in Jewish Society of Late Antiquity," in *Continuity and Renewal: Jewish and Judaism in Byzantine-Christian Palestine*, ed. L. I. Levine, Jerusalem, pp. 67–106 (in Hebrew).

Levine, L. I. 1992. "Judaism from the Destruction of Jerusalem to the End of the Second Jewish Revolt: 70-135 C.E.," in *Christianity and Rabbinic Judaism: A Parallel History of Their Origins and Early Development*, ed. H. Shanks, Washington, DC, pp. 125–49.

Levine, L. I. 2000. *The Ancient Synagogue: The First Thousand Years*, New Haven.

Kraeling, C. H. 1956. *The Excavations at Dura Europos Conducted by Yale University and the French Academy of Inscriptions and Letters: Final Report VIII, Part I: The Synagogue*, New Haven.

Kuhnel, B. 1986/87. "Jewish Symbolism of the Temple and the Tabernacle and Christian Symbolism of the Holy Tabernacle and the Heavenly Tabernacle," *Journal of Jewish Art* 12–13, pp. 147–168.

Ma'oz, Z. 1981. "The Synagogue of Gamla and the Typology of Second-Temple Synagogues," in *Ancient Synagogues Revealed*, ed. L. I. Levine, Jerusalem, pp. 35–41.

Mazar, B. 1973. *Beth She`arim, Report on the Excavations during 1936–1940. Volume I: Catacombs 1–4*, New Brunswick, NJ.

Neusner, J. 1977. *The Tosefta*, New York.

Neusner, J. 1988. *The Mishnah, A New Translation*, New Haven.

Rajak, T. 2002. "Jewish Millenarian Expectations," in *The First Jewish Revolt. Archaeology, History, and Ideology*, ed. A. M. Berlin and J. A. Overman, New York, pp. 164–88.

Revel-Neher, E. 2004. "An Additional Key to the Program of the Dura-Europos Synagogue Frescoes: Ezekiel 37," in *And Let Them Make Me a Sanctuary, Synagogues from Ancient Times to the Present Day*, ed. Y. Eshel, E. Netzer, D. Amit, and D. Cassuto, Ariel, pp. 67–75 (in Hebrew).

Rostovtzeff, M. I. 1943. "*Res Gestae Divi Saporis* and Dura," *Berytus* 8, pp. 17–60.

Schwabe, M. and B. Lifshitz. 1974. *Beth She`arim. Volume II: The Greek Inscriptions*, New Brunswick, NJ.

Runesson, A. 2001. "The Synagogue at Ancient Ostia: The Building and its History from the First to the Fifth Century," in *The Synagogue of Ancient Ostia and the Jews of Rome, Interdisciplinary Studies*, ed. B. Olsson, D. Mitternacht, and O. Brandt, Stockholm, pp. 29–99.

Schiffman, L. H. 1994. *Understanding the Dead Sea Scrolls*, Philadelphia.

Simon, M. 1960-. *The Soncino Talmud: Hebrew-English Edition of the Babylonian Talmud*, London.

Sukenik, E. L. 1947. *The Synagogue of Dura-Europos and its Frescoes*, Jerusalem 1947 (in Hebrew).

Swartz, M. D. 1996. *Scholastic Magic: Ritual and Revelation in Early Jewish Mysticism*, Princeton.

Weitzmann, K. and H. L. Kessler. 1990. *The Frescoes of the Dura Synagogue and Christian Art*, Washington, DC.

Welles, C. B. 1967. *The Excavations at Dura-Europos Conducted by Yale University and the French Academy of Inscriptions and Letters, Final Report VIII, Part II: The Christian Building*, New Haven.

White, L. M. 1997. "Synagogue and Society in Imperial Ostia: Archaeological and Epigraphic Evidence," *HTR* 90.1, pp. 23–58.

Wischnitzer-Bernstein, R. 1941. "The Conception of the Resurrection in the Ezekiel Panel of the Dura Synagogue," *JBL* 60, pp. 43–55.

CHAPTER NINE

SIGHT LINES OF SANCTITY AT LATE ANTIQUE MARTYRIA

Ann Marie Yasin

The year is 386, the place Milan, and the bishop has just arranged for the disinterment of two corpses from a cemetery outside the walls of the city. The bodies had been revealed as those of two extraordinary men, the local saints Gervasius and Protasius, and their relocation was intended to provide them with a more suitably grand resting place.[1] And majestic it was, for Ambrose, the bishop, moved them within the very walls of his newly constructed church, known as the Basilica Ambrosiana, for reburial under the altar. This is not the earliest known example of repositioning saints' relics,[2] but it is particularly noteworthy because it is so well documented, and the surviving literary sources provide access into the way in which the event was justified and orchestrated by the presiding bishop.[3]

Ambrose's relocation of Gervasius and Protasius's bodies served to distinguish them from the ordinary dead. The special treatment of their physical remains and the honored location they would receive are emblematic of a period in which those who had suffered the ultimate price for their faith were increasingly placed in a separate category, apart from ordinary humans.[4] The burgeoning cult of martyrs was fueled by a belief that their trials had earned them a particular closeness to God and that their prayers were thus particularly effective.[5] They had a special ability to intercede on behalf of those who venerated them, and honoring them became an increasingly popular expression of Christian piety. By moving martyrs' bodies from cemeteries to church buildings, tomb violation could be cast as an act of religious piety. Ambrose's actions were deemed praiseworthy both for having rediscovered the "lost" remains of saints deserving of veneration and for his ability to satisfy the desires of his congregation for patron saints of the new basilica.[6]

At the same time, Ambrose also transformed the local sacred landscape. In repositioning the saints' relics, the bishop not only steered the topographical trajectory of the martyrs' veneration away from the cemeterial fringes and toward the institutional center of the Church, but he also forged a new spatial bond between two previously distinct types of sacred focal points – saint's tomb and liturgical altar. Ambrose himself stressed the immediacy and perceptibility of this connection. His sermon following the transportation of the skeletons to the basilica underscored the power of his audience's sight to act as witness to holiness within the space of the church building. "Behold to my right," he said, "behold to (my) left the sacrosanct relics: you see men of heavenly abode …"[7] The bishop thus demonstrated the sanctity of the martyrs by directing the gaze of the gathered congregation to the relics which flanked him on either side, and he ensured the continued physical prominence of the saints' remains by positioning them permanently under the altar.[8] The altar, then, stood as the visible marker of the holy relics buried below.

The kind of physical and visible connection between altars and saints' relics that Ambrose created in Milan grew ever stronger over the course of the late fourth to seventh centuries across the Mediterranean.[9] An early fifth-century piece of legislation from North Africa, for example, called for the destruction of any altar which did not contain martyrs' relics or sit atop a site where an event from a saint's life or death occurred.[10] By the sixth and seventh centuries we find abundant archaeological testimony for holes meant for the insertion of relics in altar bases or tables.[11]

Running parallel to this trend, however, at many important late antique holy sites, liturgical altar and saint's memorial occupied separate architectural places within a common complex. For example, at the major fifth- and sixth-century shrines of St. Felix in Nola, St. Thecla at Meryemlik, St. Euphemia at Chalcedon, St. Symeon at Qal'at Sem'an, St. Demetrios in Thessaloniki, and the pilgrimage complex in Tebessa (possibly originally dedicated to St. Crispina), saint's *memoria* and altar formed two distinct focal points. At these sites, the altar and relics were separated by architectural features such as elevation changes, framing devices and barriers in the form of stairways, columns, walls, or chancels. Thus, although a church such as Ambrose's cathedral in Milan conflated altar and relics, others deployed various architectural means to segregate the site of saint veneration from that of the eucharist. Indeed, it has been a long-standing scholarly convention to divide the corpus of late antique churches into two categories, those which bring together altar and relics into a single holy locus, and those which insist upon their separation.[12]

How are we to understand such sites which seem to buck the trend of uniting liturgical focus and center of saintly veneration so flagrantly? Building on recent work in late antique studies that has come to recognize the articulation of sanctity as increasingly visual, I suggest that we need to move beyond architectural plans and typologies to try to understand how church patrons sought to negotiate the relationship between the two types of ritual focal points and how visitors would have experienced the sacred spaces.[13] At many late antique shrines of saints the location of relics was made visually prominent, even, and perhaps especially, when the saint's memorial formed a sacred focal point distinct from that of the liturgical altar.[14] Sites such as those enumerated above certainly do not neatly fit the Ambrosian model of uniting altar and relics, but at the same time, I suggest, they were not wholly foreign to it either. Rather, the experience of visitors moving through and gazing around the architectural complexes would have constructed a spatial sanctity that bound together the two types of sacred centers. The architectural programs, in other words, provided visitors with an experiential and visual link between liturgical space and saint's memorial despite a physical separation between the two types of sacred focal points. In some cases, it is even possible to demonstrate that those responsible for the structures intentionally manipulated architectural features in order to forge a meaningful connection between the two types of sacred loci (one eucharistic and one martyrial) and construct a complex but coherent sacred space that embraced both saints' memorials and eucharistic altars.

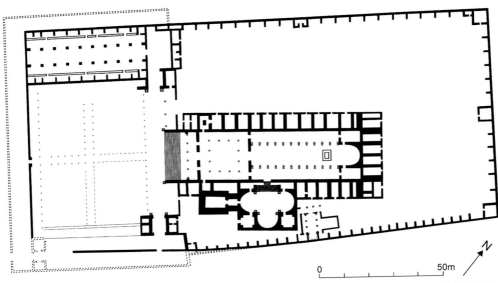

9.1. Tebessa, Algeria, plan of the Basilica complex. John Marston, after J. Christern, *Das frühchristliche Pilgerheiligtum von Tebessa. Architectur und Ornamentik einer spätantiken Bauhütte in Nordafrika*, Wiesbaden 1976, fig. 1.

Physical Separation and Visual Connection

I have examined elsewhere a number of cases in which relics are found within church complexes but *not* directly associated with the primary, liturgical altar.[15] This work stressed the way in which visitors' attention shifted between the two centers of sacred power as they moved through the ecclesiastical complexes. Witnessing the martyrium site upon entering or exiting the church could spatially frame or "bookend" the liturgical experience. At the massive basilica at Tebessa (Algeria), for example, the ornately decorated trefoil martyr shrine was approached from a staircase off the south aisle, just inside the main entrance from the nave (Fig. 9.1).[16] Dramatically different in architectural layout, but experientially not entirely dissimilar, is the pilgrimage center built circa 480–490 at Qal'at Sem'an in northwest Syria around the site of the column of the stylite St. Symeon (Fig. 9.2).[17] The cruciform plan of this church pivots around the saint's relic-column at its center, but it was the east arm of the complex, the only one equipped with an apsidal end, that housed the liturgical altar (Fig. 9.3). Access to the steeply positioned monastic

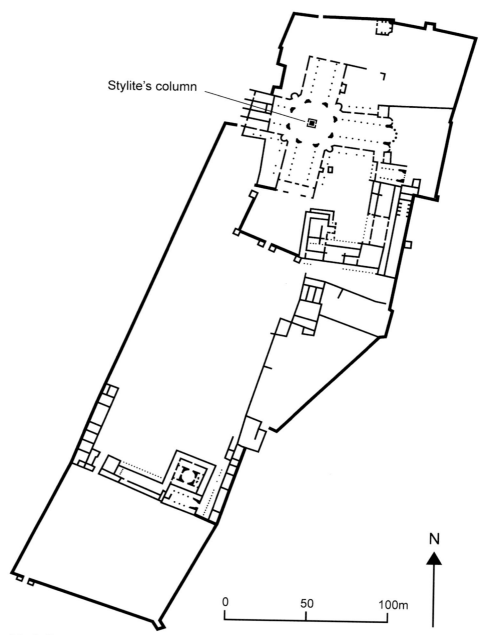

Stylite's column

N

0   50   100m

9.2. Qal'at Sem'an, Syria, plan of the complex with Church of St. Symeon the Stylite. John Marston, after J.-L. Biscop and J.-P. Sodini, "Travaux à Qal'at Sem'an," in *Actes du XIe congrès international d'archéologie chrétienne. Lyon, Vienne, Grenoble, Genève et Aoste (21–28 Septembre 1986)*, vol. 2. Vatican City 1989, p. 1676, fig. 1.

9.3. Qal'at Sem'an, Church of St. Symeon the Stylite, east arm, facing east. Photo Ann Marie Yasin.

complex was from the route leading from the nearby village of Deir Sem'an (ancient Telanissos) to the southwest; the cross-shaped structure's south arm thus served as a monumental entranceway welcoming approaching visitors. Such an arrangement meant that to attend the liturgy focused on the altar area within the east basilica, after entering from the south arm one would have passed beside and walked around the Stylite's monumental column.[18] Here, too, therefore, encountering the saint's memorial can be understood as spatially and experientially framing participation in the liturgical ritual.[19]

We might compare the major pilgrimage shine of St. Menas at Abû Mînâ southwest of Alexandria where the saint's shrine, located in a subterranean hypogaeum, was approached from a stairway to the northeast of the early-fifth-century church (the so-called Martyr Church).[20] With the construction of the large, new transept basilica (the "Great Basilica")

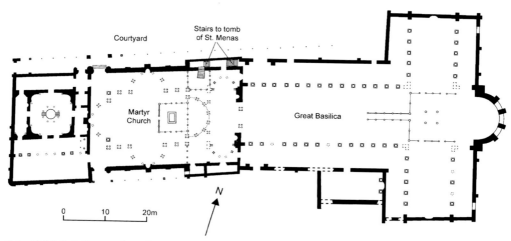

9.4. Abû Mînâ, Egypt, plan of Tomb Church (tetraconch to west) and Great Basilica (transept basilica to east) of St. Menas, Justinianic period. John Marston, after P. Grossmann, *Christliche Architektur in Ägypten*, Leiden 2002, fig. 20.

to the east at the end of the fifth century and the replacement of the first basilican Martyr Church by a tetraconch structure in the Justinianic period (527–565), the saint's shrine, with its access stairs located at the north end of the intermediate space joining the two churches, could be visited by pilgrims entering the ecclesiastical complex from the main courtyard to the north (not shown on plan) or passing between the two church structures (Fig. 9.4).[21] One's experience of the liturgy performed at the altar of the Great Basilica would thus have been shaped by seeing or passing the entrance to the underground shrine as one moved into, out of, and through the church space.

In these examples, the relationship between the saints' relics and the liturgical altar was understood and experienced spatially; they were connected through movement in and around the ecclesiastical complex. Importantly, however, the spatial distinction between the two types of sacred centers was maintained, and physical barriers (walls, floors, doors) could prevent witnessing them simultaneously.[22] The ritual activities of taking part in the liturgy and of venerating the saint were architecturally linked, but fundamentally distinct. They occurred in separate spaces: the communal liturgy in the large, open space of the church, the saint's veneration in the relatively narrow and more intimate space of the martyrium.[23] The present essay takes a closer look at shrines in which architectural barriers are in some way breached or even obliterated altogether. These are sites that walk a finer line in negotiating the relationship between centers of saint veneration and liturgical performance by simultaneously maintaining separate- ness while nonetheless allowing, even encouraging, *visual* connection between the two.

One of the most provocative instances of an overt orchestration of a visual link between separate liturgical and martyrological sacred cen- ters is found at Meryemlik (Ayatekla) outside Anatolian Seleukia (on the southern coast of modern Turkey). Here, the architectural arrangement of the church of St. Thecla, built in the second half of the fifth cen- tury, connected it to the place of the saint's veneration in a subterranean grotto below.[24] Associated with the location of St. Thecla's final years as early as the late-second-century *Acts of Paul and Thecla*,[25] since at least the late fourth century Seleukia hosted a monastic center that was a popular stop for late antique pilgrims traveling to the Holy Land.[26] The pilgrim Egeria, for example, described visiting the shrine on her return from the Holy Land in the 380s. She stayed for two days with the monas- tics; at the martyrium itself, she wrote, "we had a prayer there and read the whole Acts of holy Thecla ..."[27]

Although little is known archaeologically of the earliest phases of the site, substantial remains of the enormous three-aisled church built in the second half of the fifth century survive (Fig. 9.5). Its construction, asso- ciated with the Emperor Zeno, was carried out on a lavish scale; as the excavators note, at 81 x 43 meters it could have easily enclosed Ravenna's basilica of S. Apollinare in Classe.[28] The immense fifth-century structure at Meryemlik surmounted a natural grotto into which a subterranean basilica, the so-called Cave Church, was also constructed.[29] The subter- ranean martyrium was articulated as a space markedly distinct from, but also connected to the interior space of the above-ground basilica. The two superimposed basilicas were linked by a monumental staircase that led from a covered passage along the south exterior wall of the above- ground basilica down to the Cave Church. Passing by the south flank of the main church, one could have reached the external staircase lead- ing to the martyrium. From the massive above-ground basilica, in other words, visitors would have had to exit the building to reach the entrance to the Cave Church below.[30] At the same time, the church design also apparently allowed for direct visual access between the space of the

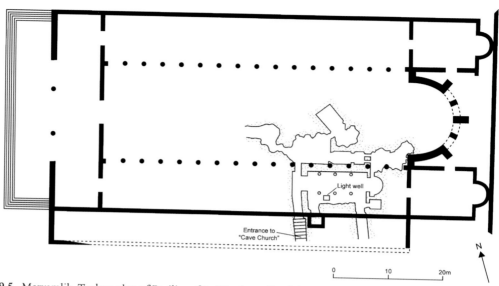

Light well

Entrance to
"Cave Church"

N

0   10   20m

9.5. Meryemlik, Turkey, plan of Basilica of St. Thecla, walls of above-ground fifth-century church are indi-
cated in black, those of the subterranean "Cave Church" stippled. John Marston, after E. Herzfeld and
S. Guyer, *Meriamlik und Korykos: Zwei christliche Ruinenstätten des rauhen Kilikiens* (*Monumenta Asiae Minoris
Antiqua* 2), Manchester 1930, figs. 6 and 7.

basilica above and martyrium below, for the excavators report a light
well cut into the floor of the above-ground church's south aisle, which
united the two spaces.[31] From within either church, whether above or
below ground, the stone-cut shaft would have signaled the direct, physical proximity of altar and martyrium and possibly even allowed for the
visitor to peer from one space into the other.

Other sites could preserve the saint's shrine and altar at the same
elevation and maintain the separateness of the two cultic focal points
while nevertheless allowing visual access between them. Perhaps the
most famous instance of this kind of arrangement is the late antique
basilica of St. Demetrios in Thessaloniki (northern Greece) where the
saint's memorial was architecturally distinct from the liturgical altar
but bound to it by visitors' experience of the space. The main liturgical focus of the large mid-fifth- to early-sixth-century basilica was the
altar located at the east end of the longitudinal nave (Fig. 9.6).[32] The
centrality of the altar as primary ritual focal point is underscored by
its position in the clerical area of the choir at the eastern end of the
basilica, its axial alignment with the main church entrance, and

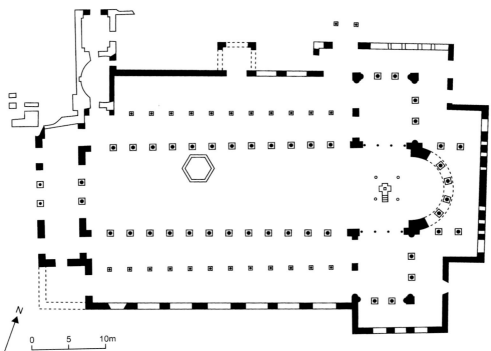

9.6. Thessaloniki, Greek plan of Basilica of St. Demetrios. John Marston, after G. Sotiriou and M. Sotiriou, *Ἡ βασιλικὴ τοῦ Ἁγίου Δημητρίου Θεσσαλονίκης*, Athens, 1952, p. 140, fig. 59 and J.-P. Spieser, *Thessalonique et ses monuments du IVe au VIe siècle: contribution a l'étude d'une ville paléochrétienne*, Athens and Paris 1984, p. 185, fig. 10.

the architectural framing provided by the basilican apse. The saint's memorial too was given distinct monumental prominence within the church. It consisted of a free-standing, hexagonal mausoleum-like structure, reportedly made of silver, which, as twentieth-century excavations of the base revealed, was located in the northwest part of the nave (see plan, Fig. 9.6).[33] According to the archbishop of the city who compiled a collection of St. Demetrios' *Miracles* at the beginning of the seventh century, this ciborium was thought by many faithful to lie over the holy relics, although the ecclesiastical author himself remained skeptical.[34] It was the site of popular prayer and veneration where, the *Miracles* text relates, candles were offered and certain visitors who were allowed entrance reportedly saw the saint on his couch.[35] The saint himself was depicted standing before this very structure receiving the prayers of his pious followers in a set of mosaic images that adorned the upper walls of

9.7. Thessaloniki, Basilica of St. Demetrios, detail of W. S. George watercolor of mosaics of north inner aisle (mosaic now lost) representing St. Demetrios before his ciborium. Reproduced with permission of the British School at Athens.

the church (Fig. 9.7).[36] The unusual form, large scale and gleaming, precious materials of the saint's ciborium, as well as its prominent location toward the west (i.e., entrance) end of the basilica, would have ensured the shrine's visibility to the church's visitors. It localized the saint's presence, serving as a place to exchange personal communication with him, while remaining fully embedded within the church space and in sight of the altar at the far end of the nave. The saint's memorial thus adorned the larger liturgical space centered on the altar and simultaneously offered a distinct locus for personal veneration. Here, as at St. Thecla's shrine at Meryemlik, discrete spaces within the church complex were arranged to accommodate distinct cultic encounters, of the eucharist, on the one hand, and the saint's veneration, on the other, but the sight line between them also ensured that the ritual experiences were spatially and sensorally linked.

Orchestrating Sight Lines

Indeed, textual sources confirm that such a visual connection was understood as desirable and could even form an explicit goal of the architectural program. The *Ecclesiastical History* of Evagrius Scholasticus and the writings of Paulinus of Nola articulate something of the aims and effects of employing such visual and architectural strategies. At the complex housing St. Euphemia's memorial at Chalcedon described by Evagrius in the late sixth century and that built up by Paulinus around the shrine of St. Felix at Cimitile in the early fifth century, the saint's tomb lay within a structure distinct from the main basilican hall. Yet, both Evagrius and Paulinus expressly emphasized the way in which the architectural arrangements granted the visitor visual access between the two cultic focal points.

Situated directly across the Bosphoros from Constantinople, St. Euphemia's martyrium was visited by the pilgrim Egeria in the late fourth century, and the church that stood there in 451 served as the splendid venue for the Council of Chalcedon. Although the location of the church remains unknown, based on the description in Evagrius's history, the martyrium that housed the silver casket containing the saint's remains was one of three principal structures of the ecclesiastical complex, together with an open porticoed courtyard and a covered basilica.[37] The martyrium was apparently circular in plan, two stories high, and ringed with interior columns. It attached to the end of one of the basilica's aisles and communicated with the side aisle at ground level as well as from an upper story gallery.[38] As part of his admiring ekphrasis, the author explained one function of the rotunda's upper level: "so that from there it is possible, for those who wish, both to supplicate the martyr and to be present at the services."[39] Evagrius thus explicitly praised the spatial configuration between Euphemia's martyrium and basilica for allowing visitors to witness the eucharistic celebration and to venerate the martyr's remains simultaneously. The arrangement, in other words, allowed a visual connection between the different spaces and thereby facilitated a kind of ritual multitasking.

An analogous separation between cult center and liturgical focus is preserved in an important, early pilgrimage center in the heart of Italian Campania. Cimitile, the northern cemetery zone of Nola and home to the tomb of St. Felix, monumentalized its patron saint's relics at the heart of the complex, but distinct from the liturgical center of the altar. Here we are fortunate to possess both literary and archaeological testimony regarding the physical and symbolic organization of sacred space. Indeed, the surviving textual attention the site received during Paulinus's time at Nola (395–431), first as monk and priest, later as bishop, is unique in the early Christian world.[40]

By the time Paulinus's tenure at Nola began, Felix's late-third-century tomb had been enclosed within an early fourth-century single-aisled structure, the so-called Aula Apsidata, which had a triple-arcade entrance on the south and an apse on the north (Fig. 9.8).[41] Sometime probably in the third quarter of the fourth century, a small three-aisled church with an eastern apse was built to the east of the Aula. This structure, dubbed the Basilica Vetus (to distinguish it from Paulinus's later Basilica Nova or "New Basilica"), was certainly integrated with the Aula, but many details of its architectural arrangement remain unclear due to the still-extant parochial church of Cimitile constructed on the site in the late eighteenth century. The altar of the Basilica Vetus would have been situated, as usual, at the east end of the structure before the apse.[42] Therefore, the altar was certainly, at the minimum, separated from the site of Felix's tomb in the Aula by that structure's still functioning east wall.[43] It appears, therefore, that the earliest monumental cult structures at Cimitile were neither directly centered on the saint's grave nor joined his tomb to a liturgical altar. Here the saint's memorial was, within the context of the larger ecclesiastical and pilgrimage complex, linked to the liturgical space within the basilica proper by the trajectory of the visitor's path.

For his part, Paulinus was very clear that the altar at the heart of the monumental Basilica Nova he built at the beginning of the fifth century was not physically assimilated to St. Felix's tomb (Fig. 9.9). In fact, with Paulinus's expansion of the complex, the saint's *memoria* and the

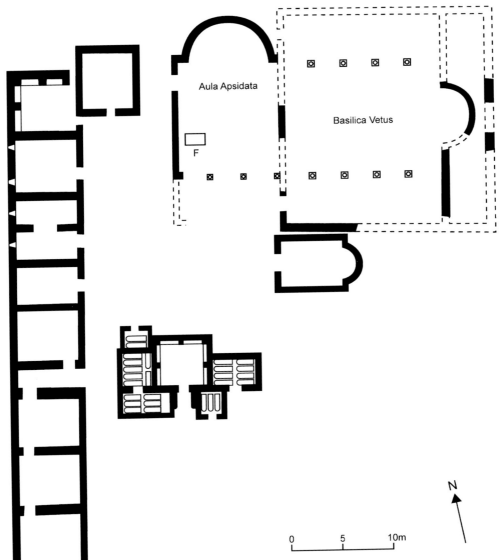

9.8. Cimitile, Italy, plan of Christian complex, third quarter of the fourth century; Grave of St. Felix is labeled "F." John Marston, after T. Lehmann, *Paulinus Nolanus und die Basilica Nova in Cimitile/Nola*, Wiesbaden 2004, fig. 26.

new liturgical altar of the Basilica Nova were distanced by more than the entire length of that church's nave. Excavations of the Basilica Nova have revealed its plan to be a three-aisled structure extending north from the area around Felix's tomb.[44] The church's main altar stood within a

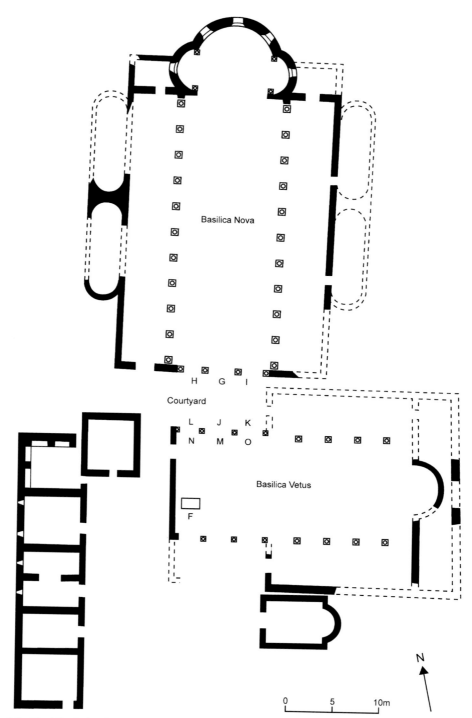

9.9. Cimitile, Italy, plan of Christian complex, early fifth century (including Paulinus's construc-tions); Grave of St. Felix is labeled "F." John Marston, after T. Lehmann, *Paulinus Nolanus und die Basilica Nova in Cimitile/Nola*, Wiesbaden 2004, fig. 27.

trefoil choir area at the northern end of the basilica, that is, at the opposite end from the direction of the saint's grave located across a narrow courtyard in the renovated Basilica Vetus to the south.

Although scholarship on Paulinus's inventions at Cimitile have focused primarily on his promotion of Felix's cult, it is clear from his material and literary attention to the relics under the altar of the Basilica Nova that the saint's tomb was not the sole repository of sanctity at the site. On the contrary, Paulinus's description of the complex at Cimitile explicitly emphasized that it possessed two sacred focal points. Writing in a letter to Sulpicius Severus, another church-building cleric, Paulinus stressed the pair of holy sites: "The basilica, therefore … is venerable not only on account of the honor of blessed Felix, but also by virtue of the consecrated relics of apostles and martyrs under the altar within the trilobed (*trichora*) apse."[45] Felix's tomb and the liturgical altar of the Basilica Nova with its own deposit of relics provided Cimitile with a doubly rich sacred pedigree.

This duality, however, while here cast as a strength, could also be a potential source of discordance, and Paulinus repeatedly sought to counter this perception by underscoring the coherence and harmony of the complex as a whole. One mechanism he used to achieve this was the crafting of a visual dialogue between sacred focal points. The texts Paulinus left us reveal the significant lengths he went to publicize the visual line he created between St. Felix's grave and the altar of his new church. He writes, for example, of the renovations he carried out at the site which included the demolition of the apsidal wall of the old *Aula* building: "For because the wall obstructed by the interfering apse of a certain monument would have cut off the new church from the old one, it was opened from the confessor's side … and thus this wall gives a view … to those gazing from one church into the other …"[46] Paulinus thus replaced what had been a solid barrier between Felix's tomb and the new basilica (cf. Fig. 9.8) with a set of permeable triple-arched passage-ways, the southern one of which can still be seen at the site (Figs. 9.9 and 9.10).[47]

Paulinus further emphasized the linking of the two sacred centers and the creation of a line of sight between them by monumental inscriptions that adorned the arches of the passageway between the two structures.[48] For example, he drew attention to the visitor's transition

9.10. Cimitile, Italy, Basilica Nova, view south along nave toward triple-arched entrance to the Basilica Vetus (left/east opening walled in). Photo Ann Marie Yasin.

from one space to another by positioning on one of the arches of the triple arcade he built between the Basilicas Vetus and Nova an inscription that addressed readers directly (labeled "N" on the plan, Fig. 9.9): "Leave the old hall of St. Felix, (and) cross to Felix's new structure."[49] While this inscription underscored the spatial shift as viewers moved from "old" to "new" buildings, to those passing through in the opposite direction, from the Basilica Nova to the old basilica, the central opening (indicated "J" on Fig. 9.9) spoke in overtly flattering terms of eliminating barriers and creating union: "Just as Jesus, our peace, opened the middle of the wall and, extinguishing (our) discord through the cross, has made two into one, so we see that, since the division of the old building has been destroyed, the new roofs are united by the marriage of (their) entrances …"[50] Similarly, he drove the message home with additional inscriptions placed on the side arches of the arcade between the Basilica Nova and Felix's old basilica. One (at position "K" on Fig. 9.9) read, "A new light is revealed to astonished eyes, and standing on a single threshold one beholds simultaneously the twin halls," and the other (at "L") read, "Three times the twin halls are opened by twin arches, and they admire their own decoration from mutual thresholds."[51] Paulinus thus crafted the martyrium complex so that it overtly and repeatedly encouraged visitors to take notice of the sight-line afforded between the old and new structures. The building complex was highly self-conscious, indeed proud, of its double centers. It celebrated the duality of its sacred focal points as well as the wonderment engendered by the experience of beholding both simultaneously.

At the same time, while forging a link between physically distinct memorials and altars, the architectural arrangement at this and other sites nevertheless can also be seen to have asserted a relative hierarchy between the two types of sacred loci. At Cimitile, the elevated sanctuary and wide, triple-lobed apse of the spacious Basilica Nova highlighted the liturgical altar's prominence as a ritual focal point (Fig. 9.9). Similarly, the longitudinal basilican plans of St. Demetrios's church in Thessaloniki, of St. Thecla's upper church at Meryemlik, and of the huge basilica at Tebessa pointed directly to the altar in each case (Figs. 9.1, 9.5, and 9.6). Likewise, at Qal'at Sem'an, while the cruciform plan of the complex does indeed focus attention on the column at its center, the structure is also overwhelmingly linear and hierarchical as one approaches the liturgical altar (Fig. 9.2). The stylite's column, in other words, was not *the* center of the complex, but *a* center. It dominated the space – and the visitor's experience – immediately before the entrance to the east wing. But the east wing itself, which is in effect a semi-independent basilica structure, and specifically the altar situated before its apse, was the primary center, the culmination of both the architectural program and the liturgical drama.[52] Distinct eucharistic and saintly focal points housed within a common complex, even when they were visually connected, were not necessarily on par.

More Relics Under the Altar

This kind of relative hierarchy also informs our interpretation of the complicated sacred topography of sites that housed multiple loci of saints' presence within a single structure by incorporating a saint's presumed tomb site *and* relics under the altar. In these cases, the architectural arrangements crafted a spatial and visual relationship not only between two different kinds of ritual focal points – of saint veneration and eucharistic liturgy – but also between two distinct manifestations of saintly presence. The link between them was important, but so too were their distinctive roles in supporting an architecturally inscribed system of ecclesiastical authority.

Of the complexes discussed here, the sanctuaries of St. Demetrios and St. Felix both offer evidence for multiple locales of saintly presence within the ecclesiastical complex. Returning to St. Demetrios's basilica in Thessaloniki, we recall that the saint's ciborium in the nave provided one venue for appealing to and encountering the saint. The ciborium, however, was not the only place in the late antique church which drew on the power of saintly presence. At the east end of the nave the altar stood atop a reliquary deposit covered by a marble plaque and once accessible (presumably only to clergy) by a narrow set of three stairs at the altar's southern side (Fig. 9.6).[53] At the center of the small chamber at the bottom of the steps, set within a conical masonry support, early-twentieth-century archaeological investigations unearthed a small marble box. Inside the box the excavators discovered an intact glass vial whose dark contents they identified as dried blood.[54] These relics so carefully installed at the site under the altar no longer preserve an identification, though the church's patron saint Demetrios has been presumed.[55] Comparison with the evidence from Paulinus's church at Cimitile, however, reminds us that such an identification is not a given. It attests to the possibility that an altar deposit could bring to the site a different set of sacred associations altogether, with relics distinct from the church's patron saint.

The arrangement Paulinus effected with his ambitious building program at Cimitile both glorified Felix's tomb and also put it into explicit relationship with the new liturgical altar located in the choir of the Basilica Nova (see Fig. 9.9). This new altar was in its own right a spiritually, architecturally, and politically critical element in the transformation of the sanctuary's sacred topography. It not only formed the axial linchpin of the longitudinal basilica's plan and center stage of the eucharistic drama but also contained a valuable collection of newly acquired holy relics that connected Nola to a larger Christian world. Paulinus trumpeted the deposition of this new cache of relics under the Basilica Nova's altar in a description of the church composed on the occasion of St. Felix's feast day in 403, as construction on the Basilica Nova was nearing completion:

For the ashes even of apostles have been set beneath that table of heaven, and consecrated amongst other holy offerings they emit a fragrance pleasing to Christ from their living dust. Here is father Andrew, the fisherman sent to Argos ... and who later by shedding his blood brought condemnation to Thessalian Patras. Here, too, is John, who both preceded and baptized the Lord, who is both the holy gateway to the Gospel and the finishing point of the Law.... Nearby lies the doubter Thomas.... Here lies Luke, a physician first by profession and later by preaching.... Joined with these apostles in devotion and faith, power and honor, are the martyrs Agricola and Vitalis together with Proculus, and Euphemia who as martyr in the area of Chalcedon marks and consecrates that shore with her virgin's blood.... Here too is the martyr Nazarius, whom I received in humility of heart as a gift of faith from the noble Ambrose....[56]

This roster of apostles and martyrs is extraordinary both in terms of the saints' importance as individuals and in terms of the great number of diverse figures whose bodily remains Paulinus managed to assemble into a single collection.

Paulinus also visually advertised the presence of these impressive relics in a monumental inscription on the wall behind the altar, the text of which he spelled out in a letter to Sulpicius Severus:

This *titulus* indicates the holy of holies which has been deposited under the altar:

'Here is the piety, here nourishing faith, here the glory of Christ;
here is the cross joined with its own martyrs.
For a little piece of the wood of the cross is a great pledge,
and the whole power of the cross is present in (even) a small piece of it.
This greatest good brought to Nola by the gift of Saint Melania
came from the city of Jerusalem.
The holy altar veils a double honor to God:
it brings together the ashes of Apostles with the cross.
How well are the bones of the pious joined to the wood of the cross,
so that those who were killed for the cross, find rest on the cross.'[57]

This monumental text informed its readers of the sacred treasures covered by the altar, and it advertised Paulinus's pride in Nola's possession of both a fragment of the True Cross as well as the relics of numerous apostles and saints. Like the passage from the feast-day poem quoted in the previous paragraph, the inscription's language stressed the place-ness of the these precious relics reiterating through the fourfold repetition of the deictic "hic" that they are "right here" in a single deposit under the altar before viewers as they stand in the newly constructed basilica.

The inscription, moreover, did not merely indicate the presence of relics, but put forth claims about their pedigree, provenance, and programmatic rationale. Conspicuously, it elaborated the Cross fragment's Holy Land point of origin and its relocation to Cimitile-Nola thanks to the actions of Melania the Elder.[58] Melania herself was not only a formidable holy figure whose asceticism made her, as one scholar has recently written, "a legend in her own lifetime," she was also a well-connected aristocrat who, upon returning from her twenty-seven-year sojourn in the Holy Land, visited Nola with a whole entourage of wealthy and influential relatives in tow.[59] Indirectly the apse inscription, and the letter in which it was transcribed, thus also highlighted Paulinus's role as patron whose connections to the likes of Melania made such an exchange of rare and precious sacred property possible.

In addition to stressing his community's benefit thanks to his own close relationships with other aristocratic and ascetic elites, Paulinus elsewhere emphasized that the collection of relics under the new basilica's altar placed Nola squarely within a larger network of cities blessed by God with saintly remains. In *Carmen* 19, composed in honor of St. Felix's feast day in 405, Paulinus explains the theological justification for the translation of relics: "Since the faith had initially not been spread through the whole world alike, many areas of the earth were without martyrs. This I think is why Christ has both inspired princes ... and acquainted His servants with His most generous decision to summon martyrs from their earlier homes and translate them to fresh lodgings on earth."[60] His poem goes on to cite the historical precedents of Bishop Ambrose's translation of martyrs in Milan and the emperor Constantine's relocation of the bodies of apostles Andrew and Timothy to Constantinople.[61] Moreover, Paulinus casts Constantine's actions as a divinely inspired strategy for elevating the new capital to the status of Rome: "... so Constantinople now stands with twin towers, vying to match the hegemony of great Rome, and more genuinely rivaling the walls of Rome through the eminence that God bestowed on her, for He counterbalanced Peter and Paul with a protection as great since

Constantinople gained the disciple of Paul and the brother of Peter."[62] When therefore Paulinus's verse then turns to praise Nola for its *own* collection of apostles' relics, it is in clear comparison with the preeminent centers of Milan, Rome, and Constantinople hailed in the immediately preceding section of the poem. Likening the particles of saints' bodies to dewdrops from which fountains of holy grace spring, he writes, "From this source Christ's abundance, so rich in its tiniest forms, has fallen on us also; for we too have received, in the form of a fragment of dust, the sacred tokens of the apostles' flesh …"[63] In other words, Paulinus publicly cast the acquisition of fragments of apostles, martyrs, and the True Cross as a development that placed Nola in the company of the most politically and religiously powerful cities of his day.

The promotion of the sacred relics that Paulinus deposited under the altar of the Basilica Nova throws into relief the embellishment of St. Felix's tomb at the west end of the Basilica Vetus. While St. Felix's cult site became increasingly monumentalized and glorified by Paulinus's interventions at Cimitile, in some way its status as holy center was also mediated by the new relation into which it was put with the relic-rich liturgical altar of the Basilica Nova. The altar, as site of the performance of the liturgy, was the place at which the clergy's status was most architecturally and ritually manifest. The altar relics and the monumental inscription that promoted them both served as a backdrop to the clergy's own ritual performance and declared the sanctuary's (and its ecclesiastical patron's) elevated position within a larger sacred and political topography. In this way the altar relics presented a global counterpart to Felix's claims to local, home-grown sanctity at Cimitile.

Conclusion

The ecclesiastical complex and martyrium of St. Felix at Cimitile-Nola is unique in terms of the range and depth of surviving evidence, but the insight it offers into a cleric's orchestration of sacred space may help us understand other sites' spatial and decorative programs. In the fifth and sixth centuries, the same period that saw the increased deposition of relics under altars, a wide range of other architectural and epigraphic devices were simultaneously developed to negotiate more complex spatial relationships between distinct focal points of saint veneration and liturgical ritual. At a number of sites which possessed multiple sacred focal points visitors would have linked the two ritual centers by virtue of moving into, out of, and gazing around the church complex. At these sanctuaries, the visual and spatial connection created between martyrial and eucharistic nodes enabled the two types of ritual experiences to remain separate, but not completely so. Complexes such as those examined here facilitated a direct, personal encounter with an authentic, tangible, and place-bound (i.e., unique and local) holy site (the martyrium) while simultaneously focusing attention on the collective, shared ritual experience led by ecclesiastical personnel at the altar. Indeed, as Paulinus's case exemplifies, it was at the liturgical altar that architecture, ritual, and the presentation of relics came together most directly to underscore the authority of local church officials and the community's connection to the universal Church.

Notes

Unless otherwise noted, translations are my own. For advice and assistance with various aspects of the article or images, I am grateful to Victoria Cain, Peter Grossmann, Cecily Hilsdale, Scott Johnson, Jaś Elsner, John Marston, Anne McKnight, Robert Ousterhout, Danny Richter, Sean Roberts, Galina Tirnanić, and Günder Varinlioğlu.

1. As the bishop Ambrose's biographer, Paulinus of Milan, relates, relocating the bodies was justified since in their original location the tombs were neither recognized nor protected, but profaned by the pedestrian traffic to the tombs of Felix and Nabor: ... *sed sancti martyres Nabor et Felix celeberrime frequentabantur, Protasii vero et Gervasii martyrum ut nomina ita etiam et sepultura incognita erat, in tantum ut supra ipsorum sepulcra ambularent omnes qui vellent ad cancellos pervenire quibus sanctorum Naboris et Felicis martyrum ab iniuria sepulcra defendebantur* (V. Ambr. 14: Pellegrino 1961, p. 70).

2. The relics of Sts. Timothy, Andrew, and Luke were, famously, taken to Constantinople in the fourth century to be deposited in the Church of the Holy Apostles, but sources disagree on whether this occurred in 336 or 356-7 (Mango 1990a and id. 1990b; Brandenburg 1995, pp. 71-72; Woods 1991). St. Babylas's corpse was moved from its third-century burial site, probably at Antioch, to Daphne between 351 and 354 and removed again on Julian's order in 362 (Mango 1990a, p. 52; Downey 1938).

3. Ambrose wrote a letter to his sister Marcellina (*Ep.* 77[Maur. 22]) that includes the texts of the sermons he delivered in days following the translation of the relics, and he also wrote a hymn for the occasion (*Hymn.* 11). See also *Vit. Ambr.* 14, and Augustine's *Conf.* IX.7.16 and *Serm.* 318.1. On the literary sources see Bastianensen 1976; Den Boeft 1991; and Zangara 1981. On Ambrose's promotion of saints' cults, see Dassmann 1975 and McLynn 1994, esp. pp. 209-19 and 226-37. On the Basilica Ambrosiana (under the extant Romanesque structure of S. Ambrosio), see Krautheimer 1983, pp. 74, 77-9.

4. Brown 1981; Markus 1990.
5. Yasin 2009; Y. Duval 1988.
6. McLynn 1994, pp. 209–19. Ambrose's discovery and translation of the bodies of Sts. Gervasius and Protasius is also an early example of a *topos* which was to gain considerable currency in following centuries, with subsequent medieval narratives capitalizing on the notion of the maltreatment or neglect of saint's remains to justify relic theft (Geary 1990).
7. *Ep.* 77[22].4: *Aspicite ad dexteram meam, aspicite ad sinistram reliquias sacrosanctas: videtis caelestis conversationis viros* (Zelzer 1982, p. 129).
8. *Ep.* 77[22].13. Dassmann in particular stresses the connection Ambrose created between the site of the martyrs' remains and the liturgy (1975, pp. 53–55). The last stanza of Ambrose's hymn to the two saints resounds with rejoicing at the relics' most vital quality, the tangibility which both demonstrates their sanctity and justifies their translation (*Hymn.* 11.29–32).
9. See Wieland 1912; and Stiefenhofer 1909, esp. pp. 88–101; Kötting 1965; Brandenburg 1995; Deichmann 1970; and the recent state of the field overview on early Christian altars by N. Duval (2005).
10. *De falsis memoriis martyrum*, Council of Carthage, 401 C.E. (Munier 1974, pp. 204–5; Kemp 1948, p. 15; Yasin 2009, p. 153).
11. Cf. N. Duval 1994; Braun 1924, esp. pp. 125–227; Michaud 1999, pp. 201–3; Ripoll and Arnau 2005; Michel 2001, pp. 77–9.
12. Grabar 1946.
13. Hahn 1997; James 2000; Schmitt 1999; on visuality and living holy men, see Frank 2000; on icons, see especially Belting 1994; Cormack 1997. See now also the essays in Hourihane 2010.
14. Mitchell (2001) suggests that the asymmetrical position of certain features within religious architecture lends those features enhanced sacred power, but the author does not go on further to explore how this works or why this should be so.
15. Yasin 2009, pp. 151–89.
16. Christern 1976; Yasin 2009, pp. 161–4; MacMullen 2009, pp. 65–7.
17. On the archaeology and dating of the complex, see Sodini 2001; Biscop and Sodini 1984; and Biscop and Sodini 1989; plus the older report of Krencker 1939 (whose reconstruction of the roofing system is nevertheless no longer accepted).
18. Such a trajectory was, however, apparently only open to men; women, Evagrius tells us, were only allowed to look in toward the column from the threshhold of the entrance (*Hist. Ecc.* I.14; trans. Whitby 2000, pp. 40–41).
19. Sodini 2001; Yasin 2009, pp. 170–2.
20. Shortly after the constuction of the first church, this stairway was enclosed by an annex built against the church's eastern end (Grossmann 1989, esp. pp. 49–50; see also the overviews of the site offered by Grossmann 1998; Grossmann 2002, pp. 401–9; and McKenzie 2007, pp. 288–93).
21. Grossmann 1989, pp. 70–73, 156, and 212. Note that the Great Basilica also went through multiple phases (Grossmann 2002, pp. 405–9): depicted in Figure 9.4 is the second, enlarged structure as it appeared in the Justinianic period. For a plan of the surrounding complex showing the main pilgrimage road opening onto the large courtyard to the west of the ecclesiastical complex over the saint's tomb, see Grossmann 1998, diagram 1; and the slightly updated version in McKenzie 2007, p. 292.

22. Additional examples are presented in Donceel-Voûte who, citing Severus of Antioch's testimony of a monophysite vistor to a Chalcedonian martyrium, argues that the separation of martyrial and eucharistic space may have allowed visitors of diverse confessional persuasions to venerate in the martyrium without encroaching on the liturgical services held in the main church (1995, esp. p. 203).

23. While most martyria spaces are fairly constrained and would have contrasted sharply with the spaciousness of the associated church interiors, this is less likely to have been strongly sensed by visitors to St. Symeon's shrine where the complex provided generous room for moving and gathering around the column.

24. Herzfeld and Guyer 1930, pp. 1–46, esp. p. 8; Hild and Hellenkemper 1990, v. 1, pp. 441–3; Grabar 1946, v. 1, p. 65; see also Davis 2001; and Dagron 1978. Krautheimer follows Kautzsch in a date of circa 480 based on forms of the surviving column capitals (1986, p. 472, n. 21; Kautzsch 1936, pp. 87–88).

25. *Acta* 43: "And when she had borne this witness she went away to Seleucia; and after enlightening many with the word of God she slept with a noble sleep" (Schneemelcher 1992, p. 246). The mid-fifth-century *Life of St. Thecla* specifies that Thecla did not die (hence there are no bodily relics), but left the earth alive (on this critical "revision" of the earlier text, see Johnson 2006). The place, the author says, of her miraculous departure in the cave is "the very place of the … altar [of the Cave Church], gleaming with silver and surrounded by columns" (PG 85.559, quoted in Wilkinson 1971, p. 292, n. 2, my interpolation). The authorship of this text is attributed in the manuscript tradition to Basil of Seleukia, bishop in the second third of the fifth century, but modern scholarship has refuted this attribution preferring to refer to the author as Pseudo-Basil (Dagron 1978, pp. 13–19, and Davis 2001, pp. 40–41; see also Delehaye 1925, pp. 49–57, and Johnson 2006).

26. Gregory of Nanzianzus, *In laudem Athanasii orat.* 22 and *Carmen de vita sua* 545–51 (Herzfeld and Guyer 1930, pp. 5–6; Maraval 2004, pp. 356–7).

27. 23.5 (translation Wilkinson 1971, p. 122; see also Wilkinson 1971, pp. 288–92).

28. Herzfeld and Guyer 1930, p. 17. The fifth-century complex replaced an earlier structure on the same site, about which little besides the orientation of the apse is certain. The existence of a fourth-century basilica on the site is indicated by Egeria's account of her visit and references by Gregory of Nanzianzus (see previous two notes as well as Hill 1996, p. 217; and Hild and Hellenkemper 1990, v.1, p. 442). There is debate over the identification of the smaller church found during excavations of the eastern half of the above-ground, fifth-century basilica (the walls of which are indicated in grey on Figure 9.5). The original excavators considered it a later structure conforming to the reduced spatial needs of the shrine in the medieval period, possibly the turn of the millenium (Herzfeld and Guyer 1930, pp. 34–38), though some recent scholarship has preferred a fourth-century date for this structure (Hill 1996, pp. 218–19).

29. For the date of the larger, above-ground structure, we have the testimony of Evagrius's *Ecclesiastical History* (written in the late sixth century) that the emperor Zeno had erected a church at Seleukia in honor of St. Thecla after 477 (*Hist. Ecc.* III.8). For the discussion of whether this passage refers to this large basilican church or the so-called Domed or Cupola Church of Meryemlik, both of which date to the late fifth century, see Hill 1996, pp. 225–34. Wilkinson has revised Herzfeld and Guyer's plan of the Cave Church based on observations

of architectural features not visible at the time of their investigations. Most significantly, he noted an in situ fragment of mosaic pavement, which was cut by the stylobate of the fifth-century church and therefore indicated an earlier structure, which he suggests was a fourth-century church, on the site (1971, pp. 288–92; note that this section with a reconstruction and commentary on the martyrium site has been omitted in the most recent edition of Wilkinson's text [1999]). See also the summary in Hild, Hellenkemper, and Hellenkemper-Salies 1984, pp. 228–36.

30. On the arrangement of the south-side open entrance hall, see Hild and Hellenkemper 1990, v.1, p. 442. Hill suggests that there may have been a direct means of access between the south side of the above-ground sanctuary and the Cave Church (1996, p. 223), but even so this would undoubtedly have been only accessible to the clergy.

31. A photograph of the south-aisle light well taken from the Cave Church appears in Hild and Hellenkemper 1990, v. 2, fig. 385. The original excavators' report indicates that two light wells were cut into the ceiling of the lower church below the upper church's south aisle, but their statement that the light shafts "zugleich auch eine Verbindung mit der oberirdischen Kirche herstellten" (Herzfeld and Guyer 1930, p. 40) remains enigmatic. The plans published in the excavation report are also inconsistent. On one plan of the upper church, there is one feature labeled "Lichtschacht zur Krypta" (Herzfeld and Guyer 1930, fig. 6, fold-out facing p. 8; this is the light well reproduced here on Fig. 9.5), while two appear on the plan of the Cave Church (Herzfeld and Guyer 1930, fig. 39). Hahn suggests that the hole(s) could also have been used to create contact relics by facilitating the lowering of objects down into the grotto (1997, p. 1087).

32. The chronology of the church, complicated by devastating fires in the early seventh and twentieth centuries, is frought. Some scholars argue a late-fifth-century date (e.g. Cormack [1985] 1989, pp. 52–58 and Krautheimer 1986, pp. 125–8 and p. 474, n. 49); others prefer an early-sixth-century foundation (e.g., Spieser 1984, pp. 165–214 and Spieser [1992] 2001, pp. 561–9; see also the summary in Skedros 1999, pp. 7–40).

33. The ciborium is described at the end of Book 1 of the *Miracles* (Bakirtzis 2002, p. 176; see also Pallas 1979), and the base was revealed in the excavations conducted after the massive fire of 1917 (Soteriou and Soteriou 1952, pp. 100–1).

34. Lemerle 1979–1981, and, importantly, Cormack 1985, pp. 50–94. See also Mitchell 2001, esp. pp. 213–14, and Brenk 1994.

35. Cormack [1969] 1989, p. 35; Cormack 1989, pp. 548–9; Bakirtzis 2002, p. 178.

36. Two late antique mosaics known from the church appear to depict the saint before his ciborium. One, from the north wall of the north inner aisle, was lost in a devastating fire in 1917 but is documented by earlier photographs and watercolors (Fig. 9.7); the other remains in situ on the west wall of the south inner aisle (Yasin 2009, pp. 174–5 and 234–7; Cormack [1969] 1989; Cormack [1985] 1989; Cormack [1969] 1989; Brubaker 2004).

37. *Hist. Ecc.* II.3 (full passage): Τρεῖς δ' ὑπερμεγέθεις οἶκοι τὸ τέμενος· εἷς μὲν ὑπαίθροις, ἐπιμήκει τῇ αὐλῇ καὶ κίοσι πάντοθεν κοσμούμενος, ἕτερός τ' αὖ μετὰ τοῦτον τό τε εὖρος τό τε μῆκος τούς τε κίονας μικροῦ παραπλήσιος, μόνῳ δὲ τῷ ἐπικειμένῳ ὀρόφῳ διαλλάττων· οὗ κατὰ τὴν βόρειον πλευρὰν πρὸς ἥλιον ἀνίσχοντα, οἶκος περιφερὴς ἐς θόλον, εὖ μάλα τεχνικῶς ἐξησκημένοις κίοσιν, ἴσοις τὴν ὕλην, ἴσοις τὰ μεγέθη καθεστῶσιν ἔνδοθεν κυκλούμενος. Ὑπὸ τούτοις ὑπερῷόν τι μετεωρίζεται ὑπὸ τὴν αὐτὴν ὀροφήν, ὡς ἂν κἀντεῦθεν

ἐξῆ τοῖς βουλομένοις ἱκετεύειν τε τὴν μάρτυρα καὶ τοῖς τελουμένοις παρεῖναι. Εἴσω δὲ τοῦ θόλου πρὸς τὰ ἕῷα εὐπρεπής ἐστι σηκός, ἔνθα τὰ πανάγια τῆς μάρτυρος ἀπόκειται λείψανα ἔν τινι σορῷ τῶν ἐπιμήκων – μακρὰν ἔνιοι καλοῦσιν – ἐξ ἀργύρου εὖ μάλα σοφῶς ἠσκημένη. Καὶ ἃ μὲν ὑπὸ τῆς παναγίας ἐπί τισι χρόνοις θαυματουργεῖται, πᾶσι Χριστιανοῖς ἔκδηλα (Bidez and Parmentier 1898, p. 40): "The precinct consists of three huge structures: one is open-air, adorned with a long court and columns on all sides, and another in turn after this is almost alike in breadth and length and columns but differing only in the roof above. On its northern side towards the rising sun there stands a circular dwelling with a rotunda, encircled on the interior with columns fashioned with great skill, alike in material and alike in magnitude. By these an upper part is raised aloft under the same roof, so that from there it is possible for those who wish both to supplicate the martyr and to be present at the services. Inside the rotunda, towards the east, is a well-proportioned shrine, where the all-holy remains of the martyr lie in a lengthy coffin – some call it a sarcophagus – which is very skillfully fashioned from silver" (trans. Whitby 2000, pp. 63–64). In the seventh century, Euphemia's remains were transferred to Constantinople (Berger 1988).

38. Krautheimer 1986, p. 105; Maraval 2004, pp. 364–5.
39. *Hist. Ecc.* II.3, see full passage quoted in n. 37.
40. On Paulinus's biography and career at Nola, see Trout 1991 and id. 1999. Particularly valuable evidence for Paulinus's building campaign at Cimitile and its promotion are his *Carmina* 27 and 28 and *Epistula* 32, which discuss the site explicitly (Goldschmidt 1940, and importantly Herbert de la Portbarré-Viard 2006).
41. Unfortunately, archaeological remains of this so-called *Aula Apsidata* are scant, but recent work at the site has allowed the foundation wall of the apse to be mapped and dated relative to adjacent features (Lehmann 2004, p. 45). Significantly, even in this earliest monumental construction at the site, Felix's tomb was neither centrally nor axially positioned, but in the current state of our knowledge it is not clear how the grave of the saint was made accessible to visitors in this phase (Lehmann 2004, p. 46). See also Yasin 2009, pp. 181–3, and MacMullen 2009, pp. 91–3.
42. Lehmann 1992, p. 251; although later an altar was situated over Felix's grave, there is no evidence for such an installation before the early sixth century (Korol 1987, pp. 160–1).
43. It is, however, possible that there was an opening in the Aula's east wall that could have provided physical or visual access between the Basilica Vetus and Felix's tomb (Lehmann 2004, p. 48).
44. Lehmann 2004, pp. 53–119.
45. *Ep.* 32.10: *Basilica igitur... reliquiis apostolorum et martyrum intra absidem trichora sub altaria sacratis non solo beati Felicis honore venerabilis est* (Hartel 1999b, p. 286); cf. Herbert de la Portbarré-Viard 2006, pp. 101–2; Goldschmidt 1940, pp. 38–9.
46. *Ep.* 32.13 (full passage): *Nam quia novam a veteri paries abside cuiusdam monumenti interposita obstructus excluderet, totidem ianuis patefactus a latere confessoris, quot a fronte ingressus sui foribus nova reserabatur, quasi diatritam speciem ab utraque in utramque spectantibus praebet ...* (Hartel 1999b, pp. 288–9); Herbert de la Portbarré-Viard 2006, pp. 168–78 discusses the difficulties with this passage; cf. Goldschmidt 1940, pp. 42–3.
47. Ebanista 2003, p. 138.

48. In *Ep.* 32.13–15 Paulinus transcribed various inscriptions he had placed throughout the complex; see Herbert de la Portbarré-Viard 2006, pp. 186–208; and Lehmann 2004, pp. 160–4. Though the actual inscriptions are no longer extant, Paulinus's letter indicates their location with sufficient clarity to allow them to be plotted onto the site plan (see Lehmann 2004, pp. 179–88).

49. *Ep.* 32.15: *Antiqua digresse sacri Felicis ab aula, in nova Felicis culmina transgredere* (Hartel 1999b, p. 290; cf. Goldschmidt 1940, pp. 44–45).

50. *Ep.* 32.15: *Ut medium valli, pax nostra, resoluit Iesus / et cruce discidium perimens duo fecit in unum, / sic nova destructo veteris discrimine tecti / culmina conspicimus portarum foedere iungi...* (Hartel 1999b, pp. 288–9); Herbert de la Portbarré-Viard 2006, pp. 188–91; cf. Goldschmidt 1940, pp. 42–43.

51. *Ep.* 32.15: *Adtonitis nova lux oculis aperitur, et uno / limine consistens geminas simul adspicit aulas. In alio: Ter geminis geminae patuerunt arcubus aulae, / miranturque suos per mutua limina cultus* (Hartel 1999b, p. 290); cf. the translations of Herbert de la Portbarré-Viard 2006, p. 186 and Goldschmidt 1940, pp. 44–45.

52. Sodini 2001; Yasin 2009, p. 171.

53. Soteriou and Soteriou 1952, pp. 61; Grabar 1946, vol. 1, p. 455; Laskaris 2000, p. 343; Sodini 1987; Mentzos 2006. The date of the sub-altar relic installation is not secure. Most scholars, myself included, see it as belonging to a late antique phase of the site. Mentzos (2006) argues that the pit postdates the seventh-century reconstruction of the church and suggests that it could be as late as the early tenth century. He admits, however, that the relic vial and incised marble slab that surmounted the deposit likely came from an earlier iteration of a relic deposit on the site.

54. Soteriou and Soteriou 1952, pp. 58, 61–3; Laskaris 2000, pp. 342–5; and Yasin 2009, pp. 173–4. There was also a crypt with hydraulic installations (Bakirtzis 1995, p. 65; Skedros 1999, pp. 48–56; Bakirtzis 2002, pp. 185–6; Laskaris 2000, pp. 337–42), and later phases of the church also facilitated the saint's cult through the production of fragrant oil (*myron*) from at least the mid eleventh century (Bakirtzis 2002).

55. E.g., Soteriou and Soteriou 1952, p. 58; Mentzos 2006, p. 268.

56. *Carm.* 27.403–37: *... et apostolici cineres sub caelite mensa depositi placitum Christo spirantis odorem pulveris inter sancta sacri libamina reddunt. hic pater Andreas, hic qui piscator ad Argos missus ... qui postquam ... Thessalicas fuso damnavit sanguine Patras. hic et praecursor domini et baptista Iohannes, idem evangelii sacra ianua metaque legis ... hic dubius ... Thomas adiacet; ... hic medicus Lucas prius arte, deinde loquella, bis medicus Lucas; ... his socii pietate fide virtute corona martyres Agricola et Proculo Vitalis adhaerens et quae Calcidicis Euphemia martyr in oris signat virgineo sacratum sanguine litus ... hic et Nazarius martyr, quem munere fido nobilis Ambrosii substrata mente recepi ...* (Hartel 1999a, pp. 280–1; trans. Walsh 1975, pp. 285–6). For the chonology of this and the other *natalicia*, I follow Trout (1999, summarized on p. xv).

57. *Ep.* 32.11: *... hic titulus indicat deposita sub altari sancta sanctorum: Hic pietas, hic alma fides, hic gloria Christi, / hic est martyribus crux sociata suis. / Nam crucis e ligno magnum brevis hastula pignus / totaque in exiguo segmine vis crucis est. / Hoc Melani sanctae delatum munere Nolam, / summum Hierosolymae venit ab urbe bonum. / Sancta deo geminum velant altaria honorem, / cum cruce apostolicos quae sociant cineres. / Quam bene iunguntur ligno crucis ossa piorum, / pro cruce ut occisis in cruce sit requies* (Hartel 1999b, pp. 286–7). The inscription described in this passage no longer survives. See Herbert de la Portbarré-Viard 2006, pp. 125–34; Goldschmidt 1940, pp. 38–41; Trout 1999, p. 140; Brandenburg 1995, pp. 76–85; MacMullen 2009, pp. 92–3; and Yasin 2009, pp. 183–5.

58. Saxer 1995, p. 50.
59. Mratschek 2001, pp. 539–41. On Melania, see also Murphy 1947. Compare the roster of aristocratic visitors to the celebration of Felix's feast day in 407, including several of Melania's relatives (notably her granddaugher Melania the Younger, her husband, and their family), on whom Paulinus lavishes praise and whose familial connections he emphasizes in *Carm.* 21 (see Mratschek 2001, pp. 543–7; Trout 1999, pp. 282).
60. *Carm.* 19.317–24: *nam quia non totum pariter diffusa per orbem prima fides ierat, multis regionibus orbis martyres afuerant, et ob hoc, puto, munere magno id placitum Christo nunc inspirante potentes … nunc famulis retegente suis, ut sede priori martyras accitos transferrent in nova terrae hospitia …* (Hartel 1999a, p 129; trans. Walsh 1975, p. 142).
61. *Carm.* 19.320–37. See nn. 2–3. On Paulinus's possible slippage, in this passage, of Constatine for Constantius, and his omission of St. Luke, see Mango 1990a, p. 53, and Mango. 1990b.
62. *Carm.* 19.337–42: *geminis ita turribus extat Constantinopolis, magnae caput aemula Romae, verius hoc similis Romanis culmine muris, quod Petrum Paulumque pari deus ambitione conpensavit ei, meruit quae sumere Pauli discipulum cum fratre Petri.* (Hartel 1999a, p. 130; trans. Walsh 1975, pp. 142–3).
63. *Carm.* 19. 363–365: *inde in nos etiam stillavit copia Christi dives et in minimis; nam hoc quoque sumpsimus istic, carnis apostolicae sacra pignora pulvere parvo …* (Hartel 1999a, pp. 130–1; trans. Walsh 1975, p. 143).

Works Cited

Bakirtzis, C. 1995. "Le culte de Saint Démétrius," in *Akten des XII. Internationalen Kongressus für christliche Archaölogie, Bonn, 22.-28. September 1991.* v. 1, Münster, pp. 58–68.

Bakirtzis, C. 2002. "Pilgrimage to Thessalonike: The Tomb of St. Demetrios," *DOP* 56, pp. 175–92.

Bastiaensen, A. 1976. "Paulin de Milan et le culte des martyrs chez Saint Ambrose," in *Ambrosius episcopus. Atti del Congresso internazionale di studi ambrosiani, Milano 1974*, vol. 2 (*Studia patristica Mediolanensia 7*), ed. G. Lazzati, Milan, pp. 143–4.

Belting, H. 1994. *Likeness and Presence: A History of the Image before the Era of Art*, trans. E. Jephcott, Chicago.

Berger, A. 1988. "Die Reliquien der heiligen Euphemia und ihre erste Translation nach Konstantinopel," *Hellenika* 39, pp. 311–22.

Bidez, J. and L. Parmentier, eds. 1898 (repr. 1979). *The Ecclesiastical History of Evagrius with the Scholia*, London.

Biscop, J.-L. and J.-P. Sodini. 1984. "Qal'at Sem'an et les chevets à colonnes de Syrie du Nord," *Syria* 61, pp. 266–330.

Biscop, J.-L. and J.-P. Sodini. 1989. "Travaux à Qal'at Sem'an," in *Actes du XIe congrès international d'archéologie chrétienne. Lyon, Vienne, Grenoble, Genève et Aoste (21–28 Septembre 1986)*, vol. 2. Vatican City, pp. 1675–95.

Brandenburg, H. 1995. "Altar und Grab: Zu einem Problem des Märtyrerkultes im 4. und 5. Jh.," in *Martyrium in Multidisciplinary Perspective*, eds. M. Lamberigts and P. van Deun, Leuven, pp. 71–98.

Braun, J. 1924. *Der chistliche Altar in seiner geschichtlichen Entwicklung*, Munich.

Brenk, B. 1994. "Zum Baukonzept von Hagios Demetrios in Thessaloniki," *Boreas* 17, pp. 27–38.

Brubaker, L. 2004. "Elites and Patronage in Early Byzantium: The Evidence from Hagios Demetrios at Thessalonike," in *Elites Old and New in the Byzantine and Early Islamic Near East: Papers of the Sixth Workshop on Late Antiquity and Early Islam*, ed. J. Haldon, L. I. Conrad, and A. Cameron, Princeton, pp. 63–90.

Christern, J. 1976. *Das frühchristliche Pilgerheiligtum von Tebessa. Architectur und Ornamentik einer spätantiken Bauhütte in Nordafrika*, Wiesbaden.

Cormack, R. [1969] 1989. "The Mosaic Decoration of S. Demetrios, Thessaloniki: A Re-examination in the Light of the Drawings of W. S. George," in *The Byzantine Eye: Studies in Art and Patronage*, London, essay I.

Cormack, R. 1985. *Writing in Gold: Byzantine Society and its Icons*, New York.

Cormack, R. [1985] 1989. "The Church of St. Demetrios: The Watercolours and Drawings of W. S. George," in *The Byzantine Eye: Studies in Art and Patronage*. London, essay II.

Cormack, R. 1989. "The Making of a Patron Saint: The Powers of Art and Ritual in Byzantine Thessaloniki," in *World Art: Themes of Unity in Diversity. Acts of the XXVIth International Congress of the History of Art*, v. 3, ed. Irving Lavin, University Park, pp. 547–54.

Cormack, R. 1997. *Painting the Soul: Icons, Death Masks and Shrouds*, London.

Dagron, G. 1978. *Vie et miracles de Sainte Thècle*, Brussels.

Dassmann, E. 1975. "Ambrosius und die Märtyrer," *JAC* 18, pp. 49–68.

Davis, S. J. 2001. *The Cult of Saint Thecla: A Tradition of Women's Piety in Late Antiquity*, Oxford.

Deichmann, F. W. 1970. "Märtyrerbasilika, Martyrion, Memoria und Altargrab," *RömMit* 77, pp. 144–69.

Delehaye, H. 1925. "Les recueils antiques de miracles des saints," *AB* 43, pp. 5–85.

Den Boeft, J. 1991. "'Vetusta saecula uidimus' Ambrose's Hymn on Protasius and Gervasius," in *Eulogia. Mélanges offerts à A. R. Bastiaensen à l'occasion de son soixante-cinquième anniversaire (Instrumenta patristica 24)*, ed. G. J. M. Bartelink, A. Hilhorst, and C. H. Kneepkens, The Hague, pp. 65–75.

Donceel-Voûte, P. 1995. "Le rôle des reliquaires dans les pèlerinages," in *Akten des XII. Internationalen Kongressus für christliche Archäologie, Bonn, 22.-28. September 1991*. v. 1, Münster, pp. 184–205.

Downey, G. 1938. "The Shrines of St. Babylas at Antioch and Daphne," in *Antioch On-the-Orontes*, vol. II: *The Excavations 1933–1936*, ed. R. Stillwell, Princeton, pp. 45–48.

Duval, N. 1994. "Les installations liturgiques dans les églises paléochrétiennes," *Hortus Artium Medievalium* 5, pp. 7–30.

Duval, N. 2005. "L'autel paléochrétien: les progrès depuis le livre de Braun (1924) et les questions à résoudre," *Hortus Artium Medievalium* 11, pp. 7–17.

Duval, Y. 1988. *Auprès des saints corps et âme. L'inhumation 'ad sanctos' dans la chrétienté d'Orient et d'Occident du IIIe au VIIe siècle*, Paris.

Ebanista, C. 2003. *'Et manet in mediis quasi gemma intersita tectis': La basilica di S. Felice a Cimitile storia degli scavi, fasi edilizie, reperti*, Naples.

Ferrua, A. 1963. "Graffiti di pellegrini alla tomba di San Felice," *Palladio* n.s. 13, pp. 17–19.

Frank, G. 2000. *The Memory of the Eyes: Pilgrims to Living Saints in Christian Late Antiquity* (The Transformation of the Classical Heritage 30), Berkeley, CA.

Geary, P. 1990. *Furta Sacra: Thefts of Relics in the Central Middle Ages*, rev. ed., Princeton.

Goldschmidt, R. C., trans. 1940. *Paulinus' Churches at Nola. Texts, Translations and Commentary*, Amsterdam.

Grabar, A. 1946. *Martyrium: Recherches sur le culte des reliques et l'art chrétien antique*, 2 vols., Paris.

Grabar, A. 1950. "Quelques reliquaires de saint Démétrios et le martyrium du saint à Salonique," *DOP* 5, pp. 18–28.

Grossmann, P. 1989. *Abû Mînâ I. Die Gruftkirche und die Gruft*, Mainz.

Grossmann, P. 1998. "The Pilgrmage Center of Abû Mînâ," in *Pilgrimage and Holy Space in Late Antique Egypt*, ed. D. Frankfurter, Leiden, pp. 281–302.

Grossmann, P. 2002. *Christliche Architektur in Ägypten*, Leiden.

Hahn, C. 1997. "The Sight of the Saint in the Early Middle Ages: The Construction of Sanctity in Shrines East and West," *Speculum* 72, pp. 1079–1106.

Hartel, W. von, ed. 1999a. *Sancti Pontii Meropii Paulini Nolani. Carmina*, 2nd ed. (CSEL 30), Vienna.

Hartel, W. von, ed. 1999b. *Sancti Pontii Meropii Paulini Nolani. Epistulae*, 2nd ed. (CSEL 29), Vienna.

Herbert de la Portbarré-Viard, G. 2006. *Descriptions monumentales et discours sur l'édification chez Paulin de Nole. Le regard et la lumière (epist. 32 et carm. 27 et 28)*, Leiden and Boston.

Herzfeld, E. and S. Guyer. 1930. *Meriamlik und Korykos: Zwei christliche Ruinenstätten des rauhen Kilikiens* (Monumenta Asiae Minoris Antiqua 2), Manchester.

Hild, F. and H. Hellenkemper. 1990. *Kilikien und Isaurien* (Tabula Imperii Byzantini 5), 2 vols, Vienna.

Hild, F., H. Hellenkemper, and G. Hellenkemper-Salies. 1984. s.v. "Kommagene – Kilikien – Isaurien," *RBK* 4, cols, 182–356.

Hill, S. 1996. *The Early Byzantine Churches of Cilicia and Isauria* (Birmingham Byzantine and Ottoman Monographs 1), Aldershot, UK.

Hourihane, C., ed. 2010. *Looking Beyond: Visions, Dreams and Insights in Medieval Art and History*, Princeton.

James, L. 2000. "Dry Bones and Painted Pictures: Relics and Icons in Byzantium," in *Eastern Approaches to Byzantium*, ed. A. Lidov, Aldershot, pp. 119–132.

Johnson, S. F. 2006. *The Life and Miracles of Thekla: A Literary Study*, Cambridge, MA.

Kautzsch, R. 1936. *Kapitellstudien: Beiträge zu einer Geschichte des Spätantiken Kapitells im Osten vom vierten bis ins siebente Jahrhundert*, Berlin.

Kemp, E. W. 1948. *Canonization and Authority in the Western Church*, London.

Korol, D. 1987. "Zu den gemalten Architekturdarstellung des NT-Zyklus und zur Mosaikausstattung der 'Aula' über den Gräbern von Felix und Paulinus in Cimitile/Nola," *Jarhbuch für Antike und Christentum* 30, pp. 156–71.

Kötting, B. 1965. *Der frühchristliche Reliquienkult und die Bestattung im Kirchgebäude*, Cologne.

Krautheimer, R. 1986. *Early Christian and Byzantine Architecture*, 4th ed., rev. R. Krautheimer and S. Ćurčić, New Haven.

Krencker, D. 1939. *Die Wallfahrtskirche des Simeon Stylites in Kal'at Sim'ân. 1. Bericht über Untersuchungen und Grabungen im Frühjahr 1938, ausgeführt im Auftrag des Deutschen Archäologischen Instituts* (Abhandlungen der Preußischen Akademie der Wissenschaften, Jahrgang 1938, nr. 4), Berlin.

Laskaris, N. G. 2000. *Les monuments funéraires paléochrétiens (et byzantins) de la Grèce*, Athens.

Lehmann, T. 1992. "Eine spätantike Inschriftensammlung und der Besuch des Papstes Damasus an der Pilgerstätte des Hl. Felix in Cimitile/Nola," *ZPE* 91, pp. 243–81.

Lehmann, T. 2004. *Paulinus Nolanus und die Basilica Nova in Cimitile/Nola*, Wiesbaden.

Lemerle, P. 1979–81. *Les plus ancient recueils des miracles de saint Démétrius et la penetration des Slavs dans les Balkans*, 2 vols, Paris.

MacMullen, R. 2009. *The Second Church: Popular Christianity A.D. 200–400*, Atlanta, GA.

Mango, C. 1990a. "Constantine's Mausoleum and the Translation of Relics," *BZ* 83, pp. 51–61.

Mango, C. 1990b. "Constantine's Mausoleum: Addendum," *BZ* 83, p. 434.

Maraval, P. 2004. *Lieux saints et pèlerinages d'Orient: histoire et géographie des origines à la conquête arabe*, 2nd ed., Paris.

McKenzie, J. 2007. *The Architecture of Alexandria and Egypt c. 300 BC to AD 700*, New Haven.

McLynn, N. B. 1994. *Ambrose of Milan: Church and Court in a Christian Capital*, Berkeley, CA.

Mentzos, A. 2006. "The Bema and Altar Crypt of the Church of St. Demetrios," in *Early Christian Martyrs and Relics and their Veneration in East and West* (Acta Musei Varnaensis 4), Varna, pp. 259–71.

Michaud, J. 1999. "Culte des reliques et épigraphie. L'exemple des dédicaces et des consécrations d'autels," in *Les reliques. Objects, cultes, symboles. Actes du colloque international de l'Université du Littoral-Côte d'Opale (Boulogne-sur-Mer) 4–6 septembre 1997*, ed. E. Bozóky and A.-M. Helvétius, Turnhout, pp. 199–212.

Michel, A. 2001. *Les églises d'époque Byzantine et Umayyade de la Jordanie Ve-VIIIe siècle: typologie architectural et aménagements liturgiques*, Turnhout.

Mitchell, J. 2001. "The Asymmetry of Sancity," in *Raising the Eyebrow: John Onians and World Art Studies*, ed. L. Golden, Oxford, pp. 209–22.

Mratschek, S. H. 2001. "*Multis enim notissima est sanctitas loci:* Paulinus and the Gradual Rise of Nola as a Center of Christian Hospitality," *JECS* 9:4, pp. 511–53.

Munier, C., ed. 1974. *Concilia Africae a. 345–525* (*Corpus christianorum, Series Latina,* 149), Turnhout.

Murphy, F. X. 1947. "Melania the Elder: A Biographical Note," *Traditio* 5, pp. 59–77.

Pallas, D. I. 1979. "Le ciborium hexagonal de Saint-Démétrios de Thessalonique," *Zograf* 10, pp. 44–58.

Pellegrino, M., ed. and trans. 1961. *Paolino di Milano: Vita di S. Ambrogio (Verba seniorum n.s. 1)*, Rome.

Ripoll, G. and A. C. Arnau. 2005. "El altar en Hispania. Siglos IV-X," *Hortus Artium Medievalium* 11, pp. 29–47.

Saxer, V. 1995. "Pilgerwesen in Italien und Rom im späten Altertum und Frühmittelalter," in *Akten des XII. Internationalen Kongressus für christliche Archäologie, Bonn, 22.-28. September 1991*. v. 1, Münster, pp. 36–57.

Schmitt, J.-C. 1999. "Les reliques et les images," in *Les reliques. Objets, cultes, symbols. Actes du colloque international de l'Université du Littoral-Côte d'Opale (Bologne-sur-Mer) 4–6 septembre 1997*, ed. E. Bozóky and A.-M. Helvétius, Turnhout, pp. 145–59.

Schneemelcher, W. 1992. "Acts of Paul," in *The New Testament Apocrypha*, ed. W. Schneemelcher, trans. R. McL. Wilson, v. 2, rev. ed. Louisville, KY, pp. 213–70.

Skedros, J. C. 1999. *Saint Demetrios of Thessaloniki: Civic Patron and Divine Protector 4th-7th Centuries CE*, Harrisburg, PA.

Sodini, J. P. 1987. "Les cryptes d'autel paleochrétiennes: essai de classification," *Travaux et mémoires* 8, pp. 437–58.

Sodini, J. P. 2001. "La hiérarchisation des espaces à Qal'at Sem'an," in *La sacré et son inscription dans l'espace á Byzance et en Occident: études comparées*, ed. M. Kaplan, Paris, pp. 251–62.

Soteriou, G. and M. Soteriou. 1952. Ἡ βασιλικὴ τοῦ Ἁγίου Δημητρίου Θεσσαλονίκης, Athens.

Spieser, J.-P. 1984. *Thessalonique et ses monuments du IVe au VIe siècle: contribution a l'étude d'une ville paléochrétienne*, Athens and Paris.

Spieser, J.-P. [1992] 2001. "Remarques sur saint-Démétrius de Thessalonique," in *Urban and Religious Spaces in Late Antiquity and Early Byzantium*, Aldershot, essay XI.

Stiefenhofer, D. 1909. *Die Geschichte der Kirchweihe vom 1.-7. Jahrhundert*, Munich.

Trout, D. 1991. "The Dates of the Ordination of Paulinus of Bordeaux and of His Departure for Nola," *Revue des études augustiniennes* 37, pp. 237–60.

Trout, D. E. 1999. *Paulinus of Nola: Life, Letters, and Poems*, Berkeley, CA.

Walsh, P. G., trans. 1975. *The Poems of St. Paulinus of Nola*, New York.

Wieland, F. 1912. *Altar und Altargrab der christlichen Kirchen im 4. Jahrhundert*, Leipzig.

Wilkinson, J., trans. 1971. *Egeria's Travels: Newly Translated (from the Latin) with Supporting Documents and Notes*, London.

Wilkinson, J., trans. 1999. *Egeria's Travels: Translated with Supporting Documents and Notes*, 3rd ed., Oxford.

Whitby, M., trans. 2000. *The Ecclesiastical History of Evagrius Scholasticus (Translated Texts for Historians 33)*, Liverpool.

Yasin, A. M. 2009. *Saints and Church Spaces in the Late Antique Mediterranean: Architecture, Cult and Community*, Cambridge.

Zangara, V. 1981. "L'inventio dei corpi dei martiri Gervasio e Protasio. Testimonianze di Agostino su un fenomeno di religiosità popolare," *Augustinianum* 21, pp. 119–33.

Zelzer, M., ed. 1982. *Sancti Ambrosi Opera, pars X: Epistulae et Acta*, vol. 3 (*CSEL* 82.3), Vienna.

CHAPTER TEN

THE SANCTITY OF PLACE AND THE SANCTITY OF BUILDINGS: JERUSALEM VERSUS CONSTANTINOPLE

Robert G. Ousterhout

In *To Take Place*, a provocative discussion of ritual theory, Jonathan Z. Smith sets out some fundamental distinctions between medieval Jerusalem and Constantinople (Figs. 10.1–10.2).[1] Because they could be regarded as two of the three most important Christian cities of the Middle Ages (Rome being the third), Smith's argument merits further exploration. In both cities, sanctity – that is, the sanctity of place and the sanctity of buildings – appeared as part of a larger, politically inspired formulation that interwove power and status. And yet the construction and perception of sanctity remained remarkably different in each. This distinction is borne out by the analysis of the most important churches of these two cities, the Holy Sepulchre in Jerusalem and the Hagia Sophia in Constantinople. The construction histories and the recorded responses emphasize their fundamental differences.

Simply put, in Christian Jerusalem sanctity was embedded in the topography, particularly in the sites associated with the Passion of Christ. Each *locus sanctus* was fixed precisely where the event had occurred, and in Christian practice it was provided with a monumental frame and a ritual of commemoration. As Smith explains, "the specificity of place is what gives rise to and what is perpetuated in memorial."[2] Within the context of its urban development, its sanctity was fixed and immutable, and history, ritual, and *loca sancta* merged in the experience of the faithful. This is a constant theme in the accounts of early Christian visitors to Jerusalem. For example, St. Jerome told of the efficacy of worship within the holy places, where the events commemorated could be

10.1. Jerusalem, aerial view with the Church of the Holy Sepulchre in the foreground and the Dome on the Rock in the background. Photo Duby Tal, Albatross Aerial Photography, Jerusalem.

10.2. Istanbul (Constantinople), view looking toward Hagia Sophia from Galata. Photo Robert Ousterhout.

made spiritually present through ritualized veneration: "Whenever we enter [the Tomb of the Lord]," he wrote, "We see the Savior lying in the shroud. And lingering a little, we see again the angel sitting at his feet and the handkerchief wound up at his head."[3] Because the exact locations of the Crucifixion, Entombment, and Resurrection were fixed, set precisely where the sacred events had occurred, the faithful could experience there the "real presence" of holy persons and events; this belief gave the *loca sancta* power in the Christian imagination. The specificity of place is emphasized in pilgrimage literature as a validation of the scripture.[4] As Jerome relates, following the psalm, it is the Christian obligation to worship "where his feet have stood."[5]

Constantinople, on the other hand, had no significant Christian history prior to its refoundation as an imperial capital by Constantine in 324–330. In fact, prior to Constantine, it had *no* significant history at all. Thus, in contrast to Jerusalem, Smith emphasizes the novelty of Constantinople as a ritual site, which could be "deliberately crafted as a stage for the distinctive drama of the early Byzantine liturgy and for the later complex elaboration of imperial-Christian ritual."[6] Yet, from the standpoint of ritual, although novelty may result in functional gain and freedom to innovate, it may also result in ideological loss and lack of resonance in the relationship of old and new. Because Constantinople did not suffer the restrictions of a memorialized past, it could, in effect, free-associate. In a recent study of the public sculptural displays in the early city, Sarah Bassett emphasizes that Constantine's city was very much an intellectual construct, consciously or even self-consciously crafted to resonate historically, mythically, and religiously. It could be New Rome, but it could also be celebrated as New Athens, or even New Troy.[7] All were potent metaphors, but none of these associations existed prior to Constantine's refoundation. They were consciously constructed.

As with much of its historical and mythical symbolism, the sanctity of Constantinople was also consciously constructed. The city became head of the Orthodox Church through political means, rather than because of any previous sacred associations. The latter was obviously a matter of some concern and was compensated in several ways – most notably by the acquisition of relics, for which the city became famous. More than thirty-six hundred relics are recorded, representing at least 476 different saints, most of which were imported.[8] It was thus celebrated as New Jerusalem as well. We can trace the beginnings of the city's imported sanctity to the Church of Holy Apostles, begun by Constantine to be his place of burial. Both its early architectural history and the date of the arrival of relics at the site are highly contested. By mid-century, the church consisted of a cruciform basilica with an adjoining, centrally planned mausoleum containing the tomb of Constantine. Surrounding the altar, the basilica housed twelve *thekai* representing the twelve Apostles, to which were added the mortal remains of Timothy, Andrew, and Luke, brought in from different locations. Although rebuilt under Justinian and destroyed in the fifteenth century, one important message of the early building remains clear: with the possession of relics, any church could be a martyrium; any church could become the goal of pilgrimage.[9] That is, holy sites and venerated tombs, whose locations may have been originally fixed and immutable, could be relocated to more advantageous situations. This translation signals the beginning of a flood of holy relics into Constantinople.

But few of the city's important relics were site-specific. For example, St. Euphemia, one of the city's few local martyrs, was originally venerated in the Asiatic suburb of Chalcedon, where a martyrium was constructed, with her tomb in a chapel adjoining the sanctuary. In the troubled seventh century, when the Asian shore was threatened by Persian attack, her relics were transferred into the city by the Emperor Heraclius for safekeeping, either in 615 or 626.[10] Eventually they came to be housed in a more centrally located church dedicated to her, by the Hippodrome, formerly the triclinium of the fifth-century palace of Antiochos. It is not entirely clear when this occurred, but once Euphemia was established near the Hippodrome, tombs and mausolea were added around the building as her cult grew in importance.[11] Curiously, rather than being fixed and immutable, her original place of burial seems to have been gradually forgotten. That is to say, the relics, wherever they were, assumed greater importance than her original place of burial. Another telling example, the robe of the Virgin, was kept at the Blachernai Church since its arrival in Constantinople in the fifth century.[12] Regarded as the sacred palladion of the city, its resting place was considerably less important than its activated presence. In its protective role, the robe was empowered by parading it along the city walls in times of crisis.[13] Indeed, the efficacy of the relic as protector of the city seems to have depended on its movement through space.

Of course, architecture contributed to the construction of a spiritual landscape, but in Constantinople its role is primarily as ceremonial setting; monumental buildings almost never appear as commemoration of place. The Great Palace of the Byzantine Emperors, for example, was regarded as sacred because it was the home of Christ's earthly representative, but more specifically because it was the setting of the rituals and ceremonies that guaranteed *taxis,* the order of the well-governed Christian cosmos, as the *Ceremony Book* explains.[14] That is, rather than commemorating events that had occurred in a specific location in the historical or legendary past, its significance as setting was directly related to universal – not site-specific – concerns of the present and future. The palace was also a great repository of relics, many of which figured prominently in court ceremonial.[15] Like the Blachernai relic, however, they seem to have been more important when activated in the rituals of the court than as markers of sacred sites. Moreover, site selection for the Great Palace ultimately depended on the location of the pre-existing Hippodrome rather than any specific topographic association. It had become standard by late antiquity for the imperial residence

10.3. Istanbul (Constantinople), Hagia Sophia, as seen from west. Photo Robert Ousterhout.

to connect to a hippodrome, following the model established in Rome. One recalls that in Rome, the Domus Augustana on the Palatine Hill was associated with the hut of the city's legendary founder Romulus, as well as the sites of a variety of other events in the urban mythology.[16] Its ceremonial association with the adjacent Circus Maximus developed only gradually but ultimately set the model for situating the palace in Constantinople.[17]

Just as the meaning of Constantine's city was consciously constructed, so too was the meaning of Justinian's church of the Hagia Sophia (Figs. 10.3–10.4). Hagia Sophia, the church of the Holy Wisdom, famously dedicated to a concept and not to a person, originally had no specific sacred associations and contained no important relic.[19] More correctly, at the time of its initial construction in the mid-fourth century, the Holy Wisdom had come to be identified with the second person of the Trinity, that is, Christ. There were also other "conceptual" churches in Constantinople, dedicated to Eirene (Peace), Dynamis (Power), Homonia (Concord), and Anastasis (Resurrection).[20] One wonders if the choice of dedications might be considered part of a larger *intellectual* construct in the formation of an urban identity for the new capital. When

10.4. Istanbul (Constantinople), Hagia Sophia, interior looking east. Photo Sébah & Joaillier, ca. 1869, collection of Robert Ousterhout.

the first Hagia Sophia was rebuilt in 415, the relics of Joseph (son of Jacob) and Zaccharias (father of John the Baptist) were deposited at the dedication. But these were never particularly important. Hagia Sophia did not commemorate any specific site, nor any specific event.

Rebuilt by Justinian, it was in the words of Cyril Mango a "gigantic, novel and ruinously expensive pile."[21] The church of the Holy Wisdom was, more than anything, a symbol of the rule of Emperor Justinian, and its construction came at a critical point in his reign. In 532, the feuds between the various political factions in Constantinople culminated in a rebellion, called the Nike Rebellion for the shouts of "Victory!" by the participants. Much of the city was set ablaze, including the old cathedral. A new emperor was proclaimed by the rabble, and Justinian was said to have been on the verge of fleeing but was rallied by the courage of his consort Theodora. The riot was quelled, with thousands massacred, and Justinian emerged secure in his imperial power.

Much of Constantinople had been devastated, and Justinian set about to rebuild the city in his own image, so to speak. The reconstruction of

Hagia Sophia was his first project. He engaged two architects with theoretical backgrounds, Anthemius of Tralles and Isidorus of Miletus, to
create a unique monument. They designed a building that was more
of a study in geometry than anything else. It is worth emphasizing the
theoretical backgrounds of the architects, for no one with a practical
background would have attempted such an experimental building on
such a grand scale.[22]

In plan, Hagia Sophia follows the model of an Early Christian basilica,
with a nave flanked by side aisles, but it differs dramatically in elevation,
with vaulting introduced throughout the building, framing an enormous, centrally positioned dome. Thus, in addition to the longitudinal
axis of the plan, a centralizing focus is introduced into the interior. The
great dome, 100 feet in diameter, is the dominant theme of the building's
design, as it soars 180 feet above the nave. We normally discuss Hagia
Sophia today in terms of its structural system, but Justinian's biographer Procopius emphasized the quality of the space in Hagia Sophia. He
notes the effect of early morning sunlight, which gave the impression
that the light is generated by the building itself. The original dome, as he
describes it, was "… wonderful in its beauty yet altogether terrifying by
the apparent precariousness of its composition. For it seems somehow
not to be raised up in a firm manner, but to soar aloft to the peril of those
who are in there … "[23] His comments are not addressed to the structural
system, but to the aesthetic effect of the interior. The architects consciously created a dematerialized impression in the interior, emphasizing the transcendental. All surfaces were lush and reflective: the vaults
were covered with more than four acres of gold mosaic, the walls and
floors with "meadows" of many-colored marble revetments and inlays.
Even the structural elements lose the appearance of support: the solidity
of the piers vanishes behind such lavish coverings, and the lack of vertical alignment in the nave and gallery colonnades denies their structural
role and reduces them to decorative screens. The carved marble details
encourage such an interpretation: capitals, spandrels, and decorative
borders are heavily undercut, the vegetal patterns executed with a drill.
The delicate and lacelike surface is emphasized, and these pieces seem
unable to support anything of substance. The sense of weightlessness,
despite the great mass of the building, led Procopius to conclude that

great dome was not supported from below but suspended by a golden chain from heaven.[24]

Hagia Sophia is all about architecture – a building, and the process of building as metaphor. It was a flexible symbol that could be read in a variety of ways and whose meaning shifted with fundamental changes in Byzantine society. As a potent visual symbol of the sacred character of the city, it acted as a magnificent stage for the intersection of imperial and religious ceremonies that underscored Byzantine social order. It was through ritual that the sanctity of the building was invoked. The architecture of Hagia Sophia was meant to remove the ceremonies it housed from common existence, to transform them into heavenly dramas. By the tenth century, the *Ceremony Book* lists seventeen special events in which the emperor officially participated.[25] Set in the magnificent interior, the Kiss of Peace between the emperor and the patriarch would have emphasized the unity of church and state. In 987, when the ambassadors of the Russian Prince Volodymir attended the liturgical celebrations in Constantinople, they responded: "We knew not whether we were in heaven or on earth ... we only knew that God dwells there among men ... we cannot forget that beauty."[26] It is a rare historical event when a nation is converted on the impression of a building.

In spite of damage and repairs, including the complete or partial collapse of the great dome on three separate occasions, Justinian's church retained its impressive appearance throughout the Byzantine period. With its great, gilded dome seeming to float above its immense nave, the church still inspires awe, as well as metaphor. Justinian's unique creation may have been meant to evoke the Heavenly Jerusalem, or the Throne of God, or the Temple of Jerusalem, or quite possibly all three. Procopius writes, "Whenever anyone enters to pray, he understands at once that it is not by human power and skill, but by God's will that this work has been so finely finished. His mind is lifted up to God and floats on air, feeling that God cannot be far away, but must especially love to dwell in this place, which He has chosen."[27] Similar themes echo in the ninth- or tenth-century, semilegendary *Diegesis*, which recounts that the bricks of the building were stamped with the verses of Psalm 45, reading "God is in her midst, she shall not be moved." Gilbert Dagron extends the metaphor to suggest that as Hagia Sophia increased in prestige, it came to be regarded as the new Temple of Solomon, thereby equating Constantinople with Jerusalem.[28] Generations of Byzantine rhetoricians waxed eloquent on the subject of the meaning of the Great Church. I wonder sometimes if the interpretation of Hagia Sophia could have been a standard exercise in Byzantine schools of rhetoric, much as we assign our Art History students similar essays today.

The excavation and study of the church of Hagios Polyeuktos, built shortly before Hagia Sophia by Justinian's political rival, Anicia Juliana, encourage an Old Testament interpretation.[29] As the excavator Martin Harrison has argued, H. Polyeuktos replicated the Temple of Solomon in its measurements, translated into Byzantine cubits: measuring 100 royal cubits in length, as was the Temple, and 100 in width, as was the Temple platform – following both the unit of measure and the measurements given in Ezekiel. Harrison estimates the sanctuary of the church to have been 20 royal cubits square internally, the exact measurement of the Holy of Holies. Similarly, the ostentatious decoration compares with that described of the Temple, if we let peacocks stand in for cherubim, we have cherubim alternating with palm trees, bands of ornamental network, festoons of chainwork, pomegranates, network on the capitals, and capitals shaped like lilies (Fig. 10.5).[30]

A powerful noblewoman, Anicia Juliana was one of the last representatives of the Theodosian dynasty, who could trace her lineage back to Constantine. When her son was passed over in the selection of emperor in favor of Justin I and subsequently Justinian, the construction of H. Polyeuktos became her statement of familial prestige. It was the largest and most lavish church in the capital at the time of its construction. The adulatory dedicatory inscription credits Juliana with having "surpassed the wisdom of the celebrated Solomon, raising a temple to receive God."[31] In this context, Hagia Sophia could be seen as part of a larger, competitive discourse between political rivals. Justinian's famous, if legendary, exclamation at the dedication, "*Enikesa se Solomon!*" "Solomon, I have vanquished thee!" may have been directed more toward Juliana than toward Jerusalem.[32] In addition to the *double entendre*, there might also be a pun here: *Enikesa : Anikia*. Procopius uses similar Temple-like language about Hagia Sophia, insisting that God "must especially love to dwell in this place which He has chosen."[33] The discourse, I would

10.5. Istanbul, (Constantinople) H. Polyeuktos, remains of decorated niche from the nave, with inscription, now in the Archaeological Museum. Photo Robert Ousterhout.

argue, was ultimately more about the construction of divinely sanctioned kingship than about sacred topography. Clearly, both Juliana and Justinian understood the symbolic value of architecture, with which they could make powerful political statements.

Recent studies have offered a more nuanced history to the architectural discourse, suggesting that HH. Sergios and Bakchos appeared as an intermediary between H. Polyeuktos and H. Sophia, and revising the dates of the first two churches.[34] Although the new chronology would place the initial construction into a somewhat different context than the rivalry between Juliana and Justinian, J. Bardill insists that it "was doubtless intended to make a striking political and religious statement."[35] With all of its ostentation, however, H. Polyeuktos never figured prominently in the sacred landscape of Constantinople. By contrast, the idea of a sacred presence at Hagia Sophia relied more on its scale and magnificence than on any intended architectural symbolism.

In Byzantine accounts of Hagia Sophia, what is *not* said may be just as important as what is: no specific historic events are associated with the building; nor is there any explanation of why the building is situated

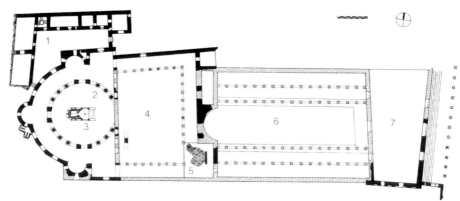

10.6. Jerusalem, Holy Sepulchre, plan of fourth-century complex: (1) Patriarchate, (2) Anastasis Rotunda, (3) Tomb Aedicula, (4) Courtyard, (5) Calvary, (6) Constantinian Basilica, (7) Atrium. Robert Ousterhout with A. Papalexandrou.

where it is. At the Holy Sepulchre, it is exactly the opposite. Historic events and specific associations with place are precisely what give the building its meaning. Constantine's biographer Eusebius refers to the church as "witness to the resurrection," "scene of the great struggle," "the place of the saving sign," a "memorial of eternal significance," and "a trophy of victory over death."[36] Marking the sites of Christ's Crucifixion, Entombment, and Resurrection, the spiritual significance of the church of the Holy Sepulchre guaranteed the building a tumultuous history.

As begun by Constantine the Great in 326, the Holy Sepulchre isolated the most significant holy sites – Calvary and the Tomb – and established the basic architectural features to glorify them (Figs. 10.6–10.7). The complex of buildings included an atrium, a five-aisled basilica with its apse oriented to the west, a courtyard with the rock of Calvary in the southeast corner, and, finally, the great Rotunda of the Anastasis (Resurrection), housing the Tomb of Christ.[37] Eusebius claimed that all remains of an earlier Roman temple had been removed to purify the site; in fact, as the archaeologist Virgilio Corbo has shown, several Roman walls and foundations were incorporated into the Constantinian complex, and these help to explain many of its irregularities.[38]

Following its destruction in 1008, the church complex was rebuilt circa. 1048 with the financial support from Byzantium.[39] As reconstructed, the Holy Sepulchre followed Byzantine architectural ideas,

10.7. Jerusalem, Holy Sepulchre, interior of the Anastasis Rotunda, looking west toward the Tomb Aedicula. Photo Robert Ousterhout.

probably directed by a master mason from Constantinople. Neither the basilica nor the atrium was reconstructed. The Anastasis Rotunda was provided with an apse, and the courtyard was enveloped by numerous annexed chapels organized on two levels. Along its eastern perimeter, the chapels marked events from the Passion of Christ, including the Prison of Christ, the Flagellation, the Crown of Thorns, the Division of the Garments, and, in an elevated position, the chapel of Calvary, above the so-called Chapel of Adam. Stairs led down to a grotto, identified as the site of the Invention of the Cross. There were additional chapels on the gallery level, above Calvary.

With the conquest of Jerusalem at the completion of the First Crusade in 1099, the complex was given a more unified appearance, incorporating elements associated with Western European pilgrim-age architecture (Figs. 10.8–10.9). The crusaders' project seems to have been motivated by the limited scale of the existing building. William of Tyre noted that at the time of the First Crusade, " … there was only a rather small chapel here, but after the Christians, assisted by divine mercy, had seized Jerusalem with a strong hand, this building seemed to them too small. Accordingly, they enlarged the original church and added to it a new building of massive and lofty construction, which

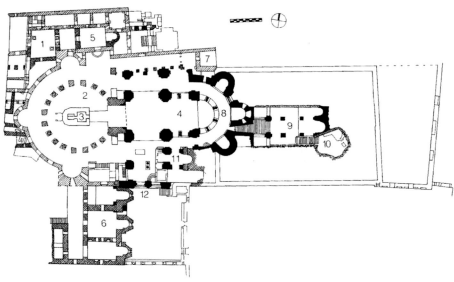

10.8. Jerusalem, Holy Sepulchre, plan of twelfth-century complex: (1) Patriarchate, (2) Anastasis Rotunda, (3) Tomb Aedicula, (4) Crusader Choir, (5) Chapel of St. Mary (eleventh century), (6) Subsidiary chapels (eleventh century), (7) Prison of Christ, (8) Ambulatory and radiating chapels, (9) Chapel of St. Helena, (10) Chapel of the Finding of the Cross, (11) Calvary, (12) Monumental entrance. Robert Ousterhout with A. Papalexandrou.

10.9. Jerusalem, Holy Sepulchre, view toward the south transept façade. Photo Robert Ousterhout.

enclosed the old church and in marvelous wise included within its precincts the holy places ... "[40]

Beginning circa 1114, the Cloister of the Canons was built to the east of the Byzantine complex, on the site of the Constantinian basilica. The subterranean chapel of St. Helena was built into its foundations.[41] The Anastasis Rotunda was left in its eleventh-century form, but the Byzantine courtyard and its subsidiary chapels were replaced by a domed transept and pilgrimage choir, with its three apsidioles replacing the Byzantine chapels. The chapel of Calvary was expanded, but contained within the eastern portions of the south transept. To connect the crusader transept to the Anastasis Rotunda, the Byzantine apse was removed, and the portals to either side were enlarged. The choir was dedicated (although certainly not completed) in 1149 to celebrate the fiftieth anniversary of the conquest of Jerusalem.[42] For the first time, all of the Holy Sites were both visually connected and housed under one roof. As one entered the building through the south transept, one could experience a panoramic view that swept from Calvary to the extreme right, across the crusader transept, and to the Tomb of Christ on the left side, visible through the enlarged doors to the Rotunda. Nevertheless, in its final form the Holy Sepulchre is as awkward as the Hagia Sophia is monumental. There is an old joke that a camel is a horse designed by a committee; in architectural terms, the Holy Sepulchre is a camel.

Throughout the Middle Ages, descriptions of the architecture of the Holy Sepulchre are at best vague and have led to all sorts of amusing reconstructions. When architectural references appear, they are meant to situate the reader in relationship to the holy places. The construction of the Holy Sepulchre never inspired detailed descriptions as the Hagia Sophia did. The architectural setting may have been appropriate to the sanctity of the site, but it was certainly *not* wonderful – it never inspired awe. If anything of the character of the building is emphasized in the historical accounts, it is the its venerable antiquity. But it was the awe-inspiring sacred contents – the Tomb of Christ and Calvary – that gave the architectural setting its meaning, not the quality of its space. Moreover, because of the fundamental importance of the events it commemorates, the Holy Sepulchre does not allow any flexibility to its interpretation; it inspires no metaphorical flourishes, for the meaning of the building is firmly grounded in the Crucifixion, Entombment, and

Resurrection. Unlike Hagia Sophia, in which ritual invokes the sanctity of the building, at the Holy Sepulchre, it is the inherent sanctity of place that inspires ritual – and gives meaning to the architectural forms.

What the Holy Sepulchre shares in common with the Hagia Sophia is that in both buildings the very fabric came to be regarded as sacred, and that with the passage of time the church itself came to be treated as a holy object. In the accounts of Russian pilgrims to Constantinople, for example, they "visit" other churches, but they "venerate" Hagia Sophia.[43] To be sure, Hagia Sophia acquired a collection of relics, including many associated with the Temple of Jerusalem, but they were clearly secondary to the architecture – that is to say, they were as important to the experience as the Guggenheim art collection is to Frank Geary's new museum in Bilbau. The building speaks for itself.

In contrast, the architecture of the Holy Sepulchre came to be regarded as sacred by virtue of what is housed. In this respect it could be regarded as a venerable reliquary or perhaps more appropriately as a contact relic. This ultimately compromised the unity of design in medieval rebuildings, in which as much as possible of the older building was maintained as new portions were added. The masons were obliged to balance aesthetic and structural decisions with spiritual concerns: the revered antiquity of the building constituted a more potent expressive force than the latest imported architectural features. I am reminded of Abbot Suger's explanation of his additions to the monastery church at St.-Denis: to "respect the very stones, sacred as they are, as if they were relics."[44] The architecture became an inextricable element in the experience and meaning of the place.

Within Constantinople, we may witness the construction of a sacred topography in many different ways, but it was not the topography of Jerusalem, and its sanctity was both constructed and perceived differently. Constantinople became "the city" (*he polis*) but it never became "the place" (*ho topos*). Like Gertrude Stein's Oakland, there was no there there. As it gained in sacred character, it could be likened to Jerusalem, in its heavenly and earthly aspects, which it neither replicated nor replaced. The distinction becomes readily apparent when we examine the Byzantine attitude toward pilgrimage. Even the Byzantine terminology marks the process as something different from the familiar, western medieval concept. Our word pilgrimage derives from the Latin *peregrinus*, meaning stranger or foreigner, and thus *peregrinatio* implies travel to foreign lands. The equivalent Greek word for pilgrimage is *proskynesis* – the same used for prayer or veneration, and scholars have argued that after the Early Christian period, pilgrimage as we think of it was literally a foreign concept within Byzantium.[45] There is ample evidence for veneration of relics, healing shrines, miraculous interventions of saints, and the like, but site-specific veneration was almost entirely a local phenomenon.

Henry Maguire has noted the discrepancy between Byzantine and Western medieval attitudes toward pilgrimage in his comparative studies of Byzantine rhetoric and Latin drama. In Sicily, which had coexistent Latin and Greek Christian populations, the interpretation of sacred texts could stand in sharp contrast.[46] For example, Christ's appearance at Emmaus was popularly reenacted in the Latin Peregrinus Play, presented during the Easter liturgy. In the rubrics, Christ is described as a pilgrim, and in south Italian depictions of Christ's appearance at Emmaus, he is dressed in pilgrim's garb. As represented at S. Angelo in Formis, for example, painted before 1086, Christ wears a cap and a shoulder bag and carries a double staff.[47]

By contrast, in the sermons of the Greek Philagathos, who preached throughout Sicily and southern Italy in the mid-twelfth century, the story of Emmaus is presented differently – and probably in response to the Latin drama. In his Emmaus homily, Philagathos emphasizes the appearance of Christ: not recognized by his disciples, they take him to be a man from Jerusalem based on his outward appearance. As he feigns ignorance of the Crucifixion, the disciples question him, "Are you the only one to sojourn (*paroikeis*) in Jerusalem who does not know the things that have happened in these days?" As Maguire notes, the Greek *paroikeis* is rendered in Latin as *peregrinus*, which could mean pilgrim, and was elaborated thusly in the Latin play. Educated in the Byzantine cultural tradition, Philagathos will have none of it, and his homily indicates his disapproval of the Latin drama, the misinterpretation of the Gospel, and his lack of appreciation for the phenomenon of pilgrimage at this time.[48]

Although we know of Byzantine pilgrims traveling to Jerusalem, we have virtually no evidence of a Byzantine ever going to Constantinople solely for the purpose of pilgrimage.[49] There is no genre of pilgrimage

literature in Byzantium, as developed in the West; most of our pilgrims'
guidebooks to Constantinople were written by Western Europeans or
Russians, who came from a different tradition.[50] The concept of place, as
locus of sanctity, is constructed differently in Byzantium. For example,
writing in the early thirteenth century, Nicholas Mesarites recounted
the adventures of his brother John, who had attempted secretly to make
a pilgrimage to the Holy Land but was arrested and returned to the capital before he had traveled very far. His father subsequently reprimanded
him: Why would he want to travel to the Holy Land when he could find
the same things in Constantinople? Christ's tomb is there, but his
shroud is in Constantinople; Golgotha is there, but Constantinople has
the Cross, the Crown of Thorns, the sponge, the lance and the reed. He
concludes, "This place ... is Jerusalem, Tiberias, Mount Tabor, Bethany,
and Bethlehem."[51] The relics he mentions were all housed in the church
of the Virgin of the Pharos, located within the confines of the Great
Palace. To be sure, Byzantine criticism of pilgrimage appears as early as
the fourth century, but here Mesarites deconstructs the notion of place,
condensing the entire Holy Land into the relic collection of a diminutive palace chapel. Moreover, in Mesarites's view, the relics represent the
sanctity of the city, not a specific place.

In the Byzantine figuration, architecture did not simply house holy
objects, it symbolized the sacred presence. Meanings associated with
place in Jerusalem and the Holy Land came to be associated with
church architecture in Byzantium. This might explain the popularity
of the architectural *ekphrasis*, by which detailed descriptions of buildings appear in texts to represent larger, abstract concerns.[52] From the
Byzantine perspective, the journey to sacred topography was not necessary because the church mystically represented sacred topography. In
the often-quoted words of the eighth-century *Historia mystagogica*, attributed to Patriarch Germanos,[53]

> The church is a heaven on earth where in the heavenly God "dwells and
> walks." It typifies the Crucifixion, the burial, and the Resurrection. It is
> glorified above Moses's tabernacle of testimony.... It was prefigured by
> the patriarchs, foretold by the prophets, founded by the apostles, and
> adorned by the angels.

The same text gives a decidedly topographical interpretation to the various parts of the church:

10.10. Chios, Nea Moni Katholikon, interior, looking south, showing so-called Feast Cycle in the transitional zone. Photo Robert Ousterhout.

> The apse is after the manner of the cave of Bethlehem where Christ was born, and that of the cave where he was buried.... The altar is the place where Christ was buried, and on which was set forth the true bread from heaven ... It is also the throne upon which God ... had rested. At this table too he sat down at his Last Supper ...

The idea that the Byzantine church could represent the Holy Land was developed by Otto Demus. He termed a common interpretation of the Middle Byzantine pictorial program the *topographical*: the images of the so-called Feast Cycle, which depicted scenes from the lives of Christ and the Virgin Mary, could transform architecture framework into sacred space (Fig. 10.10). In other words, sacred places could be collapsed into sacred space. Demus wrote:

> The building is conceived as the image of (and so magically identified with) the places sanctified by Christ's earthly life. This affords the possibility of very detailed topographical hermeneutics, by means of which every part of the church is identified with some place in the Holy Land. The faithful who gaze at the cycle of images can make a symbolic pilgrimage to the Holy Land by simply contemplating the images in their local church. This, perhaps, is the reason why actual pilgrimages to Palestine played so unimportant a part in Byzantine religious life.[54]

What this passage suggests is that we should understand the Byzantine church as more representational than functional, more symbolic than practical. While the meaning of the church building rendered the practice of pilgrimage unimportant, at the same time, when a Byzantine church housed a special, venerated object, there is little in its outward form to indicate a sacred presence. There does not seem to have been a distinctive type of Byzantine church architecture created in response to pilgrimage or to the special requirements of veneration, as is found in Western Europe, with crypts or chevets designed to accommodate the visits of the faithful to venerated tombs and relics. In fact, for Byzantium in general, we only have a vague idea of the setting for special veneration – that is, where within the churches relics were kept and how they were displayed. The typology of Byzantine church architecture seems to depend more on scale than on function.[55]

To sum up: In Jerusalem, sanctity was imbedded in its topography. Architecture could add validation to the *loca sancta*, but it was clearly secondary to the experience of place itself. It is worth noting that the majority of holy sites memorialized in the fourth century came with distinctive topographical markers: the rock-cut Tomb, the cave of the Nativity, the cave of the preaching, the footprints in the rock at the site of the Ascension.[56] In Constantinople, by contrast, sanctity was introduced and perpetuated within a complex system that interwove power and status, and architecture functioned as a setting for the rituals that emphasized the interweaving. God could choose to dwell in Hagia Sophia, just as he had chosen to dwell in Solomon's Temple, because of the piety of its patron and the skill of its builders. As with Justinian's legendary outburst, "Solomon I have vanquished thee!" we are repeatedly invited to compare Hagia Sophia with the Temple. In both, if we discount possible angelic appearances, the building preceded and inspired the sacred presence, but both buildings could have been built anywhere.

Part of the meaning of the Holy Sepulchre also comes from its association with the Temple, but the relationship of the two is constructed differently. Eusebius calls the Holy Sepulchre "the new Jerusalem, facing the far-famed Jerusalem of olden time."[57] But here we are invited to contrast, not to compare. Constantine's new church complex rose in visual juxtaposition to the ruins of the Temple, across the Tyropeon Valley. An imposing new work of architecture could testify to the success of the

New Covenant, just as the empty and abandoned remains of the Temple opposite it could represent the failure of the Old Covenant. But place was always more important than building: it didn't really matter what the church complex looked like. What mattered was the fact that the Holy Sepulchre was – both topographically and symbolically – exactly where it was supposed to be.

Notes

1. Smith 1987. A shorter version of this paper appeared as Ousterhout 2006.
2. Smith 1987, p. 22.
3. Jerome, *Ep.* 46.5, *PL* 22; 426.
4. This theme is developed in several essays included in Ousterhout 1990, in particular MacCormack 1990; see also Vikan 1986.
5. Jerome, *Ep.* 46.7, *PL* 22, 488; as noted by MacCormack in Ousterhout 1990, p. 21.
6. Smith 1987, p. 75.
7. Fenster 1968, p. 177; see also the analysis by Bassett 2004.
8. Meinardus 1970, pp. 130–3. See the discussion by Wortley 1982, p. 254; Maraval 1985, pp. 92–104.
9. See Cameron and Hall 1999, chs. 58–60, pp. 176–7; with commentary, pp. 337–9; also Mango 1990, pp. 51–62.
10. AASS, Sept., V: 275; Nauman and Belting 1966, pp. 23–4.
11. Naumann and Belting 1966, pp. 49–53; with limited remains, the dates of the mausolea remain uncertain. Mathews had argued for a sixth-century conversion for building on the overwhelming sixth-century character of its liturgical furnishings – that is, he proposed that the conversion had occurred before the transfer of relics: Mathews 1977, pp. 61–7. However, a close examination of the evidence suggests that the sixth-century marbles are spolia, and thus a later conversion sees more likely – perhaps even as late as the 796 restoration by Eirene and Constantine VI: Mango 1999, pp. 79–87. I thank Jordan Pickett for his observations of H. Euphemia.
12. Baynes 1949a, pp. 87–95; Baynes 1949b, pp. 165–77 (both reprinted in Baynes 1955); Cameron 1978; Cameron 1979.
13. As above, n. 12, esp. Cameron 1979.
14. McCormick 1991; *De ceremoniis*, book 2, praefatio, ed. Reiske 516.
15. Kalavrezou 1997.
16. Platner and Ashby 1929, pp. 101–2.
17. Platner and Ashby 1929, pp. 114–20.
18. The literature on Hagia Sophia is voluminous; see Mainstone 1988, with earlier bibliography.
19. As emphasized by Mathews 1971, pp. 105–80; see also Mainstone 1988.
20. Mango 1997, p. xxiii: all but Concord, part of the pagan or imperial vocabulary, would refer to Christ.
21. Mango 1997, pp. xxvi–ii.
22. For the Byzantine architect, see Downey 1946–1948; and more recently, Ousterhout 1999, esp. pp. 39–85.
23. Procopius, *Buildings*, I.i. 33–34; ed. Dewing, p. 16; trans. Mango 1972, p. 74.

24. Procopius, I.i.47; Mango 1972, p. 75.
25. Vogt 1935–39, passim; note also Baldovin 1987, pp. 167–226, on the stational liturgy of Constantinople; also Cameron, 1987.
26. For text, Zenkovsky 1963, pp. 66–67.
27. Procopius, I.i. 62–63; Mango 1972, p. 76.
28. Dagron 1984, pp. 293–309.
29. Harrison 1986, esp. pp. 410–11; Harrison 1989; Harrison 1984, pp. 276–9.
30. Harrison 1986.
31. Harrison 1986, pp. 5–7.
32. Ed. Preger, I, 105; Dagron 1984, pp. 303–9.
33. Procopius, *Buildings*, I.i.61–62.
34. Bardill 2004, pp. 62–4 and 111–16, dates the bricks from the substructure to the period 508/9 to 511/2, and those of the superstructure to 517/8 to 521/2; see also review by Ousterhout 2005.
35. Bardill 2006, pp. 339–70, with a thorough bibliography; note esp. pp. 339–40. All the same, it is difficult to argue that the specific model for Juliana's church was Ezekiel's Temple, particularly when the dedicatory inscription refers to Solomon. Whereas the underlying symbolism derives from the Temple, most likely it was not a representation of one particular Temple, although Ezekiel's or Solomon's might have been called to the fore as the political or religious occasion prompted. Note also Croke 2006, for an earlier date for HH. Sergios and Bakchos; and Ousterhout 2010, for a review of Solomonic themes in Byzantine architecture.
36. Eusebius, *V. Const.* 3.33.1–2, trans. Cameron and Hall 1999, p. 135; extensive commentary, pp. 273–91.
37. The standard monograph remains Vincent and Abel 1914, vol. 2. The history of the building is summarized in Ousterhout 1989; and Ousterhout 2003. Corbo 1981, 3 vols., is indispensable and has superseded all previous publications on the subject, but without providing a full analysis of its architectural remains. A less satisfactory account, with imaginative reconstruction drawings is provided by Couasnon 1974. More recently, see Taylor and Gibson 1994, for important observations on the site of the Constantinian building, although their essays at reconstruction are less useful. Biddle, 1999, offers important observations on the building's history while focusing on the present condition of the tomb aedicula.
38. Corbo 1981, I, 41–42; Eusebius, *Vita Constantini*, 3:26.
39. Ousterhout 1989; Biddle 1999, pp. 77–81, has questioned the attribution of the Byzantine reconstruction with Constantine Monomachus, preferring his predecessor Michael IV (1034–41). The association with Constantine Monomachus was recorded after ca. 1165 by William of Tyre, based on local tradition, although the reconstruction may have been begun several decades earlier.
40. William Archbishop of Tyre 1943, p. 344; Folda 1995, p. 503, n. 121.
41. Folda 1995, pp. 57–60, and 517, n. 3; and fig. 5 for plan of the cloister (reproduced from Enlart).
42. Folda 1995, esp. p. 178.
43. Majeska 1984, p. 199.
44. Panofsky 1946, pp. 100–1.
45. Mango 1995, pp. 2–3; Carr 2002, esp. pp. 76–77 (and other studies in the same volume devoted to Byzantine pilgrimage); see also Vikan 1991; Ousterhout 2000.
46. Maguire 2001; Maguire 2003.

47. Maguire 2001, pp. 222–5, and fig. 2.
48. Ibid., pp. 225–7.
49. Greenfield 2000; see also Kaplan 2002, pp. 109–27; Talbot 2002.
50. Ciggaar 1996; Majeska 1984.
51. Heisenberg 1922, p. 27; see Magdalino 2004 (whom I thank for the reference).
52. Ousterhout 1999, pp. 36–7; James and Webb 1991.
53. Brightman 1908; significant portions are translated in Mango 1972, pp. 141–3.
54. Demus 1948, p. 15.
55. See comments by Ousterhout 1996.
56. Ćurčić 2006.
57. Eusebius, *V. Const.* 3.33.1–2; Smith 1987, p. 83.

Works Cited

Baldovin, J. 1987. *The Urban Character of Christian Worship*, Orientalia Christiana Analecta 228, Rome.

Bardill, J. 2004. *Brickstamps of Constantinople*, 2 vols., Oxford.

Bardill, J. 2006. "A New Temple for Byzantium: Anicia Juliana, King Solomon, and the Gilded Ceiling of the Church of St. Polyeuktos in Constantinople," in *Social and Political Life in Late Antiquity*, ed. W. Bowden, A. Gutteridge, and C. Machado, Leiden, pp. 339–70.

Bassett, S. 2004. *The Urban Image of Late Antique Constantinople*, Cambridge.

Baynes, N. 1949a. "The Finding of the Virgin's Robe," *Annuaire de l'institute de philology et d'histoire orientales et slaves* 9, pp. 87–95.

Baynes, N. 1949b. "The Supernatural Defenders of Constantinople," *Analecta Bollandiana* 67, pp. 165–77.

Baynes, N. 1955. *Byzantine Studies and Other Essays*, London.

Biddle, M. 1999. *The Tomb of Christ*, Sutton, UK.

Brightman, E.F., 1908. "The *Historia* Mystagogica and Other Greek Commentaries on the Liturgy," Journal *of Theological Studies*, 9, pp. 248–67 and 387–97

Cameron, Av. 1978. "The Theotokos in Sixth-Century Constantinople: A City finds its Symbol," *Journal of Theological Studies* n.s. 29, pp. 79–108.

Cameron, Av. 1979. "The Virgin's Robe: An Episode in the History of Early Seventh-Century Constantinople," *Byzantion* 49, pp. 42–56.

Cameron, Av. 1987. 'The Construction of Court Ceremonial: the Byzantine *Book of Ceremonies*,' in *Rituals of Royalty*, ed. D. Cannadine and S. Price, Cambridge, pp. 106–36.

Cameron, Av. and S. G. Hall, 1999. *Eusebius Life of Constantine*, Oxford.

Carr, A. W. 2002. "Icon and the Object of Pilgrimage in Middle Byzantine Constantinople," *Dumbarton Oaks Papers* 56, pp. 75–92.

Ciggaar, K. N. 1996. *Western Travellers to Constantinople: The West and Byzantium 962–1204*, Leiden.

Corbo, V. C. 1981. *Il Santo Sepolcro di Gerusalemme*, Jerusalem, 3 vols.

Couasnon, C. 1974. *The Church of the Holy Sepulchre in Jerusalem*, The Schweich Lectures 1972, London.

Croke, B. 2006. "Justinian, Theodora, and the Church of Saints Sergius and Bacchus," *Dumberton Oaks Papers* 60, pp. 25–63.

Ćurčić, S. 2006. "Cave as Church. An Eastern Christian Hierotopical Synthesis," in *Hierotopy: The Creation of Sacred Spaces in Byzantium and Medieval Russia*, ed. A. M. Lidov, Moscow, pp. 225–36.

Dagron, G. 1984. *Constantinople imaginaire: Etudes sur le recueil des "Patria,"* Paris.

De ceremoniis aulae byzantinae, ed. J. J. Reiske, Bonn, 1829–1830.

Demus, O. 1948. *Byzantine Mosaic Decoration*, London.

Downey, G. 1946–48. "Byzantine Architects: Their Training and Methods," *Byzantion* 18, pp. 99–118.

Eusebius, 1999. *Life of Constantine*, ed. Av. Cameron and S. Hall, Oxford.

Fenster, E. 1968. *Laudes Constantinopolitanae*, Munich, 1968.

Folda, J. 1995. *Art of the Crusaders in the Holy Land, 1098–1187*, Cambridge and New York.

Greenfield, R. P. H. 2000. *The Life of Lazaros of Mt. Galezion: An Eleventh-Century Pillar Saint*, Washington, DC.

Harrison, M. 1984. "The Church of St. Polyeuktos in Istanbul and the Temple of Solomon," *Okeanos: Essays Presented to Ihor Sevcenko on His Sixtieth Birthday by His Colleagues and Students*, ed. C. Mango, O. Pritsak, U. M. Pasicznyk, Cambridge, MA, pp. 276–9.

Harrison, M. 1986. *Excavations at the Saraçhane in Istanbul*, Princeton, vol. I.

Harrison, M. 1989. *A Temple for Byzantium*, Austin.

Heisenberg, A. ed., 1922. *Neue Quellen zur Geschichte des lateinischen Kaisertums und der Kirchenunion*, I: *Der Epitaphios des Nikolaos Mesarites auf seinen Bruder Johannes*, Munich.

James, L. and R. Webb. 1991. "'To Understand Ultimate Things and Enter Secret Places': Ekphrasis and Art in Byzantium," *Art History* 14/1, pp. 1–17.

Kalavrezou, I. 1997. "Helping Hands for the Empire: Imperial Ceremonies and the Cult of Relics at the Byzantine Court," *Byzantine Court Culture from 820 to 1204*, ed. H. Maguire, Washington, DC, pp. 53–79.

Kaplan, M. 2002. "Les saints en pèlerinage à l'époque mésobyzantine (7e-12e siècles)," *Dumbarton Oaks Papers* 56, pp. 109–27.

MacCormack, S. 1990. "Loca Sancta: The Organization of Sacred Topography in Late Antiquity," in Ousterhout 1990, pp. 7–40.

Magdalino, P. 2004. "L'église du Phare et les reliques de la Passion à Constantinople (VIIe/VIIIe-XIIIe siècles)," in *Byzance et les reliques du Christ*, ed. J. Durand and B. Flusin, Centre de recherché d'histoire et civilization de Byzance, Monographies 17, Paris, pp. 15–30.

Maguire, H. 2001. "Medieval Art in Southern Italy: Latin Drama and the Greek Literary Imagination," in *L'Ellenismo italiota dal VII al XII secolo: Alla memoria di Nikos Panagiotakis*, Athens, pp. 219–39.

Magurie, H. 2003. ""Byzantine rhetoric, Latin drama and the portrayal of the New Testament," in *Rhetoric in Byzantium*, ed. E. Jeffreys, Aldershot, pp. 215–33.

Mainstone, R. 1988. *Hagia Sophia: Architecture, Structure and Liturgy of Justinian's Great Church*, New York.

Majeska, G. 1984. *Russian Travelers to Constantinople in the Fourteenth and Fifteenth Centuries*, Washington, DC.

Mango, C. 1972. *Art of the Byzantine Empire 312–1453*, Englewood Cliffs, NJ.

Mango, C. 1990. "Constantine's Mausoleum and the Translation of Relics," *Byzantinische Zeitschrift* 83, pp. 51–62.

Mango, C. 1995. "The Pilgrim's Motivation," in *Akten des XII. Internationalen Kongresses für christlichen Archäologie*, Münster, pp. 2–3.

Mango, C. 1997. *Hagia Sophia: A Vision for Empires*, Istanbul.

Mango, C. 1999. "The Relics of St. Euphemia and the Synaxarion of Constantinople," in S. Luca and L. Perria (eds.), *Studi in onore di mgr Paul Canart*, published as *Bolletino della Badia Greca di Grottaferrata* 53, pp. 79–87.

Maraval, P. 1985. *Lieux saints et pèlerinages d'Orient*, Paris, pp. 92–104.

Mathews, T. F. 1971. *The Early Churches of Constantinople: Architecture and Liturgy*, University Park, PA.

McCormick, M. 1991. "Taxis," *Oxford Dictionary of Byzantium*, Oxford, vol. III, p. 2018.

Meinardus, O. 1970. "A Study of the Relics of Saints of the Greek Church," *Oriens Christianus* 54, pp. 130–3.

Naumann R. and H. Belting. 1966. *Die Euphemia-Kirche am Hippodrom zu Istanbul und ihre Fresken*, Berlin.

Ousterhout, R. 1989. "Rebuilding the Temple: Constantine Monomachus and the Holy Sepulchre," *Journal of the Society of Architectural Historians* 48, pp. 66–78.

Ousterhout, R. 1996. "An Apologia for Byzantine Architecture," *Gesta* 35, pp. 20–29.

Ousterhout, R. 1999. *Master Builders of Byzantium*, Princeton.

Ousterhout, R. 2000. "Pilgrimage Sites, Byzantine," in *Trade, Travel, and Exploration in the Middle Ages: An Encyclopedia*, ed. J. B. Friedman and K. M. Figg, New York, pp. 483–5.

Ousterhout, R. 2003. "Architecture as Relic and the Construction of Sanctity: The Stones of the Holy Sepulchre," *Journal of the Society of Architectural Historians* 62, pp. 4–23.

Ousterhout, R. 2005. Review of Bardill, *Brickstamps of Constantinople*, BZ 98, pp. 575–7.

Ousterhout, R. 2006. "Sacred Geographies and Holy Cities: Constantinople as Jerusalem," in *Hierotopy: The Creation of Sacred Space in Byzantium and Medieval Russia*, ed. A. Lidov, Moscow, pp. 98–116.

Ousterhout, R. 2010, "New Temples and New Solomons," in *The Old Testament in Byzantium*, eds. R. Nelson and P. Magdalino, Washington, DC, pp. 223–54.

Ousterhout, R. ed., 1990. *The Blessings of Pilgrimage*, Urbana, IL.

Panofsky, E. ed. & trans. 1946. *Abbot Suger on the Abbey Church of St.-Denis and Its Art Treasures*, Princeton.

Platner, S. M., and T. Ashby. 1929. *A Topographical Dictionary of Ancient Rome*, London.

Procopius, 1954. *Buildings*, I.i. 33–34; ed. H.B. Dewing, Cambridge, MA.

Smith, J. Z. 1987. *To Take Place: Toward Theory in Ritual*, Chicago.

Talbot, A.-M. 2002. "Pilgrimage to Healing Shrines: The Evidence of Miracle Accounts," *Dumbarton Oaks Papers* 56, pp. 153–67.

Taylor, J., and S. Gibson. 1994. *Beneath the Church of the Holy Sepulchre*, London.

Vikan, G. 1986. *Byzantine Pilgrimage Art*, Washington, DC.

Vikan, G. 1991. "Pilgrimage," *Oxford Dictionary of Byzantium*, Oxford, vol. III, pp. 1676–77.

Vincent, H., and F.-M. Abel, 1914. *Jérusalem nouvelle*, Paris, vol. 2.

Vogt, A., ed. 1935–39. *Le livre de ceremonies*, Paris.

William Archbishop of Tyre, 1943. *A History of Deeds Done beyond the Sea*, trans. E. A. Babcock and A. C. Crey, New York.

Wortley, J. 1982. "Iconoclasm and Leipsanoclasm: Leo III, Constantine V, and the Relics," *Byzantinische Forschungen* 8, pp. 254.

Zenkovsky, S. Z., ed. 1963. *Medieval Russia's Epics, Chronicles, and Tales*, New York.

CHAPTER ELEVEN

DIVINE LIGHT: CONSTRUCTING THE IMMATERIAL IN BYZANTINE ART AND ARCHITECTURE

Slobodan Ćurčić

When Moses came down from Mount Sinai with the two tablets of the testimony in his hand as he came down from the mountain, Moses did not know *that the skin of his face shone* because he had been talking with God. And when Aaron and all the people of Israel saw Moses, *behold, the skin of his face shone*, and they were afraid to come near him. But Moses called to them; and Aaron and all the leaders of the congregation returned to him, and Moses spoke with them. And afterward all the people of Israel came near, and he gave them in commandment all that the Lord had spoken with him in Mount Sinai. And when Moses had finished speaking with them he put a veil on his face; but whenever Moses went in before the Lord to speak with him, he took the veil off, until he came out; and when he came out, and told the people of Israel what he was commanded, the people of Israel saw the face of Moses, *that the skin of Moses' face shone*; and Moses would put the veil on his face again, until he went in to speak with him.[1]

The quoted passage from the Book of Exodus refers to the visible evidence of Moses' encounter with God atop Mt. Sinai – "the skin of his face shone." The following passage from the Book of Matthew describes the Transfiguration of Jesus atop Mt. Tabor:

And after six days Jesus took with him Peter and James and John his brother, and led them up a high mountain apart. And he was transfigured before them, and *his face shone like sun and his garments became white as light*. And behold there appeared to them Moses and Elijah talking with him. And Peter said to Jesus, 'Lord it is well that we are here; if you wish, I will make three booths here, one for you and one for Moses and one for Elijah.' He was still speaking, when lo, a bright cloud overshadowed them, and a voice from the cloud said, 'This is my beloved Son, with whom I am well pleased; listen to him.' When the disciples heard this, they fell on their faces, and were filled with awe. But Jesus came and touched them, saying, 'Rise and have no fear.' And when they lifted up their eyes, they saw no one but Jesus only.[2]

The quoted accounts of the two quintessential biblical theophanies are key reminders of the invisibility of God in both the Old and the New Testament traditions. In both instances it is *light* that appears as the only manifestation of divine presence. Reflecting the Second Commandment that states: "You shall not make for yourself a graven image, or any likeness of anything that is in heaven above …" (Ex. 20:4) in each of the two theophanies, a human being – Moses and Christ – became instruments of transmission of Divine Light for the benefit of human perception. There is a fundamental difference between the two theophanies, however, that also must be underscored. While in both accounts it was the faces – of Moses and of Christ – that shone, in the case of Christ, his garments also "became as white as light." Moses, we must remember, was a man *chosen by God*; consequently, we might say, he was "irradiated" by Him. Christ, by contrast, was God incarnate, made visible on earth by virtue of his flesh and his distinctive, human form.

While in Judaism the message of the Second Commandment was clear and was universally observed, the Christian tradition grappled with the issue of representation of God for a long time with eventually differing approaches in the Eastern and Western Christian traditions. This paper cannot and will not presume the task of exploring the various aspects and histories of the Christian debate regarding representations of divinity. It will only consider the role of certain specific means of representing Divine Light in the Eastern Christian or Byzantine artistic and architectural tradition. Specifically, I intend to explore how Byzantine painters and builders employed common symbolic language – expressed in media as different as mosaic, fresco painting and brick and mortar – to convey the notion of Divine Light in physical terms.[3] What I hope to demonstrate is that the concept of "construction of sanctity," to which this volume is dedicated and as it applies to this context, had not only the predictable symbolic, but also distinctly

11.1. Dorset, England, Hinton St. Mary, Roman villa. Floor mosaic, fourth century. Photo © The British Museum.

tangible, even three-dimensional characteristics in art and architecture of Eastern Christendom.

The problem of depicting Divine Light arose already in the early stages of monumental Christian art. One of the earliest known representations of Christ, on a third-century vault mosaic in a mausoleum discovered in the necropolis under St. Peter's basilica in Rome, depicts Him glorified by a halo and with an arrangement of rays emanating from his head in such a way that they could at once be understood as a *symbol* referring to his name ICOYC XPICTOC (Jesus Christ, in Greek), as well as a *depiction* of rays of Divine Light.[4] Another fourth-century image image – from the Roman villa at Hinton St. Mary in Dorset, England – while using the very same formula is a bit more intelligible, not to say "literal" – the Greek letters XP here made clearly visible (Fig. 11.1).

The formula, as illustrated in the mentioned examples, is of interest because it appropriated a pagan idea of the radiant crown as a means of conveying the notion of divinity in the Christian context. Generally understood as coming from the East, the radiant crown became commonplace in the Roman world of the third century, appearing on statues

11.2. Gold coin, minted in Siscia (after 330?). A. Constantine I wearing radiant crown (obverse); B. God Helios (reverse). Photo Belgrade City Museum.

of oriental divinities, and eventually within the context of Roman imperial iconography, linked to the growing significance of the cult of Sun God, Helios. Common on late-third- and early-fourth-century coinage, it appears also on the coinage of Constantine I, as the coin minted in Siscia, now in the Belgrade City Museum, illustrates (Fig. 11.2).[5]

The importance of Divine Light in relationship to Christ became an issue of prime importance in the work of early theologians. Thus, according to the fourth-century Cappadocian Church Father, Gregory Nazianzos, the light that illuminated Jesus on Mount Tabor was *one* of the visible forms of Divinity. The sixth-century Byzantine artist, who set the famous apse mosaic of the basilica in the Monastery of St. Catherine on Mount Sinai, must have relied on such a theological formula in making one of the earliest known pictorial renditions of the event on Mount Tabor (Fig. 11.3).[6] Thus – as though illustrating Evangelist Matthew verbatim – he made Jesus garments "white as light." Additionally, he chose eight linear rays to illustrate radiant energy emanating from the transfigured Jesus and affecting the present witnesses – the three fallen Apostles and the standing Prophets, Elijah and Moses. The iconographic model thus created, became a virtual norm in subsequent Byzantine art, as the Transfiguration mosaic in the Cappella Palatina in Palermo, executed by Byzantine mosaicists for the Norman King Roger II, around 1142–1143 illustrates (Fig. 11.4).[7] "Divine Light made visible" was here rendered

11.3. Mt. Sinai, Monastery of St. Catherine, Church, Christ Transfigured; detail from apse mosaic, sixth century Photo Roberto Nardi.

even more emphatically – the rays having been given rigidly defined, almost metallic shapes. Finally, in the closing century of Byzantine artistic production, an image of the Transfiguration demonstrates that its iconographic scheme was still faithfully maintained. Yet, the spiritual followers of the influential Hesychast mystic, Gregory Palamas, also produced a new visual expression of "uncreated light," or emanation of

11.4. Palermo, Cappella Palatina, Transfiguration mosaic, 1142–1143. Photo Slobodan Ćurčić.

"divine energy" as Palamas himself referred to it. The full-page illumination from the Theological Works of John VI Kantakouzenos, now in the Bibliotheque National in Paris (Ms.Gr. 1242), painted circa 1370–1375, effectively depicts the dramatic release of "divine energy."[8] Despite the vastly increased complexity of the rays of light in this composition, their visual rendition would nonetheless have been intelligible to the beholders.

The last point was one of the key challenges of Byzantine art, in general given over to the central objective of communicating things immaterial, and therefore invisible, by visual means. This paradoxical aspect of Byzantine art is well known and hardly requires further elaboration. Yet, Byzantine scholarship is still far from having reached the level of full comprehension of the range of possibilities relative to the means by which Byzantine artists achieved this goal. In the remainder of this chapter, I intend to explore how Byzantine painters and builders employed common symbolic language – expressed in media as different as mosaic, fresco painting and brick and mortar – to convey the notion of Divine Light in physical terms. Though my remarks will be mostly limited to the Middle and Late Byzantine periods (roughly ninth through the fifteenth centuries), we must bear in mind that the conceptual framework for examples I will be considering was already fully articulated in late antiquity.

To set the stage for my exploration I will refer to two well-known monuments – the late-eleventh-century Katholikon of the monastery of Daphni and the twelfth-century apse of the Cathedral of Cefalù in Sicily. The dome of the main church of Daphni monastery contains the paradigmatic image of Christ the Pantokrator (the Universal Ruler) (Fig. 11.5). Notwithstanding the controversy regarding the mosaic restoration that may have affected some of its details, the authenticity of the image of Christ depicted book in hand, within a rainbow mandorla against the background of gold tesserae, is not in doubt and, as such, it has been used in most general books on Byzantine art. The rainbow mandorla has also been noted as a paradigmatic image of the heavenly glory (H DOXA).[9] Its band made up of beautifully composed small squares organized in five concentric rings, each of a different color, together producing the "rainbow" effect with its unmistakable allusion to the Divine Light emanating from Christ, its source. "I am the light of the World" – according to the Gospel by John 9.5 – are the words spelled out in Greek and in Latin on the opposite pages of the open book held by Christ in the famous apse mosaic from Cefalù (Fig. 11.6), assuring us of the correct manner of interpreting this type of an image.[10] We should also note that both, the idea of the heavenly glory, and the manner of its representation at Daphni, have their unmistakable roots in late antique art, as the detail from the late fourth-century mosaic in the dome of the Rotunda in Thessaloniki illustrates (Fig. 11.7).[11] Though the order of colors varies in the two representations, the symbolic message in both is unquestionably the same – the circular rainbow frame *is* a rendition of Divine Light.

As already alluded to in my earlier comments, complexities in the manner of depicting heavenly glory increase in later Byzantine art. One of the more characteristic forms of depicting the heavenly glory takes

11.5. Daphni, Monastery church, dome mosaic, circa 1100. Photo Wikipedia Commons (public domain).

the form of zigzag lines contained within a circular band outlining the medallion with a bust of Christ, the late-twelfth-century example from Lagoudera in Cyprus being a good example of this scheme (Fig. 11.8).[12] Here, the zigzag pattern consists of a red and a blue band with individual elements that make up the bands given an illusion of *three-dimensionality* by virtue of shading and by setting the "folded" band elements against a black background. Thus, the symbolic reference to the Divine Light – in this case — has been given a curious, almost paradoxical, illusion of the third dimension.

11.6. Cefalù, Cathedral, apse mosaic, Christ Pantokrator. Photo Wikipedia Commons (public domain).

One of the most explicit manifestations of the phenomenon of "three-dimensionality" of Divine Light is undoubtedly the thirteenth-century narthex fresco from Hagia Sophia at Trebizond (present Trabzon in Turkey) (Fig. 11.9).[13] The unusually complex scene on the large cross vault of the central narthex bay depicts the hand of God at the apex of the vault, surrounded by a burst of Divine Light framed by the four Evangelist symbols each holding a jewel-studded Gospel Book. From the four corners of the Light-Burst emanate four streams of light depicted in the form of what may be described as "three-dimensional rainbows." The three-dimensional effect is achieved by using a folded-plate method of depiction, with one side of each of the folded-plate ridges rendered in darker tones than the opposite side, thus creating the desired illusion of three-dimensionality.[14] This method of rendering a multicolored folded-plate illusion is also known from late antiquity, as may be seen in floor mosaics and other media.

In Hagia Sophia at Trebizond we note that, placed in a diagonal manner, the four "streams" recall vault ribs. Spreading toward the bottom of

11.7. Thessaloniki, Rotunda, dome mosaic, detail of mandorla and Archangel, circa 400. Photo 9th Ephoreia of Byzantine Antiquities, Thessaloniki.

the vault, they acquire an almost architectural character at its springing points. Thus, both in terms of their illusionistic rendition *and* by virtue of their placement, the four streams confront us with a contradictory impression – by conveying the notion of the intangible and uncontainable through the employment of artistic devices of two media – the

11.8. Lagoudera, Panagia Araka, dome fresco, 1192. Photo Annemarie Carr.

11.9. Trebizond, H. Sophia, narthex, vault fresco, thirteenth century. Photo Robert
Ousterhout.

11.10. Canon Table, detail; Gospels (Ms. 9422), Matenádarán collection, Yerevan, circa 1280, f. 8. Photo E. M. Korkhmazian.

formal logic of architecture and the illusion-making potential of painting. Subject of a discussion in a recent publication by Antony Eastmond, the four multicolored streams are described by him as " ... perhaps an attempt to match in paint the light-reflecting quality of mosaic ... "[15] While correct as an observation of physical realities, this assessment falls short of detecting the intent to convey the idea of Divine Light by relying on conventions of *two* visual media.

Discussing the mentioned fresco at Hagia Sophia at Trebizond and its origins, Eastmond also made a passing comment regarding the possible " ... influence of the decoration of canon tables in contemporary Armenian manuscripts ... "[16] Beyond an example cited by him, we may profitably turn to two other Armenian examples of special relevance in the context of our discussion. The first is a canon table from the Gospels (Ms. 9422) in the Matenádarán collection in Yerevan (Fig. 11.10).[17] Dated around 1280, the canon tables appearing on f. 8 is a work of an unknown, but accomplished painter. The second canon table is from the Gospels in the Walters Art Museum in Baltimore (MS. W.539). Dated precisely to 1262, this canon table, in this case also on f. 8, is the work of a distinguished Armenian illuminator, T'oros Roslin (Fig. 11.11).[18] Rigidly defined, and elaborately decorated architectural frames characterize both examples. Both feature prominent arches

11.11. Canon Table, detail; Gospels (Ms. W. 539) Walters Art Museum, Baltimore, f. 8. Photo T. F. Mathews.

whose faces are articulated by the familiar "three-dimensional" folded-plate pattern executed in multiple colors with typical tonal shading creating the illusion of depth.

The Yerevan canon table arch is embedded within fields filled with scrolls of exotic plants populated by different creatures. In the geometric center of the arch we find a small disc executed in stippled gold leaf, in imitation of mosaic technique. Its shimmering effect was clearly the goal of the illuminator whose objective was to allude to the source of light in this symbolic display. The Baltimore canon table features a personification of the Sun in exactly the same position – the geometric center of the arch – with undoubtedly the same symbolic massage. What furthermore distinguishes both canon tables is the elaborately lush depiction of exotic plants and animals in a clear allusion to Paradise. The Armenian manuscripts, then, may be said to combine the symbolic representations of Divine Light and of Paradise in a highly imaginative fashion.

The idea of a "three-dimensional" folded-plate, that I have attempted to define, became a standard feature in Byzantine monumental painting, manuscript illuminations, icons, and so on during the thirteenth and fourteenth centuries. Used particularly in bands, featuring double, triple, or even multitiered arrangements this motif appears especially in

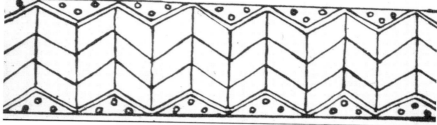

11.12. Fresco border details. Top Serbian churches, thirteenth century. After Z. Janc. Bottom Chora Monastery church, Constantinople, circa 1320. After D. Pugher.

horizontal bands. Treated in scholarship as elements of a distinct "decorative vocabulary" and used for separating pictorial compositions, these motifs have been recorded, as a group from the Serbian thirteenth- and fourteenth-century churches illustrates (Fig. 11.12 top).[19] An essentially identical band from the Monastery of Chora in Constantinople, painted ca. 1320, underscores the geographic spread of the motif, all of its essential details included (Fig. 11.12 bottom).[20] While the practice could be, and has been, discussed as evidence of the general reliance of painters on pattern books, the far more important question of the significance and meaning of this motif has *not* been addressed.

The same motif, it should be noted, also appears regularly on the exteriors of Middle and Late Byzantine churches. Made of brick, and more rarely of stone, this motif has been ascribed a banal name in English – *dog-tooth*, or *saw-tooth frieze* – and has thus suffered even greater ignominy than its painted interior counterpart. I would argue, in fact, that the two share not only similarities of form, but that they are bearers of the same symbolic meaning and should be associated with Divine Light. The term "dogtooth frieze," under these circumstances reveals at once the initial inability of scholars to recognize the potential of meaning in what have been referred to as "purely decorative" forms, but also a pressing need to find an alternative term that would adequately respond to the current investigation. Another term – *chevron* – used in writings on western medieval architecture, is also formally descriptive and fails to address the issue of symbolic intent.[21] For our purposes, therefore, I will adopt the term *"radiant freeze"* as a tentative solution to this dilemma.

The "radiant frieze" makes an early appearance on the facades of the tenth-century church of the Panagia at the monastery of Hosios Loukas in central Greece. Though perhaps not the earliest, this is certainly the best known of the monuments on which the feature in question was used extensively (Fig. 11.13).[22] It appears characteristically in two distinctive ways – as a corbelled frieze below the roof eves and as multiple recessed bands on the upper portion of the east and south facades of the church. The manner in which the bands wrap around the apses and windows of the eastern end of the church underscore the location of the "holy of the holies," the church sanctuary, highlighting it, along with the dome, as the most important parts of the church building. The so-called Pseudo-Kufic letters that also appear on the east façade of the church have been subject of considerable scholarly attention. At the same time, the "radiant friezes" have been all but ignored. In my opinion, they are to be understood together, as references to the holy; the "radiant friezes" specifically underscoring the notion of illumination by the Divine Light.

11.13. Hosios Loukas Monastery, Church of the Panagia; east end, tenth century. Photo Slobodan Ćurčić.

The clearest confirmation of such an association comes from the appearance of the same motif in church interiors, in the context of their painting programs. One of the most prominent places where the motif commonly appears is on the face arches framing the entrance into church sanctuaries. Several churches in the Göreme region of Cappadocia, for example, have arches in those positions decorated in just such a manner. Elmalı Kilise and a parekklesion at Kılıçlar, both from the eleventh century, illustrate the point in very clear terms.[23] The motif also appears in the same position in the small, late-twelfth-century church of St. George at Kurbinovo in the F.Y.R.O.M (Fig. 11.14).[24] Treated more elaborately,

11.14. Kurbinovo, Church of St. George, Annunciation fresco, 1191. Photo L. Hadermann-Misguich.

here it relates to the scene of the Annunciation in which the Divine Light plays the central role.

The "radiant frieze" also appears in a curious "shorthand" symbolic fashion in the scene of the Annunciation in the Psalter and New Testament Ms., illuminated circa 1084, now in the Dumbarton Oaks Collection in Washington, DC.[25] Here a single "radiant frieze" band may be understood as a capping of the wall enclosing Virgin Mary's house garden (Fig. 11.15). At the same time, however, it links the blessing Archangel Gabriel and Virgin Mary as a substitution for the here curiously missing ray of Divine Light and the dove commonly part of the Annunciation iconography.

Once introduced as an aspect of church façade articulation, the "radiant frieze" became a common aesthetic feature, but its symbolic role has

11.15. Annunciation, illumination; Psalter and New Testament Ms. circa 1084, Dumbarton Oaks Collection, Washington, D.C. Photo Dumbarton Oaks.

gone undetected in modern scholarship. Even a simple listing of monuments where the motif appears would probably fill pages. Highlighting but a few more interesting ways in which the motif was employed during the Late Byzantine period will suffice. The east façade of the thirteenth-

11.16. Arta, Church of H. Vasileios, east end; detail, gable, twelfth century. Photo Slobodan Ćurčić.

century church of H. Vasileios at Arta, in Epiros, displays the use of a single-banded "radiant frieze" under its roof eave and as a means of framing a window flanked be two shallow niches that contain two ceramic icons (Fig. 11.16).[26] Other decorative bands made of specially cut bricks produced for this purpose enhance the decorative character of the east façade and add to its symbolic reading as the enclosure of the holy of the holies. Below the window one notices the reduced version of the "rainbow band" a familiar reference to the Divine Light that we have encountered before.

An even more dramatic manifestation of this phenomenon may be seen on the east façade of the thirteenth-century church of the Archestrategos at Kostaniani in Epiros. Here, the entire tympanum of the east façade is completely filled with multiple parallel bands of "radiant friezes" – ten in all (Fig. 11.17). The effect is stunning and may be conceptually likened with a flickering surface covered with gold mosaic. The church at Kostaniani reveals another popular device related to the radiant frieze motif – a frieze of pitched bricks set in such a way that their thicknesses form a zigzag line of larger dimensions than a simple radiant frieze band. Its face within the wall plane, this motif is essentially two-dimensional, graphic, in nature.

11.17. Kostaniani, Church of the Archestrategos, east end, thirteenth century. Photo Robert Ousterhout.

The same motif, on occasion, acquired a three-dimensional quality by virtue of the fact that the areas surrounding individual bricks that form the zigzag line were not filled with mortar, thus creating dark voids against which the zigzag line appears in an even more emphatic way. Combined with the conventional "radiant frieze" band, as in the case of the thirteenth-century Panagia tou Vrioni at Arta, and again concentrated on the east façade of the church, the motif is effective, leaving little doubt as to its symbolic message (Fig. 11.18).[27] Coming even closer to the actual wall surface of the Panagia tou Vrioni we note that the theme of the zigzag line recurs – on a much smaller scale – on individual faces of each brick (Fig. 11.19). With the help of a sharp tool, each visible flat brick surface was incised before firing with a zigzag pattern of its own. This miniaturized texturing, reminiscent of woodcarving in its effect, was clearly an aesthetic as well as a symbolic choice. It should be noted that among the rare preserved fragments of painted church façades we also find the mini-zigzag motif, as for example that

11.18. Arta, Church of Panagia tou Vrioni, thirteenth century; east end, detail, upper part of apse. Photo Slobodan Ćurčić.

on the apse of the twelfth-century church of the Panagia at Asinou in Cyprus (Fig. 11.20).[28]

Another related architectural motif that appears in the course of the Middle Byzantine period is a frieze consisting of large corbelled triangular elements each made of several rows of bricks of variable dimensions. These usually appear as corbel-table friezes below church roof eaves, on domes, and so on, as seen on the early fourteenth-century parekklesion of the Virgin Pammakaristos in Constantinople and the Katholikon of Hilandar Monastery on Mount Athos.[29] Their practical function in such positions is clear, but given our investigation of the symbolic meaning of certain architectural forms, such friezes should also be added to the list of features with a symbolic meaning related to the concept of Divine Light. This is illustrated even more effectively by such features appearing on church domes as, for example, on the twelfth-century church of Hagoi Apostoloi at Pyrgi on Chios (Fig. 11.21).[30] Here the triangular elements are arranged radially in relationship to the arches above the dome windows, creating an effect resembling that of a radiant crown. The form of this zigzag arched band was in all likelihood plastered and painted,

11.19. Arta, Church of Panagia tou Vrioni, thirteenth century; apse, detail, wall masonry. Photo Slobodan Ćurčić.

as several later partially preserved examples suggest. The partially preserved exterior painted decoration on the complex of churches of the Serbian Patriarchate at Peć has been a subject of an important study that has provided invaluable insights into the probable appearance of these churches around the middle of the fourteenth century when their exteriors were evidently fully plastered over and painted. Reconstruction drawings of the dome on the Church of the Mother of God illustrate

11.20. Asinou, Church of the Panagia, twelfth century; apse, detail of preserved exterior painting. Photo Slobodan Ćurčić.

vividly the emphasis placed on the radially disposed "folded plate" multi-colored band with all the characteristic details (Fig. 11.22).[31] The arched multi-colored band is echoed in a somewhat smaller, horizontal multicolored "radiant frieze" band. The third element in this composition is an arched arrangement involving intersecting palmette-bearing vines depicted against white background directly above each of the dome windows. The motif is certainly a symbolic reference to Paradise. The pairing of this motif with that of the "folded-plate" multicolored band and its symbolic allusion to Divine Light was certainly no accident, as we have already seen in other contexts, such as the two Armenian canon tables referred to earlier.

Invaluable additional insights into this symbolic language may be gleaned also from the east façade of the twelfth-century Church of SS. Maria e Donato at Murano, an island in the Venetian lagoon. In this case the entire façade is spanned with a double zigzag band situated at its mid-height. Partially restored, this double zigzag band still preserves some of its original exterior revetment in the form of triangular marble slabs richly decorated with different patterns, all of them based on variations of vine-scrolls, palmettes and split-palmettes.

11.21. Pyrgoi, Chios, Church of Hagioi Apostoloi, twelfth century; dome exterior. Photo Slobodan Ćurčić.

These elements have not been studied closely since the days of John Ruskin, who lovingly recorded them in two drawings published in his *The Stones of Venice* (Fig. 11.23).[32] We are reminded of the links between Venice and Byzantium in the course of the twelfth century.[33] The motif, here under investigation, has unmistakable aesthetic and symbolic parallels in Byzantium, as another look at the arch framing the apse of Kurbinovo will convince us (Fig. 11.14). Despite the fact that the Kurbinovo arch is internal and its face painted in fresco technique, the differences between its and the Murano symbolic vocabulary are those between two dialects of the same language. This observation can be extended to include a great many Byzantine monuments of the twelfth and thirteenth centuries with their subtle variations on the same theme. Underlying these similarities and differences is the basically firm, geometric structure alluding to the notion of Divine Light, and an equally telling inclusion of the sinuous vine-scroll motifs alluding to the Garden of Paradise. As such, together, they echo early formulas that were being explored already by the sculptors in the age of Justinian, as the superb capital now in the garden of the

11.22. Peć, Serbian Orthodox Patriarchate, Church of the Mother of God, 1324–1337, single face of a dome drum exterior, reconstruction of painting. V. J. Djuric.

Archaeological Museum in Istanbul illustrates (Fig. 11.24). This capital is also significant because examples of exactly the same type exist in locations as widely scattered as Parenzo (modern Poreč), Venice, and Jerusalem. The universal Byzantine artistic language of abstract symbolism, therefore, much like the figural language that we are more familiar with, was clearly in the making already in the period before

11.23. Murano, Church of SS. Maria e Donato, twelfth century; east façade, detail of window arch. Watercolor by J. Ruskin.

11.24. Istanbul Archaeological Museums, Byzantine capital, Constantinople, twelfth century. Photo Slobodan Ćurčić.

Iconoclasm. Its fruition, as in the case of figural iconography, however, took place only during the Middle Byzantine period.

It was during the twelfth and the thirteenth century that the impact of this new symbolic language became major, its effects felt over a vast

11.25. Bivongi, Church of S. Giovanni Vecchio, 1122; domed bay, interior view. Photo M. Johnson.

geographic territory from as far as Sicily and Calabria in the southwest, to Novgorod and Vladimir in Russia, in the northeast. The church of S. Giovanni Vecchio at Bivongi, near Stilo in Calabria, dedicated in 1122, for example, reveals uses of the "radiant frieze" that were completely consistent with the Byzantine practice.[34] On the exterior we find such a frieze executed in brick wrapped around the upper part and the base of the apse, while inside we see a monumental three-dimensional version of the same motif executed in stone, prominently placed directly under the main dome (Fig. 11.25).

A similar attitude – using a large-scale "radiant frieze" depicted in fresco technique – is found in prominent places in the church of the Assumption at Volotovo Polye, near Novgorod in Russia.[35] Painted in 1363, this remarkable ensemble of frescos was destroyed in 1941 during World War II. Detailed records of the church have been published that illustrate practically all aspects of the original program. For our purposes, the monumental "radiant frieze" band demonstrates the significance attached to this feature within the building interior. Nearly a century later, frescoes in the church of Hag. Giorgios in Apáno Symi at Monofatsi on the island of Crete, painted in 1453, unmistakably speak the same visual language, despite enormous geographic and cultural distances that separate the two painted church interiors.[36] Associated with the Christological fresco cycle, the "radiant frieze" in both cases reverberates with the notion of "Christ, the Light of the World" with which my analysis began.

We should not leave these observations without noting an interesting phenomenon of cultural appropriation of the "radiant frieze" motif that took place in the context of Ottoman religious architecture. Occurring in symbolically relevant places, the motif appears on exteriors and interiors of many Ottoman mosques. Externally, it appears in familiar three-dimensional form on monuments such as the sixteenth-century minaret of the Ibrahim Pasha Cammi, a converted medieval church in the town of Rhodos. Internally, we see it employed at the dome base of the Mustafa Pasha Camii, built in 1492 in Skopje. The painted variation of the radiant frieze motif appears here in the company of other distinctly Islamic elements, but it preserves its folded-plate characteristics seen in many Byzantine churches in precisely the same position. What the eyes of the Islamic believers may have perceived in this motif is unclear, but its visual and architecturally contextual similarity with its Byzantine uses could hardly have been totally accidental.

My remarks have sought to demonstrate that certain so-called decorative features in Byzantine architecture and painting were actually imbued with important symbolic messages. Prominent among these, as we have seen, was the "radiant frieze" used to convey the notion of Divine Light. Whether executed in paint, in brick and mortar, or some other material, the rendition of this symbol depended on the medium in which it was executed, but its ultimate visual effect, regardless of the medium, was invariably three-dimensional. The exact implications of this observation do not have a ready answer, though its appearance in the context of an artistic tradition that generally tended to play down the significance of three-dimensionality is striking. Are we entitled to contemplate three-dimensionality in Byzantine art as a distinctive manifestation, generally off-limits to humans, and therefore by extension – in its selective symbolic use – as an exclusive prerogative of Divinity? The question and its implications are too great to have received adequate treatment here. If the question that I have posed is the right question, then my goal for now will have been accomplished.

Notes

1. Exodus, 34: 29–35.
2. Matthew 17:1–8.
3. A different approach to the subject of "Divine Light" in the context of the Monastery of St. Catherine on Mt. Sinai was published recently by Nelson 2006, pp. 1–38, who considers the issues of relationship between "natural" and "Divine Light."
4. Grabar 1968, p. 80.
5. Christodoulou 1998, pp. 56–57.
6. Andreopoulos 2005. The apse of the basilica in the Monastery of St. Catherine has been a subject of several studies. Of particular relevance here is Elsner 1994, pp. 81–102.
7. Regarding the iconographic implications of the Transfiguration scene in the Cappella Palatina, cf. Krönig 1956; also Ćurčić 1987, esp. pp. 127–38.
8. Lowden 2004, pp. 286–7; cf. also Andreopoulos 2005, pp. 228–9 ("The Hesychastic Mandorla").
9. On the "mandorla," see a useful overview with older literature in Andreopoulos 2005, pp. 83–86.
10. Demus 1949, p. 11.
11. Cleaned and conserved following the 1979 earthquake that damaged the Rotunda, the dome mosaics have not yet been published. For a brief overview with several good photographs cf. Kourkoutidou-Nikolaidou and Tourta 1997, pp. 50–68.
12. Stylianou and Stylianou 1985, esp. p. 159, where the bust of the Pantokrator in the dome medallion is described without even a mention of the zig-zag band within the rim of the medalion frame.
13. Eastmond 2004, pp. 120–3, where special emphasis is placed on their iconographic significance in the fresco program as a whole.
14. Eastmond 2004, p. 120, where what I refer to as the "three-dimensional rainbows" is described as " ... perhaps an attempt to match in paint the light-reflecting qualities of mosaic ...," a notion that ignores their sophistication of design and symbolic implications.
15. Eastmond 2004, p. 120.
16. Eastmond 2004, p. 120.
17. Korkhmazian 1984, pp. 132–9, fol. 8.
18. Mathews and Wieck 1994, pp. 149–50, and pl. 12.
19. For the illustration of the Serbian examples cf. Janc 1961, Tab. XVI, nos. 100–1.
20. Pulgher 1878, pl. XXII, fig. 16.
21. Borg 1967, pp. 122–40.
22. Stikas 1970, pp. 148–73, with several helpful photographs that illustrate the method of laying the masonry elements of the "radiant frieze."
23. Restle 1967, vol. 2, pl. 160; Rodley 1985, pl. 37.
24. Hadermann-Misguich 1975.
25. Vikan 1973, pp. 100–3, and fig. 35.
26. Papadopoulou 2002, pp. 125–7. Trkulja 2004 (a revised updated version as a book is currently in preparation) is an important general contribution to the study of aesthetics and symbolism of decorative elements in Middle and Late Byzantine architecture.

27. Velenis 1988, esp. pp. 279–80, with the basic information and older literature.
28. Ćurčić 2000, pp. 29–30, and fig. 30.
29. Vokotopoulos 1981, esp. p. 558, who refers to the motif as "pendant triangles."
30. Bouras 1974, pp. 42–45; esp. p. 44, uses the term "saw-tooth bands."
31. Ćurčić 2005, esp. p. 25.
32. Ruskin 1853, vol. 2, pl. V (facing p. 45).
33. Richardson 1988, pp. 1–8, and passim.
34. Romano 1988, pp. 176–9, pls. 58–62.
35. Alpatov 1977, pl. 1; and a more detailed study: Vzdornov 1989, pls. 65–66 (Documentation)—Crucifixion and Deposition frescoes.
36. Gallas, Wessel, and Borboudakis 1983, pp. 447–9; pl. 139.

Works Cited

Alpatov, M.V. 1977. *Frescoes of the Assumption at Volotovo Polye*, Moscow.

Andreopoulos, A. 2005. *Metamorphosis. The Transfiguration in Byzantine Theology and Iconography*, Crestwood, NY.

Borg, A. 1967. "The Development of the Chevron Ornament," *Journal of the British Archaeological Association* 120, pp. 122–40.

Bouras, Ch. 1974. *Chios*, Athens.

Christodoulou, D. N. 1998. *The Figures of Ancient Gods on the Coinage of Constantine the Great (306–326 AD)*, Athens.

Ćurčić, S. 1987. "Some Palatine Aspects of the Cappella Palatina in Palermo," *Dumbarton Oaks Papers* 41, pp. 127–38.

Ćurčić, S. 2000. *Middle Byzantine Architecture on Cyprus: Provincial or Regional?*, Nicosia.

Ćurčić, S. 2005. "Nezapazeni doprinosi Hilandara razvoju srpske srednjovekovne arhitekture," *Cetvrta kazivanja o Svetoj Gori*. Belgrade, pp. 17–37 (Engl. sum.: "Unobserved Contributions of Hilandar Monastery to the Development of Medieval Architecture in Serbia," pp. 467–8).

Eastmond, A. 2004. *Art and Idenitity in Thirteenth-Century Byzantium. Hagia Sophia and the Empire of Trebizond*, Aldershot, UK.

Elsner, J. 1994. "The Viewer and the Vision: The Case of the Sinai Apse," *Art History* 17, pp. 81–102.

Demus, O. 1949. *The Mosaics of Norman Sicily*, London.

Gallas, K., K. Wessel and M. Borboudakis. 1983. *Byzantinisches Kreta*, Munich.

Grabar, A. 1968. *Early Christian Art from the Rise of Christianity to the Death of Theodosius*, New York.

Hadermann-Misguich, L. 1975. *Kurbinovo: les fresques de Saint-Georges et la peinture byzantine du XIIe siècle*, Brussels.

Janc, Z. 1961. *Ornamenti fresaka iz Srbije i Makedonije od XII do sredine XV veka* (Ornaments in the Serbian and Macedonian Frescoes from the XII to the Middle of the XV century), Belgrade.

Korkhmazian, E. M. 1984. *Armenian Miniature of the 13th and 14th Centuries from the Matenadaran Collection, Yerevan*, Leningrad.

Kourkoutidou-Nikolaidou, E., and A. Tourta. 1997. *Wandering in Byzantine Thessaloniki*, Athens.

Krönig, W. 1956. "Zur Transfiguration der Cappella Palatina in Palermo," *Zeitschrift für Kunstgeschichte* 19, pp. 1962–79.

Lowden, J. 2004. "Theological Works of John VI Kantakouzenos," in *Byzantium: Faith and Power (1261–1557)*, ed. H. C. Evans, New York, pp. 286–7.

Mathews, T.F., and R. S. Wieck. 1994. *Treasures in Heaven. Armenian Illuminated Manuscripts*, Princeton.

Nelson, R. 2006. "Where God Walked and Monks Pray," in *Holy Image, Hallowed Ground. Icons from Sinai*, Los Angeles.

Papadopoulou, V. N. 2002. *Hê Vyzantinê Arta kai ta mnêmeia tês,* Athens.

Pulgher, D. 1878. *Les anciennes églises byzantines de Constantinople*, Vienna.

Restle, M. 1967. *Byzantine Wall Painting in Asia Minor*, Greenwich, Conn.

Richardson, J. 1988. "The Byzantine Element in the Architecture and Architectural Sculpture in Venice, 1063–1140," Diss. Princeton University.

Rodley, L. 1985. *Cave Monasteries of Byzantine Cappadocia*, Cambridge.

Romano, C. G. 1988. *La Basilicata, la Calabria*, Milan.

Ruskin, J. 1853. *The Stones of Venice*, London.

Stikas, E. G. 1970. *To oikodomikon chronikon tês monês Osiou Louka Fôkidos*, Athens.

Stylianou, A., and J. A. Stylianou. 1985. *The Painted Churches of Cyprus. Treasures of Byzantine Art*, London.

Trkulja, J. 2004. "Aesthetics and Symbolism of Late Byzantine Church Façades, 1204–1453," Diss., Princeton University.

Velenis, G. 1988. "Thirteenth-Century Architecture in the Despotate of Epirus: The Origins of the School," *Studenica et l'art Byzantine autour de l'année 1200*, ed. V. Korać, Belgrade.

Vikan, G. ed. 1973. *Illuminated Greek Manuscripts from American Collections*, Princeton.

Vokotopoulos, P. L. 1981. "The Role of Constantinopolitan Architecture during the Middle and Late Byzantine Period," *Jahrbuch der Österreichischen Byzantinistik* 31, pp. 551–73.

Vzdornov, G. I. 1989. *Volotovo. Freski tserkvi Uspeniia na Volotovom pole bliz Novgoroda*, Moscow.

CHAPTER TWELVE

STRUCTURE, AGENCY, RITUAL, AND THE BYZANTINE CHURCH

Vasileios Marinis

Byzantinists have tended to shy away from developments in modern theory, sometimes with good reason. Theories founded on premises bearing no demonstrable relevance to medieval or Byzantine reality contribute little more than an impression of methodological sophistication. The ideas applied by scholars in the observation of the ceremonial systems of contemporary societies have little to offer to the study of Byzantine society's ritual engagements; not least because, unlike the social models from which these theories are derived, Byzantine society can no longer be observed. By contrast, ritual theory does offer some useful tools that, properly adjusted for differences of context, may enable a deeper understanding of some of Byzantium's structures and ritual expressions. Thus, I begin with some methodological clarifications. In this chapter I reiterate the basic dichotomy between belief and ritual.[1] Belief is a set of tenets accepted as true by a group of people. Ritual, on the other hand, enacts, performs, and objectifies belief. To cite an example pertinent to the topic at hand, the Byzantines believed that the prayers of the living for the deceased functioned as appeals to God, who would take them into consideration during the final judgment of the souls. This is the belief. The ritual of memorial services performed adjacent to the tombs objectifies and expresses this belief with an assortment of prayers and acts. There exists an aspect of ritual that is largely ignored, even though it is crucial: ritual is *situational*.[2] That is, much of what is important about ritual cannot be understood outside the specific context in which it occurs. Byzantine ritual usually

12.1. Istanbul (Constantinople), Monastery *tou Libos*, from the southeast. Photo Robert Ousterhout.

took place in a very specific framework – the actual church building and its environs – in which both belief and ritual found accommodation and were expressed through the architectural arrangement and interior decoration of spaces. Nevertheless, a Byzantine church was not a mere shell for ritual but rather an essential interlocutor in a constant dialogue.

Several scholars have observed the interaction and integration of architecture and ritual in various contexts and eras.[3] In this paper I investigate the ways in which architecture, ritual, and belief intertwined in a single monastic complex, the monastery *tou Libos* in Constantinople (Figs. 12.1–12.6). I argue that the architectural forms of the monastery's two surviving churches was the result of a negotiation between inherited social, religious, and cultural structures and individual agency.[4] Structures entailed primarily canonical regulations, extended and informed by theological developments, which guided church building, as well as considerations for the accommodation of the ritual and symbolic divisions of space; nonnegotiable architectural elements (such as an altar, a templon, a space for the congregation); and established decorative and iconographic practices. Individual agency refers to the desires of patrons, masons, and artists, and their responses to such economic realities as budget and availability of materials.[5]

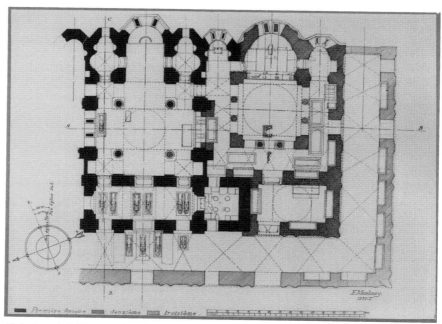

12.2. Istanbul (Constantinople), Monastery *tou Libos*, ground plan. After E. Mamboury in T. Macridy, "The Monastery of Lips (Fenari Isa Camii) at Istanbul," *DOP* 18, 1964, fig. 5.

The complex is now located in the intersection of Adnan Menderes Vatan Bulvarı and Halıcılar Caddesi, southwest of the Fatih Camii. All the auxiliary buildings of a typical Byzantine monastery, including cells, a refectory, a circuit wall with a gatehouse,[6] a bath, and even a hospital,[7] have disappeared, leaving only two churches and an outer ambulatory. The buildings were damaged by several fires, which resulted in a number of reconstructions. Consequently, their original appearance has been significantly altered. In 1929 Theodore Macridy, then assistant curator of the Istanbul Archaeological Museum, undertook the first serious investigation of the site.[8] In the 1960s the Byzantine Institute of America and Dumbarton Oaks restored the building.[9] It has been used as a mosque ever since.

The original foundation dates to the ninth century.[10] Constantine Lips, a high-ranking military official in the imperial army,[11] was the patron of the monastery, which he dedicated to the Theotokos (Figs. 12.1–12.3, 12.5).[12] Its consecration took place in 907, with the participation of emperor Leo VI.[13] The history of the monastery *tou Libos* during the Middle Byzantine period is not well documented. It is possible

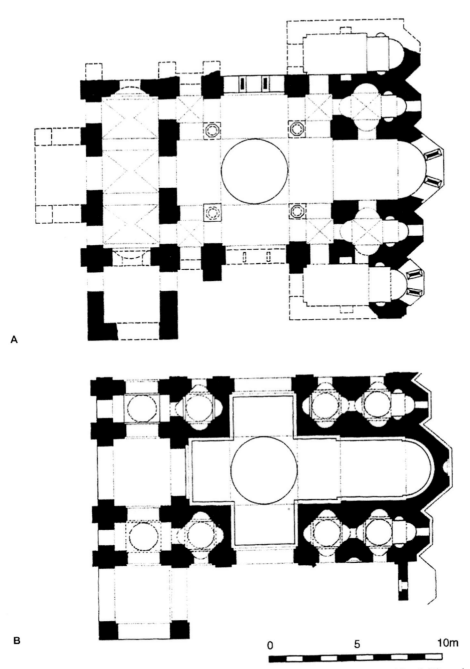

12.3. Istanbul (Constantinople), Monastery *tou Libos*, Theotokos, plan at ground level (A), and gallery level (B). Drawing Robert Ousterhout, after Slobodan Ćurčić.

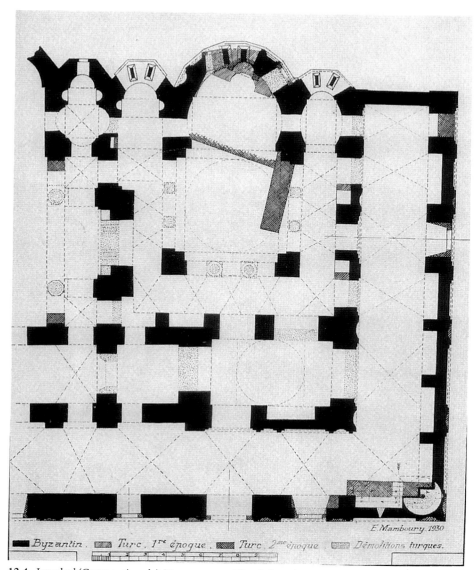

12.4. Istanbul (Constantinople), Monastery *tou Libos*, Saint John, ground plan. After E. Mamboury in T. Macridy, "The Monastery of Lips (Fenari Isa Camii) at Istanbul," *DOP* 18, 1964, fig. 8.

that it followed the fate of many other religious foundations during the Latin occupation of Constantinople (1204–1261) and was abandoned. At the end of the thirteenth century the dowager empress Theodora, widow of Michael VIII Palaiologos, restored the monastic complex adding a second church, dedicated to St. John the Baptist, to the south

12.5. Istanbul (Constantinople), Monastery *tou Libos*, Theotokos Panachrantos, interior. Photo Vasileios Marinis.

12.6. Istanbul (Constantinople), Monastery *tou Libos*, Saint John, interior. Photo Vasileios Marinis.

of the existing, tenth-century church (Figs. 12.1–12.2, 12.4–12.6).[14] An outer ambulatory, enveloping the two churches along the west and south sides, was added shortly after the completion of the church of St. John (Figs. 12.1–12.2, 12.6).

More than 350 years separated the two churches of the monastery *tou Libos*. They differed from each other not only in terms of building technique, architectural style, and decoration but also, and most importantly, in terms of the interior articulation of spaces. The north church of the Theotokos was a typical cross-in-square church (Figs. 12.2–12.3, 12.5).[15] It was built with alternating bands of brick and ashlar stone up to circa 5.5 meters from the floor. The arches and vault were constructed exclusively of brick. The naos, or main part, was relatively large by middle Byzantine standards, measuring circa 15.5 meters from the sill of the western door to the inner wall of the central apse, and circa 9.4 meters at the full extent of the north and south cross-arms. It was divided into nine bays. The central bay, which was originally defined by four columns, is the largest, measuring approximately 6 meters by 4 meters. The tripartite bema was located to the east of the naos. It comprised a large central apse, where the altar would have been, flanked by two identical smaller apses, the prothesis to the north and the diakonikon to the south. The main apse was connected to the prothesis and diakonikon through doors in its lateral walls. To the west of the naos was the narthex, a rectangular space measuring 9.1 by 3.2 meters; it is divided into three bays. The narthex was accessible through three doors on the west, of which the central one was the largest and opened into a small porch.

The most distinguishing feature of the church of the Theotokos was the six additional chapels, two at ground-level flanking the prothesis and diakonikon and four on the roof (Fig. 12.3). While the northern ground-level chapel has long since disappeared, part of the foundation of its apse has been excavated.[16] In the late thirteenth century, the chapel next to the diakonikon was incorporated into the south church to serve as its prothesis and was partially preserved. The four roof chapels survive in part. Their appearance today is largely due to the extensive reconstruction undertaken in the 1960s. The two western chapels were situated over the western corner bays of the naos. The western chapels were located over the diakonikon and prothesis at the east end of the building. A staircase located in the square compartment in the south of the narthex provided access to the roof and the chapels (Fig. 12.3).[17]

In comparison to the north church, the plan of the south church of St. John differed significantly (Figs. 12.2, 12.4, 12.6). This later church belonged to the ambulatory type, with the central bay under the dome separated from the rest of the church by columns and piers that create a corridor surrounding the central bay on three sides.[18] Its plan was affected by the fact that it was attached to the preexisting church of the Theotokos, while incorporating parts of it.

As it stands today, the interior of the south church's naos gives the rather misleading impression of a very open space (Fig.12.6). This is the result of alterations during the Ottoman period. The naos is a rectangle, measuring 10.5 meters in length from the sill of the western door to the threshold of the bema, and 13.1 meters from the end of the south passageway to the end of the north passageway. The large central bay, defined by four piers in the corners, measures 8.1 by 7.5 meters. Between the piers on the north, west, and south sides were pairs of columns. All of them were removed after the building's conversion into a mosque and replaced by large pointed arches. Nevertheless, the previous configuration of the space is evident: on all three sides the remains of the original arches are visible. The masonry technique is apparent in the exposed interior wall surfaces. Bands from one to five bricks are interspersed with single ashlar courses without exhibiting any regular pattern. The masonry turns to brick only above the marble cornice that marks the springing of the vaults. The bricks are long and thin, while the stones are roughly but regularly hewn. The interior was decorated with marble revetments up to the springing of the vaults, as indicated by the numerous small holes in the masonry for the nails holding the marble panels together. The dome and the rest of the vaulting were decorated with mosaics.

Originally, the narthex in the church of St. John was truncated (8.6 by 1.4 meters) due to the existence of the tenth-century staircase compartment. A door in the west wall provided access to the narthex from the outer ambulatory: opposite it stands the single entrance into the naos of St. John. Another door to the naos was opened in the east wall of the tower. The narthex was crowned by a large dome. Finally, the outer ambulatory enveloped the complex on the south and west sides. The length of the south arm is approximately 22 meters; the west one approximately 28 meters long; both are circa 3.50 meters wide. It is unclear whether the ambulatory extended to the north side of the complex.

This brief description of the two churches in the monastery *tou Libos* reveals the dissimilarities between them. Some of them, such as the differences in the masonry techniques or in the decoration of the exterior walls, may be attributed to the distinct architectural styles of the tenth and thirteenth centuries. However, the fundamental differences lay in the architectural forms and particularly of the interior articulation of the two buildings. These differences reflected the divergent functions of each church. But they were also the result of the negotiation between the wishes of the two patrons and what was theologically and socially acceptable.

The tenth-century church of the Theotokos is the earliest extant securely dated cross-in-square church in Constantinople.[19] Scholars still debate the origins of this type, which would become very popular both in the capital and the provinces in subsequent centuries. Very often the narratives have disintegrated into linear evolutionary formalism, wherein older types beget new ones with the obligatory mediation of "transitional" buildings.[20] Regardless of its origins, examples of the type dating to as early as the eighth century are found in Bithynia, in northwest Asia Minor.[21] Because of its modest size and lack of internal divisions, the type was favored in monasteries, although there is also evidence of its use in secular, specifically palatial contexts.[22]

Why did the cross-in-square type become so widespread? In part, the answer has to do with the particulars of the transmission of architectural knowledge in medieval Byzantium.[23] A cross-in-square church did not pose any significant structural challenges or demands beyond practical mathematics while at the same time, depending on the training and experience of the masons, it allowed for relatively large, tall, and elegant interior spaces and exterior façades. If the type was indeed transmitted from Constantinople and was associated with palatial structures (both religious and secular), an element of prestige was surely attached to it.

A further reason for the type's popularity was certainly the fact that it provided a suitable setting for the celebration of the Divine Liturgy in the form that it acquired after Iconoclasm.[24] During the Middle Byzantine period, and under the increased influence of monastic practices (which were, by necessity, self-contained), the Divine Liturgy became intimate and introverted. All the action took place mostly inside the church, for the most part in the sanctuary. Two brief ritualized appearances of the clergy constituted the dramatic high points of the service. Thus, during what became known as the First or Little Entrance, the clergy carried the Gospel book from the altar into the nave and then back to the altar. The second entrance, called the Great Entrance, consisted of transferring the eucharistic elements from the prothesis, the space where they had been prepared, to the altar, following a "U" path to the center of the main church and back to the sanctuary.

The cross-in-square type provided fitting accommodation for these ritual entrances (Fig. 12.3). The naos was a centralized, self-contained, and unified space, interrupted only by the columns supporting the dome. The worshippers would have congregated in the corridor around the central bay and thus were able to see the celebration of the liturgy while at the same time leaving adequate space for the two processions. The bema, where most of the ritual took place, was visible from almost anywhere inside the naos. Furthermore, the clearly defined zones of holiness (sanctuary, naos, narthex on the horizontal axis) corresponded to the divisions of the people.[25] Because of the dome, such churches also had a vertical heaven-to-earth hierarchical axis often underscored by the iconographic program. This is not to say that other architectural types were not popular or even better suited for the celebration of the liturgy. Nonetheless, it appears that the cross-in-square type offered an ideal combination of practicality in execution and suitability for ritual and decoration, as well as sufficient size and prestige.

The north church *tou Libos* was surely an expression of such considerations. It conformed to the exigencies of inherited structures pertaining to the accommodation of rituals and the symbolic divisions of space. And yet, aspects of the building manifested the wished and aspirations of the patron, Constantine Lips. I have suggested elsewhere that the tombs uncovered by Macridy in the narthex and the porch of the north church belonged to Constantine and members of his family.[26] Most importantly, the Theotokos *tou Libos* was different from other comparable churches in its incorporation of six additional chapels, two at ground level flanking the sanctuary and four more on the roof (Fig. 12.3). It is difficult to discern the function of these spaces.[27] There is clear evidence that most if not all chapels contained consecrated altars, but at least the chapels on the roof could not have been much frequented. Their existence should be seen as fulfilling the wishes of

Constantine Lips and associated with the Byzantine perception of the intercessory role of saints in a person's salvation.[28] This is evident in the dedicatory inscription, parts of which still survive on the exterior walls of the sanctuary of the north church. From it we learn that Constantine offered the church to the Mother of God in the hope that she would grant him citizenship in heaven. This inscription also suggests that perhaps some of the chapels were dedicated to the Apostles.[29] Another source reveals that one chapel was dedicated to Saint Irene.[30]

Let us turn now to the thirteenth-century church of Saint John (Fig. 12.4). The ambulatory plan of this building presents some challenges when one considers the form of the liturgy, which, as noted earlier, was distinguished by a series of circular processions that started and ended in the sanctuary. An opposed to a cross-in-square building, an ambulatory church is not well suited to this kind of ritual: the columns and piers that screen off the main bay not only would have inhibited the processional movement of the celebrants, but also hindered the view of the people attending the service. How then can we interpret these peculiarities?

Several scholars have traced the evolution of the ambulatory type.[31] Apart from the fact that an evolutionary approach to Byzantine architecture has proven to be highly problematic,[32] an important functional aspect of the ambulatory churches in Constantinople has not been emphasized enough: its funerary character. Based on a theory first put forward by Robert Ousterhout,[33] I have suggested that the emergence of the ambulatory type in the Middle and Late Byzantine period might be connected to its funerary function, a proposition confirmed by some of the surviving ambulatory churches in Constantinople.[34]

In the case of the monastery *tou Libos*, Theodora's foundation document, (in Greek *typikon*), confirms the funerary character of the church of St. John.[35] This document provides invaluable information regarding the life of the nuns and the administration of the monastery (including matters such as the length of the novitiate, division of labor, selection of the superior), along with the nuns' liturgical duties. More important for our purposes, the document makes it clear that the church of St. John was to be used as the mausoleum for Theodora's imperial family. There are some very specific instructions concerning the burials in the south church, including her own:

It is now time to be mindful of death, since there is no one "that lives and never sees death." First I will make clear to my family and descendants my wishes concerning my own burial. The body of my daughter is buried to the right of the entrance to the church of [Saint John] the Forerunner. My tomb and that of my honored mother (for I cannot bear to be separated from her even after my death) should be built after the intervening door. In the future, any of my children or sons-in-law, who request during their lifetime to be laid to rest here, shall be suitably buried. The same shall apply to my grandsons and granddaughters, daughters-in-law, and the husbands of granddaughters, for all of whom there are to be annual commemorations. The opposite side, on your left as you leave for the old church of the Virgin, will be totally reserved for whatever purpose desired by my son the emperor.[36]

From the information in the *typikon* and later sources we can compile a list of people buried in the monastery *tou Libos*. They included Theodora's mother and Anna, her daughter;[37] Constantine, the younger brother of Andronikos II who died in 1304;[38] Eirene, first wife of Andronikos III, who died in1324;[39] Andronikos II himself who died in 1332;[40] and Anna, the Russian first wife of John VIII Palaiologos, who died in 1418.[41] A funerary stele now in the Istanbul Archaeological Museum depicting a nun called Maria, "the faithful sebaste and a daughter of Palaiologos" might have come from the monastery *tou Libos*.[42] Evidently the south church was a popular place, since twelve masonry tombs and two ossuaries were discovered in the naos along with the seven masonry tombs located in the outer ambulatory.

Other ambulatory churches in Constantinople exhibit a similarly pronounced funerary character. The church of Theotokos Peribleptos was built by Romanos III Argyros (1028–1034) (Fig. 12.7);[43] shortly thereafter an adjoining monastery was added. Romanos was buried in the church of Peribleptos. Later, Nikephoros III Botaniates (1078–1081) restored the monastery and was also buried in the church. The exact location of the two tombs is unclear, but some information comes from Ruy González de Clavijo, the Spanish ambassador who went to Constantinople in 1403 and visited the church of Peribleptos. Clavijo narrates that:

In the body of the church are five altars, and the body itself is a round hall, very big and tall, and it is supported on jasper [columns] of different colors; ... This hall is enclosed all round by three aisles which

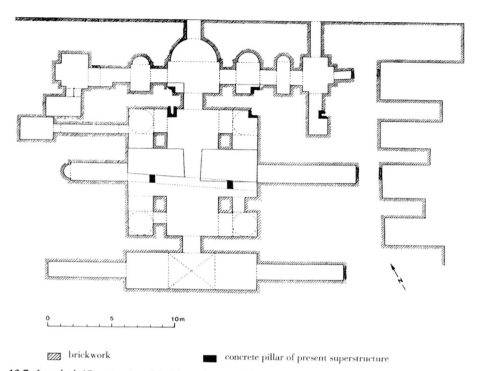

brickwork   concrete pillar of present superstructure

12.7. Istanbul (Constantinople), Theotokos Peribleptos, circa 1028–1034. After F. Özgümüş, "Peribleptos, Sulu, monastery in Istanbul," *Byzantinische Zeitschrift* 93, 2000, plan 2. Reproduced with permission of the author.

are joined to it, and the ceiling of the hall and the aisles is one and the same, and is completely wrought in rich mosaic. And at the end of the church, on the left side, was a big tomb of colored jasper wherein lies the said Emperor Romanus.[44] And they say that this tomb was once covered with gold and set with many precious stones, but that when, ninety years ago [sic], the Latins won the city, they robbed this tomb. And in this church was another big tomb of jasper in which lay another emperor.[45]

According to Clavijo the tomb of Romanos was located in the north arm of the church's ambulatory; the second tomb was undoubtedly that of Nikephoros Botaniates. Based on Clavijo's description, Cyril Mango suggested that the church was of the ambulatory type.[46] The original building has disappeared but a recent investigation was carried out after a fire had exposed some vaulted substructures: these were surveyed and photographed.[47] Based on the plan of the substructures one can very

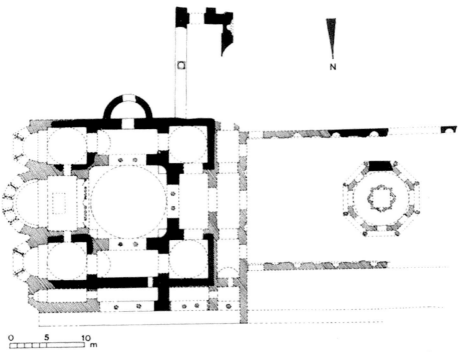

12.8. Istanbul (Constantinople), Saint George ton Manganon, circa 1042–1057. Redrawn from E. Mamboury and R. Demangel, *Le quartier des Manganes et la première région de Constantinople*, Paris, 1939, pl. V.

easily suggest that Peribleptos was indeed an ambulatory church, where at least one of the imperial tombs was placed in the ambulatory in a fashion not unlike the church of St. John *tou Libos*.[48]

The church of St. George *ton Manganon* (Fig. 12.8) was built by emperor Constantine IX Monomachos (r. 1042–1055), third husband of the empress Zoe.[49] Unfortunately only some substructures survive of this famous foundation. Mamboury suggested that the church was of the ambulatory type, although other reconstructions are also possible. Constantine Monomachos was buried in his foundation and close to his tomb he placed a sarcophagus for his mistress Skleraina.[50]

The katholikon of the Pammakaristos monastery also belongs to the ambulatory type and although some of its features are still debated, there is a general consensus that it is a Komnenian construction (Fig. 12.9).[51] From a now lost inscription we know that the church was built by a certain John Komnenos and his wife Anna Doukaina.[52] From a description

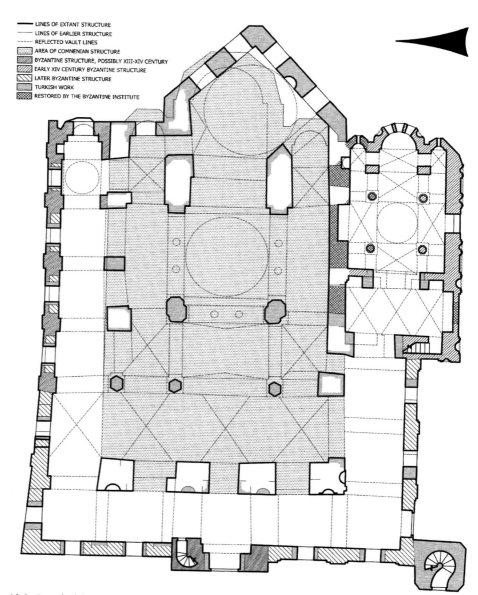

12.9. Istanbul (Constantinople), Theotokos Pammakaristos, twelfth century and later. Redrawn after H. Belting, C. Mango, D. Mouriki, *The Mosaics and Frescoes of St. Mary Pammakaristos (Fethiye Camii) at Istanbul*, Washington, DC, 1978, fig. 1.

of Pammakaristos contained in a document now in the Trinity College Library at Cambridge, it is very clear that the main church was used as a resting place for the founder's family.[53] The document is vague about the exact location of the tombs[54] but the arrangement would have been similar to the south church *tou Libos*.

This brief survey of some ambulatory churches in Constantinople indicates that there are good reasons to link the plan with churches of predominantly funerary character.[55] But still, why the choice of this specific spatial arrangement to accommodate tombs? Burials occurred inside churches throughout the empire, despite explicit canonical prohibition against the practice.[56] Very often this prohibition was circumvented by confining the tombs to spaces of secondary symbolic, liturgical, and spiritual importance, such as narthexes, chapels, crypts, and outer ambulatories as was the case with the tombs of the Lips Family in the church of the Theotokos. The narthex, for example, was not considered as holy as the naos or the sanctuary.[57] However, only rarely do we find burials inside the naos, as it is the case with St. John *tou Libos*.[58]

I consider this another case of the negotiation between overarching structures (in this case the canonical framework regulating the function of a church, including the prohibition of burials) and personal agency – specifically Theodora's desire to secure for herself and some members of her family the most spiritually beneficial burial location. Scholars have interpreted burials inside churches as the continuation of early Christian *ad sanctos* burials, and connected it with the relics of martyrs deposited under the altar during the consecration ceremony.[59] However, there may have been a different reason for this practice. First, the souls of the deceased were believed to benefit from the prayers of monastics and visitors and from the frequent celebration of the liturgy, in addition to regular memorial services.[60] The eagerness to preserve the memory of the deceased and to encourage prayer on his or her behalf is evident in the decoration of tombs. Although there is little evidence left in St. John,[61] the partially preserved tombs in the parekklesion of the Chora monastery (Kariye Müzesi) offer some parallels: the tombs included funerary portraits, sculpted decorative frames, and extensive inscriptions that addressed the viewer directly and ask him or her for prayers on behalf of the souls of the deceased.[62] By virtue of their prominent position inside the naos, the figural and textual decoration of the St. John *tou Libos* tombs intended to take advantage of both the regular attendants and occasional visitors to the church. In addition, the location of the tombs was another instance of the Byzantine preoccupation with proximity to holiness. The ambulatory created a space that could easily accommodate tombs and sarcophagi inside the naos and close to the bema, the holiest part of the church. In fact, Theodora's tomb, which according to the *typikon* was located in the southeastern arcoso-lium in the church of St. John, was the one closest to the sanctuary.[63] At the same time, the main liturgical area – the central bay and the bema – remained separate. There is another reason for this separation of spaces, one connected with the practicalities of memorial rituals. Memorial services usually took place alongside the tombs, and the ambulatory created the necessary space for the people to congregate around them. Following a process of creating zones of differing spiritual importance and function, the columns and piers in the naos of St. John separate spaces that served different purposes, with the liturgical core isolated from the funerary ambulatory. Therefore, the ambulatory plan, at least in Constantinople, can be interpreted as a solution that accommodated the juxtaposition of liturgical and funeral spaces within the same build-ing. The distinction of these spaces was apparently very desirable.

Another functional and symbolic distinction of spaces occurred with the construction of the outer ambulatory. Even given the privi-leged position of any tomb inside a church, there existed degrees of importance associated with location. Annexed structures, whether exonarthexes, ambulatories, or lateral aisles, built anew or added to preexisting buildings, were very common in the Palaiologan architec-ture of the capital and its sphere of influence. The obvious purpose of the outer ambulatory in the monastery *tou Libos* was to provide space for further burials.[64] The burial niches are set into the thickness of the wall, and from the masonry it is evident that all of them were part of the original planning. The funerary character of such spaces is reinforced by the primary sources. Thus, the twelfth-century *typikon* of the con-vent of the Mother of God Kecharitomene in Constantinople offered these instructions concerning the descendants of its founder, Empress Eirene Doukaina:

> If ever any of our daughters or daughters-in-law or even of our granddaughters, to whom the *ephoreia* of the convent has been assigned and the use of the more sumptuous buildings, should choose to be buried in this convent (for it is not unreasonable to discuss this also), this will be possible for her if she has assumed the monastic habit, but not at all otherwise, and she will have a place in the exonarthex for the burial of her remains, making her own tomb according to her own wishes.[65]

Analogous directives concerning the burial and memorial service –
this time of monks – in the exonarthex are given in the twelfth-century
typikon of Athanasios Philanthropenos for the monastery of St. Mamas
in Constantinople.[66]

Because much of the archaeological evidence for the tombs at the
monastery *tou Libos* has disappeared, it is impossible to know if the outer
ambulatory was constructed after all the tombs within the church of
St. John were filled. I believe that this was not necessarily the case. The
outer ambulatory accommodated tombs of persons who were important, but not as important as the ones inside the naos: this is evident
from the surviving fragments of the decoration of the tombs. The arco-
solium of Theodora's tomb was decorated with her mosaic portrait.[67]
However, all the decoration that has survived in the outer ambulatory is
in fresco,[68] which was less expensive. It appears that the tombs located
there were not considered as privileged as the ones inside the church
because they were not located so close to the altar. Textual evidence also
confirms this distinction: Constantine, the younger son of Theodora,
a rather shady character, was condemned and imprisoned in 1293 and
died in 1304. The relevant passage from the historian Pachymeres mentions that Constantine "was buried like the common men in the outer-
most tombs [of the monastery *tou Libos*]."[69] The liturgical use of these
spaces corroborates the idea that they were considered of lesser importance. According to monastic *typika*, some minor service, such as com-
pline, were celebrated in narthexes and outer narthexes.[70]

In conclusion, in both the church of the Theotokos and that of St.
John at the monastery *tou Libos*, the arrangement of spaces was the
product of a negotiation between the beliefs and desires of the patrons
and socio-cultural structures that dictated what was required and permissible in a church. Furthermore, architecture was used functionally
and symbolically to indicate degrees of importance. Principal services
were celebrated and eminent people were buried inside the churches;
minor services and less important people found their place in the outer
ambulatory.

The Byzantine world view was informed by a complex set of beliefs
expressed in an intricate array of rituals that took place in a specific
architectural setting. Belief is abstract and difficult to gauge, whether
in the past or the present; ritual, while more recoverable, nevertheless

remains elusive. Architecture, as the locus of so much ritual practice in Byzantine society, can help us recreate, however imperfectly, ritual customs that have otherwise left no trace; by extension, it can help us gauge the beliefs that underpinned those rituals. Often these three areas – belief, ritual, architecture – are dealt with as separate subjects or their affinities are denigrated by an explain-all "form follows function" formula. In the case of Byzantium, as in other cultures, belief, ritual, and architecture were intrinsically interdependent. The subtleties and ramifications of their interaction repay close attention.

Notes

1. Geertz 1973, pp. 86, 126–31. This rudimentary division has been ramified and even challenged, although it still stands true for Byzantium. For an extensive discussion, see Bell 1992, pp. 182-96. See also Kreinath, Snoek, and Stausberg 2006 and especially Snoek 2006.
2. On this, see Bell 1992, p. 81.
3. See, for example, Heitz 1963 for the Carolingian era; Thompson 1988 for Japan; Scott 2003 for Turin; Moore 2006 for Masonic Temples in the United States; Sears 2008 for medieval India.
4. On the topic of structures and personal agency see selectively Giddens 1984; Thompson 1989; Bryant and Jary 1991; and most importantly Sewell 1992 (essentially reprinted in Sewell 2005, pp. 124-51). For application of Giddens in the created environment, although not specific buildings, see Pred 1984; Saunders 1989.
5. The loss of artistic and archaeological evidence from Constantinople, as well as the idiosyncratics of the written sources, allow only for educated guesses regarding some of these categories.
6. Delehaye 1921, pp. 114–15, 117; *Typikon of Lips*, pp. 1270, 1271.
7. Delehaye 1921, p. 134; *Typikon of Lips*, pp. 1265, 1269, 1273, 1275, 1279, 1281.
8. Macridy 1929, pp. 343–4; Macridy 1964.
9. Megaw 1964; Mango and Hawkins 1964, 1968.
10. Van Millingen 1912, pp. 122–37; Ebersolt [1913] 1979, pp. 211–23; Macridy 1964; Janin 1969, pp. 307–10, 417–18; Mathews 1976, 322–45; Marinis 2004.
11. The "synoptic" chronicles, Constantine Porphyrogennetos, and the Patria offer conflicting accounts of the life and career of Constantine Lips. See Adontz 1965, pp. 222–5; *De administrando imperio*, pp. 162–3, 179; Mango and Hawkins 1964, pp. 299–300; Marinis 2004, pp. 23–31.
12. Fragments of the dedicatory inscription are still located in a cornice that runs along the exterior of the three apses of the church, see Mango and Hawkins, pp. 300–1, fig. 1.
13. Theophanes Continuatus, p. 371.
14. For Theodora Palaiologina see Talbot 1992, pp. 295–303.
15. The original form of the north church has been the subject of significant debate. Brunoff argued that the church belonged, along with several other monuments in Constantinople, to a "five-aisled" plan, which was later transplanted to Russia, see Brunoff 1927, 1927a, 1968, Popov 1968. Excavations performed by

A. H. S. Megaw did not confirm the existence of an outer aisle in the north side of the building, Megaw 1964. More recently, Lioba Theis reintroduced the idea of outer aisles, although this is contradicted by Megaw's findings and by the evidence in the masonry of the north wall of the church. See Theis 1995, 2005, pp. 56–64. For some new observations see Marinis 2004, pp. 43–70.

16. Macridy 1964, fig. 27.
17. Megaw 1954, pp. 283–91, 294–5.
18. Eyice 1959 (Eyice's suggestion that the "ambulatory" type is a Palaiologan creation is erroneous); Krautheimer 1986, p. 517; Vokotopoulos 1992, pp. 126–31; Chatzetryphonos 2004, especially pp. 152–63.
19. For the cross-in-square type, see selectively Millet 1916, pp. 55–94; Orlandos 1939–1940; Mavrodinov 1940; Mango 1976, pp. 178–80; Krautheimer 1986, pp. 340–3; Lange 1986. Buchwald has suggested a ninth-century date for another cross-in-square church, Hırami Ahmet Paşa Camii, usually identified with St. John Prodromos *en to Troullo*, see Buchwald 1977, p. 290, n. 95.
20. For a summary of the proposed theories, see Lange 1986. See also Toivanen 2007, pp. 140–152.
21. Mango 1976, pp. 96–98.
22. Ćurčić 2010, pp. 271–2.
23. Ousterhout 1999, esp. pp. 39–85; Bouras 2002, 2005, 2010.
24. For the evolution of the Byzantine rite see primarily Taft 1992. See also Mateos 1971; Arranz 1976; Schulz 1986; Wybrew 1989; Taft 1978, 1980–1981, 1988, 1995; Pott 2000. For the parallel developments in architecture, see Marinis 2009, 2011.
25. These would have been clergy in the sanctuary, laity in the naos, and individuals who were not permitted to attend services in the naos, such as penitents, in the narthex.
26. Marinis 2009, pp. 158–61.
27. Mathews 1982.
28. Marinis 2010, pp. 297–8.
29. Mango and Hawkins 1964, pp. 300–1.
30. *Typikon of Lips*, p. 1267.
31. See the comprehensive summary in Chatzetryphonos 2004, p. 152, with further bibliography.
32. See, for example, the criticisms in Striker 2001.
33. Ousterhout 1999, pp. 124–5.
34. Marinis 2004, pp. 179–99.
35. The *typikon* is preserved in a single manuscript, British Library Additional 22748, which is likely the original version. The Greek text can be found in Delehaye 1929, pp. 106–36. English translation by A.-M. Talbot in *Typikon of Lips*, pp. 1265–82. Talbot offered a number of amended readings based on her examination of the manuscript. See also suggested that the date of composition can be narrowed down to sometime between 1294 and 1301, see Talbot 1992, p. 299.
36. Delehaye 1929, p, 130; *Typikon of Lips*, pp. 1278–9.
37. Theodora had three daugthers named Irene, Eudokia, and Anna, who was probably the one buried in the church of St. John, see Mango and Hawkins 1964, pp. 301–3; Talbot 1992, p. 299.
38. *Pachymeres*, vol. 4, p. 467.
39. *Kantakouzenos*, vol. 1, pp. 193–4.

40. *Gregoras*, vol. 1, p. 463.
41. *Phrantzes*, p. 110. The tomb of Anna is also reported by the Russian traveler Zosima the Deacon who visited Constantinople in the early fifteenth century: see Majeska 1984, pp. 188, 309–12.
42. Evans 2004, pp. 104–5, with older bibliography on the stele. Macridy uncovered a fragment of a pseudo-sarcophagus bearing the name "Theodosia." See Macridy 1964, p. 269 and n. 52b.
43. Janin 1969, pp. 218–22; Mango 1992, pp. 473–93.
44. Clavijo perhaps mistook the porphyry stone of the sarcophagi for jasper, which is also red.
45. Mango 1986, pp. 217–18.
46. Mango 1992, pp. 476–7.
47. Dark 1999; Özgümüş 1997–1998, 2000.
48. For an alternative reconstruction of the Peribleptos as a domed-octagon church, see Dalgıç and Mathews 2010.
49. The site where the remains of the church are located today is virtually inaccessible. The most complete archaeological survey of the site, conducted by the French troops occupying Constantinople in 1921–1922, is published in Mamboury and Demangel 1939. See also Janin 1969, pp. 70–76.
50. After the Latin occupation of the city the sarcophagus of Skleraina was used for the burial of Count Hughes de Saint-Pol. Clavijo, who visited also Mangana, mentions a "great tomb of jasper covered with a pall of silk, and here lies an empress," see Mango 1986, p. 220.
51. Hallensleben 1963–1964; Belting, Mango, and Mouriki 1978.
52. Published in Siderides 1907, pp. 271–2. The inscription was located on the cornice of the bema, which has long been destroyed. It was preserved in an eighteenth-century manuscript at the Greek Theological School at Chalke, which was also perished in 1894 when an earthquake leveled the school. Another copy of this epigram is found in Vind. med. gr. 27, fol. 124r, see Hunger 1961, vol. II, p. 75.
53. The document was published in Schreiner 1971. English translation in Belting, Mango, Mouriki. 1978, pp. 39–42.
54. Effenberger 2007, where a summary of earlier opinions.
55. The other extant building that belongs to the type is the Koca Mustafa Paşa Camii. It has suffered extensive alterations. Eyice identified it with the church of Saint Andrew *en te Krisei*, a foundation known already in the eighth century but restored shortly after 1284 by the *protovestiarissa* Theodora Raoulaina, niece of Michael VII Palaiologos. If Eyice's identification is correct, then the building is very close in date and type to the south church of Lips. All evidence for the original interior arrangements, including tombs or sarcophagi, has long disappeared. But from the sources we know that the relics of patriarch Arsenios were immediately moved to the restored monastery from Hagia Sophia. Theodora Raoulaina herself along with Simonida, daughter of Andronikos II, were buried there. See Eyice 1955, pp. 184–90; 1959; 1980; pp. 5–10; Janin 1969, pp. 28–31. See also Van Millingen 1912, pp. 106–21; Mathews 1976, pp. 3–14. No evidence of tombs has survived in the interiors of Gül Camii (c. 1100?) and Kalenderhane Camii (c. 1200), both of comparable plans.
56. Such legislation dates to as early as the fourth century and was repeated often. For example, the twelfth-century canonist Theodore Balsamon indicates that << Οὐκ ἔξεστιν θάπτειν τινὰ ἐν ἐκκλησίᾳ, ἐὰν δηλονότι μάρτυρος ἐκεῖσε σῶμα

ἀπόκειται,>> Ralles and Potles 1852, vol. 4, p. 479. For a survey of the sources, see Marinis 2009, where also earlier bibliography on the topic.

57. See, for example, *Symeon of Thessaloniki*, col. 704: "Thus, the narthex is the earth, the naos is the heavens, and the most holy bema represents those things beyond heavens."

58. On this, see Marinis 2009.

59. Emmanouilidis 1989, pp. 185–6, 189, 206–23.

60. As explained in *Kabasilas*, pp. 210–5.

61. With the exception of a marble arch decorated with busts of Apostles, which probably decorated a tomb, Belting 1972, pp. 63–100 and esp. pp. 67–70.

62. Brooks 2004 and 2006.

63. On the position of Theodora's tomb, see Marinis 2009, pp. 163–5.

64. The funerary character of ambulatories has been noticed also by Chatzetryphonos 2004, pp. 80–85.

65. Gautier 1974, p. 131; *Typikon of Kecharitomene*, p. 704. I do not differentiate between exonarthex and outer ambulatory in the monastery *tou Libos*.

66. Eustratiades 1928, pp. 256–314; *Typikon of St. Mamas*, p. 1020.

67. Mango and Hawkins 1964, p. 302, fig. 2.

68. Mango and Hawkins 1968, pp. 177–8, figs. 1–3.

69. <<καὶ ὑπὸ δαψιλέσι φωσὶ καὶ λαμπάσι καὶ ψαλμῳδίαις μεσούσης ἡμέρας, τῇ τοῦ Λείψη μονῇ παραπέμπεται καὶ οὕτω λαμπρῶς καὶ πολυτελῶς, μόνον δὴ φέρων εἰς μνήμην τὴν εἰς Χριστὸν δουλείαν καὶ ψιλὸν ὄνομα, κατὰ τοὺς πολλοὺς τοῖς ἐξωτάτω σορίοις ἐνταφιάζεται,>> *Pachymeres*, vol. 4, p. 467.

70. Gautier 1974, pp. 81, 83, 85; Marinis 2009, pp. 294–5; *Typikon of Kecharitomene*, pp. 687, 688; *Symeon of Thessaloniki*, col. 360B.

Works Cited

Adontz, N. 1965. *Études arméno-byzantines*, Lisbonne.

Arranz, M. 1976. "Les grandes étapes de la liturgie byzantine: Palestine-Byzance-Russie: essai d'aperçu historique," in Liturgie de l'église particulière, liturgie de l'église universelle, Rome, pp. 43–72.

Babić, G. 1969. *Les chapelles annexes des églises byzantines. Fonction liturgique et programmes inconographiques*, Paris.

Baldovin, J. F. 1987. *The Urban Character of Christian Worship. The Origins, Development, and Meaning of Stational Liturgy*, Rome.

Bell, C. 1992. *Ritual Theory, Ritual Practice*, Oxford.

Belting, H., C. Mango, D. Mouriki. 1978. *The Mosaics and Frescoes of St. Mary Pammakaristos (Fethiye Camii) at Istanbul*, Washington, DC.

Belting, H. 1972. "Skulptur aus der zeit um 1300 in Konstantinopel," *Müchener Jahrbuch der Bildenden Kunst* 23, pp. 63–100.

Bouras, Ch. 2002. "Master Craftsmen, Craftsmen, and Building Activities in Byzantium," in A. Laiou, ed., *The Economic History of Byzantium: From the Seventh through the Fifteenth Century*, Washington, pp. 539–54.

Bouras, Ch. 1976. "Τυπολγικὲς παρατηρήσεις στὸ καθολικὸ τῆς μονῆς τῶν Μαγγάνων στὴν Κωνσταντινούπολη," *Archaiologikon Deltion* 31, pp. 136–51.

Bouras, Ch. 2005 "Originality in Byzantine Architecture," in *Mélanges Jean-Pierre Sodini. Travaux et Mémoires* 15, pp. 37–65.

Bouras, Ch. 2010. *Τρόποι ἐργασίας τῶν βυζαντινῶν ἀρχιτεκτόνων καὶ ἀρχιμαστόρων*, Athens.

Brooks, S. T. 2004. "Sculpture and the Late Byzantine Tomb," in H.C. Evans, ed., *Byzantium: Faith and Power* (1261–1557), New York.

Brooks, S. T. 2006 "Poetry and Female Patronage in Late Byzantine Tomb Decoration: Two Epigrams by Manuel Philes," *Dumbarton Oaks Papers* 60, pp. 223–48.

Brunoff, N. 1926. "Rapport sur un voyage à Constantinople," *Revue des études grecques* 39, pp. 1–30.

Brunoff, N. 1927. "Die fünfschiffige Kreuzkuppelkirche in der byzantinischen Baukunst," *Byzantinische Zeitschrift* 27, pp. 63–98.

Brunoff, N. 1927a. "L'église à croix inscrite à cinq nefs dans l'architecture byzantine," *Echos d'Orient* 26, pp. 257–86.

Brunoff, N. 1968. "K voprosu o srednevekovoi arkhitekture Konstantinopolia," *Vizantiiskii vremenik* 28, pp. 159–91.

Bryant C. G. A. and D. Jary 1991. *Giddens' Theory of Structuration: A Critical Appreciation*, London.

Buchwald, H. 1977. "Sardis Church E – A Preliminary Report," *Jahrbuch der Österreichischen Byzantinistik* 26, 265–99.

Chatzetryphonos, E. K. 2004. *Το περίστωο στην Υστεροβυζαντινή εκκλησιαστική αρχιτεκτονική*, Thessaloniki.

Ćurčić, S. 2010. *Architecture in the Balkans: From Diocletian to Süleyman the Magnificent*, New Haven and London.

Dalgıç, Ö. and T. F. Mathews 2010, "A New Interpretation of the Church of Peribleptos and its Place in Middle Byzantine Architecture," in *First International Sevgi Gönül Byzantine Studies Symposium: Change in the Byzantine World in the Twelfth and Thirteenth Centuries*, ed. A. Ödekan et al., Istanbul, pp. 424–31.

Dark, K. 1999. "The Byzantine Church and Monastery of St Mary Peribleptos in Istanbul," *The Burlington Magazine* 141, pp. 656–64.

Administrando imperio = G. Moravcsik, ed. 1967. *Constantine Porphyrogenitus, De administrando imperio*, 2nd ed., Washington, DC.

Delehaye, H. 1921. *Deux typica byzantins de l'époque des Paléologues*, Brussels.

Ebersolt, J. [1913] 1979. *Les églises de Constantinople, repr.* London.

Effenberger, A. 2007. "Zu den Gräbern in der Pammakaristoskirche," *Byzantion* 78, pp. 170–96.

Emmanouilidis, N. E. 1989. *Τὸ δίκαιο τῆς ταφῆς στὸ Βυζάντιο*, Athens.

Eustratiades, S. 1928. "Τυπικὸν τῆς ἐν Κωνσταντινουπόλει μονῆς τοῦ ἀγίου μεγαλομάρτυρος Μάμαντος," *Hellenika* 1, pp. 256–314.

Evans, H. C. 2004. *Byzantium: Faith and Power* (1261–1557), *exh. cat.*, New York.

Eyice, S. 1955. "Remarques sur deux anciennes églises Byzantines d'Istanbul: Koca Mustafa Paşa camii et l'église de Yuşa tepesi." In Πεπραγμένα 9ου Διεθνοῦς Βυζαντινολογικοῦ Συνεδρίου, Athens, vol. 1, pp. 184–95.

Eyice, S. 1959. "Un type architectural peu connu de l'époque des Paléologues à Byzance." *Anadolu Araştirmalari* 1–2, pp. 223–34.

Eyice, S. 1980. *Son devir Bizans mimarisi*, 2nd ed., Istanbul.

Gautier, P. 1974. "Le typikon du Christ Sauveur Pantokrator," *Revue des Études Byzantines* 32, pp. 1–145.

Geertz, C. 1973. *The Interpretation of Cultures*, New York.

Giddens, A. 1984. *The Constitution of Society: Outline of the Theory of Structuration*, Berkeley, CA.

Hallensleben, H. 1963–1964. "Untersuchungen zur Baugeschichte der ehemaligen Pammakaristoskirche der heutigen Fethiye Camii in Istanbul," *Istanbuler Mitteilungen* 13/14, pp. 128–93.

Heitz, C. 1963. *Recherches sur les rapports entre architecture et liturgie à l'époque carolingienne*, Paris.

Janin, R. 1969. *La géographie ecclésiastique de l'empire byzantin, I: Le siège Constantinople et le patriarcat oecuménique, 3: Les églises et les monastères, 2 ed.* Paris.

Gregoras = I. Bekker, ed. 1829–1855. *Nicephori Gregorae historiae Byzantinae*, 3 vols., Bonn.

Hunger, H. 1961. *Katalog der griechischen Handschriften der Österreichischen Nationalbibliothek*, Vienna.

Kabasilas = P. K. Christou, ed. 1979. Νικολάου Καβάσιλα Εἰς τήν Θείαν Λειτουργίαν καὶ Περὶ τῆς ἐν Χριστῷ ζωῆς, Thessaloniki.

Kantakouzenos = *Ioannis Cantacuzeni eximperatoris historiarum libri iv*, 1828–1832. 3 vols, Vienna.

Krautheimer, R. 1986. *Early Christian and Byzantine Architecture*, 4th ed., New York.

Kreinath, J., J. A. M. Snoek, and M. Stausberg ed. 2006. *Theorizing Rituals*. 2 vols. Leiden and Boston.

Lange, I. D. 1986. "Theorien zur Entstehung der byzantinischen Kreuzkuppelkirche," *Architectura* 16, pp. 93–113.

Macridy, T. 1929. "Les recéntes fouilles de Constantinople," *Archäologischer Anzeiger*, pp. 343–58

Macridy, T. 1964. "The Monastery of Lips (Fenari Isa Camii) and the Burials of the Palaeologi," *Dumbarton Oaks Papers* 18, pp. 249–77.

Majeska, G. P. 1984. *Russian Travellers to Constantinople in the Fourteenth and Fifteenth Centuries*, Washington, DC.

Mamboury, E. and R. Demangel. 1939. *Le quartier des Manganes et la première région de Constantinople*, Paris.

Mango, C. and E. J. W. Hawkins. 1964. "The Monastery of Lips (Fenari Isa Camii) at Istanbul: Additional Notes," *Dumbarton Oaks Papers* 18, pp. 299–315.

Mango, C. and E. J. W. Hawkins 1968. "Additional Finds at Fenari Isa Camii, Istanbul," *Dumbarton Oaks Papers* 22, pp. 177–84.

Mango, C. 1976. *Byzantine Architecture*, New York.

Mango, C. 1986. *The Art of the Byzantine Empire, 312–1453: Sources and Documents*, Toronto.

Mango, C. 1992. "The Monastery of St. Mary Peribleptos (Sulu Manastir) at Constantinople Revisited," *Revue des Etudes Arméniennes* 23, pp. 473–93.

Mavrodinov, N. 1940, "L'apparition et l'évolution de l'église cruciforme dans l'architecture byzantine," in *Atti del V Congresso Internazionale di Studi Bizantini*, Rome, pp. 343–52.

Marinis, V. 2004. "The Monastery tou Libos. Architecture, Sculpture, and Liturgical Planning in Middle and Late Byzantine Constantinople" (diss. Univ. of Illinois at Urbana-Champaign).

Marinis, V. 2009. "Tombs and Burials in the Monastery tou Libos in Constantinople," *Dumbarton Oaks Papers* 63, pp. 147–66.

Marinis, V. 2010. *"Defining Liturgical Space in Byzantium,"* in P. Stephenson, ed., *The Byzantine World*, London and New York, pp. 284–302.

Marinis, V. 2011 "Some Notes on the Functional Approach in the Study of Byzantine Architecture: The case of Constantinople," in *New Approaches to Medieval Architecture*, ed. R. Bork, W. W. Clark, and A. McGehee, Farnham and Burlington, pp. 21–33.

Mateos, J. 1971. *La célébration de la parole dans la liturgie byzantine*, Rome.

Mathews, T. F. 1971. *The Early Churches of Constantinople. Architecture and Ritual*, University Park.

Mathews, T. F. 1976. *The Byzantine Churches of Istanbul. A Photographic Survey*, University Park.

Mathews, T. F. 1982. "'Private' Liturgy in Byzantine Architecture," *Cahiers Archéologiques* 30, pp. 125–38.

Megaw, A. H. S. 1964. "The Original Form of the Theotokos Church of Constantine Lips," *Dumbarton Oaks Papers* 18, pp. 279–98.

Millet, G. 1916. *L'École grecque dans l'architecture byzantine*, Paris.

Moore, W. D. 2006. *Masonic Temples. Freemasonry, Ritual Architecture, and Masculine Archetypes*, Knoxville.

Orlandos, A. K. "Ή Ἁγία Τριάς τοῦ Κριεζώτη," *ABME* 5, pp. 3–16.

Ousterhout, R. 1999. *Master Builders of Byzantium*, Princeton.

Özgümüş, F. 1997–1998. "Peribleptos Manastiri (Sulu Manastir)," *Sanat Tahiri Arastirmalari Dergisi* 14, pp. 21–32.

Özgümüş, F. 2000. "Peribleptos ('Sulu') monastery in Istanbul." *Byzantinische Zeitschrift* 93, pp. 508–20.

Pachymeres = A. Failler, ed., 1984–2000. *Georges Pachymérès relations historiques*, 5 vols.

Phrantzes = I. Bekker, ed., *Georgius Phrantzes, Ioannes Cananus, Ioannes Anagnostes, Corpus scriptorum historiae Byzantinae*, Bonn 1838.

Popov, A. N. 1968. "Iavliaiutsia li ostatki kammenikh balok v stene severnoi tserkvi Fenari-Issa v Stambule ostatkami opor balkona?" *Vizantiiskii vremenik* 28, pp. 192–4.

Pott, T. 2000. *La réforme liturgique byzantine: Étude du phénomène de l'évolution non-spontanée de la liturgie byzantine*, Rome. Engl. trans. *Byzantine Liturgical Reform: A Study of Liturgical Change in the Byzantine Tradition*, Crestwood, NY, 2010.

Pred, A. R. 1984. "Place as Historically Contingent Process: Structuration and the Time-Geography of Becoming Places," *Annals of the Association of American Geographers* 74: 2, pp. 279–97.

Ralles G. A. *and* M. Potles 1852, *Σύνταγμα τῶν θείων καὶ ἱερῶν κανόνων*, 6 vols., Athens.

Saunders, P. 1989. "Space, Urbanism and the Created Environment," in D. Held and J. B. Thompson, eds., *Social Theory of Modern Societies: Anthony Giddens and his Critics*, Cambridge, pp. 215–34.

Schreiner, P. 1971. "Eine unbekannte Beschreibung der Pammakaristoskirche (Fethiye Camii), und weitere Texte zur Topographie Konstantinoples," *Dumbarton Oaks Papers* 25, pp. 216–48.

Schulz, H.-J. 1986. *The Byzantine Liturgy: Symbolic Structure and Faith Expression*, New York.

Scott, B. J. 2003. *Architecture for the Shroud. Relic and Ritual in Turin*, Chicago.

Sears, T. I. 2008. "Constructing the Guru: Ritual Authority and Architectural Space in Medieval India," *Art Bulletin* 90:1, pp. 7–31.

Sewell, Jr., W. H. 1992. "A Theory of Structure: Duality, Agency, and Transformation," *The American Journal of Sociology* 98:1, pp. 1–29.

Sewell, Jr., W. H. 2005. *Logics of History: Social Theory and Social Transformation*, Chicago and London.

Siderides, C. A. 1907. "Περὶ τῆς ἐν Κωνσταντινουπόλει μονῆς τῆς Παμμακαρίστου καὶ τῶν κτιτόρων αὐτῆς," Ὁ ἐν Κωνσταντινουπόλει Ἑλληνικὸς Φιλολογικός Σύλλογος 29, pp. 271–2.

Snoek, J. A. M. 2006. "Defining 'Rituals'," in *Theorizing Rituals: Issues, Topics, Approaches, Concepts*, ed. J. Kreinath, J. A. M. Snoek, and M. Stausberg, Leiden and Boston, pp. 3–14.

Stethatos = J. Darrouzès, ed. *Nicétas Stéthatos: Opuscules et letters*, Paris 1961.

Striker, C.L. 2001. "The Findings at Kalenderhane Camii and Problems of Method in the History of Byzantine Architecture," in *Byzantine Constantinople: Monuments, Topography and Everyday Life*, ed. N. Necipoglu Leiden, pp. 107–16.

Symeon of Thessaloniki = J. P. Migne, ed., 1866. *Symeon Thessalonicensis Archiepiscopus, in Patrologiae Cursus Completus, Series Graeca*, vol. 155, Paris.

Taft, R. F. 1978. *The Great Entrance. A History of the Transfer of Gifts and Other Preanaphoral Rites*, 2nd ed., Rome.

Taft, R. 1980–1981. "The Liturgy of the Great Church: An Initial Synthesis of Structure and Interpretation on the Eve of Iconoclasm," *Dumbarton Oaks Papers* 34, pp. 45–75.

Taft, R. 1992. *The Byzantine Rite: A Short History*, Collegeville, MN.

Taft, R. 1995. "Church and Liturgy in Byzantium: the Formation of the Byzantine Synthesis," in *Liturgy, Architecture, and Art in the Byzantine World*, Saint Petersburg, pp. 13–29.

Taft, R. 1997. *Beyond East and West: Problems in Liturgical Understanding*, Rome.

Talbot, A.-M. 1983. *Faith Healing in Late Byzantium. The Posthumous Miracles of the Patriarch Athanasios I of Constantinople by Theoktistos the Studite*, Brookline.

Talbot, A.-M. 1992. "Empress Theodora Palaiologina, Wife of Michael VIII," *Dumbarton Oaks Papers* 46, pp. 295–303.

Talbot, A.-M. 2002. "Pilgrimage to Healing Shrines: The Evidence of Miracle Accounts," *Dumbarton Oaks Papers* 56, pp. 153–73.

Theis, L. 1995. "Überlegungen zu Annexbauten in der byzantinischen Architektur," in *Studien zur byzantinischen Kunstgeschichte: Festschrift für Horst*

Hallensleben zum 65 Geburtstag, ed. B. Borkopp, B. Schellewald and L. Theis, Amsterdam, pp. 59–64.

Theis, L. 2005. *Die Flankeräume im mittelbyzantinischen Kirchenbau*, Wiesbaden.

Theophanes Continuatus = I. Bekker, ed., *Theophanes Continuatus, Ioannes Cameniata, Symeon Magister, Georgius Monachus*, Bonn, 1838.

Thompson, F.S. 1988. *Ritual and Space*, Waterloo.

Thompson, J.B. 1989. "A Theory of Structuration," in *Social Theory of Modern Societies: Anthony Giddens and his Critics*, ed. D. Held and J. B. Thompson, Cambridge, pp. 56–76.

Toivanen, H.-R. 2007. *The Influence of Constantinople on Middle Byzantine Architecture* (843–1204), Helsinki.

Typikon of Kecharitomene = "Kecharitomene: Typikon of Empress Irene Doukaina Komnene for the Convent of the Mother of God Kecharitomene in Constantinople," in *Byzantine Monastic Foundation Documents: A Complete Translation of the Surviving Founder's Typika and Testaments*, ed. J. Thomas and A. Constantinides Hero, Washington, DC, 2000, pp. 649–724.

Typikon of Lips = "Lips: Typikon of Theodora Palaiologina for the Convent of Lips in Constantinople," in *Byzantine Monastic Foundation Documents: A Complete Translation of the Surviving Founder's Typika and Testaments*, ed. J. Thomas and A. Constantinides Hero, Washington, DC, 2000, pp. 1254–86.

Typikon of St. Mamas = "Mamas: Typikon of Athanasios Philanthropenos for the Monastery of St. Mamas in Constantinople," in *Byzantine Monastic Foundation Documents: A Complete Translation of the Surviving Founder's Typika and Testaments*, ed. J. Thomas and A. Constantinides Hero, Washington, DC, 2000, pp. 973–1041.

Van Millingen, A. 1912. *Byzantine Churches in Constantinople*, London.

Vokotopoulos, P. 1992. *Ἡ ἐκκλησιαστικὴ ἀρχιτεκτονικὴ εἰς τὴν Δυτικὴν Στερεὰν Ἑλλάδα καὶ τὴν Ἤπειρον ἀπὸ τοῦ τέλους τοῦ 7ου μέχρι τὸ τέλος τοῦ 10ου αἰῶνος*, 2nd ed., Thessaloniki.

Wybrew, H. 1989. *The Orthodox Liturgy: The Development of the Eucharistic Liturgy in the Byzantine Rite*, London.

AFTERWORD

Bonna D. Wescoat and Robert G. Ousterhout

The construction of sanctity through architecture within the early historical cultures of the Eastern Mediterranean forms the main theme of the essays in this volume. We take construction of sanctity in its dual sense to mean the way in which ancient and medieval patrons, architects, and masons physically shaped the environment in sacred cause, as well as in a metaphorical sense as the way in which ideas and situations generated by the built environment contributed to the cultural formulation of the sacred. Both meanings presuppose intimate human participation, and each informs the other. For the latter sense, human engagement in a sacred context finds its most recognizable expression through cult practice, which consists principally of structurally organized, repeated, privileged, performed actions or rites that signal to all involved that engagement with the divinity has been properly transacted; in a word, rituals.[1]

Ritual actions stand in service of belief; they are a constitutive part of religion. As Smith succinctly explains, "Ritual is, first and foremost, a mode of paying attention."[2] Throughout the Orthodox Christian liturgy, for example, the officiant reminds the congregation of this fact: "Let us be attentive," he instructs. In the cases discussed in this volume, architecture serves as a "focusing lens" – to use Smith's terminology, although in many instances the relationship of action to setting is far from clear. Sometimes we have precise accounts of ritual movements that can be tied to specific places and buildings, such as that provided by the *typikon* of a Byzantine monastery or by the text of a pilgrims' guide.

In other instances actions may be inferred from physical evidence that appears – at least to our eyes and minds – heightened or to stand out of the ordinary, as at the Theatral Circle at Samothrace or the monumental stairs of so many ancient Greek sanctuaries. Without doubt, in the cultures under consideration here, events that may be defined as rituals occurred in contexts other than the sacred, and no doubt many actions in addition to those that can be called rituals occurred within sanctified spaces. Indeed, private rituals of worship occurred within domestic settings during all periods under consideration. Markets and fairs overlapped temporally and spatially with religious festivals; sacred settings could also be employed for not-so-sacred activities. One need think, admittedly anachronistically, of St. Paul's in London, which outside of service became a thoroughfare and a market. Moreover, as Rose makes clear in his essay, sacred rituals conducted within sacred space may be inextricably intertwined with political, social, and cultural aims.[3] While all of the authors of this volume would agree that neither ritual nor sacred space is a neatly bounded concept, our focus has been the sacred aspects of sacred spaces that can be recognized and understood as such.

The architectural investigations offered here are micro-histories. As the authors point out in a range of ways, architecture is site-specific and ritual is situational. They attempt to explain the sacred parameters of particular spatial or architectural phenomena found in the archaeological and architectural record of particular places. Taken together, these studies may begin to shape a dialogue that returns place to the center of studies regarding sacred experience, regardless of whether that experience was pagan, Christian, or Jewish. Although the case studies span multiple religious traditions over two millennia, certain themes recur with such frequency that they take on a defining function in our understanding of the construction of sanctity. They are worthy of review.

Shaped Actions: The Passage of the Body and Eye. In the first chapter to this volume, Jaś Elsner warns of the dangers of inferring actions from architectural forms: "the material cultural frame of a ritual center – architectural, topographic, decorative – may offer no clues at all as to what people choose to do liturgically with it." To be sure, the configuration of solids and voids will not ever allow us to recover all the actions that ever took place within sacred spaces, especially in places of great accumulation. But "no clues at all" stands counter to the very nature of architecture, which, although itself chiefly static, exists and serves to shape human actions. Ritual actions, while hardly exclusive to sacred contexts, lie at their core. It is thus no surprise that almost every paper presented here concentrates on movement and encounter within the architectural environment. Although not articulated as such, most of the essays have the phenomenological basis that architecture is understood through experience and that the two are not only inseparable but also mutually transformative.[4] The authors explore their interconnectedness through a full range of sensory apprehensions.

Thus Hollinshead begins her discussion of monumental stairs with the weight of the body and the tread of a foot; the difference of feeling and of seeing in the acts of going up or going down. In her overview of monumental stairs and ramps in Greek sanctuaries, she demonstrates just how tactile the management of the celebratory crowd would have been. Miles tracks Pausanias along the monument-littered 22-kilometer road between Eleusis and the City Eleusinion, the termini of which are framed by twin propyla. The physical and visual experience engendered by gathering in an architecturally constructed circle within the entrance of the Sanctuary of the Great Gods interests Wescoat. Rose recreates the route of the ancient tour guide around the highly charged memory monuments of Troy reinvented at Ilion. Perry notes the formidable role of the Temple of Jupiter Optimus Maximus as the ending point of triumphal procession and the starting point of the religious procession inaugurating the *Ludi Romani*. Yasin asserts that we may understand the configuration of the Late Antique martyria that explicitly separate altar and relic only by connecting the pilgrims' twin experiences of physical passage and lines of sight. The portable Tabernacle, with its capacity to reformulate place, provides for Branham a model for mapping new territory, juxtaposing representational space with performance. And as Marinis makes clear, Byzantine church design provides unobstructed space to accommodate the processional entrances of the liturgy while allowing clear observation by the congregation.

Reciprocity of Architecture and Ritual, or Space, Building and Place. By framing topography and shaping space, sacred architecture can establish the conditions for religious ritual; the two are, as Rose says, mutually reinforcing. But each site examined here differs in significant ways; this point come through forcefully in Ousterhout's comparison of the Holy Sepulchre and the Hagia Sophia, and in turn the places of Jerusalem and Constantinople. In the cultures under consideration, there is a clear language of sacred architecture. While the component forms do not differ so markedly from those used in secular architecture, in one or more categories of placement, composition, scale, material, elaboration, or decoration, they communicate a sacred or ritual setting. We have come to have such clear assumptions and can so readily recognize a sacred "constellation" of features that sometimes that which is right before our eyes, so to speak, goes unrecognized. Ćurčić's paper, for example, asks us to look again at some standard features of Byzantine architecture and architectural decoration as signifiers of divine light. While not every dogtooth brick band or every zigzag pattern would fit the bill, he argues convincingly that in select instances these decorative details should be read symbolically. Similarly, Wescoat argues for special meanings of interiority and regeneration associated with the use of the Corinthian order at Samothrace. Again, not every application of the Corinthian order should be interpreted in this way, but its unique usage and special position in the Sanctuary of the Great Gods call out for special consideration.

Social and Spatial Boundaries. Just as there were zones of increasingly sacred character and increasingly limited access at the Temple of Jerusalem, similar zones appear in many of the sites discussed here. In the church of the Monastery *tou Libos* discussed by Marinis, these zones may be understood in relationship to both the liturgy and to the privileged burials within the complex. In other examples, the distinction is between space within and space without, and efforts to find meaning in architecture often center on the negotiation of boundaries. One way to construct sanctity is to set it apart. The root of the word temenos (sacred precinct) is in *temenein*.[5] As with the Holy of Holies in the Temple, the bema of a Byzantine church or the naos of a pagan temple were areas of limited, privileged access. The threshold marks a zone of liminality. To be able to enter that space was a mark of status. In a like manner, cutting oneself off from the larger world and forging an alternate sacred community involves the establishment of boundaries. This is certainly what happens in the Theatral Circle on Samothrace. In contrast, the Sacred Way between Athens and Eleusis and its framing propyla, are overtly part of the urban fabric. While the propyla mark the transitions into temenoi, the road itself is a public thoroughfare; it becomes sacred space through its active engagement in processions. Processions similarly connected the churches of Byzantine Constantinople. While monasteries or churches marked sacred space, set off and treated differently from the world outside, they could be linked by means of ritual procession into a web of sanctity. The Great Palace formed a separate, isolated zone of sanctity within the city, highlighted by its chapels, its relics, and the ceremonies that bound them together; clearly part of its sacred aura came from its isolation from the rest of the city.

Construction of a Sacred Topography. In the cultures under discussion, sacred experience can be linked directly to the extraordinary nature of a place. In the late nineteenth century, the Anatolian archaeologist and religious historian Sir William M. Ramsay had associated the concept of *religious awe* with special localities marked by distinctive natural features. As places that communicated with the divine, oracles were often associated with topographical phenomena. Similar themes emerge in the writings of Rudolph Otto, Emile Durkheim, and Mircea Eliade. There are places on earth where natural forces interact to exude a numinosity, and we might argue that Samothrace is one such place – or at least this is how it was perceived in Antiquity. In opposition to this view – and in specific reference to Eliade, Smith argues that sanctity is a political construct. Following his argument, we might post the question, is place inherently sacred, or is it made sacred by human response? Some places came to be regarded as sacred by the occurrence of an event regarded as holy, such as the sites of Christ's Crucifixion and Resurrection, or the place where the ascetic St. Symeon the Stylite lived atop his column. In these and other examples, architecture plays a significant role. Both received distinctive architectural frameworks to heighten the experience of the place, such that architecture *becomes* place. Elsewhere, in many religious contexts, a sacred presence might have been introduced into an architectural setting by the mortal remains of a holy figure, as at the tomb of Felix at Nola addressed by Yasin, or in a unique Jewish example discussed by Magness, the enigmatic bone deposit at the synagogue of Dura Europos.

Architecture may be used to both frame the experience of place and to establish between reciprocity between places that frame ritual experience.

In offering a new reconstruction for the Propylon to the Eleusinion in Athens, Miles shows just how closely connected the two entrances termini graphically demonstrates the way in which architecture and its decoration mirrored. Rose, too, notes the "related design strategies" tapping into the ancestral past at work on the Athenian Acropolis and the Ilion's Athenaion and ties them to the shared Panathenaic festival and the structurally related traditions of the *arrhephoroi* in Athens and the Lokrian Maidens at Ilion.

History and Memory. History and memory are powerful and essential instruments in the architect's toolbox. For architecture to signify, it must appeal to shared instincts and experiences, even when exploring new territory. For ritual to mean anything, there has to be a collective memory of the action and its significance, even as it is reconstituted with each enactment. Both are simultaneously fixed and protean. Visual associations, historical appeal, and cues to memory form central themes in several of the papers presented here. Memory and historicism play a critical role in the crafting of sacred spaces investigated by all of the authors working in the Roman period. Miles points to the intense historicism of the Second Sophistic as a guiding idea in forging ritual experience between the gates of the Eleusinian sanctuaries, with the Athenian karyatids mirroring their sacred sisters in Eleusis. Twenty-two kilometers and six centuries separate the Propylaia on the Athenian Acropolis and the Greater Propylaia at Eleusis, but shared architectural forms collapses the distance conceptually and binds the two places; the iconography of the Lesser Propylaia and the new gate to the City Eleusinion erected in the second half of the second century C.E. employ the same iconography (here separated by only two centuries) to remind the participants of where they are and what the cult offers.

Rose traverses an even greater panorama, exploring the weave of the ritual-historical ties between Ilion, Athens, and Rome through the invention, replication, and manipulation of architecture, landscape, and cult. For Perry, the sanctity of the Temple of Jupiter Optimus Maximus resides in the premise that the building, in each of its incarnations, recaptures enough of the original form to physically tie the building to the sacred foundations of the city. That it actually looked "the same" was, as Perry demonstrates, far less important than the idea that it could be relied upon to encapsulate the historical memory and tradition of

Rome. The portable Jewish Tabernacle holds the collective memory of the house of Israel, transforming each place it rests into the sacred center of the tribe. Allusions to Tabernacle sacrifice and sacrificial imagery (either in metaphor or paint), become, for Branham, a way for Jewish religious communities to map their post-Temple identity in meaningful historical terms.

On the opposite side of the spectrum, the fixed and immutable loci of the events of the Christian passion form the historical armature for the sanctity of place in Jerusalem, as Ousterhout demonstrates. Of course, not all appeals to memory need be historically based; architects in the premodern Mediterranean rely on the powerful adhesive of familiarity to fix recognizable actions, utterances, and forms into powerful new configurations in sacred landscapes. The monumental staircases of Hellenistic Greek sanctuaries both generate and facilitate procession; and when they are empty, the bear the memory of the processions past and those to come. In sum, by framing actions and creating social environments, architecture shapes and maintains memory.

Iconography and Signifiers. If spaces were crafted with the express and nonneutral aim of shaping sacred experience in sacred settings of the eastern Mediterranean, the manner in which the framing walls, colonnades, windows and doors were adorned was equally, and to modern eyes, more obviously charged. Studies of pagan, Jewish, and Christian sacred iconography are legion, but the authors in this volume bring new vigor to the enterprise by concentrating more specifically on the interaction of iconography, space, and movement. Perhaps the most overt declaration of iconography interacting both with place and participants can be found in the karyatids representing Eleusinian priestesses that mirror the procession of worshippers entering the sacred precincts of the City Eleusinion and the Sanctuary of Demeter at Eleusis, which Miles discusses. Equally declarative are the symbols of the cult – myrtle, wheat, boukrania, kistai, plemochoai, phialai – displaying in stone above the entrances the same objects that were plied back and forth by the cult personnel and participants. For Wescoat, it is the act of departing through the remarkable Corinthian façade of the Propylon of Ptolemy II in the Sanctuary of the Great Gods that gives the order meaning. Similarly, Magness and Branham focus on the direct interaction of iconic imagery with the liturgical space of the early synagogue. In so doing Magness stands in sharp opposition to Elsner's pessimism that the focus on priestly rituals in the Dura paintings may have no connection with the activities within the building.

Other instances of iconographic signifiers may be more abstract (to our eyes) but no less powerful, especially when surrounding windows and doors, the most volatile parts of a sacred structure. Ćurčić, in an extraordinary bold stroke, locates powerful theological meaning in one of the most ubiquitous decorative forms of Byzantine architecture, which he has now named "radiant light." Magness combines the painted imagery surrounding the Torah Shrine at Dura with the inscriptions on ceiling tiles to demonstrate priestly influence and connecting that, in turn, with the potential for apocalyptic expectations. Ousterhout reveals the way the Hagia Sophia itself becomes the sacred object, even an iconic image. While containing no significant relic and commemorating no important event, by dint of its audacious architectural expression, it came to be venerated by pilgrims. Implicit in all essays stands the notion that iconography facilitates the formation of cultural and religious identity; Branham draws these ideas out by exploring the way in which the strategy of mapping sacrifice from one object, person, or place to another transforms, reorients, and recreates early Christian and Jewish "theological cartography."

Architecture and Ritual Accoutrement. Architecture does not operate independently of the humans who animate it and the accoutrement they use to communicate and accomplish sacred acts. The papers presented here do not focus on the archaeological accoutrement of cult, but in certain instances, the intersection of cult objects in archaeological contexts provides essential evidence for interpreting sacred space. In establishing the evidentiary base for hero-worship at Ilion from the inception of the Iron Age city, Rose points to the geometric pottery assemblages that signal feasting on circular platforms hard up against the Bronze Age wall of Troy. Miles combines the archaeological evidence for the ritual vessels known as *plemochoai* discovered in the City Eleusinion with the iconography of the Ninnion plaque and the representation of *plemochoai* on propylaia at both ends of the Sacred Way to establish a greater claim for the vessel in the rituals of the cult. Wescoat seeks to make sense of the extraordinary quantity of curiously shaped conical bowls found in the region of the Theatral Complex as evidence for cult activity in the entrance complex in the Sanctuary of the Great Gods. In a quite different trajectory, the lost accoutrement of ancient Jewish sacrifice – altar, thymiaterion, and incense – resurfaces metaphorically in the virtuous bodies of Christian widows and virgins.

Buildings, Actions, and Texts. The authors refrain from engaging the once popular and largely rhetorical strategy of 'reading' the building. As architectural historians, they appreciate that the act of reading a text is fundamentally different from the experience of architecture, which requires a radically different engagement with time, motion, and sensory perception.[6] Ćurčić's contribution most closely approaches Elsner's urging to look again to the ancient texts "as a series of theological proposals instantiated through liturgical performance and ritual artifacts." The nature of biblical theophany in both Old and New Testaments forms the theological proposal that Ćurčić finds instantiated in the three-dimensional "radiant frieze" framing first painted programs and ultimately windows, doors, and the upper zone of Byzantine churches. Rabbinical texts provide the theological framework within which Magness debunks notions that human bones in all contexts were impure. Yasin charts the transformations in the early Medieval sacred landscape at Cimitile/Nola, with its dual sacred focal points through the synchronized evidences of architectural forms, Paulinus's writings, and the inscriptions embedded in the fabric of the complex, which give directions to the pilgrims as to how to move, and where to look. The repeated textual invocation of sameness presented by ancient authors, set against literary description and archaeological evidence, leads Perry to question what is meant by sameness in a sacred context of the Temple of Jupiter Optimus Maximus, and why being the same matters to the construction of sanctity in Rome's oldest and most defining temple. Mining the *typikon* for religious establishments allows Marinis to identify the primary function of certain establishments, such as the church of St. John at the monastery *tou Libos*, and from there to conclusions regarding the divergent architectural designs within the monastery.

Architectural Process and the Cumulative Aspect of Sanctity. By and large, our way of understanding architecture centers on its culminating moment; we often cannot resist finding the accomplished program within the germinating idea. The classical Athenian Acropolis stands as a case in point, for the monuments are so artfully related that scholars find it hard to resist the idea that they must all have been part of a fully articulated ingenious master plan conceived c. 449 B.C.E., which was then faithfully executed over the second half of the fifth century, despite war, plague, and changing financial circumstances. However, the authors of this volume repeatedly point out the cumulative nature of architectural thinking and practice. As one architectural idea builds upon another, ritual experience is shaped and recrafted. The several monumental stairs and stoas at Lindos and Kos developed over two centuries; similarly, the full potential of a seamless grandstand and closed orchestra in the Theatral Circle at Samothrace was not realized until after the open plan had been built and experienced. The monuments and memorials that form the "fingerposts" for Eleusis accumulate over centuries to shape the path of the second century C.E. initiate; those that define "Holy Troy" reach back to the Bronze Age.

With the striking exception of Hagia Sophia in Constantinople (an outrageously bold and theoretically engendered project), Early Christian and Byzantine sacred places are in a constant state of architectural accumulation. With each addition or revision we witness a combination of practical response to circumstance (the pilgrims need to venerate the dead or witness the eucharist), a striving to define an idea (how to create the right spiritual conditions for witness; how to combine the polar experiences of eucharist and saint veneration), and the intense desire to lay claim to sacred experience. Paulinus, in fact, celebrates the virtue of accumulation by adding halls, joining buildings, and giving directions to the pilgrims that emphasize the rich experience of passing through and visually enjoying the several conjoined sacred spaces. The architecture of the Church of the Holy Sepulchre hardly survives the trauma of its accumulated sacredness. The point is that very few constructions of sanctity are found to be sufficiently perfect in the experiences and minds of their users to remain untouched. They do not hold satisfaction for very long; not because they are incomplete ideas or inferior executions but because the construction of sanctity cannot remain static. It exists in a constant state of revalorization, accomplished by the reenactment of rituals as part of religious expression and by the need to take ownership of sacred place and experience as a socially (Burkert would argue biologically) defining aspect of being human.[7] Our interpretations, of course, contribute to that revalorization.

Notes

1. Much of Kyriakidis 2007 is devoted to the question of defining ritual, with very different views proposed. Elsner, here, addresses the fundamental concerns, and while he comes down on the somewhat more pessimistic side, we favor the more optimistic, e.g, Renfrew (2007). While fully recognizing that ritual plays a significant cultural role in nonsacred settings (we have all just finished witnessing the inauguration of the forty-fourth president of the United States), it is possible to distinguish between daily habits and customs, on the one hand, and ritual actions, on the other.
2. Smith 1987, pp. 103–4.
3. In his essay, Elsner notes the ritualization of things other than the sacred, e.g., power.
4. The concept has a rich philosophical tradition explored by M. Heidigger and H.-G. Gadamer, but as Lindsay Jones (2000 p. 45) writes, "Whether deriving this insight from [R.] Ingarden, [H.-G.] Gadamer, reader-response criticism, or elsewhere, we need to accept the profound ramifications of conceiving of peoples' interactions with architectural works as dynamic, open-ended, interactive processes (or events) in which both buildings and beholders make substantial contributions and both are significantly transformed."
5. Note the important study by Branham 1992.
6. See Lefebvre 1991, pp. 7, 143–4; Sullivan 1990. Reviewed by Jones 2000, pp. 121–33.
7. Burkert 1996.

Works Cited

Branham, J. R. 1992. "Sacred Space Under Erasure in Ancient Synagogues and Early Churches," *The Art Bulletin* 74, pp. 375–94.

Burkert, W. 1996. *Creation of the Sacred. Tracks of Biology in Early Religions*, Cambridge, MA.

Jones, L. 2000. *The Hermeneutics of Sacred Architecture. Experience, Interpretation, Comparison*, Vols. 1–2, Cambridge, MA.

Kyriakidis E., ed. 2007a. *The Archaeology of Ritual*, Los Angeles.

Lefebvre, H. 1991. *The Production of Space*, trans. D. Nicholson-Smith, Oxford and Cambridge, MA.

Renfrew, C. 2007. "Archaeology of Ritual, of Cult and of Religion," in Kyriakidis 2007, pp. 109–122.

Smith, J. Z. 1987. *To Take Place; Toward a Theory of Ritual*. Chicago.

Sullivan, L. E. 1990. "'Seeking an End to the Primary Text' or 'Putting an End to the Text as Primary,'" in *Beyond the Classics? Essays in Religious Studies and Liberal Education*, ed. F. E. Reynolds and S. L. Burkhalter, Atlanta, pp. 41–59.

INDEX

377